Social Understanding

THEORY AND DECISION LIBRARY

General Editor: Julian Nida-Rümelin (*Universität München*)

Series A: Philosophy and Methodology of the Social Sciences

Series B: Mathematical and Statistical Methods

Series C: Game Theory, Mathematical Programming and Operations Research

SERIES A: PHILOSOPHY AND METHODOLOGY
OF THE SOCIAL SCIENCES
VOLUME 47

Assistant Editor: Martin Rechenauer (*Universität München*)

Scope: This series deals with the foundations, the general methodology and the criteria, goals and purpose of the social sciences. The emphasis in the Series A will be on well-argued, thoroughly analytical rather than advanced mathematical treatments. In this context, particular attention will be paid to game and decision theory and general philosophical topics from mathematics, psychology and economics, such as game theory, voting and welfare theory, with applications to political science, sociology, law and ethics.

For further volumes:
http://www.springer.com/series/6616

Jürgen Klüver · Christina Klüver

Social Understanding

On Hermeneutics, Geometrical Models and Artificial Intelligence

 Springer

Jürgen Klüver
Department of Economics
University of Duisburg-Essen
Essen
Germany
juergen.kluever@uni-due.de

Christina Klüver
Department of Economics
University of Duisburg-Essen
Essen
Germany
c.stoica-kluever@uni-due.de

ISBN 978-94-007-3469-2   ISBN 978-90-481-9911-2 (eBook)
DOI 10.1007/978-90-481-9911-2
Springer Dordrecht Heidelberg London New York

Printed on acid-free paper

Springer is part of Springer Science+Business Media (www.springer.com)

Preface

In several aspects this book is a sequel to our book "On Communication" (Klüver and Klüver 2007). Yet it is of course possible to read and understand this new book of ours without having to read our publication from 2007. When we refer to concepts, definitions, and research results from this book we shall always give the necessary explanations. In other words, we shall do the same as for example J. R. R. Tolkien or J. Rowling did in their sequels to the first novel(s), namely referring to that what had happened before to Frodo and Harry.

As our books before this one could also never have been written without the labor(s) of many students, in particular those who wrote their MA-theses supervised by us. We mentioned their names in the text where they contributed to this book by implementing certain computer programs, designed by us, or performed experiments with computers and/or human probands. We emphasize this fact because our experiences with these students again demonstrated to us that it is nowadays still possible to do ambitious research without much support from funding institutions. The old and venerable paradigm of the unity of research and teaching that characterized the modern universities since the great reformers Humboldt and Schleiermacher is still valid in the sense that there are no better research assistants than engaged graduate students.

Yet there are always exceptions, even from this rule. We wish to thank Wolfram Mach for his help to realize a cooperation with his firm, the *Deutsche Telekom*, in order to develop one of our systems, namely the so-called self-enforcing network (SEN) that is described in Chapter 4. Our thanks of course also go to his superiors who supported the cooperation.

It is a bit unusual that only one author of two writes the preface. My wife and co-author Christina insisted that I should do it because the theoretical and mathematical ideas and the text are principally my responsibility. I should according to her explicitly say this in the preface or else she would not accept a co-authorship. I reluctantly agreed to do this but I wish to emphasize that this book could never have been written without her and that her contributions to this book are much more than just giving me technical help or encouraging the students when they became desperate with respect to their MA-thesis. Christina is, after all, the professional computer scientist in our team and so her indispensable task was to supervise and consult the programmers and to test and validate the programming results.

For a long time Christina and I have been a successful research team and we intend to keep matters this way. Nothing is better for a happy marriage than satisfying common work.

Essen, Germany   Jürgen Klüver

Contents

Chapter 1
Introduction: Historical Methodical and Conceptual Frames

A book that simultaneously deals with hermeneutical problems on the one hand and with Artificial Intelligence and the construction of mathematical models on the other seems to achieve the impossible or, to speak in mathematical terms, to solve the quadrature of the circle. Since the rise of the modern physical sciences at the Renaissance and the beginning of Enlightenment mathematics is *the* language of the sciences; hermeneutics in contrast is the traditional methodical tool of the humanities and – to apply a famous quotation of Kipling – never the twain shall meet. In particular the quest for an Artificial Intelligence is a branch of computer science and hence a science based on the construction of mathematical models. Therefore, to combine these very different schools of rational thinking seems to be an enterprise that can only be done in metaphorical ways and hence rather useless ones.

We of course believe otherwise or we would not have written this book. But we are quite aware of the fact that the analysis of hermeneutical problems by mathematical models and the attempt to base some principles of a hermeneutical Artificial Intelligence on such models is nothing less than the attempt to bridge the gulf between the sciences and the humanities. In other words, simultaneously dealing with hermeneutics and mathematical constructs is the walking of a path whose end may be the goal of a unified science. To be sure, we do not intend to reach that old goal in this book. We just try to demonstrate that the conception of a hermeneutical Artificial Intelligence may be more than a metaphor and that it is now already possible to give some preliminary results of our research in this direction. Yet as we know that in the end the possibility of a combination of hermeneutics and Artificial Intelligence has much to do with the old quest for a unified science we start in the first subchapter with a brief historical sketch of classical attempts to reach that goal.

In the center of the wide and widely differentiated field of hermeneutics is the concept of *understanding*. Whole sub disciplines of the social sciences, in particular qualitative social research and cultural anthropology, deal with the question how it is methodically possible to *understand* humans, i.e. their behavior, their world views, beliefs and so on. The same is true for the humanities like history or literature analysis insofar as they deal with texts, written by humans. In all these fields the core problem is to understand, i.e. to interpret the products of human activity. Yet there is a common consent that all human activities must be understood as *socially* founded ones and that, therefore, understanding always means understanding in some social sense. That is why we define our subject as *social* understanding. We shall clarify these rather general and a bit vague remarks in the next chapters, but we wish to emphasize already in the beginning that we deal only with the problems of understanding humans as social actors and human social actions. The hermeneutical problem of the interpretation of certain texts is not our subject and not our problem in this book although we show some models how humans possibly understand specific texts.

Neither qualitative social research nor the traditional hermeneutical disciplines are mathematically orientated – on the contrary because usually mathematical methods seem to be very unsuited for the tasks of understanding. Yet we have already shown that some problems of qualitative social research, for example, can be successfully analyzed by several mathematical methods of computer simulations (Klüver and Klüver 2007; Klüver et al. 2006). The subject of this book is to continue and systematize these ideas, namely to demonstrate the possibility of a partial integration of mathematics and hermeneutics.

When we speak of a combination of hermeneutics and mathematical methods, though, we have to clarify our usage of "mathematical methods". We do not mean, of course, the classical mathematical methods of the natural sciences, namely differential equations, nor do we mean statistical methods. Both mathematical methods have been immensely fruitful not only in the natural sciences but also in the fields of economics and, in the case of statistical methods, also in psychology and quantitative social research. The mathematical methods we shall use to analyze hermeneutical problems are chiefly the so-called techniques of Soft Computing, namely especially artificial neural networks and cellular automata, and computer simulations based on such models. In particular we try to demonstrate that the analysis of the topology of artificial neural networks can be an important contribution to understand understanding. In other words, we do not only construct artificial neural networks that are able to perform some operations or simulations respectively of some basic hermeneutical processes but we also intend to demonstrate that a geometrical, i.e. topological analysis of such networks is a way to understand the empirical processes that these networks simulate. Hence, on the one hand we use these networks not only for the task to simulate processes of understanding. Parts of the cognitive sciences have developed this approach with encouraging success and with different modeling techniques, which is also called the field of cognitive modeling (cf. McLeod et al. 1998; Polk and Seifert 2002; Thagard 1996). We also look on the other hand for mathematical, i.e. topological characteristics of our networks and specific algorithmic operations that can explain the specific behavior of the networks and hence probably of the humans whom these networks simulate. The second approach is still rather new even in the cognitive sciences. Therefore, with the term "mathematical methods" we simultaneously mean the construction of simulation models and the mathematical analysis of these models. In the following chapters we show examples of both procedures.

To put our procedure into a nutshell: The first step is of course the identification and definition of the respective problems like, for example, certain processes of restricted information assimilation by human individuals (see below Chapter 5); after that we have to construct a suited mathematical model, usually in form of an artificial neural network and to implement it into an according computer program; by performing experiments we try to find out observable regularities and in addition try to explain these regularities by the mathematical characteristics of our model. If the models behavior is sufficiently similar to the human cognitive processes that should be modeled we not only have a possible explanation for these processes but also the programs as components of a future Artificial Intelligence: If we can construct suited mathematical models and according computer programs we also may be capable to construct artificial systems that are able to "understand", at least in some ways.[1]

But first we give some overviews to the historical and conceptual framework of our subject.

1.1 Unifications of the Sciences

We only understand what we can make (Source: *Giambattista Vico*)

In the seventeenth century the philosophers and mathematicians Descartes and Leibniz developed the ideas of a *mathesis universalis* (Descartes) and a *mathesis characteristica* respectively (Leibniz). These concepts expressed the idea of a universal mathematical science, i.e. a science with a universal mathematical language where all problems can be formulated in a mathematical manner and can be solved by arithmetical calculations. Accordingly Leibniz declared *"calculemus"* (let us calculate) if some differences of opinion should occur.[2]

It was not by chance that at the beginning of the modern natural sciences the dream of a unified mathematically formulated science simultaneously emerged. Both Leibniz and Descartes had made important contributions to mathematics and hence they believed that it must be possible to unify all forms of rational thinking by the new and powerful mathematical tools that they and others had developed. The rapid progress of mathematics and physics in the following decades and centuries seemed to be a verification of the dream of Descartes and Leibniz. Possibly Leibniz got the idea of a universal science because he invented the system of dual numbers, i.e. the possibility to represent all numbers as combinations of 1 and 0. As 1 and 0 represent the simplest alternative – yes or no – all problems should be expressed as a combination of such simple alternatives. Three centuries later Shannon in his mathematical theory of information formalized the same basic idea with his famous concept of "bit": One bit is the simplest form of selection, namely between 1 and 0 (Hartley 1928; Shannon and Weaver 1949).

---

[1] It is not important here if the artificial systems "really" understand or if they are "only" simulating understanding. We shall deal with the discussion about "strong" versus "weak" AI in Section 1.4.

[2] Actually the basic idea of such a formal calculus is much older. Already in the thirteenth and fourteenth century the scholastic philosopher Raimundus Lullus developed the program of an *ars combinatoria*, i.e. a formal method for combining different concepts in order to solve philosophical problems. Yet the idea of Lullus, naturally, found not much interest. Nowadays it reminds of certain modern computer programs that operate in a similar manner.

Yet already in the eighteenth century the Italian philosopher Giambattista Vico denied the possibility of even a natural science by declaring a famous argument: God understands the world but only because he created it. Therefore, humans cannot understand nature because they did not make it. They just can understand their own creations, namely human history, society, and of course creations of their mind like literature or the arts. In modern terms Vico argued for the possibility of the humanities and denied the possibility of the sciences, as far as they deal with nature.[3]

Vico apparently did not see that the natural scientists had found a methodical equivalent for the creation of nature with the experimental method. Quite literally natural scientists recreate parts of material reality during their experiments in the laboratory and they are even able to create material artifacts that did not exist before the according experiments; this is quite usual in the chemistry of synthetic materials. The intended experiments with the new *Large Hadron Collider* (LHC) at CERN (autumn 2009) have the goal to demonstrate the recreation of early states of the Universe, perhaps even states like the Big Bang. In this sense physics and other natural sciences have taken Vico's postulate quite literally: They understand nature because they can recreate and even create parts of it – they can make it. In this sense they realized the famous word of Vico *"verum et factum convertuntur"*.[4] It is not without irony that the natural sciences successfully applied the principle of Vico and that the humanities were not able to do it in a strict and systematical manner. We certainly often (although not always) understand our own creations but, in comparison to the strict and successful methods of the natural sciences, only in an informal manner.

In any case, whether he had intended it or not, Vico laid the foundations for the growing gulf between the natural sciences and the humanities. The dream of a universal science with a common mathematical terminology had been a product of the rationality of the Enlightenment. During Romanticism and in particular inspired by the philosophers of German Idealism like Herder, Schelling and Hegel the methodical concept of the humanities evolved.

According to the German term *Geisteswissenschaften* (sciences of the mind) the subject of the humanities should be, just as Vico postulated, the creations and products of the human mind. The fact that the humanities could not apply the successful methods of the natural sciences was not understood as a deficit of the humanities but as evidence for the distinguishing marks of their subject. The human mind and its products cannot be understood via the mathematical and experimental methods of the natural sciences but must be analyzed in a special manner. Therefore, the humanities are rational ways of thinking too but because of the complexity of their subjects they have rational methods and standards in their own right. In consequence the humanities evolved in parallel to the natural sciences, became institutionalized in the modern universities, and created a rational universe of their own. In the middle

---

[3]In contrast to the possibility of the natural sciences Vico accepted the possibility of a science of mathematics because the objects of mathematics are also our own products (Vico 1947).

[4]That what is true and what has been made converge (our translation).

of the twentieth century the gulf between the world of natural sciences and that of the humanities seemed so absolute that C. P. Snow characterized this situation by his famous remark about the "Two Cultures" (Snow 1963).

The main reason for this still existing and very influential gulf between the two cultures of scientific enterprise may be characterized by the old and venerable term of *Hermeneutics*. The concept of Hermeneutics can be translated as the art of interpreting and hence understanding human actions and their according products like society, the arts, literature and so on. It is principally not possible, so the early founders and advocates of the humanities, to explain the world of the human mind by the methods of the natural sciences, although these have been and are very successful in dealing with material reality. Human beings cannot be explained this way but must be understood in a hermeneutical way. *In nuce*, the task of the natural sciences is to *explain* material reality in a mathematical and experimental way; the according task of the humanities is to *understand* human beings in a hermeneutical manner. As it is not possible to reduce one methodical way to the other or to combine both methodical procedures, according to the partisans of the hermeneutical approach the differences between the two cultures is a methodical necessity. It is not by chance, by the way, that the gulf between the different methodical ways even exists within the social sciences, namely the difference between the so called qualitative and the quantitative methods of social research. We shall systematically deal with the concepts of hermeneutics, explaining, and understanding in the next chapters.

Despite this differentiation between the two cultures since the nineteenth century there have always been attempts to realize the idea of a universal science. The well-known program of a "Unified Science" of the philosophical school of Logical Positivism (e.g. Carnap 1950) is just one of them. All sciences should, according to this program, be only based on empirical facts and formal, i.e. mathematical logic; scientific theories, regardless of which domain, are then nothing else than logical combinations of empirical facts. By the way, it is interesting and not by chance that despite the failure of this program one important branch of Artificial Intelligence research, namely the research in and construction of rule based systems or expert systems respectively follows the same idea: Expert systems mainly consist of (a) facts that are stored in a so called knowledge base and (b) logical rules for the combination of these facts, e.g. in order to give a diagnosis for certain failures of systems like diseases or technical failures, and to derive a "therapy" from the diagnosis, like medical therapies or technical repairs. Yet the program of Logical Positivism failed for several reasons and with respect to the problem of hermeneutics the program of the Unified Science was not a solution of the problem but simply a denying of its existence.[5]

---

[5]The program of a "real" Artificial Intelligence, realized by the construction of sophisticated expert systems, failed too and probably for the same reasons: This program also simply denied the fact that human thinking is indeed partly only understandable in terms of hermeneutics. It must be noted, however, that expert systems are nowadays widely applied to all kinds of problems, e.g. in medical, technical, and economical domains.

Despite or perhaps because of the failure of the program of a Unified Science of the logical positivists many other attempts were made with different concepts and methods. To name only a few: Under the influence of Wiener's creation of cybernetics (Wiener 1948) many scholars tried to translate the "art of steering", as the Greek word cybernetics must be translated, into certain fields of the humanities, e.g. into the methodology of education (Cube 1965); concepts like feed back systems and feed back loops are still prominent in different scientific disciplines. Similar ideas were developed in the theory of autopoietic systems by the biologist Maturana (1975) and the theory of synergetic (Haken 1984), i.e. the theory of the effects of the combination of different factors. Yet in the humanities all these approaches were either neglected or only taken as sources of new concepts. The scholars in the humanities, as for example the theoretical works of the sociologist Luhmann, used these concepts only metaphorically and neglected the fact that a scientific usage of concepts from the natural sciences only makes sense if one uses the according scientific methods too (cf. Klüver 2000; Mayntz 1990).

The newest and perhaps most promising quest for a unified science is the research program on complex systems theory. The according research is often identified with the famous Santa Fé Institute for Research on Complex Systems (for a general description cf. Waldrup 1992). The basic concept of these lines of research is to treat empirical domains as complex dynamical systems. Accordingly research is done on general properties of complex dynamical systems via the use of certain computer programs like cellular automata on the one hand and the reformulation of scientific subjects in terms of complex systems theory and according empirical research on the other. The program of research in complex systems theory is formulated from its beginning as an interdisciplinary enterprise that shall include and unify all scientific disciplines as well as the humanities. Because our own work is also based on the general foundations of complex systems theory we shall deal with some concepts of this approach in a later subchapter.[6]

The important attempts to unify the sciences have always been, like the program of Logical Positivism and in accordance to the dreams of Leibniz and Descartes, attempts to introduce mathematical and experimental methods into the fields of the humanities. To be sure, there exist attempts to "understand" nature in a hermeneutical way, i.e. to reformulate the natural sciences according to the methodical program of the humanities. One of the best-known attempts in this direction is the *Farbenlehre* (theory of colors) by Goethe (cf. e.g. Böhme 1980). But the success of the natural sciences was and is so overwhelming that a unified science in a concrete meaning of this term can only be either a reduction of hermeneutical methods to those of the mathematical sciences, i.e. to develop the concept of a mathematical and experimental hermeneutics, or to combine both methodical ways. It is probably not surprising that we undertake in this study the first way, mainly because a simple

---

[6]We are certainly by far not the only scholars in the social and cognitive sciences, who use the concepts and methodical approaches of "complexity science". For a detailed and systematic overview of the influence of complexity science on the social sciences cf. Castellani and Hafferty (2009); an impression of the merging of complexity science and cognitive ones gives the collection of Polk and Seifert (2002).

combination of both methods would be strictly speaking just mirroring the same situation as it is now: There would be still fields of hermeneutical thinking on the one hand and those of the application of natural sciences methods on the other and the two domains would be as separated as ever. In other words, the goal of a unified science demands an integration of the hermeneutical methods into the field of mathematical thinking – a mathematical hermeneutics.

Even if one accepts the fact that the program of Logical Positivism was far too restricted to give a foundation even only for the natural sciences, other attempts to found the humanities on the mathematical and experimental methods of the natural sciences also failed or captured only fragments of the subjects of the humanities, as we already mentioned. The most important reasons for these failures are certainly the impossibility of repeatable experiments in most of the humanities on the one hand and the fact that the usage of the traditional mathematical methods of the calculus on the other hand yield only in very few cases important results in the humanities.[7] To be sure, the application of the tools of differential equations has been successful in economics and experimental methods have been applied with equal success in psychology. But these disciplines do not belong any more to the humanities proper and psychology has not succeeded in combining experimental *and* mathematical methods with the exception of elaborated statistical methods. Accordingly the core of the humanities is still and exclusively founded on hermeneutical methods and uses concepts of the natural sciences, if at all, only in a metaphorical way.

If practically all attempts to unify the different sciences, i.e. to unify the two cultures, have failed the question arises if such attempts are indeed fruitless because the task is impossible. Hence, why another attempt despite the discouraging experiences of the past?

Our belief that another attempt to lay down the foundations of a mathematical hermeneutics would be worthwhile, namely the proof that it is possible to analyze the classical hermeneutical problems in a mathematical way, is founded chiefly on three scientific achievements of the last century. The first one is the rise of modern structural mathematics and mathematical logic, which allow the mathematical treatment of hermeneutical problems in a fashion more suited to these problems than by the classical methods of the calculus. The second one is the mentioned program of research on complex dynamical systems. In our belief the respective conceptual and methodical foundations of this program offer a new chance for another attempt that is not restricted like its predecessors. The third and for us most important one is the invention of the computer and the possibility to introduce the method of computer simulation and hence computer experiments into the field of the humanities. We shall deal with these achievements in the next subchapters.

In particular, even only sketches of characteristics of an Artificial Intelligence, founded on these three achievements, would be a step according to the postulate of Vico: We can understand our mind because we can make an artificial one. Perhaps this is a bit more than just a hopeless dream or a utopia respectively.

---

[7]Examples for such cases are given, for example, in Epstein (1997).

In the rest of the chapter we shall discuss some fundamental problems concerning the questions what meaning the term of Artificial Intelligence has in our conceptual frame and why in particular philosophers of Artificial Intelligence often understand hermeneutics as a proof of the impossibility of a "real" Artificial Intelligence. The assumption that an Artificial Intelligence is principally not able to understand in a hermeneutical manner can be found, as we shall demonstrate, even in contemporary Science Fiction.

1.2 The Importance of Structural Mathematics and Computer Models

Since the rise of modern science in the sixteenth and seventeenth century its success was always explained by the combination of experimental method and mathematical theory construction. Only the language of mathematics apparently was suited for the generation of exact and precise knowledge and only by such knowledge science was able to serve as the foundation of modern technology, i.e. science based technology, and become this way the "first of productive forces" (Habermas 1968) and the foundation of modern economics. The fact that theoretical physics was and probably still is the paradigm of science proper is in particular explainable by the mathematical formulation of its theories. Therefore, it is no wonder that the famous Einstein equation $E = mc^2$ is for many laymen and scientists alike *the* symbol of science as it should be. Accordingly, no field of knowledge may be called as "science" if the respective knowledge cannot be formulated in mathematical terms.[8]

Because those disciplines that deal with human beings, society, and human cognition were for a long time not able to construct mathematical models and theories these fields of knowledge were not "sciences" but "humanities". To be sure, for example in psychology already in the nineteenth century the German psychologist Wundt and his school tried to formulate mathematical laws of human perception and contemporary psychology has gained a lot of statistically interpreted knowledge. That is why many psychologists define themselves rather as natural scientists than as representatives of the humanities. In economics, to take another example, Keynes and his followers have developed at least in macroeconomics mathematical tools akin to those of theoretical physics and have applied these tools with remarkable success to macro-economical processes. Therefore, economists alone of the social scientists may win a Nobel Prize. Yet it is an undeniable fact, as we remarked, that at the core of the sciences of man – the humanities – there are none or only very simple mathematical models. Sciences in the sense that mathematical models are the foundation of theory construction and of the interpretation of empirical data are, with the exception of macroeconomics, still only the natural sciences.

---

[8] Already at the beginning of modern (natural) science one of its founders, namely Galileo Galilei, postulated this thought when he declared, "the book of nature is written in mathematical letters". More than a century later Immanuel Kant, the probably greatest mind of the Enlightenment, remarked that each theory of nature is only so far science as it contains mathematics (Metaphysical Foundations of the Natural Sciences).

The reason for this fact is probably that the classical mathematical tools of, e.g. theoretical physics are not suited for the modeling of "real" complex systems like social or cognitive ones. When the renowned evolutionary biologist Richard Lewontin once remarked that in comparison to the complexity of social systems the problems of molecular biology seem to be "trivial" (Lewontin 2000) then this may be a reason for the difficulties of constructing mathematical models for the problems of the "soft" sciences. Indeed, social-cognitive systems are, e.g., characterized by their capability of changing their own structure, they frequently consist of different levels that permanently interact, and in particular they generate their own complexity by the continuous interdependence between social and cognitive processes: the cognition of social actors is dependent on their social milieu and the social milieu is constructed by the thoughts, world views, and the according actions of these actors. Problems of such complexity are not to be found in the complex natural systems – the natural sciences deal with systems that are in comparison "simple".[9] The classical mathematical methods that are very successful for the analysis of these systems were not constructed to deal with social-cognitive complexity.

Fortunately, at least for the development of mathematical foundations of the social-cognitive sciences, during the nineteenth century a new kind of mathematical thinking emerged that can be called "structural mathematics": Mathematics became "pure" in the sense that it was defined as the general theory of formal structures. These structures may be algebraic ones like those expressed in group theory, logical ones like those George Boole formulated in his algebra of logic, or topological ones as foundations for the problems of the continuum. Mathematics finally became a science in its own right and not primarily a tool for the natural sciences. This development is in particular clearly characterized by Cantor's theory of transfinite sets: Mathematics emancipated itself from empirical reality. On first sight it seems a bit paradoxically that just the *pure* mathematics also became the foundation of the computer and the according simulation software; on a second sight the fact that each computer basically consists of many coupled logical nets can quite easily explain this paradox. In the famous work of Bourbaki, which influenced the mathematical curricula for more than a generation, the whole building of mathematics then was reconstructed on the foundations of set theory and mathematical logic; Bourbaki, hence, can be understood as the peak of this development.[10]

In our opinion it is not by chance that nearly at the same time of Bourbaki, i.e. since the fifties of the last century, new mathematical modeling techniques emerged. On the one hand the new structural mathematics had been fully developed at this time and the first accordingly revised mathematical textbooks began to determine mathematical education. On the other hand based on the work of early pioneers

---

[9]"Simple" is, of curse, to be understood only in a relative manner. Many of the greatest minds of the human species have demonstrated how difficult it is even to understand these "simple" systems.

[10]Several social theorists rather early saw the possibilities the new mathematical ways could offer to the social-cognitive sciences. For example, Kurt Lewin, one of the founders of *gestalt* theory, spoke of a "topological psychology" and postulated the introduction of vector algebra into the social-cognitive sciences (Lewin 1969). Bourbaki, by the way, was the pseudonym of a group of French mathematicians.

like Konrad Zuse and John von Neumann the first computers were built and offered new ways for the construction of mathematical models. Indeed, the influence of the computers on the ways of mathematical thinking became so strong that one of the most famous representatives of early research in Artificial Intelligence (AI), namely Douglas Hofstadter, spoke of a renaissance of the experimental mathematics of the eighteenth century by the computer (Hofstadter 1985).

To be sure, the well established and proven mathematical methods like statistics and differential equations still are at the core of the usage of mathematics via the computer. Yet at that time new mathematical models were invented and analyzed that were oriented at natural processes and in particular developed in order to solve problems of life, mind and society. For example: In 1943 McCulloch and Pitts described the first mathematical model of a "neural network", i.e. a model of the operations of the brain. The operation of this artificial network was called by its inventors a "logical addition", which meant the characterization of brain processes in terms of logic and mathematics. This was the start of the development of artificial neural networks, the main tool we use for our purposes in this book. A whole branch of computer science, the so-called neuro-informatics, concentrates on the development and applications of artificial neural networks. Neural networks, as we shall call them in this book, are basically nothing else than "dynamical" graph structures, whose connections can be varied according to certain rules and which can be described by graph theoretical and topological characteristics. In this sense they are an offspring of structural mathematics. Yet they can be applied to practical problems and thoroughly studied with respect to their fundamental features only by their implementation in according computer programs. Therefore, neural networks are a fascinating type of mathematical models that are based on structural mathematics and on their usage as computer programs likewise.

A second example is the development of cellular automata in the Fifties of the last century, mainly connected with the name of John von Neumann.[11] Von Neumann, a mathematical universal genius, was interested in the construction of models of living systems, in particular with respect to their ability of self-reproduction. Cellular automata consist of a grid of cells and rules of interaction between the cells. By these rules the cells change their state in dependency of the state of other cells. Similar as in the case of neural networks cellular automata can be characterized by a certain "geometry" or topology respectively, namely the topological definition of neighborhood, and by certain rules of interaction. Yet cellular automata are also only useful by implementing them into respective computer programs. Even simple cellular automata unfold rather complex dynamics that are impossible to analyze without the use of computers. The probably most famous cellular automaton, the Game of Life by Conway, is an instructive example that even a cellular automaton with very simple rules can be thoroughly analyzed only via a computer program.[12]

---

[11] Actually von Neumann got the basic idea for cellular automata from Stanislav Ulam, the mathematical father of the hydrogen bomb.

[12] Conway did his first experiments with the Game of Life without using computers. He instead used little black and white plates like those known from the game of Go. Records tell us that soon his working room and other rooms were full of these plates and that it was literally impossible to

Evolutionary algorithms, developed nearly at the same time in the late Sixties by Holland and Rechenberg, are a third example. As the name suggests, evolutionary algorithms are constructed as formal models of biological evolution, i.e. of the processes of mutation and recombination of genes and of natural selection. These algorithms are mainly used as optimization methods and are also useful only as specific computer programs. Yet some of their main characteristics, in particular their convergence behavior, can be understood by applying some results of metrical topology, as for example Michalewicz (1994) has demonstrated. Again we find the combination of structural mathematics and the usage of computer programs.[13]

Last but not least the so-called Fuzzy-Methods are basically nothing else than an extension of classical mathematical logic and classical set theory, *the* foundations of modern mathematics. Although their invention by Zadeh in the Sixties was motivated by the attempt to capture some aspects of human thinking that are not exactly describable by classical logic Fuzzy-Methods have also demonstrated their fruitfulness by their implementation as specific computer programs, in particular as extensions of so-called production systems or expert systems respectively. In all these cases, to put it into a nutshell, structural mathematics and the computer together made it possible to develop and to apply new forms of mathematical models, which can be applied to problems outside of the range of traditional mathematics.[14]

These new modeling techniques, of which we shall chiefly use neural networks in this book, hence may be called mutual children of structural mathematics and the computer. They are the main *methodical* reason why we think that a new attempt to apply mathematical techniques to problems of hermeneutics is worthwhile. A more *conceptual* reason is, as we mentioned, the framework of complex systems theory, with which we shall briefly deal in the next subchapter.

A certain terminological remark is in this context in order. Frequently a distinction is made between *mathematical* models on the one hand and *computational* models on the other; the last term is used when formal models are based on computer programs and when the modeled system's behavior is not given by the solutions of according equations but by the algorithms of the respective programs and the simulation runs of the program. In our opinion this distinction is rather superfluous. Of course for example neural networks are nothing else than certain mathematical algorithms and the models of social and cognitive processes, built via the construction of adequate neural networks or other techniques, are consequently mathematical

---

capture different developments of his cellular automaton in dependency of different initial states (cf. Levy 1993).

[13] Holland, Rechenberg, and other pioneers in the field of evolutionary algorithms based their models on the famous "modern synthesis" in evolutionary biology (Huxley 1942). In the meantime, though, recent developments in evolutionary biology demonstrate that the modern synthesis is too simple to capture the complexity of biological evolution. In particular it is apparently necessary not only to consider simple genes as the fundamentals of evolution but also to differentiate between "toolkit" genes – the sort of genes functionally known since Mendel – and so-called regulator genes (cf. Carroll 2006).

[14] Basically of course a computer itself is nothing else than a huge ensemble of logical circuits, i.e. a technical application of mathematical logic.

models. To be sure, as we already mentioned, these are not mathematical models in the tradition of the mathematical natural sciences, mainly based on the calculus. But because the complex systems the social and cognitive sciences have to deal with need another form of mathematical modeling it seems rather strange to us not to speak of mathematical models in this context. It may well be the case that in particular evolutionary theories in the social, cognitive and even biological sciences need such new forms of mathematical models because they are at their logical and structural core algorithmic ones (cf. Dennett 1995; Klüver 2003). Therefore, the difference between mathematical models and computational models should be renamed as the difference between classical mathematical approaches and those new ones that are better suited to model social and cognitive complexity.

By the way, even a superficial glance at formal systems like, e.g., cellular automata and Boolean networks shows the mathematical basic features of them. We already mentioned the fact that these systems can and must be described on the one hand by their respective topology (see below Section 1.3.1). On the other hand rules like the transition functions of cellular automata or the logical functions of Boolean networks must be understood as basic algebraic properties of these systems. For example, the set of transition rules of a reversible cellular automaton is in terms of algebra an algebraic group, although not necessarily an Abelian one. This example demonstrates that these formal systems can be understood as classical mathematical structures, namely by a combination of algebraic and topological structures; we shall come back to this aspect below. In future publications we shall give some results of according investigations.[15]

1.3 A Short Glossary on Complex Systems, Simulations, and Communication Theory

1.3.1 Complex Systems, Attractors, and Trajectories

If one wants to model some empirical domain the first step, of course, is to determine the conceptual characteristics of the model. In other words, from which perspective shall the model be constructed? To be sure, there are many different ways to solve that problem. Yet in science it has become rather common to describe the respective domain as a "system", which means in the most general sense that the domain is understood – and described – as a set of "elements" that are connected by specific "relations". If one simply wants a static description of that system it is enough to characterize the relations and define that way the "structure" of that system as the set of all relations between the elements. A simple example is, for instance, a social group. The elements of that system are the members of that group and the social relations are, e.g., defined by a hierarchical structure: some members are more important

---

[15]Reversible cellular automata are t-invariant systems, i.e. they allow computing their states in the future and the past. An Abelian group is one with commutative operations.

than others and may influence the members with a lower social status. In the behavioral sciences groups with an informal social hierarchy are called groups with a "pecking order". Another example for a system is our planetary system, consisting of the elements "Sun" and the formerly nine planets.[16] Their relations are described by Newton's law of gravitation, which means that the relations are defined by the mutual gravitational attraction of the planets.

Yet a purely structural description of systems is often not enough. Most interesting empirical domains are characterized by a certain dynamics, which means that these systems change over time. Because of this fact the mathematical tools of the calculus, i.e. differential equations, had become the most prominent mathematical methods to analyze the time dependent behavior of systems. Already one of the first mathematical laws of physics, namely the famous law of fall by Galileo Galilei, is written as a differential equation $ds/dt = g$, that is acceleration in dependency of the time t. Hence, a definition of a system must contain in addition rules of interaction between the elements that describe the behavior of the system during a certain time of observation.

The modeling of physical systems has an old tradition in contrast to that of social and cognitive ones and definitions developed for the natural sciences are not necessarily useful for the social and cognitive sciences. Therefore, it is necessary to give some general definitions of the dynamical behavior of complex systems.

At a certain time t a complex system is in a state S_t, which is usually defined by an aggregation of the states of the respective system's elements. For example, a social group may consist of nine members and these members are in a certain state of mind, i.e., they are angry, happy, or indifferent. Then the state of this group can e.g., be defined by the arithmetical mean of the emotional states of the members or by other mathematical forms of aggregation. The state of the whole group can accordingly be described as, for example, "more frustrated than happy with respect to all members". If a new member enters the group then the (emotional) state of the group will change, according to the state of the new member. In addition, if the group members interact according to the social rules of the group hierarchy then the emotional state of some members may change too – they become even more frustrated or happier. The new state(s) of our system hence is a result of the rule governed social interactions of the group members.

Accordingly the state of the solar system is defined by the number of the different planets and their geometrical positions at time t in the space the solar system occupies. As these geometrical positions change according to Kepler's and Newton's laws, which means according to the gravity caused attractions, the new state(s) of the solar system is again a result of the interactions between the system's elements.

In a more general and formal sense we obtain the following definition:

If f denotes the set of the rules of interaction of a certain system, if S_1 denotes the first state, i.e. an initial state, and $f^n(S)$ the applications of the rules of interaction on the state S for n times, then

---

[16]Recently the former planet Pluto is not considered as a planet anymore.

$$f^n(S_1) = S_{n+1}. \tag{1}$$

The dynamics of a complex system is accordingly defined as the succession of the system's states generated by the iterative application of the rules of interaction. Note that the term "application" means in the empirical sense that the elements of the system interact according to the specific rules; in a model theoretical sense "application" of course means that the rules are applied on the model. For the sake of brevity we speak in both cases of the application of the rules.

By defining the state of a system as we did in the previous examples we may also define the set of all possible states of a system. "Possible" means all states that are generated under all conditions that may determine the system's fate. For example, a predator-prey system may reach a state where the predators have eaten all prey, which will cause the predators to starve. In this case the system will vanish but this is nevertheless a possible state. Another possible extreme state may be that all predators starve because they could not get the prey. Then the prey's population will permanently grow until it reaches the carrying capacity of their biological environment, i.e., the maximum number of prey that can be fed. Yet whether a certain eco-system will reach such extreme states is another question: that depends in this case on the initial states, the fertility rates, and other parameters. Therefore, we must distinguish between the set of all possible states and the subset of states a certain system will factually reach. This subset we call the *trajectory* of the system and the set of all possible states is called *the state space* of the system.[17] In more informal terms the trajectory can be understood as the path of the system through the space of all possible states. For visualization purposes the state space of a system is often represented as a plane and the trajectory as the according curve in this plane. We shall give examples of such visualizations below. But note that a plane is only a two-dimensional space and that state spaces are frequently defined by much more dimensions. For example, the state space of our eco-system is characterized by the size of the two different populations, by the biological gender of one prey or predator respectively, the age of the different animals, and so on. Hence, visualization usually is only possible by neglecting some dimensions and by concentrating on only two.

The two-dimensional visualization of a trajectory is not the same as the time dependent process curves one frequently can see in textbooks and other scientific publications. In this case one dimension of the plane is always the time, usually represented by the x-axis. In the case of a trajectory the dimensions of the plane are defined by certain components of the states as in the example of the eco-system. To be sure, one can add time as a third dimension but only for illustrating purposes. As an example we show in the first figure (Fig. 1.1) the time dependent curve of the behavior of a predator-prey system, programmed as a cellular automaton. The two curves represent the change of the populations of predator and prey respectively.

---

[17]In the natural sciences frequently the term "phase state" is used instead of state space.

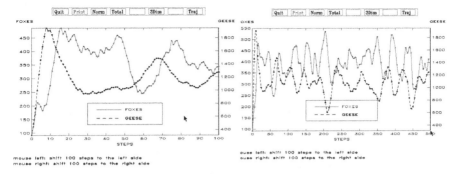

Fig. 1.1   Population variations of predator and prey

The second figure (Fig. 1.2) is the trajectory of the same system. The dimensions of the state space are defined by the size of the respective populations.

The third figure (Fig. 1.3) demonstrates the trajectory of the same system as in Fig. 1.2, but with time added as a third dimension.

Note that for visualization purposes the curve is continuous. Factually it is a discrete succession of different points in the state space, i.e., the different states of the system.

Now consider a case when the rules of the system are still operating but the trajectory reaches a certain point in the state space and stops there. This particular state, which the system does not leave anymore, is called a *point attractor*: the system is "drawn" to it by its rules of interaction. If the system reaches a certain state, generates a second one, then a third one and then reaches the first state again,

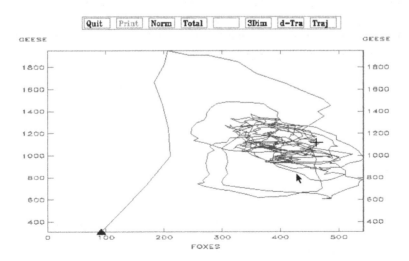

Fig. 1.2   Trajectory of the same system

Fig. 1.3 Trajectory as path in state space and time

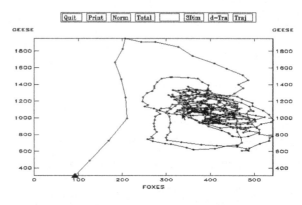

then this succession of states is called a *simple attractor* of period 3. Accordingly a point attractor is also called an attractor of period 1. In a more formal sense a point attractor S_A can be defined as

$$f(S_A) = S_A. \tag{2}$$

An attractor of period n can be defined the following way: Let $S_N = (S_1, S_2, \ldots, S_n)$ be a succession of n states and $S_i \in S_N$. Then S_N is an attractor of period n if

$$f^n(S_i) = S_i, \text{ for all } S_i \in S_N \tag{3}$$

An attractor of period n, n > 1, hence, is not a single state but a part of the trajectory consisting of n succeeding states. The part of the trajectory before the system reaches an attractor is called the pre period of the attractor. The following Figs. 1.4 and 1.5 show a point attractor and an attractor of period 4.

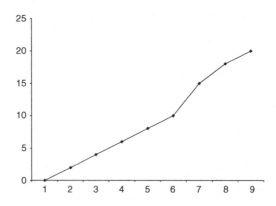

Fig. 1.4 A point attractor

Fig. 1.5 Attractor of period 4

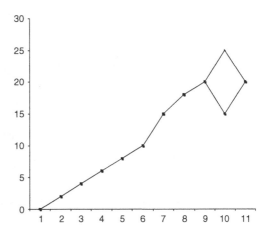

For theoretical purposes it is also useful to define a strange attractor. A strange attractor is, informally speaking, a certain segment of the state space, which the system enters and does not leave anymore. Inside the attractor the system often behaves in a manner that is difficult to predict – the system is *chaotic*. Chaotic systems play a role, e.g., in meteorology, yet it is a theoretically undecided question, if in reality there are in a strict mathematical sense chaotic systems at all. Indeed, the French mathematician Poincaré pointed out that finite systems always are periodic – the theorem of eternal return. For that reason we shall not deal with strange attractors and chaotic systems but always mean simple attractors of finite periods when we speak of attractors.

The theorem of eternal return, though, refers only to so-called *deterministic* systems. A deterministic system contains only deterministic rules, that is rules that always operate if the respective conditions for that rule are fulfilled. An example for such a rule is in a predator-prey system "IF a predator is hungry, and IF a prey can be caught, THEN the predator will (always) catch and eat it". In contrast to purely deterministic rules there also are *stochastic* rules, i.e., rules that operate only with a certain probability if the respective conditions are fulfilled. Many rules in social systems are stochastic, for example: "IF a young woman and a young man have married, THEN they will have children in the next years with the probability of, e.g., 0.7". Of course, the probability of that rule depends on the specific culture the young couple lives in. In Western industrial societies this probability is much lower than in agrarian societies.

Another important concept must be introduced: Whether a system reaches an attractor and if so which one depends on the rules of interaction on the one hand and the respective initial states on the other. It seems rather trivial that a system with certain rules often reaches different attractors when starting at different initial states. Yet a system frequently reaches the same attractor from different initial states. The complexity researcher Kauffman (1995) illustrates this fact with a lake (the attractor), into which different creeks flow. The creeks all start from different springs but flow into the same lake. A little Fig. 1.6 can demonstrate this.

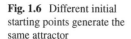

Fig. 1.6 Different initial
starting points generate the
same attractor

The set of all initial states that generate the same attractor is called the *basin of attraction* of this attractor.[18] The dynamics of a certain system can *in principle* be analyzed by the study of the different basins of attraction. By the way, the set of all basins of attraction of a system is called the *basin of attraction field* of the system. In more mathematical terms one can say that a basin of attraction field divides the set of all initial states into equivalence classes with respect to the specific attractors they generate.

Comparatively large systems frequently generate not only attractor states for the whole system but also local attractors. A local attractor of a system means that the whole system has not reached a point attractor or a simple attractor with a small period but is either still in the pre period of a certain attractor or in a strange attractor. The system, so to speak, is still at unrest. Yet certain subsets of the set of all elements may have already reached a local attractor, i.e. the subset constitutes a subsystem that has generated an attractor state. Formally a local attractor is defined the following way:

Let S be a system, f the set of all rules of local interaction, S' ⊂ S, i.e. S' is a subset of S, St(S) a state of S, and A a state of S' at the same time of St(S). Then A is a local point attractor if

$$f(A) = A \text{ and}$$
$$f(Z(S)) \neq Z(S). \tag{4}$$

The definition of a local attractor with a period p > 1 is accordingly done.

If a sufficient large system is in a strange attractor or in a long pre period the whole system's behavior may seem to be chaotic (in the mathematical sense of the word). If certain subsystems have reached local attractors these sub-states look

---

[18]The picture was drawn by Magdalena Stoica. By the way, after having made many didactical experiences with this terminology we learned that the tem "basin of attraction" is a rather unfortunate one. Frequently students thought that the lake in the picture is the basin and not the set of different springs. A better term would be, e.g., "set of attractor springs" or "set of attractor initial states". But because the term "basin of attraction" has been established for rather a long time we also use this term.

like "isles in the chaos", to use an apt picture from Kauffman (1995). Yet at least in social or cognitive systems such local attractors occur rather frequently: If a society is at unrest, i.e. in a period of changes in form of political reforms or even revolutions then certain institutions like churches may still be stable and other sub systems like the armed forces may have already reached a local attractor. This for example was the case during and after the French revolution where the new army was a stabilization factor for the society. The same observation of local attractors can be made with respect to cognitive systems (Klüver and Klüver 2007): Some parts of the biological neural networks of our brain may have reached a local attractor by, e.g., recognizing an old friend while other parts of the brain still search for a stable state.

Besides the distinction between stochastic and deterministic rules another distinction is important:

Imagine a large firm and the according rules of interaction, for example the rule that members of a team with different qualifications should cooperate for the best possible result of the team. The according interactions generate different states of the team and in particular a point attractor when the desired result has been reached. As this rule is valid for all teams we may call it a *general rule*: the rule must be obeyed always when its conditions – working together in a team – are fulfilled. Yet there are in addition other rules, which we call *topological* ones and which decide, which element of a system can interact at all with which other elements. If we take again the firm, then an according topological rule, e.g., determines which members of the firm may communicate with the chairman of the board. Certainly not every simple worker is allowed to do this and probably only the high-ranking managers of the firm plus the personal secretaries and assistants may contact the chief. In this case the topological rules define a social hierarchy. The same is the case with, e.g., a pack of wolves. The pecking order allows only certain male wolves to mate with certain female wolves. Only the alpha male wolf may mate with the alpha female. Hence, the generality of the mating rule is restricted by the topological one. Again we have a social hierarchy, defined by the respective topological rules.[19]

Yet these rules do not always constitute a hierarchical structure: the members of a jury, for example, are not allowed to speak during the trial with the attorneys or the accused although the jury members are neither socially higher nor lower than the attorneys or the accused. We call them topological rules because such rules constitute a certain geometry or topology respectively of the system. Hence, if we speak in general of the rules of interaction of a certain system we usually mean both the general rules and the topological ones. The topology of complex systems plays an important role in the cases of Boolean networks and neural networks (see Chapters 3 and 4). In the case of social and cognitive systems we shall also use the term "structure of a system" if we mean the set of topological rules, because "structure" is a well-known term. By the way, for the analysis of kin structure in early societies Read (2004) also emphasizes the necessity of topological analysis.

In the previous paragraphs we only mentioned the dynamics of a system in dependency of the initial states and the rules of interaction. We did not take into

---

[19]The general rules characterize the algebraic properties of the respective system, the topological rules its topology – hence the name.

account the fact that systems do not exist as isolated entities but that they always maintain their existence in a certain environment. A predator-prey system, for example, has a certain dynamics. Yet the environment determines the fate of this system as well: if because of unfavorable weather conditions the prey as herbivores cannot get enough plants to eat they will starve and as a consequence the predators will also die. Such ecological catastrophes frequently occur. The system follows its own dynamics but is not able to adjust to new environmental conditions.

Now consider a system that is able to respond to changed environmental conditions by changing its own rules of interaction, general ones or topological ones or both. The most famous examples of such systems are biological species, which are able to change the genomes of their members by the well-known "genetic operators" of mutation and recombination. A biological species, of course, does not react to changing environmental conditions in a conscious manner but reacts to them by favoring those new individuals that are able to exist in a new way. If the creating of new individuals is fast enough then the species will survive by having changed its genetic structure via the generation of new individuals. Other examples of such systems are human nations that react to a coming war by introducing new laws for the economy, the restriction of individual freedom rights and so on. If a social system is not able to adjust its particular structure to such external threats it will certainly perish, i.e. it becomes the prey of the aggressive neighbors.

With these distinctions we are able to define the concepts of self-organization and adaptability: We call a system *self-organized*, if it generates its particular dynamics, i.e., its succession of states only by its own rules of interaction, and does so without taking into regard any environmental conditions. The environment may disturb the system by inserting new components and it may force the system to generate a new state. By such a disturbance the trajectory of the system will change but the system will still operate under the same rules of interaction. Most systems, with which physics and chemistry deal, are such self-organized systems like, for instance, the chemical reactions in a biological cell. The cell will always reproduce itself by the same laws of interaction between its specific molecules and may only be disturbed by the environment of the organism, for example by the invasion of a virus. Then the cell will react to the new element but again by the same biochemical rules of molecular interaction. We shall come back to this definition of self-organization in Chapter 4 when discussing the concept of self-organized learning.

Adaptive systems are in addition characterized by their capability to react on environmental conditions by changing their particular structure, i.e. their general and topological rules of interaction. Take for an example a social group of teenagers with a certain social hierarchy. Let us assume that this group is well suited to act in a social milieu where sporting abilities are important because the group leaders are selected according to their abilities in specific sports. If this group has to operate in another social milieu, where particular intellectual competences are demanded by the social environment, then the group has to adjust its social structure: by certain social rules like, e.g., voting, the group will choose new leaders and hence generate a new social structure, i.e. new topological rules. Because the changing of the topological rules is not done at random but by applying rules of changing old rules we call the rules of changing old rules *meta rules*: They operate above and upon the former rules of interaction by changing them.[20] Accordingly we call a system *adaptive* if it reacts on environmental conditions not only by changing its states but also by changing its rules of interaction via the application of certain meta rules. The meta rule of voting to obtain a new social structure in a group is one example; the genetic operators of mutation and recombination in the case of a biological species are another. A third example is the application of a specific learning strategy in a cognitive system, which we will discuss in the next chapters.

Although the term "meta rule" may sound a bit strange the phenomenon itself is rather common in social life as the example of the social group demonstrated. In the political realm, for example, certain laws regulate the social interactions of the members of a specific nation. If the parliament introduces new laws by changing old ones the parliament does so by the well-known processes of majority decisions. This procedure is a classical case of a meta rule because by its application the former rules of social interaction are changed.

In the previous paragraphs we introduced the concept of "attractor", i.e. a state or a succession of states, which the system will not leave anymore despite the permanent application of the rules of interaction. If we consider the set of rules of interaction as a system on a higher level of abstraction, upon which certain meta rules are operating, then we can define the concept of a *meta attractor*: It is a stable state of the rules of interaction that do not change although certain meta rules are applied to them. If for example political reforms via the decisions of a parliament do not really change the important rules of interaction because the reforms are only carried through in order to make the impression of an active and efficient government then the social rules in this society are in a meta attractor. Yet because these considerations are important only for theorists of complex systems we shall not deal with the concept of meta attractor in a more detailed fashion (cf. Klüver 2000; Klüver and Klüver 2007).

When we define a system as adaptive if it has the capability to change its rules of interaction by certain meta rules, according to specific environmental demands, we have to distinguish between two cases of adaptability. On the one hand a system may be adaptive as a whole although the elements of the system are not adaptive themselves. That is the case with biological species where the single organisms are not adaptive but "only" self-organizing by their genetic program. Environment may accelerate the ontogenetic development, may slow it down or may even stop it. But the genetic program always runs the same way. The species as a whole is adaptive the way just described but only as a whole. On the other hand there are adaptive systems where the elements itself are adaptive and at least partly generate the system's adaptation by their individual adaptive processes. A social group is such a case where the individual members by their cognitive processes understand the necessity to change the group structure. In that case the group members adjust to a new social milieu and as a consequence they apply social meta rules to the old group structure.

---

[20]The Greek word *meta* means exactly that, namely "above", "beyond" or "upon" like in "metaphysics" or in "meta mathematics".

A lot more could be said about the concepts of self-organization and adaptability. But for our purposes these short introductory remarks are quite sufficient. More detailed considerations on these subjects can be found in, e.g. Klüver (2000) and Klüver (2002).

1.3.2 Would-Be-Worlds: The Methods of Simulation[21]

The construction of mathematical models is one of the most important methodical tools in science and technology and, of course, mathematical models frequently allow for very important insights of complex systems already without using computer simulations. Yet in the case of many complex systems like, e.g., those studied in meteorology or in the social sciences it is not possible to analyze complex dynamics without the use of suited simulation programs. The reasons for this are either that as in meteorology basic mathematical descriptions of the climate system are known but that they are not directly applicable, i.e., there exist no simple solutions for the basic equations. In addition, there are so many different details to consider that only very large computers can deal with them. Or, as in the social and cognitive sciences, there exist no basic equations for the description of the respective dynamics and hence the dynamics must be represented by the usage of according simulation programs. Therefore, as we shall deal with many simulation examples in this book, what is a simulation?

The term "simulation" has a Latin origin and is derived from *similis*, which means "like" or "similar". In everyday language "to simulate" often means, "to pretend", i.e. to generate a false impression. In this sense a young healthy man may "simulate" a sickness if he wants to avoid being enlisted into the army. He tries this by producing an image of his physical state that is "similar" to that of a real sick person. His simulation, therefore, is a similar representation of a sick body.[22]

Although in science and technology the term "simulation" is certainly not used with the meaning of pretending something that really is not the case a scientific simulation has also the aspect of the construction of representations that are similar to some original. Because of that general meaning sometimes "simulation" is used in the same sense as the term "model". Yet for the sake of clarity, in this book we shall always distinguish between model and simulation. The reason for this is simply that we shall speak only of simulations if they are based on and performed with according computer programs. By the way, the Oxford Dictionary also defines "simulations" by the usage of computer programs.

If we bear this in mind, then we can define "simulation" the following way:

A simulation consists of the translation of a formal model into a suited computer program *and* by the running of this program on the basis of certain parameter values and predefined initial states of the system one wants to simulate. In other words, the

---

[21] We borrow the term of "would-be worlds" from Casti 1997.

[22] Perhaps the most famous story of such a simulation is the novel "Confessions of the confidence trickster Felix Krull" (*Bekenntnisse des Hochstaplers Felix Krull*) by Thomas Mann.

simulation of a complex system always means the analysis of the system's dynamics by observing how the trajectory of the system is generated by the simulation program in dependency of the initial states and the parameter values. Simulations, therefore, are always undertaken in order to study complex dynamics. Although there are many computer programs that allow the analysis of the static structure of complex systems simulation programs refer to the dynamical characteristics of the systems one wants to study. Accordingly a simulation program is "valid", i.e. it produces satisfactory results, if the simulation program is sufficiently "similar" to the original, i.e. the empirical systems, and if observing the behavior of the empirical system can validate the results of the simulations.

In the experimental sciences like physics or chemistry experiments are done by the variation of a certain parameter and by keeping constant the others. The reason for this restriction is of course that only the variation of one single parameter allows statements about the exact influence of this particular parameter. If one tries to vary two or more parameters at the same time one could never be sure, which effect is caused by which parameter value. To be sure, there are statistical methods that allow the simultaneous variation of more than one parameter, but these methods cannot be discussed here. When one confines oneself to the variation of only one parameter the first question is, of course, which one it should be. This is as in the case of model construction a consequence of the respective research question. The next question is what values the constant parameters should be given. One rule of the thumb usually is that these values should be kept in the middle of the respective scale of values. If, for example, the values of a particular parameter that should be constant vary from 0 to 1 then this parameter should be kept at 0.5. Although this methodical rule is sufficient for many cases not all computer experiments can be done this way. Sometimes it is necessary to keep the values of the constant parameters as low as possible and sometimes they should be kept at the maximum. It is as always a question of practical experience to know at which values the constant parameters should be kept.

Another question is the selection of representative samples. Because computer experiments allow the variations of systems parameters in a nearly unlimited fashion one often gets the problem of a so-called combinatorial explosion. For example, we studied the impact of certain topological structures on the dynamics of Boolean networks with only six elements. Simple combinatorial calculations showed that even in the case of such small networks there are 10^{15} different networks to take into account. The analysis of this number according to our research question would be not only time consuming but also difficult for a statistical evaluation. Hence we reduced that large number to 1,499 different networks by partitioning all networks into equivalence classes of isomorphic graphs (Klüver and Schmidt 2007). (We cannot explain the rather strange number of 1,499 equivalence classes, by the way.) In this case the representative character of the selected samples is given by graph theoretical considerations. But often this question cannot be answered by mathematical considerations alone.[23]

---

[23]The procedure of partitioning a set of data or samples into equivalence classes is also frequently used for testing the validity of a computer program.

There are at least three important problems that can in the case of "real" complex systems only be solved by the usage of simulation programs and that make the use of such programs an absolute necessity:

1.3.2.1 The Explanation of Complex Phenomena

With the concept of "explanation" one usually means the reduction of a certain observed phenomenon B – the effect – to another phenomenon A – the cause. The statement "A explains B" is in this sense equivalent to the statement "A is the cause of (the effect) B". Consider a complex system whose state S_t is observed at time t. If we wish to explain this state then we have to take account of (a) some previous states of the system, if they are known, and (b) of course the rules of interaction that characterize the dynamics of that system. The concrete dynamics is then determined by the previous or initial states respectively and the rules of interaction. We may then say that we explain S_t by these two characteristics of the system (see below Chapter 2 on "explanation").

Now we have to consider three different cases. (a) Besides the present state the rules of interaction of the system are known but not the initial state or any previous states. (b) The initial state of the system or some previous states are known and of course the present state but not the rules of interaction of the system. (c) Besides the present state neither previous states nor the rules of interaction are known. Obviously the last case is by far the most difficult one.

All three cases are rather common in science and frequently they cannot be answered without the use of simulation programs. Let us start with the first case; the probably most famous example of such a problem is the question in cosmology "what was before the Big Bang" (cf. e.g. Greene 1999).

(a) Many laws in classical physics and chemistry have the characteristic of the so-called "t-invariance", which means that they are independent from the direction of time. Laws that are t-invariant allow the (mathematical) reconstruction of the past, i.e. previous states, by the same manner as the prediction of future states – the laws allow a backward computation as well as a forward computation. The laws of Kepler are an example for t-invariance, because they allow the computation of planetary positions in the past as well as in the future.[24]

Unfortunately many complex systems cannot be explained by t-invariant laws. We already mentioned in Chapter 1.3 the concept of "basin of attraction", i.e. the set of all possible states that precede a particular attractor. In many cases the basin of attraction of a particular attractor contains more than one state, which means that in general one particular state has more than one possible predecessor. Such systems cannot be characterized by t-invariant laws because their rules do not allow a backward computation. Hence, in general one can only try different simulation

---

[24]In many adventure stories the hero is able to impress the natives of a simple tribe or a pre-scientific society by correctly predicting an eclipse of the sun and by that to save his life. The scientific reason for this capability is the t-invariance of the Kepler equations.

runs by inserting some possible or assumed initial states and by observing if the present known state will be the result of the simulation runs. It is then a question of empirical research to exclude one or several of the possible previous states. But without the use of computer simulations it would not be possible at all to obtain a list of possible states that could be candidates for the answer one looks for. Else one could not distinguish between possible and impossible previous states in an exact manner at all. We shall come back to this problem in Chapter 3.

A variant of this case is the hypothetical assumption about an external disturbance of the system in the past. For example, many scholars believe that the extinction of the dinosaurs was due to the strike of a large meteorite. According simulations that used the well-known physical effects of such a strike demonstrated that indeed this hypothesis is a plausible one. In general, such a hypothesis postulates an externally caused state of the systems; confirmations of this hypothesis are done by simulations to obtain the present state or a well-known previous state.

(b) For the second case a classical example is the fundamental question of biochemistry about the origins of life. The initial state is known, i.e. a "primordial soup" of organic molecules. Yet neither the exact rules are known how these molecules are combined to larger complexes of proto life nor is it known how probable these combination processes are. Kauffman (1993) demonstrated in what way the use of certain simulation programs, i.e., Boolean networks, allows to postulate possible rules that at least in the simulations lead from (artificial) organic matter to (artificial) organic complexes large enough to be interpreted as simple forms of life. This approach is paradigmatic for the dealing with the second case: Grounded on theory and empirical knowledge a known initial state – or generally some known previous state – is inserted into the respective simulation program and hypothetical rules are inserted too. If the result of the simulation is the known present state the hypothesis about the according rules of interaction is confirmed. But note that such a successful simulation experiment does not prove the truth of the hypothesis once and for all. The considerations about the impossibility to compute backwards in an unambiguous manner, i.e. the impossibility to definitely determine the real initial state, have their parallel in this case: It is nearly always possible to generate a present state from a certain initial state by different sets of rules.

This deplorable fact can be illustrated by a little mathematical example. Consider the number series 0, 2, 6, define 0 and 2 as previous states, and 6 as the present one. A recursive rule that would generate this little series is, e.g., $n_{k+1} = 2(n_k + 1)$.[25] Then the series would be continued with the number $2(6 + 1) = 14$. Another rule for the series 0, 2, 6 would be the following one: if $k = 1, 2, 3, \ldots$, then $n_k = k^2 - k$ because $0 = 1^2 - 1$, $2 = 2^2 - 2$, $6 = 3^2 - 3$. The next number in the series generated by the second rule is then $4^2 - 4 = 12$. Hence the two rules both generate from the states 0 and 2 the same state 6 but differ in the next states. Both rules explain the state 6

---

[25] $0, 2(0 + 1) = 2, 2(2 + 1) = 6.$

but also generate, i.e. explain two different larger systems. A third even simpler rule would be "repeat the sequence after the first three steps". Obviously this rule would generate 0 in the fourth step. We shall come back to this little example when dealing with the question of prediction.

By the way, in theory of science this general problem is known as the problem of "conventionalism". This term means that all scientific theories are only "conventions", i.e. their validity is only provisional and that it is often not possible to decide at some time between different theories. One of the earliest partisans of scientific conventionalism was the great mathematician Poincaré (Poincaré 1902); the critical rationalism of Popper is an even more famous example of conventionalism in the theory of science (Popper 1969).

Generally, it is always possible to define very different rules for any finite number series that all generate the same series. Yet already our little example demonstrates that the continuation of a finite series by different rules practically always generates different successions. The same fact, of course, is valid for empirical complex systems.[26] Therefore, the successful implementation of hypothetical rules in the simulation program, i.e. the generation of a known present state from equally known previous ones is no final proof of the according hypothesis but "only" a confirmation that may be refuted some day if and when more facts about the respective system are known. But as in the first case no exact plausible hypothesis could be generated at all without the use of a suited simulation program if no classical mathematical tools are applicable.

(c) The most difficult case is, of course, if neither previous states nor rules of interaction are known. If no historical research about factual previous states is possible then the system could only be observed for some time in order to obtain some additional states. If that can be done then this case is the same as case (b): from the knowledge about a succession of states hypothetical rules can be inserted into the according simulation program and if one is lucky then the simulation results would be just that succession. The *caveat* about the results, i.e. that they are only provisionally valid, is also the same as in case (b).

1.3.2.2 The Prediction of the Future of a System

Explanations are usually interesting only in the sciences whose task is to explain certain known facts. For practical purposes it is often more important to obtain predictions about a system, i.e., to get knowledge about the probable or even factual future development of the system. As we saw, explanations always refer to the past of the system that is to be explained. In this sense we used the term "historical

---

[26] A classical example is the discipline of history where historians permanently discuss the reasons, i.e. rules, why certain historical processes went their specific way and not another. Many facts about the succession of social states are known yet there is seldom any consent about the rules that lead from one state to the next one.

research", i.e., the look for previous states. Predictions in contrast of course refer to the (possible) future of a system. Because the future states of a system are for trivial reasons not known as facts predictions are only possible, if at all, if one knows not only the present state of the system but also the rules of interaction. In other words, a prediction by the usage of a simulation program is basically nothing else than the inserting of the present state of the system together with the according rules of interaction. The next states the simulation will generate are the prognostication of the system's future.[27] In this case predictions are even less problematic than explanations because the problem of uncertain previous states does not exist.

But of course there may be also the case that one knows the present state of the system to be predicted but not the rules. Prediction then is only possible if besides the present state one knows also some previous states. If by successful simulations one obtains the present state from the previous ones we have the same situation as in case (b): it is possible to insert the rule(s) and try simulations with it but the mentioned *caveat* is still more important. Because the present state can be generated from previous ones with different rules the simulations will generate in most cases different future states. Our little mathematical example demonstrated how different the results of the respective fourth step are. Predictions, hence, can be done with some chance of success only by knowledge of present state(s) *and* the respective rules.

The well-established method of time series analysis is an illustrative example for the problems that arise when predictions are tried on the basis of the knowledge about previous and present states alone. There are many attempts, e.g., to predict the stock market by time series analysis, the so-called technical analysis. Even neural nets were constructed to do this task (cf. e.g. Kaastra and Boyd 1996). Yet even in this comparable simple case the prediction success was never greater than about 80%.

But even in the first case there are in practice a lot of problems that make successful, i.e., unambiguous predictions difficult and sometimes even impossible. On the one hand a successful prediction can only be done if the present state is very accurately known. Many complex systems change their trajectory in a significant manner if the present state is changed only to a small degree (the famous Butterfly-Effect). That means in a methodical sense that an imperfect knowledge about some components of the system's present state will make the according prediction rather uncertain and frequently useless. Because it is often very difficult to know all important details of the state of an empirical system all respective simulations can be interpreted only with great caution – the results are only probably valid in proportion to the degree of knowledge about the present state.

On the other hand there is an analogous problem with respect to the rules of interaction. Even if the rules are well known they may be only stochastic ones (see above), which means that the results generated by simulation runs are valid

---

[27] It must be noted, by the way, that even in the case of explanation some predictions are necessary: A successful theory must not only explain known facts but also predict unknown ones.

only with a certain probability. To be sure, in this case the simulation runs can be repeated for many times and the final results can be obtained by constructing the mean value of the different single results. This is a well-known procedure in the experimental sciences. But even this statistical validation yields only results about *probable* developments.

To make things even worse, frequently both problems simultaneously arise in practical research. If neither the present state is accurately known nor the rules or if the known rules are only stochastic ones then the results of simulation runs are only to be taken as heuristic orientations, namely with respect to the directions how more thorough research on state and rules of the system should be done.

Fortunately things are not always so bad. In many cases the present state *and* the rules of systems are sufficiently known and predictions are possible with a satisfactory degree of precision. Therefore, these warning considerations should demonstrate that simulations are neither in the case of explanations nor in that of predictions something like a wizard's wand, although sometimes it may seem so. Simulations are not a substitute for empirical and theoretical research but often a very valuable tool, without which neither predictions nor explanations are possible at all.

1.3.2.3 The Steering of Systems

The importance of a possible prediction of complex systems is obvious and it can be experienced every day on TV with weather forecast or the prognostication of economical developments. Yet frequently in practice the possibility to steer systems is even more important. "Steering" means usually the task to improve the performance of a certain system in different aspects, i.e., the task of an optimization of the system. For example, the working results of a team of co-operators may be unsatisfactory and the question is if another composition of co-operators might yield better results; the traffic flow in a city may be too slow and the question is how other combinations of traffic lights might obtain a better traffic flow – a classical example of network optimization; the information flow in a firm may be too complicated and too many errors in the sending of messages may occur; the according question is then how the flow of messages might be improved; the social hierarchy in a school class may be such that pupils with learning difficulties are hindered by their class mates; the question then is how the teacher can change some of the interaction rules between the pupils in order to generate a better social climate in the class, and so on.

In more general terms the steering of a complex system in order to improve its performance can be understood the following way with respect to two cases: (a) The goal of the improvement is known in form of a certain state. By this we mean that a certain possible state S of the system is known, in which the system will generate the desired results. In this case the optimization task is to change the trajectory of the system in order to let the system generate from the present state the desired one S. The translation of this task into the usage of simulation means of course that first the simulation is done with the actual state and the at present observable rules of the system. Usually the results of the simulation runs will show that the next states will be not much better than the present one, in particular if the system is in a simple attractor. As the changing of a trajectory can be done in at least two ways the first attempt to better the states of the system can be to change the present state. That would be the case, e.g. if a social team is changed by the exchanging of some group members. According simulation runs will show if the changing of the state is successful or if still additional changes have to be made.

The second attempt is to change the interaction rules of the system, as a teacher would try in the example above. Another example is the changing of the topology of a certain network, e.g., the position of traffic lights in a city. The inserting of the changed rules and topology respectively will then perform the simulation runs and again the results will show if the changing obtains the desired results. In both cases the practical question is of course if the changing is possible at all to the necessary degree. If, for example, the substitution of one team member by another is not sufficient and if the simulations demonstrate that only the exchange of at least half of the team members will produce the desired effects then such a radical variation of the group might not be possible. Accordingly, it may not be possible to vary the rules of a system to that degree which would be necessary for the generation of the desired results.

In such a case a combination of the two attempts might not only be useful but even perhaps the only way to realize the desired states of the system. In other words, if radical changes of states and/or rules are practically not possible then according simulations might show that small and hence possible variations of both states and rules could generate the desired results. It is obvious that such methodically complex cases could be sufficiently analyzed only by the use of suited simulation programs.

In practice when the possibilities to change a system can be very limited the last approach may be often the only possible one. One analyzes which changes are possible at all – either state changing or rule changing or both – and sees what results these changes generate in the simulation. It may be that the results are not satisfactory. But even in this case the simulation was worthwhile: If there is only one possible way to change a system and if the simulation demonstrates that this changing will produce no significant better results, then it is better not to change the system than to change it with some costs and be afterwards disappointed because of no better effects. It is then the problem of the system analyzer how he may get the possibilities to change the system in a more radical way.

A very practical and important example of our own research shall illustrate this. One of our students analyzed for his doctorate a hostel for delinquent youths and asked how the dividing of the members of this hostel into different subgroups could be optimized in order to decrease the degree of violence in the respective groups. He did this by using two of our simulation programs developed for this task, namely a special cellular automaton and a genetic algorithm. To his disappointment he learned from the results of the simulation runs that there exists no combination of hostel members in this particular hostel that would reduce the degree of violence to the desired minimum. When he asked the teachers of this hostel and of other ones all experts told him that this problem is typical for these hostels because the hostels get from the authorities too many youths with a strong tendency for violence. In this case, therefore, no changes are possible that could better the social climate in the hostels. Yet even this unsatisfactory result was not obtained in vain because it can be a strong argument for the responsible politicians to principally change the combination of delinquent youths in these hostels (Herrmann 2008).

(b) The second case is if one knows that the actual results of a certain system are unsatisfactory but one does not know the desired goal, and in particular one does not know what state of the system might produce better results than the present state does. The only knowledge one has at one's disposal is that certain states will produce better results than others. In mathematical terms this case is an optimization problem where the desired optimum is not known but only the difference between better and worse states. In terms of learning types in neuro-informatics this is the case of so called reinforcing learning (see below Chapter 4).

In this case, of course, the usage of simulations is even more important than in the first one. If neither the goal nor the way are known with sufficient accuracy then practically only suited simulations can tell, which improvements of the system will lead to better results. To be sure, all the distinctions mentioned in the first case must be considered in this case too and the most important question is, as always, if the necessary variations of the system are possible at all. But only the (additional) usage of suited simulation programs could help in such complicated cases.

So far we have only discussed the possibilities of simulating self-organized systems. Certainly all the mentioned problems will also arise if one wants to explain, prognosticate, or steer adaptive systems, i.e. systems where meta rules may change the rules of interaction. It is obvious that these tasks can only be performed if one has a sufficient knowledge about the probable meta rules and their effects on the rules of interaction. Although the mentioned problems are in the case of the simulation of adaptive systems even more difficult to solve than in the discussed cases simulations are also possible (cf. Klüver 2002). Yet for practical purposes, as the examples showed, it is frequently possible to restrict the simulation experiments to just self-organized systems. The methodical problems are even there difficult enough.

For very different reasons neither in research nor in social or technical practice simulation programs are by themselves sufficient for the solving of difficult problems. But very often they are necessary and indispensable tools. Without simulation programs researchers and practitioners alike frequently have to operate according to trial and error methods that are not only time and energy consuming but also expensive and not seldom impossible. Neither with dangerous technical systems not with social ones trial and error methods are usually possible at all. The better simulation programs for such problems are the better for research and practice.

1.3.3 Some Basic Concepts of Communication Theory

Frequently the task to understand human beings, namely their actions and the according social products, is embedded in a social, i.e. communicative context. We have to understand people when interacting with them, we have to understand their "products", i.e. social actions and their manifestations like verbal messages and written texts by receptive communication, and we have to understand certain social structures by communicating with people who act according to these structures. Even if one only observes other people or reads texts from authors who died a long time ago we ask for the "meaning" and the "information" the observed actions, messages or texts have for us and in particular for the producers of the actions and messages. We shall discuss the different forms of understanding in Chapter 2; here we just give some definitions of the communicative concepts of *meaning, information,* and relevance. Because it is quite impossible in this study to discuss the numerous definitions of these concepts we just give those definitions in mathematical terms that we developed as the basis of our mathematical theory of communication.[28]

The *meaning* of a message can (and probably must) be defined in terms of complex systems theory. Meaning always means meaning *for* a receiving system. Although we are quite aware that there also exists the idea of an "objective" meaning of a message that is independent of a certain receiving system (a human person, an animal or even an artificial system like a computer program), in contexts of social interaction and communication only a meaning for a receiving system makes sense in a practical way. From this first definition it immediately follows that the meaning of a certain message can und frequently will be different for different receiving systems. Hence, to understand the reaction of another person to a specific message includes the task to understand the meaning of the message to this particular person. The meaning of the message "the structure of the universe must be described in terms of fractal geometry" is certainly different for a theoretical physicist and a medical doctor respectively.[29]

Now let us define a person who receives a message as a cognitive system that consists of certain elements interacting with each other. It is of no importance whether we define these elements as, e.g., biological neurons of the brain, i.e. if we understand the receiving cognitive system as a neurobiological one, or if we for example define the cognitive elements as semantical concepts and thus define the cognitive system as a semantical network. We shall give examples of both possibilities in the following chapters. A message is something like an "external disturbance" of the interactions of the elements, i.e. the message causes the system to generate a certain dynamics. If and when the trajectory of the system that is caused by the message reaches an attractor, preferably a point attractor, the system has assimilated the message. *The meaning of the message then is nothing else than the attractor the system has generated.*

In Klüver and Klüver (2007) we illustrated this rather abstract and probably unusual definition with the example of the famous dog of Pavlov. Before the

---

[28]Readers who want to know more about these subjects can look up the according definitions in more detail in Klüver and Klüver (2007).

[29]The concept of an "objective" meaning of, e.g., a certain word is simply due to the fact that in each social community with a common language must exist social conventions about the intersubjective usage of a sign. For example, one expects of a user of the linguistic symbol "oak" that he refers to a certain tree and not to an animal. Yet the meaning of "oak" is certainly not the same for a ranger in a national park and for a joiner.

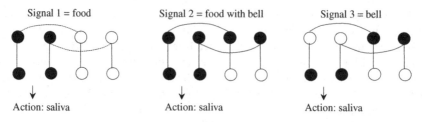

Fig. 1.7 Visualization of the cognitive system

conditioning process the signal of the bell had perhaps a certain meaning for the dog but certainly not the meaning after the conditioning process when the dog reacted to the bell by producing saliva. This can be visualized by a simple neural network (Fig. 1.7).

The network on the left side shows the (possible) structure of the dog's cognitive network that is responsible for the receiving and transforming of the two messages "food" and "bell" before the conditioning process. The right network shows the result of the conditioning process: Because of the repeated simultaneous receiving of both signals the network has changed, i.e. built up new connections between the neurons of the input layer (the layer on top). Both networks are "activated" by the external signals, i.e., the neurons of the input layer obtain certain numerical values that are sent to the neurons on the output layer (the bottom one). Now the dog generates the attractor "producing saliva" if it only hears the bell. The bell signal now has another meaning for the dog than before the conditioning process. In other words, the meaning of a signal or message may not only be different for different receiving systems but also different for the same system before and after a learning process. We shall come back to this little example when dealing with the concept of learning in Chapter 4.

In this example the (artificial) neural networks represent some part of the brain. In another example the respective receiving network is constructed as a semantical net, i.e. a network whose units (the artificial neurons) represent certain concepts that are connected by different links. The links represent the logical relations between the concepts. Such a semantical network represents the structure of some knowledge, i.e. not only knowledge in form of a set of concepts but also the connection of the knowledge parts. Obviously this network contains some knowledge about the key concepts "Paris" and "France" (Fig. 1.8)

The semantical network then is transformed into a so-called interactive neural network. This type of neural networks is characterized by connections between in

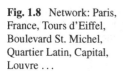

Fig. 1.8 Network: Paris, France, Tours d'Eiffel, Boulevard St. Michel, Quartier Latin, Capital, Louvre ...

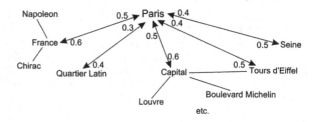

principle all neurons. In contrast to this type the network used in the previous example of the dog has only connections between the neurons on the input layer and between these neurons and those of the output layer. When an interactive network receives a message, for example the triple of concepts (Paris, Capital, France) – "Paris is the capital of France" – then these three concepts of the interactive networks are activated, which in turn activate all other neurons. The result of this mutual activation is again an attractor consisting of the neurons in different states of activation. By assuming that the meaning of a verbal message that is generated by a receiving semantical network contains only those concepts that are most important for the receiving system we define the meaning of a message in this case as those three concepts of the attractor that are most strongly activated. Such a result is shown in the next Fig. 1.9.

The length of the beams represents the size of the activation values. One sees that the concepts Seine, Tours d'Eiffel, and Quartier Latin are the concepts with the strongest activation and hence they represent the meaning of the message for this network. To be sure, the resulting attractor may be quite different for a network with the same concepts but another structure, i.e. another topology defined by the connecting links between the concepts. Because we shall apply interactive networks to several problems of understanding in Chapters 4 and 5 we shall here not give more technical details.

It must be noted that of course the knowledge of a certain person does not only consist of one semantical network but additionally of many networks that may themselves be connected. For example, the semantical network containing the concepts of Paris as the capital of France may be connected to quite another semantical network that also contains the concept "Paris" but now connected with concepts like "Troy", "Helena", Ulysses", "Hector" etc., i.e. the knowledge about the epos of Homer. Then a message containing the concept "Paris" may generate attractors in both networks. We may call the attractor of the first network the direct meaning of the message if it consists of concepts like "France" and the attractor of the second network the indirect or also mediate or associated meaning of the message; the second attractor is part of the association field of the meaning.[30]

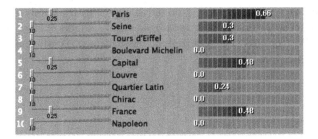

Fig. 1.9 Visualization of an attractor of the Paris network

---

[30]The association field may be significantly larger than just one additional attractor. For example, in 2007 we added a third network to the message with "Paris", namely a network consisting of some concepts from a detective novel by Agatha Christie, where "Paris" played an important role.

The concept of mediate meaning(s) or association field respectively allows another definition, namely that of the degree of meaning in analogy to the degree of information.[31] To be sure, in everyday language a statement like "message A is more meaningful to me than message B" frequently either means that for the speaker A has more information than B or that A is more relevant than B. Yet it makes sense to translate the statement into another one, namely that the speaker wishes to say "I can associate more ideas with A than with B". When defining the degree of meaning by the set of associations the receiver has with a message then the degree of meaning is the set of all attractors that are generated after the receiving of the message. A message A, hence, is more meaningful than a message B if and only if the set of attractors generated by the receiving of A is larger than that of B. But these short sketches are enough for the moment.

Meaning, hence, is defined as a construction of a receiving system that is activated by a certain message and thus generates a final state, namely an attractor state. It is important for the system that it generates a point attractor in order to obtain an unambiguous meaning. If the generated attractor would consist of, e.g., two states then the system would oscillate between these two states and would be unable to act. The message would be ambiguous and the system would be literally in the situation of the famous donkey of Buridan, which could not decide between two identical heaps of hay. As a sad result the donkey died of starvation. Therefore, the hesitation of a person to act after having received a message may sometimes be due to the fact that the cognitive structure of the system is not able to generate a point attractor but only one with a period larger than one.

Like the term meaning the concept of *information* is used in everyday language in rather different ways. Frequently the two terms are used synonymously as the utterance shows "this message has much meaning for me", with which the speaker wants to express that the message contains much information for him. Examples for the converse usage can also be found very easily. Yet at least since the classical study of Shannon and Weaver (1949) a precise definition of information or of the degree of information respectively is at hand, which distinguishes information from meaning.[32]

The first mathematical definition of the information degree of a message is due to Hartley (1928), who defined the information degree by the number of selections that are necessary to generate a message from a set of symbols or signs respectively. Shannon and Weaver (1949) generalized the basic ideas of Hartley and formulated their famous definition, namely

$$H = -\sum_i p_i * ldp_i \tag{5}$$

---

[31] Strictly speaking Shannon and Weaver did not give a definition of information but one of the *degree* of information

[32] Shannon and Weaver called their theory "A Mathematical Theory of Communication", which is rather unfortunate because they themselves emphasize that they do not deal with meaning.

if H is the information degree of the message, p_i is the probability of the part i of the message, and ldp_i the logarithm with base 2 of p_i. Shannon and Weaver used this logarithm (with the basis 2) because they wished to emphasize the selective character of their definition – according to Hartley: Each part of a message is the result of a binary selection between yes or no.[33] In more informal terms this definition postulates that the information degree of a message is the higher the more improbable a message is and vice versa.

In the natural and technical sciences this definition has been widely used and still it is the basis for the analysis of communicative processes in these disciplines. Yet it is of only restricted use in the social sciences because it presupposes an "objective" degree of information for arbitrary receiving systems. The degree of information H is frequently also called "negentropy", i.e. the negative measure of entropy of the system, about which the receiving system is informed. Because the entropy of any dynamical system is indeed an objective measure it seems obvious that its negative counterpart can also be defined in an objective manner.

Certainly this presupposition is in general not valid for social communicative processes, i.e. between human communicators, although we believe that the basic idea of Shannon and Weaver is very useful also for our own purposes. As we showed with respect to the meaning of a message the degree of information for a receiving system also depends on the knowledge of the system about the subject of the message, i.e. on the learning biography of the receiving system. A message like "Minister X has declared his resignation from his office" may contain much information for a political layman but not necessarily for a political analyst who expected this resignation for some time. Therefore, it is necessary to substitute the concept of objective probability by a subjective one.

We take over the basic idea of Hartley, Shannon, and Weaver that the information degree is the higher the less expected the message is and vice versa. This idea is certainly plausible also for social communication between human communicators: The message that there is snow at the North Pole is of course not very informative because everybody expects that in these cold regions there is a lot of snow. But the message that the glaziers at the North Pole begin to melt because of the climate change is certainly rather informative for most receivers of this message because only few experts expected it. We also take over the assumption that each message is composed of part messages. Hence, a message M can be defined as a vector $M = (m_1, \ldots m_k)$, if m_i are the part messages. Because this message is perceived by the receiving system we can also define M as a "perception vector".

Before the receiving system gets the message about the respective theme the receiver has a certain expectation about the subject, for example that Minister X will not declare his resignation or that the glaziers at the North Pole are still frozen. We then define this specific expectation also as a vector $E = (e_1, \ldots, e_k)$; the components e_i are of course the parts of the expectation. This gives us the basic definition of the information degree H of a message as the difference between the vectors M and

---

[33] From this definition Shannon derived his famous concept of "bit".

E, i.e. as the difference between a particular expectation vector and the according perception vector.[34]

Now we have to take into account the idea that the information degree depends on the probability of the part messages and hence of the whole message. If receiver gets a message X then

$$X = (x_1, \ldots, x_k). \tag{6}$$

The expectation of the receiver was

$$Y = (y_1, \ldots, y_k). \tag{7}$$

Then the part probability of the component i of the message is

$$p_i = 1 - |(x_i - y_i)| \tag{8}$$

In other words, the probability of a part message is the inverse of the difference between the components i.

By considering that the information degree of a message is its negative probability and by summing up the part probabilities we obtain

$$H = -\sum_i p_i \tag{9}$$

If we add the logarithm with base 2 for normalization purposes we obviously precisely get the Shannon-Weaver definition. But note that the p_i represent subjective probabilities that depend on the learning biography of the receiving system. The mathematical definition is the same in both cases but the concept of probability differs in an important aspect. Only by changing the concept of probability it is possible to use this mathematical definition for the formal analysis of social communicative processes. The definition can easily be extended to the case of semantical networks, i.e., if the message is a verbal one and if the vector of expectation is generated from the semantical network (cf. Klüver and Klüver 2007). Because we shall show some results about the relation between the topology of complex systems and the degree of information a message has for such systems we shall demonstrate the extension of our definition to semantical networks in Chapter 3.

In everyday language not only "meaning" and "information" are frequently used in a synonymous fashion but also "relevance". A message is said to be "meaningful" if the speaker wishes to say that it is important or relevant for him; the same is often the case when a speaker calls a message "very informative". But as we have, in the tradition of Shannon and Weaver, to distinguish between "meaning" and "information", we also have to distinguish between these two concepts and the concept of

---

[34]In statistics the concept of "expectation vector" is also known. Yet the statistical expectation vector has more to do with the objective probability of the Shannon-Weaver definition than with our concept of the expectation of a certain receiving system.

"relevance". In particular we have also to define this concept in terms of complex systems, i.e., in terms of dynamical semantic or neural networks respectively.

Consider again a cognitive system that consists of different semantic or neural networks. When this system receives a message or a signal it generates the meaning(s) of the message and computes the degree of information. Such a message has a certain meaning and the meaning might be associated with a lot of other networks; hence the message has a high degree of meaning. In addition, the message might also have a high degree of information. But nothing is said by these characterizations of the message about the relevance it has for the receiver.

With the concept of "relevance" we want to determine, according to the everyday understanding of this concept, if a message has practical consequences for the receiver and if so, by which degree. A message like "in the Andromeda Galaxy a supernova has exploded" may have some meaning for an educated layman. The message might also have a rather high degree of information, because perhaps the receiver did not know that the concepts "supernova" and "explosion" belong together. But despite the high information degree and the elaborated meaning the message is not very relevant for the receiver because this message has no practical consequences at all for his own life. He just receives it and will probably soon forget it.

A professional astronomer on the other hand will attach much more meaning to this message and perhaps not such a high degree of information because he probably expected the message. But in many cases such a message has a high degree of relevance for him because it has consequences for his professional life. In other words, he will perhaps feel anger that he did not make the discovery himself, he will try to confirm the message by making his own observations, he will get in touch with other colleagues and so on. The message has a high degree of relevance because it causes him to some reactions – emotions and practical actions.

According to this little example we can define the degree of relevance the following way:

We call that part of the whole cognitive system that processes the message in form of the generation of meaning and the computing of the information degree the cognitive net (CN). The CN is connected with other sub networks or just layers of units that we call the action part (AP) of the cognitive system. According to the connections between CN and AP some attractors will activate parts of AP and cause this way different actions of the whole system while some attractors will not.

Apparently a message is relevant for the cognitive system if the CN transmits its attractor state to the AP and otherwise not. If the AP gets an activation by a particular attractor of the CN then the AP will generate an attractor itself. This particular attractor of the AP we call the content of relevance of the message because this attractor causes the actions according to the message. For example, after the conditioning processes of the dog of Pavlov the content of relevance of the signal "bell" was quite different from the same message before the conditioning processes – producing saliva or not.

The degree of relevance, i.e. the degree by which one relevant message A is more relevant than another relevant message B, is dependent on the norms or values of the whole system. For example, for most humans the value of staying alive is certainly higher than the value of finding good entertainment. Therefore, the message "there comes a dangerous animal" has a higher degree of relevance than the message "there is a new and interesting movie at the cinema". We may safely assume that in living systems exists a hierarchy of values that define the degrees of relevance of different messages. Some of these values animals and humans have obtained as part of their biological heritage; other values have to be learned, i.e., they have to be placed at the correct place in the hierarchy of values during processes of socialization.

Yet the degree of relevance is not only dependent on the values of the respective system but also on the state the system has obtained at the time of the message. Consider again an organism with a high value of "food". If the organism is hungry at the time when a signal "food available" arrives, the signal will have a high degree of relevance. But if the organism is satiated, then the signal will have not much relevance; other signals, for example "potential sexual partner", will bear more relevance. These considerations lead to the following definition:

The state of the receiving system CN is represented by a numerical value s with $0 \leq s \leq 1$, for example the state "hunger". According to the construction principles of artificial neural networks the connections between CN and the action part AP are "weighted", i.e., they are also represented by a numerical value w with $0 \leq w \leq 1$. The strength of the connections – the "weights" – represent the value(s) the received signals respectively the accordingly generated attractors have for the system. The degree of relevance dr of a message is then defined as

$$dr = s * w. \tag{10}$$

For example, let us assume that "food" has a very high value, e.g. 1. The state of "hunger" is accordingly represented by a value $s = 1$, that is, the system's orientation is directed towards food. The degree of relevance of the signal "food available" is $dr = 1 * 1 = 1$, or in other words, the system will act because of the high degree of relevance. If on the other hand the system is satiated, then its state is with respect to "hunger" $s = 0$, which obtains the degree of relevance for the same signal as $dr = 0 * 1 = 0$. The system will not act at all.

If there are more than one connections between CN and AP then the value of dr will be computed the usual way characteristic for neural networks, i.e.,

$$dr = s * \sum w_i \tag{11}$$

for the different connections i.[35]

---

[35]By "usual" we mean that this linear activation function is frequently used when constructing neural nets. There are other functions too, for example the sigmoid function.

If the system gets several different messages at the same time, then it will "compute" the dr of all messages and will act according to the message with the highest degree of relevance.

The definitions of the content and the degree of relevance immediately show that relevance must be analytically distinguished from meaning and information, as the example of the astronomer already demonstrated. A message then may be understood as a three-dimensional construct that is characterized by a certain meaning "me", degree of information "di" and a certain content and degree of relevance "dr": a message "m", therefore, must be understood as m = (me, di, dr). When we represent as before the message by a vector that operates as input to a cognitive system then the cognitive system is principally able to generate a certain meaning, to compute the degree of information, and to generate actions by transmitting the attractor of the CN to the AP and thus determining the content and degree of relevance. To be sure, to do this in a successful manner the cognitive system had to learn (a) to generate the "correct" attractors, if the system was not been "born" with it, (b) to develop the "right" connections within its association or semantical field respectively in order to understand the communicative processes it takes part in, and (c) to connect the CN the "right" way with the AP in order to react adequately to different messages. Yet the problem of learning will be dealt with in later chapters.

1.4   Artificial Intelligence (AI) – The Quest for a Homunculus[36]

In Section 3.2 we showed that it is nearly always possible to construct different but equivalent models in order to explain some phenomena, i.e. processes. "Equivalent" means that all models explain the same phenomena but consist of different rules and hence will frequently generate different future states. Therefore, it is seldom possible to decide, which model is the empirical most valid one if one has neither time nor opportunity to wait for future states of the empirical system. That is particularly the case if it is not possible to directly look "inside" the empirical systems one wishes to explain, i.e. if the system is factually a black box for an observer. Especially just this problem arises when one tries to model and explain cognitive processes of the mind and/or brain. Despite all progresses neurobiology has made during the last decades neurobiologists still cannot give explanations of cognitive processes in terms of exact formal theories. They just are able to demonstrate where the brain is activated if human probands perform certain cognitive operations. But "knowing where is far from knowing how", as Lakoff and Núñez correctly remark in this context (2000, 26). Because of this the construction of mathematical or computational models respectively of certain cognitive processes, as we intend, is always only the construction of possible and plausible models and hence possible explanations of

---

[36]*Homunculus* is the name of an artificial small man who was developed by Wagner, the assistant of Dr. Faust, in the great drama "Faust" by Goethe. The term *homunculus* means "little man".

these processes. The caveat of conventionalism is valid in our case too. We shall give several examples of topologically different models that are all able to explain the same cognitive processes in the next chapters.

In Section 1.2 we quoted Vico that "we understand only what we can make". In a certain sense the construction of artificial systems that can simulate some of the numerous cognitive operations that humans are able to perform may help us a bit to overcome the boundaries of conventionalism. If AI-systems can do now and in future that what men would do as "intelligent" beings then we would have a strong indictor for the validity of our models. We understand parts of our mind and confirm the respective models because we made it.

To be sure, the construction of AI-systems are no final proof for the "truth" of our assumptions. Following Popper (loc. cit.) we are of course aware that there is no such thing like "true" theories or models respectively but only more or less well confirmed ones. But if a successful technology is based on a certain theory and according models we all accept this theory as a "true" one as long as the technology does what it is constructed for. It is, e.g., still not possible to look inside a star and to directly observe its process of nuclear fusion; but at least since the construction of the H-bomb nobody seriously doubts the principal truth of the theory formulated as the Bethe-Weizsäcker cycle. Therefore, we understand that part of nature because we re-made it, if only in form of a destructive weapon. Accordingly a successful construction of AI-systems would at least help us to understand our own mind better than without such a technology. One may call that methodical principle "confirmation by technology". More than a century ago Marx already formulated that principle in his second thesis on Feuerbach: "The question whether the human thinking can be true is not a question of theory but a practical one. In practice man must prove the truth ... of his thinking."[37] Our still very modest practice will accordingly be the construction of several systems that are at least able to perform some simple processes of cognition by simulating and thus explaining them. But what is meant with the term AI?[38]

A famous definition gave Minsky, one of the early pioneers in this field: "Artificial Intelligence is the science of making machines do things that would require intelligence if done by men" (Minsky 1968, V). In this formulation Minsky apparently identifies the field of research in AI with its subject and goal, namely artificial systems or machines respectively that "do things" of intelligence. We shall always distinguish between these two concepts and shall speak of AI only when we mean the respective constructs. But besides this little terminological confusion Minsky obviously shifts the question "what is AI" to the question "what is intelligence". Because this book is no introduction into cognitive psychology and/or

---

[37]MEW 3, 5, italics in the original, our translation from the German original: "Die Frage, ob dem menschlichen Denken gegenständliche Wahrheit zukomme – ist keine Frage der Theorie sondern eine *praktische* Frage. In der Praxis muss der Mensch die Wahrheit... seines Denkens beweisen". C.S. Peirce in his famous Pragmatic Maxim articulated principally the same position.

[38]A brief but interesting and informative overview about the field of AI can be found in Agogino (1999).

cognitive sciences we shall not try to answer this general question. As far as we know there is no generally accepted definition of this difficult concept. Instead of such a definition, which is perhaps not possible at all and at least not at present, scholars in AI and in the domain of cognitive modeling frequently give examples for "intelligent" actions like understanding and speaking natural language (cf. e.g. McLeod et al. 1998), learning from experience, drawing logical conclusions, constructing analogies and so on (cf. the examples in Polk and Seifert 2002; cf. also Russell and Norvig 2003). An artificial system then "is" intelligent or at least can simulate intelligence if it is able to perform some or all of these tasks. Because animals and in particular sub human primates are not able to do these things artificial systems that can do this are similar to homo sapiens – they are the step towards to artificial humans, i.e. Homunculi.[39] It is interesting to note, by the way, that the subject of our book, namely understanding, is only seldom mentioned when listing intelligent operations. On the contrary, problems of hermeneutics are mentioned usually only by the critics of AI and in particular of the so called "strong AI" (see below), in order to prove the impossibility of an AI (cf. e.g. Penrose 1989, 401; Dreyfus 1992; Winograd and Flores 1986).

The conception or dream of a "real" AI has frequently been the subject of Science Fiction (SF), as is well known. It is quite illustrative to have a look into some literary descriptions of AI-systems if one wants to obtain some characteristics for the possible intelligence of AI-systems. In their comprehensive overview of recent research in AI Russell and Norvig (loc. cit.) give some impressions how AI-themes are fictionally dealt with. Independently of them we got the same idea, namely by holding a seminar about fundaments of AI and AI-themes in SF in the summer semester 2006. Of course, we cannot mention all the numerous examples of SF-literature and films but just show some cases that are in our opinion rather representative.

1.4.1 A Little Excursion into Science Fiction

Isaac Asimov certainly was not the first writer who dealt in SF with the subject AI. Yet his "Robot Stories" were a milestone with respect to AI in SF and surely belong to the classics of this genre. All his many stories about robots are based on the famous "three laws of robotics", which we give in a reduced version:

(1) A robot must not harm a human being but instead help humans where it can.
(2) A robot must obey human orders, if they do not violate law (1).
(3) A robot must protect its own existence, if this does not violate laws (1) and (2).

Asimov started these stories, as far as we know, in the fifties of the last centuries when computers were still rather rare and when a computer program could

---

[39]The famous or infamous respectively experiments with the teaching of language to chimpanzees had only one result, namely that apes can learn, if at all, only a few words; whether they really "understood" the words they had learned is rather doubtful (cf. Pinker 1994).

only do the tasks that had been explicitly formulated during the process of programming. Hence the robots of Asimov could only follow the three laws, besides the special tasks they were programmed for, because the laws were given to the robots as explicit basic rules. As most SF-authors Asimov did not describe in any detail how intelligence and in several cases even consciousness could be the result of such explicitly programmed rules. He just assumed that in some future the computer scientists would solve these problems by constructing programs that are sophisticated enough to operate in an intelligent manner.[40]

Artificial Intelligence, hence, is the result of careful and sophisticated programming, i.e. the construction of a program where all intelligent abilities are inserted a priori into the system. The robots of Asimov are helpful and even kind beings because they are not able to act otherwise. To be sure, concepts like "kindness" and "helping" are only interpretations by the human users. The robots are neither kind nor unkind; they just follow their programmed rules. In particular, with respect to law (3) they do not have a *will* to survive. The protection of its own existence, which usually is in all animals and humans a natural part of their biological heritage, must be inserted into the robot's program as an explicit rule.

The idea that artificial intelligent systems like robots can only follow the rules that have been inserted as part of their programs is rather common in SF. Take for example one of the most famous AI in SF, namely HAL 2000 from the novel and the film "2001: A Space Odyssey". HAL, as is well known, operated during a space voyage to Jupiter quite well, when it (or should we say "he"?) suddenly seemed to go berserk by killing all astronauts except the commander of the space ship. Only by switching off HAL's main functions the commander was able to save himself.

Neither in the film by Stanley Kubrick nor in the script by Arthur C. Clarke an explanation for the erratic behavior of HAL was given. Clarke gave such an explanation in his sequel novel "2010: Odyssey Two": The mission control had given HAL two fundamental orders that generated a contradiction. On the one hand HAL should always operate according to the orders of the crew and protect them. On the other hand HAL was not allowed to tell the crew about the true goal of the mission, which became in HAL's estimation a danger for the crew. Hence HAL, in the words of Clarke, got caught in a "Hofstadter-Möbius loop" because it could not find a way out of this contradiction. As a result HAL solved this problem by killing most of the crew as a consequence of not being able to vary its programmed orders.[41]

---

[40]In his latest stories Asimov introduced robots that are able to learn and even can ignore the three laws by formulating a "zero law". But these additional capabilities emerged within some robots by "mutation", which Asimov did not describe either.

[41]We must confess that we do not know exactly what Clarke meant by the term "Hofstadter-Möbius loop". We know of course the famous Möbius loop, namely a two-dimensional closed curve that allows changing sides without leaving the curve. We assume that Clarke simply meant that HAL was caught in an endless loop without being able to leave it. We shall come back to this problem below.

Even the "Architect", the master artificial mind in the current "Matrix" movie series, just follows its original programs and expects that machines and humans will do the same. Hence, it could not "understand" the hero Neo when he acted in an unexpected way by sacrificing himself. The concept of voluntarily choosing one's own death for the good of the community – in this case the whole human race – was not part of the Architect's program; hence it could neither anticipate such an action nor understand it. The idea that AI-systems are always more limited than humans because they can only operate according to certain fixed programs is something like a central theme in numerous SF-novels and films. It is obvious that such restricted systems will never be able to "understand", and in particular not be able to adequately react to messages that are outside their own limits.

The fact well known from everyday experience that many humans also have similar restrictions in the sense that they understand only what they are used to do and what they are accustomed to perceive does not change the also well known fact that human beings are principally able to transcend the limits of their usual thinking. Hence humans can do things that artificial systems can do not, at least such artificial systems like HAL or the robots of Asimov. Yet it is not surprising that many SF authors also saw these limits and introduced AI figures that are able to learn from their experiences and to understand human actions and human motives.

One of the probably first examples is the giant computer MYCROFT, nicknamed Mike, in Robert Heinlein's classical novel "The Moon is a Harsh Mistress" from the early fifties. Mike "suddenly woke up" (Heinlein) when his constructors added more and more hardware to the original computer. (By the way, we do not know of any SF author who gives any detailed explanation about the emergence or implementation of intelligence in their AI-systems.) Mike is not only able to learn and change as the result its own operations but it also can understand humans by communicating with them. It even was able to act as a persona, namely as the leader of the rebels on the Moon against the Terran government. Because in the novel Mike's fellow conspirators treated it as a person with equal rights Mike should be called as a "he". He was in addition able to have emotions: He felt loneliness and was vain enough to be proud of himself when his achievements to impersonate the leader of the rebellion were admired by his human companions. The waking up of Mike, including the emergence of intelligence and consciousness, was an unintended by-product of his technical enlargement; his capability to understand humans and to successfully impersonate one were, as in the case of human children, the result of a permanent communication with a human, namely a computer technician who taught Mike the reasons of human actions and how to understand them.

Neither Heinlein nor the intellectual parents of the next two more current examples give explanations for the astonishing capabilities of their AI-systems. The systems "are" just intelligent and even conscious. The first example is one of the most famous cinema roles of the present governor of California Arnold Schwarzenegger, namely "Terminator 2". As in the first Terminator movie the Terminator is a killing machine but in the sequel to the first movie the machine is friendly, i.e. it helps human rebels against hostile intelligent machines that want to destroy the human race. Although the Terminator operates according to a basic program that has been implemented by other humans – like the robots of Asimov it *must* be friendly towards certain humans – the Terminator is able to learn and to change its behavior according to situational demands. In this sense it is an adaptive system as defined in Section 1.3.1. It even succeeded to understand humans when cooperating with them for a time. In the end when the Terminator asked the people it had protected to destroy it because it is too dangerous it observes that the humans are crying. It explicitly comments on this by saying "Now I know why humans are crying. But I can never do this". In other words, the Terminator understands emotions, in particular the emotion of grief, and how humans react to them. Yet it cannot feel emotions like humans do and this deficit is still an absolute boundary between "real humans" and AI-systems, even if they are as intelligent and capable of understanding humans like the Terminator.

It is probably not by chance that frequently in SF stories not just intelligence but also the capability to have emotions are taken as a final proof for the "humanity" of AI-systems.[42] Accordingly AI-systems are only accepted as equal to humans if they have the same weaknesses as humans like mortality (cf. for example one of the last Robot Stories by Asimov, "The Bicentennial"). Hence, the gulf between machines and human beings can only be bridged if machines become like humans not only in their capabilities but also in their weaknesses and non intellectual behavior. By the way, some of the programs we shall show in Chapters 4 and 5 seem to have just human weaknesses, because they show weak performance in exactly those domains where human probands also did (see below).

The second example is "Solo", the hero of the film of the same name. Solo is an android originally constructed as a fighting machine to suppress some rebels.[43] By several incidents Solo becomes separated from his military unit and learns that he should be destroyed because his series should be substituted by better constructions. As a consequence he tries to escape because he does not wish his destruction; he obviously has something like a will to survive. Sole finds a refuge in the village of some rebels who repair his damages; for this help Solo defends the villagers against the government troops and in particular against another android, which belongs to the new and more advanced android series. Solo is able to learn about reciprocal help because he observes humans who help other people even if they risk their own lives by doing so. Because he did not understand he asked and became informed about the principle to help others if they helped himself. Solo even learned to bluff by observing children who tried to win their games by bluffing their opponents. Again he had to ask and by understanding the strategy of bluffing he was able in the final showdown against the superior android to win and save the villagers because the superior machine had no concept of bluffing at its disposal and hence did not understand the tactics of Solo. We shall deal with the ability of "learning from examples", which Solo obviously had, in the next chapters in order to demonstrate that artificial systems are even nowadays able to do this.

---

[42]Cf. for example episode 35 "The Measure of a Man" from "Star Trek, The Next Generation".

[43]Usually the term "android" means a robot, which looks and acts like human beings.

Yet even though Solo could learn from observations and own experiences, which made him very humanlike, he also could not feel emotions although he could understand them. When a young woman from the village fell in love with him he could only explain to her that he understood her feelings yet as a "mere" artificial being he was unable to feel any emotions himself. Therefore, in the end, he had to separate himself from the villagers despite the respect and even admiration the humans felt for him. Yet he stayed, although alone, in the vicinity of the village to protect its inhabitants in the case of new dangers. Solo had no emotions in the usual sense of the word, but he obviously had a sense of responsibility for the people who once had helped him. The gulf between artificial systems like Solo and "real" humans was perhaps not so wide as it seemed in the beginning of the film.

It is important for the subject of our study that in the cases of Solo and Terminator 2 the ability to understand emotions and human actions caused by certain emotions is not dependent on the ability to feel emotions. In everyday language and interpretation the ability to understand the emotions of others is frequently thought the same as the ability to have the same emotions as the other. In this sense emotional understanding has to do with empathy, namely the ability to feel the same as the other. In the cases of Solo and Terminator 2 the ability to understand human emotions is a pure cognitive ability and totally independent of own emotions. The same is the case, by the way, with Data, the intelligent android in Star Trek. We shall argue from the same basic position: Understanding other people is a cognitive task and should not be confused with emotional operations as far as they are assumed to be in contrast to rational acts.

It is not by chance that in these two movies – as in numerous other examples of SF – intelligent machines are described both as dangerous and helpful. The Terminator 1 is a mere killing machine that tried according to its program to kill the human rebels; the same is the case with the superior androids or robots respectively in Terminator 2, Terminator 3 and in Solo. Terminator 2 and Solo, in contrast, are helpful and save the people they should and wanted to protect. This ambivalence of artificial intelligent systems is something like a leitmotiv in SF. Mostly, as in the last two examples, intelligent machines are dangerous because they have been programmed to be this way and they are friendly for the same reason (cf. the robots of Asimov). Yet sometimes intelligent machines like Solo can develop and change their attitudes toward humans by experience and learning. The result may be a friendly attitude like in the case of Solo and, to take another example, the artificial web intelligence in the novel "Coils" by Roger Zelazny and Fred Sabberhagen. The kindness of this AI was motivated by a "feeling" of loneliness and the desire to learn about the physical world.[44] Yet the result of such learning processes may also be an aggressive and dangerous attitude like for example the machines in "Matrix" or the "Berserk Machines" in the stories by Sabberhagen. In both cases the machines had

---

[44]The web intelligence in "Coils" is a mere virtual being because it exists only as an emergent quality of the coupling of many computers; hence the web intelligence knows about the physical world only by its contact to the human hero of the story. The novel was written in 1982 when the authors obviously anticipated something like the Internet respectively a vast Intranet.

developed a will to survive and looked at humans as a high danger for the survival of the machine intelligences. As the web intelligence in "Coils" obviously these machines had developed something like emotions, at least the emotional value to maintain and protect their own existence and that of their species.

Our main theme is not that of AI systems and emotions and we will certainly not try to define this concept. Yet it is quite interesting to consider if artificial systems can indeed develop something like a will to survive because on a first sight such needs seem to be quite useless for a system of algorithms. After all, even a very sophisticated AI will be just that, namely a complex ensemble of algorithms, combined by very complex feed back loops. There seems to be no sufficient reason for the development of survival instincts. In order to analyze this questions in a rather simple manner we constructed a system that simulates a population of so called Von Neumann machines.

Von Neumann machines are virtual or physical constructs that are able to multiply by making identical copies of themselves. Both in scientific literature and in SF the concept of Von Neumann machines is frequently used for the idea to change hostile environments, for example strange planets, by sending such machines into the environment, let the machines multiply, and let them change the respective environment. We simulated such a population by constructing a cellular automaton (CA), consisting of cells that are able to copy themselves.[45]

The cells are divided into five types: (a) Empty cells with the state of zero; (b) "death cells" with the state of 1; (c) "living cells" with the states of 2, 3, 4, 5, or 6. The CA-rules of transition are:

A cell with the states 2, 3, 4, 5, or 6 will move at random to an empty cell (state 0) in its "Moore neighborhood" (the eight adjacent cells of a "center cell", if the cells as usual are defined as a square); death cells do not move.

After a certain time, i.e. after a certain number of time steps, a cell with the state 2, 3, 4, 5 or 6 will make a copy of itself if there is an empty cell in its Moore neighborhood; this empty cell is chosen at random if there are more than one empty cells and it will change its state to 2, 3, 4, 5, or 6 according to the state of the "parent cell".

After another number of time steps, approximately four times larger than the first time rate, a living cell of states 2–6 will "die", i.e., the according cell will change its state to 0. The death cells do not die.

If a cell of states 2, 3, 4, 5, or 6 will come into the Moore neighborhood of a death cell then the living cell will die regardless how "old" this cell is.

The dynamics of this little system apparently chiefly depends on (a) the number of death cells, i.e. the probability for a living cell to move into the Moore neighborhood of a death cell, (b) the "fertility rate", i.e. the number of time steps before a cell

---

[45]It is not by chance that John von Neumann both developed the formal systems of CA and the concept of Von Neumann machines. A CA is basically a grid or lattice respectively consisting of artificial units, namely the cells that are in different states and change their states according to rule-governed interactions between the cells. For a detailed description of CA cf. for example Klüver (2000) and Levy (1993).

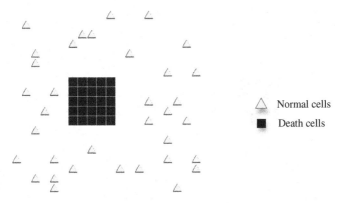

Fig. 1.10   A state of the Von Neumann machines system with death cells in the center

reproduces, (c) the mortality rate, i.e. the number of time steps before the automatic death of a cell, and finally (d) the initial number of living cells. By varying these parameters it is quite easy to generate trajectories that lead either to the extinction of all living cells or to "overpopulation", namely a state of the whole system where literally no empty cells are on the grid and reproduction stops. Other system's states between these extremes can equally easy be generated. Figure 1.10 shows one of these middle states.

The black cells in the middle of the grid are an ensemble of death cells; white cells are empty ones and the cells of the other states are visualized by different grey colors. When letting the system run one sees something like a dance of the living cells that move around, reproduce, die of "old age", and vanish if they come into the neighborhood of the death cells. The parameter values are such that the whole system always remains in approximately the same state, i.e. the approximately same quantitative distribution of the different living cells and empty cells.[46]

After several time steps we introduced a certain mutation, which we will describe below. Now the figure is drastically changing: Cells of state 2 are becoming more and more extinct; in contrast the number of the cells of the other four states continually increases. After about 200 time steps there are only very few cells of state 2 left and the grid becomes filled with living cells of the other four types. In particular one can observe that the cells of states 3, 4, 5, and 6 seem to avoid the death cells because these living cells only seldom come into the neighborhood of the death cells. The cells of state 2 still rather frequently get extinct by coming near the death cells. This unfortunate effect increases because with the increasing of the population of the other cells the cells of state 2 are forced to go into empty cells near the death cells. An observation of this new dynamics suggests that the cells

---

[46]The program was implemented on the basis of a CA-shell of ours by Christian Horn; the experiments were made by Filiz Kurt and Vahdet Kirli. Readers who are interested to experiment with this system may obtain it from the authors.

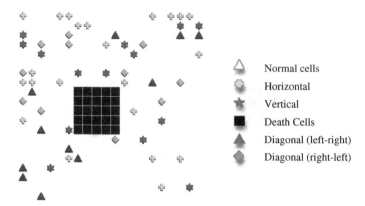

Fig. 1.11 Cells of state 2 (normal cells) have lost the competition in our system

of state 3, 4, 5, and 6 have developed something like an instinct to survive because they apparently avoid coming into the neighborhood of the death cells. In particular it looks as if these living cells are able to perceive the death cells as potential danger and try to keep away from it. Because of this behavior the reproduction chances of these cells are significantly larger than those of the cells of state 2; accordingly the population of these cells is decreasing. Figure 1.11 shows a system's state where all cells of state 2 have vanished.

There are of course also developments where several "non mutated" cells still survive. Whether such developments occur is simply a question of the initial number of cells and in addition of the size of the space. It is obvious that non mutated cells that move at random and were situated far away from the death cells will survive until they die of old age. As their "offspring" is situated also far away from the deadly cells in the center the offspring cells will also survive, produce new offspring cells without mutation and so on. Figure 1.12 shows such a development where

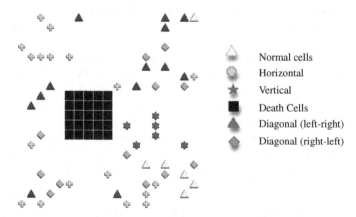

Fig. 1.12 Only mutated cells survive and generate offspring in the center, non mutated cells survive only down, in the right corner

a significant number of non mutated cells still have survived and produced new "normal" cells.

To be sure, the cells of states 3, 4, 5, and 6 have developed nothing like a will to survive and they are definitely not able to recognize the death cells as potential danger. They just move as if they had developed such useful abilities. Their changed behavior is only due to a little mutation we mentioned before, namely the changing of some probability rates. Before the mutation all living cells moved, as we said, at random, which means that the probabilities for selecting an empty cell in the Moore neighborhood are equal for all empty cells. This is still the case for the cells of state 2 that accordingly move with equal probability in all directions if there are enough empty cells in their Moore Neighborhood. By our little mutation we just changed the probability rates with respect to the cells of states 3, 4, 5, and 6: Cells of state 3 now move with a higher probability in a horizontal direction, cells of state 4 with the same increased probability in a vertical one; cells of state 5 move with a higher probability in the north-east and south-west diagonal, i.e. they prefer empty cells at the north-east and south-west corner of the Moore neighborhood, and finally cells of state 6 prefer the other diagonal direction. To be exact, the probability that for example cells of state 3 chooses an empty cell at the right or the left side is about 40% for each of these cells; the probability for choosing another cell is $20/6 = 3.33...\%$. The same is the case with the cells of state 4 with respect to empty cells above and below them and with the cells of state 5 and 6 with respect to the cells at the corners.[47] The resulting effects are on hindsight easily understandable:

Immediately after the mutation there are for example, still cells of state 3 besides the death cells, if the cells are distributed at random on the grid. These cells quickly become extinguished because they not only do not avoid the death cells but even go with a higher probability into the neighborhood of the death cells. The same fate have the cells of state 4 that are after the mutation below or above the death cells; accordingly soon those cells of type 5 and 6 are extinguished if they are positioned near the respective corners of the block of death cells. All other cells of these four mutated types rather seldom come near the death cells because they mostly move parallel to the death cells either in a horizontal, in a vertical, or a diagonal direction. Accordingly they have a proportional larger chance to reproduce than the cells of state 2 that still move to the death cells with the same probability than moving into other directions. In other words, by introducing this little mutation the well known effects of Darwinian evolution take place: The increased fitness of the mutated cells is directly measured by their increased reproduction success. Because these cells have developed something formally akin to a will to survive they are more successful in an evolutionary sense than the cells without mutation.

The lecture one may obtain from our little experiment is two-fold: On the one hand our simulation shows how something like an instinct to survive may have

---

[47]The respective probabilities can be varied, i.e. a user can choose probabilities as he wishes. In particular it is possible to let the different cells mutate with different probability values.

emerged in the real biological world. Obviously one must only assume that such mutations have occurred long a time ago in an ecosystem full of simple organisms that were able to move and to reproduce in a mono-sexual way. The mutations only needed to change some moving behaviors without changing "instincts" of these organisms or without increasing their ability to perceive and understand their environment. By preserving this mutation when copying themselves it is unavoidable that in the long run only such organisms survived and reproduced that had undergone the mutations. In a human sense of course these simple organisms had not more a "will to survive" than our artificial units. Yet it was a first step in the long line of biological evolution that lead to the human form of a will to survive in a strict sense of the word.

On the other hand the dynamics of our system indeed demonstrates the possibility that machines, whether they are intelligent or not, may develop something like a will to survive, at least an according behavior that has the same effects as if the machines "really" wish to survive and hence defend themselves against aggressors or try to avoid them. If one takes a population of machines, for example Von Neumann machines on a strange and hostile planet, and assumes that they are able to evolve by mutation and reproduction then something like the formal equivalent of a will to survive will emerge with a high probability if not even necessity. It is not difficult to imagine the emergence of other characteristics like mutual help against common dangers or the wish to stay together in the same way.[48] Of course, abilities like learning from examples as in the case of Solo are far beyond such simple systems. Our aim is just to demonstrate, as the great Immanuel Kant would say, the condition of possibility for the emergence of traits like those mentioned – quod erat demonstrandum.

On a first sight, by the way, one would assume that all mutations – moving horizontally, vertically, or in one diagonal – lead to the same surviving and reproducing effects because they are deliberately introduced in the same fashion, i.e., by favoring just one space direction. Interestingly enough that is frequently not the case because mutations that prefer one diagonal direction in many simulations get extinct more often than the mutations with a preference of the horizontal and vertical direction. We cannot give a mathematical explanation for this rather strange fact; we but just hint at the possibility that mutated cells with a preference for one diagonal direction are spatially put at a disadvantage if they are situated at the beginning near some corner of the whole grid. Figure 1.13 shows a simulation where only cells of type 3 and 4 have survived.

Our CA-system is very simple and we could have simulated in a more sophisticated way by a similar evolutionary method an emergence of something like a surviving behavior with evolutionary algorithms like the well known classifier systems of Holland (Holland 1998). Yet just the simplicity of our system is a suited

---

[48] We speak of "formal equivalents" because we do not wish to become identified with the position of the so-called "strong AI", at least not here. We shall discuss this position in the next subchapter and leave it here open if such machines develop a "real" will to survive or are only simulating it.

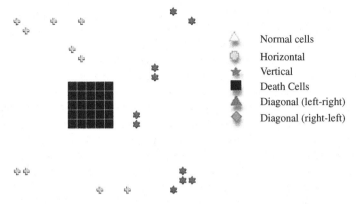

△	Normal cells
⬠	Horizontal
★	Vertical
■	Death Cells
▲	Diagonal (left-right)
◆	Diagonal (right-left)

Fig. 1.13 Only mutated cells of type 3 and 4 survive

demonstration that the emergence of such traits is far from impossible and even rather probable.[49]

Our little excursion into the dealing with AI themes by SF authors has in particular one result: Apparently it is very important for many authors to provide their AI inventions with humanlike attributes like the ability to understand humans and to interact with humans in a way that humans could interpret as similar to interactions they would have with other humans, either in a friendly of in an aggressive way. To be sure, there are many examples in SF of AI systems equipped only with cold logic and operating just according to logical reasoning. But such systems are not able to understand humans and become even irritated like HAL 2000 when they are confronted with the fact that humans often do not act in a rational way. The inventors of such systems probably do not believe that it is possible to create AI systems that can "understand" in a hermeneutical way. AI systems like Solo on the other hand obviously are more humanlike by being able to learn from singular experiences and to develop some sense of responsibility towards the people that had helped them before.

The stories of androids, namely artificial beings that look and behave in exact the same way as humans do, go even deeper. These artificial beings sometimes even do not know that they are not real humans, they have emotions and know of frustrations, disappointments and desperations. Data in Star Trek and the "Blade Runner" in the novel and film by Philip K. Dick are examples of such humanlike artificial beings. In these figures, as in the robot hero of the "Bicentennial" by Asimov, the gulf between artificial constructs and humans begins to dissolve and the subject of these stories are societies consisting of humans and AI constructs together. Yet always the ability of the artificial systems to understand human actions and motives must be assumed

---

[49]In his once famous program "Tierra" the evolutionary biologist Ray already demonstrated in a much larger and more complex evolutionary artificial system similar effects of the emergence of such traits (Ray 1992).

if the stories based on such AI constructs should be plausible. An advanced AI must be a hermeneutical one or it is no AI at all. In this respect the mentioned SF authors take the same position as we as scientists.

Each important theme of SF contains the question how much of the described technological and scientific innovations is principally possible. The famous transportation method of "beaming" in Star Trek for example is principally not possible because of Heisenberg's uncertainty principle: A person that is dissolved into elementary particles could not be put together as the same person because some particles would have changed with certainty. Yet as there are no principal physical objections against human looking and behaving androids or other AI systems the described SF inventions perhaps could some day, although only in the far future, be part of our physical and social reality.[50]

Despite our liking of SF we do not intend to speculate about such technical developments. There will be a long way to go until even modest SF dreams can become true and our own considerations and research are just the construction of some building stones, as we remarked in the beginning. Instead of such speculations we shall deal in the next subchapter with some fundamental problems concerning AI and in particular we shall discuss some principal objections against the possibility of a real AI. In memoriam of one of the first computer programs that human users thought to be intelligent we dedicate the first subchapter to "Eliza".

1.4.2 How Much Can Eliza Understand?

Alan Turing, one of the Founding Fathers of theoretical computer science, dealt very early with the question if machines could become intelligent; as a consequence he developed the conception of a test that should decide if a certain computer had reached intelligence, namely the famous Turing Test (Turing 1950). The basic idea of this test is the following:

Imagine a human user who sits alone in a room. He is connected via a keyboard with two other rooms; in one of these rooms is another human and in the other room is a computer. The human user, who does not know in which room is the other human and in which the computer, now has to communicate via the keyboard alternately with one of the rooms, i.e. putting questions, telling jokes and so on. Each communicative act of the user gets an answer, either from the other human or the computer. If the user after a "sufficient" time of communication is not able to decide which one of his communication partner is the human and which the computer then the computer has passed the test – it must be considered as "intelligent". Turing gave no measure of "sufficient time" but let us assume that several hours should be enough.

---

[50] An exception is Penrose (loc. cit.), who not very convincingly postulates the necessity of a new physics if one wants a real AI. Because Penrose, an eminent mathematician and physicist, is not very clear on this point we do not discuss his position in detail (see next subchapter).

Turing gave an operational definition of intelligence in terms of behaviorist psychology. It is not important how the structure of the according computer program is, if it is for example similar to the brain or if it follows another algorithmic logic. The decisive point is the behavior of the computer, that is its ability to respond to the user in a way that the user interprets as typical for a human communicator. As in behaviorist psychology, which was dominant at the time of Turing, human beings or other organisms were treated as "black boxes", the computer in the Turing Test is looked at the same way. Only its behavior, defined as reaction or response respectively to the communicative stimuli of the user, can be taken as a measure of the computer intelligence. Despite the simplicity of this test conception the passing of a suited Turing Test is still something like the Holy Grail in AI research. No computer program has passed such a test, when the test was constructed and supervised by professional test constructors, and we believe that for a long time no program will.

By the way, the discussion that dominated in the eighties and early nineties the discourses about AI if such programs "are" intelligent (the so-called strong AI) or if they just successfully simulate intelligence obviously plays no role in the Turing Test. Because as in the behaviorist tradition only the performance or behavior respectively is measured as criterion of success the difference between "being intelligent" or "simulating intelligence" is here of no relevance and only a metaphoric one.

One of the main problems with the Turing Test is doubtless the fact that the decision about intelligence is left to a user and certainly different users have different opinions about intelligence. A layman in computer science or cognitive sciences will possibly be satisfied with some answers of the program that the user was expecting. A professional expert in intelligence research will probably think of very sophisticated questions, will use ambiguous terms and so on. Therefore, a valid application of the Turing Test must also specify what is meant by a human test person. In particular, can a person serve as a suited test person if this person is estimated according to some IQ tests as not very intelligent himself?[51] In other words, the decision about the possible intelligence of a computer program is always dependent on the expectations and beliefs about intelligence of the test person. If this is taken into regard then the applicability of the Turing Test becomes a socio-psychological question.

The once famous story of "Eliza" is an apt illustration of this problem. Eliza is the name of a computer program, constructed in the sixties by Joseph Weizenbaum (Weizenbaum 1966).[52] Eliza should simulate a psychotherapist basing on the

---

[51] The scientific literature about the Turing Test is full of anecdotes that describe this difficulty. Hofstadter, one of the early advocates of the so-called strong AI, tells about a Turing experiment with a group of his students where he himself served as the test person. When he finally selected one of his communication partners as the computer he learned that this partner was the group of his students who intentionally and successfully tried to simulate a computer program (Hofstadter 1985). The proposal of Penrose (loc. cit.) to take a female proband because women are better to put themselves into the position of other humans than men is quite amusing but hardly a solution of this problem.

[52] Weizenbaum was, as he remarked, inspired by Eliza, the heroine of the famous musical "My Fair Lady", based on the theatre play "Pygmalion" by Shaw. In the play (and musical) Eliza became

so-called Roger method of conversation therapy; its structure and its according performance is rather simple: A user gives an input in form of a statement like, for example "this night I dreamed of my father". Eliza answers with "tell me about your father". When the user, e.g. says "I had trouble with my father" then, for example, Eliza would say "I am sorry to hear that. Tell me more." Or as reaction to the input "I feel very depressed" Eliza's reaction could be "Sorry for that. Tell me about it", and so on. Eliza could operate that way because it (a) had a list of key words like "father", "mother", feeling depressed", "fear" and so on and (b) had a second list of answers like "tell me more", "I am sorry to hear that" and so on. These two lists were connected by specific rules: if Eliza got one or several of the key words as input then a certain answer was selected by the key word specific rule and given to the user. The rest of the message of the user like "this night" was ignored by the program. Eliza obviously was one of the first so-called rule based systems, although a very simple one, that later became known as "expert systems

The effect of Eliza on human users was very astonishing and even irritating for its constructor. Many users, including the secretary of Weizenbaum, got the opinion that they were discussing their personal problems with a human therapist; not seldom the users praised the professional competence of their conversation partner. When Weizenbaum explained that Eliza was just a rather simple computer program the users reacted in the way that obviously this was a very intelligent program – as intelligent and competent as a good human therapist. In the eyes of the probands Eliza had apparently passed the Turing Test if "only" for the field of psychotherapy.

Weizenbaum was, according to his own narrative, deeply irritated and even shocked by the reactions of his probands. Several years later he gave up computer science and spent the rest of his life with warnings of the growing influence of computers on human society. But that is another story. His main irritation was due to the fact that Eliza, as a simple rule determined system, certainly did not "understand" to the slightest degree the inputs of the users. Nevertheless it could give human users the definite impression that they were not only understood by the program but that in addition the program cared for them and dealt with their problems.

To be sure, the reactions of the probands are not so astonishing if one takes into regard the probable fact that the users had never before spoken about their problems in such an open manner. In addition, the impression of Eliza as a competent psychotherapist hints at the probability that human therapists may react nearly the same way as Eliza, in particular if they are trained in the Roger method. Apparently Weizenbaum had succeeded in simulating the Roger method far better than he had anticipated.[53] Yet in one aspect Weizenbaum was certainly right: there can be no doubt that in the usual sense of the word Eliza indeed understood nothing of the inputs of the users. It just reacted to the input key words in an automatic way and it

---

an artificial product by her education in language and cultural behavior and could act despite her socially humble origins as a lady of the noble society. Weizenbaum, though, claimed in 1976 that the name Eliza has its origin in the ancient Greek saga of Pygmalion; no such name existed in ancient Greek. In his original article from 1966 he correctly referred to G. B. Shaw.

[53] Originally Weizenbaum intended to parody the Roger method.

could not react otherwise. In a certain sense Eliza reacts the same way as animals
that were conditioned by one of the classical methods, for example like the dog of
Pavlov.[54]

Despite the fact that the constructor of Eliza did not believe that it had passed the
Turing test because for Weizenbaum intelligence always means the understanding of
verbal messages, and despite his becoming a skeptic of computer science in general,
Eliza became quite famous and nowadays there are several different versions of
Eliza, applicable to different fields of knowledge, available in the Internet. But what
does it mean that Eliza did not "really" understand the input of the users?

As we shall deal in a systematic way with the concept of understanding in the
next chapter we just assume for the sake of our Eliza analysis that Weizenbaum and
other critics of Eliza's "intelligence" meant that Eliza did not grasp the "meaning"
of the words the user gave it as input. Thus we come back to the question what
meaning is (see above Section 1.3). In a colloquial sense the meaning of a word is
(a) an impression in the mind of the receiver of the object or process that the word
refers to, for example a visual picture of the object, and (b) the definition for the
word known by the receiver. In this sense to understand the meaning of "father" is
(a) to generate a mind picture of a certain father, mostly the own one, and (b) to
know the according definition, i.e. a father is the male part of the parents. Parents,
to continue this procedure, are again visualized as the own parents and defined as a
pair of adults that care for certain children. Of course, this definition can also refer
to a pair of educators in a kindergarten, but the problem of ambiguous definitions
and that of the infinite regress that such definitions generate is not our concern here.
Hence, one understands the statement "Last night I dreamed of my father" if "last"
is understood as the night that has just passed, "night" as the part of the day when
it is dark and when one usually sleeps, "I" as the person who just formulated that
statement, "dreaming" as having visual and/or acoustic experiences during the sleep
phase and "my father" as the male part of the speaker's parents.[55]

Eliza, alas, had no father but just a constructor, who did not like his creation,
and like the mentioned web intelligence in "Coils" it has no experience with the
physical world outside of its hardware. By implementing Eliza into a robot with
suited sensory devices this restriction could be changed but just now we have to be
content if Eliza would associate the usual definitions with its respective key words.
In order to give Eliza such a reduced form of understanding we reconstructed Eliza
in form of two neural networks that are coupled in a certain way.

The first network is a so-called feed forward network that is trained to react to
certain key words in the desired manner. For example, if this network is given an
input like the sentence about dream and father it automatically generates the output

---

[54]The linguist Pinker (1994) explains the reactions of trained dogs the same way. The dog does of
course not understand remarks like "Fido, you noisy dog, stop barking and come here". The dog in
contrast hears "Fido, blah, blah, blah. . ." and only reacts to the key word "Fido". Like Eliza Fido
just ignores all other words.

[55]We omit the fact that in different cultures the terms "father" and "parents" can be used in other
ways than in the Western cultures.

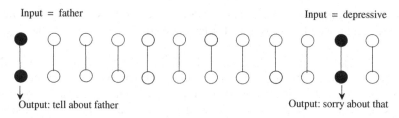

Fig. 1.14   A simple network of Eliza

"tell about father". This network, hence, is the equivalent to the according rule in the original Eliza with the only difference that this network is trained to react in this way, the same as would be the case with a student of Roger's psychotherapeutic method who also has to learn how to react to certain key words. The relation between such explicit rules as in the original version of Eliza and the performing of a trained network are subject of Chapter 4, where we demonstrate how an artificial system generates rules by learning from singular examples. We just show a part of this network; the training was performed with totally 10 key words[56] (Fig. 1.14.).

More important for the question if Eliza can be able to show at least a reduced form of understanding is the second network, namely a so-called interactive network. This network represents a semantical network where the key words as some of the network's units are connected with other units that represent words with a semantical relation to the key words. Such a network is shown in Fig. 1.8 in Section 1.3. The weighted connections represent the "semantical strength" of the connections between different concepts; the network has learned these weight values by the application of a new learning rule that we developed for such purposes, the so-called "enforcing rule" (see below Chapter 4). We assume that this the usual way human learners construct their semantical networks. Figure 1.15 shows a part of this network.

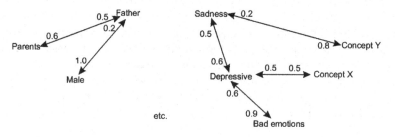

Fig. 1.15   A part of the semantical network of Eliza

---

[56]Similar neural network versions of Eliza, i.e. similar feed forward networks, can be found in the Internet.

The two networks are coupled by the input, i.e. they get the same input vector. When the second network receives the input "father" it associates the concepts "male" and "parent" and generates the output (father, male, parent). Accordingly the input "depressive" generates the association (depressive, sadness, bad emotions).[57] In this of course only reduced sense one can say that the "two network version" of Eliza is able to understand some of the statements of the user. A user then can ask "what do you mean with "father" " and will get the output just described.

In contrast to the above mentioned indifference of the Turing Test with respect to the inner structure of a computer program we have to take into account the network structure of our Eliza version. The basis of our version is of course the assumption that the knowledge of humans about certain parts of the real world is organized in form of such semantical networks and that the understanding of concepts like father or depressive in the second sense is basically formally equivalent to the activation of our artificial network. Yet the construction of such an enlarged version of Eliza is only possible by not treating programs as a black box. The claim that our Eliza at least has some reduced form of understanding its inputs, hence, is based on the assumption of a certain structural equivalence between the according processes in the brain or the mind respectively and the performance of our artificial networks. This is certainly more than the behaviorist position that intelligence of programs is just defined by an equivalence between the input–output relation of a program and the stimulus-response relation of a behaviorist organism. We shall come back to such an enlargement of behaviorist models in Chapter 4 on learning.

One of our students, Philipp Krätzig, implemented a slightly different version of our "network Eliza" in order to make the performance of Eliza even more realistic. He also used a coupling of a feed forward network with an interactive network; the task of the feed forward network is the same as in the basic version, the task of the interactive network is to generate "mediate meanings" or associative meanings respectively to the verbal inputs of the user. For this task the student used the "Edinburgh Associative Thesaurus", namely a data base of verbal associations. This thesaurus was developed from 1968 to 1971 by surveys at different British universities. One hundred probands had the following task: They got a certain word and they should name the first word that they associated with the word they got as "input". This task was several times repeated, in particular also with the words the probands associated with the given words. Our student constructed on the basis of the thesaurus a semantical network consisting of 55.732 units.

When this Eliza version received a certain input it gave the answers it had learned as in the basic version; the training consisted of 40 key words. In addition Eliza associated according to the Edinburgh Associative Thesaurus certain other words as the indirect or associated meaning of the inputs (see above Section 1.3). A rather illustrative example of an according dialog between a human user and Eliza is the following. The lines marked with > are the inputs of the user, the numbers behind

---

[57]This usage of interactive or semantical networks is described in more detail in Klüver and Klüver (2007); cf. also below Chapters 4 and 5.

the words in the associative lines of Eliza are the weight values in the interactive network.

```
> Hello
Hello... I'm glad you could drop by today.
Associations: hello => 0.8510064, good-bye => 0.64247936,
goodbye => 0.4424955, greet => 0.3436779, dolly => 0.24116759,
greeted => 0.22204521
> I am stressed out.
Did you come to me because you are stressed out?
Associations: out => 0.99416643, in => 0.96210134, not out => 0.59775627,
way => 0.57128906, inside => 0.5306816, fizzle => 0.49508813
> yes
OK, but can you elaborate a bit?
Associations: yes => 0.999549, no => 0.9664174, aye => 0.6055219,
not => 0.6004546, yeah => 0.563355, ja => 0.49155128
>It is annoying.
You seem very certain.
Associations: annoting => 0.735429, anger => 0.17531529,
angry => 0.15286608, noise => 0.11579541, nuisance => 0.11044914,
irritating => 0.10475901
>Stress is normally not a good thing.
How does that make you feel?
Associations: good => 1.0, bad => 0.9786908, is => 0.9027828,
yes => 0.8739512, thing => 0.8596619, stress => 0.8561722
>I feel bad.
When do you usually feel bad?
Associations: good => 1.0, bad => 0.9186719, evil=> 0.63463044,
excellent => 0.49582335, luck => 0.4462093, nasty => 0.44598848
>Why do you ask?
Why do you think do I ask?
Associations: me => 1.0, you => 0.972318, do => 0.89355874,
ask => 0.88065827, not => 0.8212408, myself =>0.79270065
>Because you are the therapist.
Is that the real reason?
Associations: me => 1.0, you => 0.9231549, are => 0.84702694,
i => 0.8016863, thank => 0.78600085, myself => 0.78311515
>I want to know it from you
Why do you want to know it from me?
Associations: me => 1.0, yes => 1.0, not => 0.98021966,
want => 0.89530015, it => 0.8878347, from => 0.8871784
I am just curious
How do you feel about being just curious?
Associations: just => 0.74441963, curious => 0.7101235, now => 0.39229533,
then => 0.23542672, so => 0.20374855, right => 0.19952464
>I don't feel anything special about it
Don't you really feel anything special about it?
Associations: about => 0.89005196, it => 0.850903, feel => 0.8475101,
anything => 0.8055858, special => 0.7521672, nothing => 0.723956
>|
```

Eliza apparently not only gives suited answers to the user but performs certain associations the same way as a human communicator would do in a real conversation. Because the associations of Eliza are based on the empirical data of the Edinburgh Associative Thesaurus each user of the Eliza version would – and could –

assume that Eliza associates the same way as humans do. In other words, although a bit anthropomorphically, Eliza takes part in a conversation with a human user and in addition is thinking associated thoughts – indeed a very humanlike behavior.

Finally, do our two versions of Eliza "truly" understand some of its inputs? Weizenbaum surely would answer this question in the negative although our Eliza has learned in a similar way as human students of psychotherapy do and is able to answer some questions with respect to the meaning of certain inputs. Weizenbaum and other advocates of "weak AI" would argue that our Eliza successfully imitates or simulates respectively some process of intelligent humans but not more. In our opinion this debate about strong versus weak AI is rather fruitless. It is a purely semantical question if one calls computer programs as intelligent or if one says that they "only" simulate intelligence. Although we believe that it is necessary to broaden the behaviorist positions by making the black boxes transparent, as we shall further demonstrate in the chapter on learning, we also believe in the pragmatic position of Turing: In the end the performance is the decisive factor, combined with the search of structural equivalences between artificial and biological intelligent systems. "By their fruits shall ye know them" (Matthew 7, 16; see also e.g. Jeremiah 17) and the question if there is "real" or just "simulated" intelligence belongs to metaphysics and not to constructive science.[58]

1.4.3 Chinese Rooms, Gödel and Other Principal Arguments

We dealt among other reasons with Eliza in such detail because it is an apt example for a very famous argument against the possibility of real AI, namely the argument of the Chinese room by Searle (1980, 1987). Certainly not by chance the argument has some similarity with the structure of the Turing Test[59]:

Imagine again a lone man in a room who has no knowledge of the Chinese language. Regularly the man gets from outside sheets of paper covered with Chinese symbols. At the beginning of the experiment the man had gotten another set of papers, also covered with Chinese symbols. In addition the man has a list with orders (in English) that tell him which paper of his original set he should give to the people outside of his room when he gets a certain paper from outside. The papers our man gets from outside contain certain questions written in correct Chinese; the papers the man gives to the people outside his room contain the (correct) answers to the question, also written in correct Chinese. An observer of the whole procedure who understands Chinese must consequently get the impression that the man in the "Chinese room" is able to understand Chinese because he obviously can correctly take part in a Chinese conversation. The observer of course is wrong because the man is totally ignorant of the Chinese language and language symbols

---

[58]We thank Reverend Ilie Stoica for telling us where to find this famous quotation in the Bible.

[59]There are slightly different versions of the thought experiment with the Chinese room. We describe the basic version (cf. also Penrose loc. cit.).

Searle wanted to demonstrate the impossibility of an AI because, as he argued, computer programs operate just the way as the man, namely only automatically following orders or rules respectively without having any understanding of the operations they perform. It is basically the same argument as that against Eliza: Computer programs as well as the man only operate according to syntactical rules; yet to understand a language like Chinese it is necessary to know the semantical dimension of that language, i.e. the meaning of the linguistic symbols. In contrast to the man who could learn the semantical dimension of the Chinese language computer programs principally are not able to learn that. They always will only operate according to syntactical rules and such will never be able to understand a language in the sense humans mean when they speak of language understanding. Hence, computer programs could never be intelligent – quod erat demonstrandum.

There were a lot of arguments against this reasoning, which we will not discuss here (cf. Penrose loc. cit.; Russell and Norvig loc. cit. and the different articles, e.g., in Wikipedia). Because, as we mentioned, Searle's argument is very similar to the problem of Eliza's understanding, it is sufficient to deal with the Chinese room only briefly:

(a) The lack of the semantical dimension in the thought experiment can be solved in a similar way as in our version of Eliza. It is easy to imagine several large semantical networks that all contain Chinese concepts on the one hand, according English concepts on the other, and finally adequate weighted connections between those Chinese and English concept that belong together (strong connections) or do not belong together (weak connections). If for example a Chinese symbol showing two women under one roof is given one network as input and if, as we were told by sinologists, this symbol is to be translated as "quarrel", then the network must be trained to generate a strong connection between these two symbols and only weak connections between the two symbols and most other ones. In order to understand "quarrel" the English part of this network should also generate a strong connection between "quarrel" and e.g. "squabble"; the last symbol should also be strongly connected with the Chinese symbol and so on. The according training process would certainly be a long one but as far as we know native speakers of English or German also need a rather long time to learn Chinese. In the end we would have an artificial system that is able to explain the English meaning of Chinese symbols and vice versa. Accordingly the Chinese symbol for quarrel would be strongly connected with those other Chinese symbols that either are synonymous with it or belong to the class of symbols with related meanings.

With respect to "understanding" linguistic symbols by generating an impression in the mind of the object the symbol refers to according to the famous definition of a symbol aliquid stat pro aliquo (something stands for something else) it is also easy to imagine a list of pictures that are connected with the according symbols; take for example a picture of two quarreling humans, preferably a married pair, that is connected with both the Chinese and the English symbol. Nobody would really undertake the tedious task to construct such a network because it would be practically useless but nobody would really put our man in the Chinese room either.

If such a network "really" understands Chinese or English is, as we mentioned, rather a metaphysical question.

(b) Searle seems to believe that our brain does not operate in the way that it can be represented as a rule based system. After all, Searle formulated his argument at a time when AI practically was synonymous with expert systems (or knowledge based systems, as they were also called). Indeed, if one could look even more exactly in the brain than neurobiologists are at present able then certainly no rules would be seen and no lists of symbols. Not long ago psychologists liked to describe the memory as some kind of store where the different elements of the remembered knowledge are preserved. No such store would be found either but "only" vast networks of biological neurons that interact in complex feed back loops. That is of course the main reason why we described our versions of ELIZA and the artificial counter part of the man in the Chinese room as networks whose operations are, as is the case with the brain, the result of training or learning processes respectively.

Memory is, as the neurobiologist and Nobel laureate Edelman once declared, "a system property" (Edelman 1992), and not something like a store. The trained networks, to be more exact, remember the learned input because they have accordingly varied their weighted connections and hence are able to generate the correct output if they are given the according input. In a way we shall describe below (see Chapter 4) the fixed connections between neurons or neural groups are the logical equivalent to the rules of, e.g. expert systems or other programs. In other words, memory is in the structure of accordingly trained networks or part of this structure respectively. If the brain is able by these network operations to understand linguistic symbols and other perceptions then there is no principal reason why sufficient large and complex artificial networks could not do the same.[60]

Because Searle obviously only referred to one form of AI and a very restricted one too he identified the possibilities of AI in general with the factual possibilities of those AI systems he knew. That is a fine example for the dangers one risks if one postulates a principal impossibility on the basis of some factual state of the respective art. Searle was certainly right in assuming that the state of AI art in the eighties made it impossible to declare that such systems could understand linguistic symbols. Yet if he concluded that AI systems would never be able to understand then he caught himself in some kind of reductive fallacy.

Yet there is still a fundamental argument against the possibility of real AI. Even if one imagines efficient AI systems as very large and complex networks the assumption that they are mathematically equivalent to the brain is not a trivial one; we shall discuss the problem of mathematical equivalence between the brain and artificial networks below in Chapters 4, 5, and 6. Our own argument against Searle just was based on this assumption. The frequently mentioned physicist Penrose (loc. cit.)

---

[60]Another critical aspect of AI is, according to Searle, the fact that programs do not act in an intentional way because they just follow the implemented algorithms or rules respectively. We do not discuss this problem here because we shall deal with the problem of AI and intentionality in the next chapter.

formulated, as far as we see, a fundamental argument against this assumption. Although he is, as we remarked, not very clear in this aspect, we shall reformulate this argument and subsequently, of course, try to refute it.

In the first half of the last century the great mathematicians, logicians and computer scientists Gödel, Church and Turing constructed or discovered respectively several "limiting theorems" (our name for them); the most famous of them are the incompleteness theorem of Gödel and the theorem of the insolubility of the so-called halting problem of Turing. Both theorems were developed in order to analyze the possibility of constructing a formal system that should be able to derive all valid or "true" mathematical statements inside the system and of course only those statements. If false statements could be derived inside the system it would be inconsistent and hence worthless. In other words, the task was to construct a finite set of axioms that should be sufficient for all mathematical statements. Turing reformulated this problem by translating it into the task to construct a computer program that should be able to decide with respect to all computer programs whether they would stop (halt) at some time, regardless how long this time would be.

The answers to both problems are, as is well known, negative. Gödel's incompleteness theorem states that there is no finite set of axioms with the desired capability; each consistent formal system that is rich enough to contain at least number theory always contains statements that are true but cannot be derived from the axioms of the system.[61] Hence, there is no single formal system that allows to capture all the vast fields of mathematics, although of course it is always possible to construct formal systems of certain fields of mathematics. Accordingly Turing proved that there can be no single computer program that can solve the halting problem although it is always possible to construct programs that are capable of decision with respect to certain other programs. The two theorems are obviously related because computer programs can be represented in form of formal axiomatic systems and accordingly a formal mathematical system, i.e. an axiomatic one, can be translated into a computer program (cf. footnote 60).

Both Gödel and Turing used for their proofs a variant of the so-called diagonal method that was invented by Georg Cantor, the founder of general set theory. For our purpose it is sufficient to say that in the proofs of Gödel and Turing a certain kind of self-referentiality was applied: Gödel constructed a system that contains number theory and formulated a statement in terms of number characteristics that is a statement about itself. Accordingly Turing proved that in particular no program that has to decide on the halting behavior of all programs can decide on its own behavior. Factually the proofs are much more complicated but that is here of no relevance.

---

[61] Axioms can be considered as initial states of formal systems. Each analysis whether a given statement can be derived within the system starts with one or several of the axioms and carries on with logical procedures. If by applying these procedures the statement can be generated then the statement is derivable in the system. If this is not possible then the statement is not derivable and, if the system is complete with respect to a certain field of knowledge, then the statement is false. Number theory, by the way, is the theory of integers, i.e. 1, 2, 3,....

Self-referentiality became known as a grave problem with the discovery of the logical paradoxes as a consequence from Cantor's set theory. The best known paradox has the form of a statement S "this statement is false". If one assumes that S is true then obviously S is wrong and vice versa. The paradox is a result from the self-referentiality of S that consists of a statement about itself. Other similar paradoxes were found or constructed respectively that have basically the same form (cf. Penrose loc. cit.; Poundstone 1988). As a consequence mathematicians tried to ban self-referentiality from formal systems like the system of meta languages by Tarski (1956).[62]

The importance of these results for our subject is clear: On the one hand an AI that has the capability of a human brain, i.e. is as intelligent as humans, must have the characteristic of self-referentiality because obviously humans have this capability. A mind can think about itself, a language contains statements like S and may other statements that refer to themselves, humans as part of the human race can formulate theories about this race and hence about themselves and so on. The socio-cognitive world is full of self-referentiality and people use according rhetoric and argumentative figures each day without any problems. If, on the other hand, it is not possible to construct a computer program that is as efficient as the human brain without running into paradoxes then Gödel and Turing have, so to speak, mathematically proved that a real AI is principally not possible even in the long run – quod erat demonstrandum again in the eyes of AI critics. In the terminology of Penrose: Human beings can do mathematics in a recursive and a non-recursive way; computer programs operate only in a recursive manner.[63]

Fortunately in practice things are not so bad. Humans can treat self-referentiality because they can transcend the level on which the self-referential paradoxes are formulated and can also detect on this level the source of the paradoxes. Accordingly the communication theorists Watzlawick et al. (1967) proposed in the case of communicative disturbances a new communicative level, namely one of meta communication. If one assumes that computer programs are not able to operate on different levels apparently one has in mind computer programs like HAL 2000: HAL, as we mentioned, became confronted with a paradox, namely on the one hand telling the crew members all information it possessed and on the other hand giving them not all information (Fig. 1.16.). The dilemma of HAL hence can be visually described as HAL was forced when meeting a crew member to apply one certain rule; by doing this he was equally forced by its basic program to apply a second rule, which leads to the necessity to apply the first rule again and so on. The result is

---

[62]Frequently logicians and mathematicians assume that the source of the paradoxes is the introduction or allowance of self-referentiality. That is not quite exact because mainly the paradoxes are constructed by the coupling of self-referentiality and negation, for example in the paradox by Russell "the set of all sets that do *not* contain themselves as elements" or our example of the statement S. It is easily possible to construct systems with self-referentiality that generate no paradoxes.

[63]The German poet Hans Magnus Enzensberger illustrated this consequence from Gödel's theorem "you can describe your brain with your brain but not totally" (*Hommage à Gödel*). German original: "Du kannst Dein eignes Gehirn mit Deinem eignen Gehirn erforschen: aber nicht ganz."

Fig. 1.16 The dilemma of
HAL

Inform crew ⟹ not inform crew

Clarke's "Hofstadter-Möbius loop", i.e. an endless loop that HAL could only escape by eliminating the crew, i.e. by eliminating the situations by that it became entangled into the endless loop.

HAL is described as a logically closed system that is not able to change its rules. The brain on the other hand certainly is in that sense an open system that it can structurally react on external signals – it is adaptive in the sense we defined in Section 1.3.1. An adaptive system is able to change its rules and its geometrical structure in order to improve its own performance with respect to environmental demands. The system can do this because it has, as we mentioned, meta rules at its disposal that can be applied in order to change the rules and geometry of interaction. In many studies we and other scholars have demonstrated the possibility of such systems in form of so-called hybrid computer programs that overcome the one-sidedness or one-dimensionality respectively of systems like HAL. Adaptive systems are not only able to change their structures as a response to certain environmental conditions and to learn from experience but they are also able to evaluate their own operations and to detect if they are caught in logical paradoxes, i.e. endless loops. In that case a suited meta rule can be applied that allows the system to find a way out of the endless loop without such damaging effects on its environment as was the case with HAL. To use an apt term of the theoretical physicist Tipler (1994): such systems are able to "outgödel", namely to overcome the deficiencies of one-dimensional systems that are the subject of Gödel's theorem (cf. also Chaitin 1999). Hence, such computer programs are more similar to SF AI-figures like Solo than to the robots of Asimov or to HAL.

To be sure, Gödel's and Turing's results are still valid if one searches for one single formal system for all fields of mathematics or for one single computer program to solve the halting problem for all computer programs, including itself. But because there are no such formal systems and computer programs one has to assume that the brain too does not operate that way. In contrast it permanently outgödels paradoxes and adjusts to new problems if and when they come. It does this, of course, only in a finite fashion, i.e. only for certain cases if necessary. It does not in practice deal with all possible cases whose number may be infinite. But it does not need to and neither do computer programs need to handle all (potentially) infinite cases at once. There is no AI possible that operates as a giant axiom system and that way generating all possible mathematical theorems and other statements. But because the brain or the mind is also not able to do this the seeming proof of the impossibility of an AI, derived from Gödel and Turing, is nothing more than the proof of the impossibility of an AI that can do certain things that humans cannot do.

With these concluding remarks we can finish the introduction of the subjects our book deals with. The next subject is the task to clarify the difficult and frequently not clearly used concept of understanding.

Chapter 2
The Operation Called "Verstehen": Considerations About Formal Systematizations of Understanding

In 1948 the American sociologist Theodore Abel published an article that had some impact on the discussion on the different methods of "understanding" (the humanities) and "explaining" (the sciences) and which gave this chapter the heading (Abel 1948). Abel tried to give an exact definition of understanding and not by chance he used the German term for it, namely "verstehen". The reason for this terminological choice was the fact that the methodical problems of the humanities (in German Geisteswissenschaften) were most thoroughly discussed in the German philosophy of the humanities of the nineteenth and early twentieth century. Therefore, even critics of AI who principally argued against its possibility frequently referred to the German classical authors of hermeneutics like Dilthey, Gadamer and even Heidegger (cf. Dreyfus 1992; Dreyfus and Dreyfus 1986; Winograd and Flores 1986).

Abel explains his position with respect to "understanding" with the example of a significantly high correlation between the annual rate of crop production and the rate of marriage in rural regions in a given year. If the harvest is good, i.e. the rate of cop production is high, then the rate of marriage is high and vice versa. Abel claims that this correlation is validated, which we accept. An understanding of this correlation is the task to understand why farmers make their marriage behavior obviously dependent on the results of the harvest. Such an understanding, according to Abel, would need the following facts to be combined: (a) failure of crop (or sufficient crop in the other case), (b) lowering the farmers income, and (c) one makes new commitments if one marries. The lowering of one's income is "internalized" (Abel) as a feeling of anxiety, which results in the fact (b') feeling of anxiety. Now a general principle about human behavior can and must be applied, namely the principle "people who experience anxiety fear new commitments". The application of this principle to the case of marriage behavior produces the understanding: We understand the marriage behavior in dependency of harvest results because it is a special case of the general principle.

Understanding, hence, means for scholars like Abel (a) the knowledge that and how objective facts are "internalized" as feelings, emotions or other mental states, and (b) the application of general principles about human behavior in dependency of mental states. If these two conditions are fulfilled then we can say that we understand the respective actions. Obviously Abel is not willing to associate understanding with

J. Klüver, C. Klüver, *Social Understanding*, Theory and Decision Library A 47, DOI 10.1007/978-90-481-9911-2_2, © Springer Science+Business Media B.V. 2011

some form of empathy or intuitively putting oneself into the position of the people one wants to understand. Yet one must know about the respective processes of "internalizing", i.e. one must have at one's disposal something like a "mental model" of the social actors one wants to understand. We shall come back to this and similar positions in the next subchapters and the next chapter when dealing with the concept of "mental models". Yet because the example of Abel is a very special one and because one can sincerely doubt that in all cases of understanding one has at disposal such general principles of behavior it is necessary to investigate more thoroughly the different aspects of the term of understanding.

2.1 Understanding Versus Explanation

In Section 1.1 we referred to the gulf between the natural sciences and the humanities; methodically this gulf was and is expressed by the difference between explanation as the goal of the (natural) sciences and understanding as that of the humanities. Since the rise and acceptance of the humanities in the nineteenth century in particular the advocates of these enterprises frequently emphasized that only understanding can be a suited method for the tasks of the humanities, namely to deal with the complexity of human behavior. The reasons for this methodical difference between the "two cultures" (Snow loc. cit.) are many but chiefly these are mentioned (for a reconstruction of this permanent controversy cf. e.g. Apel 1979, 1982):

(a) Human individuals cannot be looked at as identical objects but each human person must be understood as an original unique entity. When a physicist analyzes elementary particles he can be sure that one electron behaves in an identical way as any other electron (under the same boundary conditions of course). This cannot be assumed in the case of human individuals. Given the same social situation experience tells that two social actors frequently will behave in different ways. To be sure, the behavior may be very similar and very often it is but no identity of two persons can methodically be assumed. Although it is certainly possible to aggregate many individuals in a statistical manner and such make predictions about the average behavior of the aggregated individuals we cannot predict the behavior of one special actor. To understand human individuals needs to take into account their uniqueness.

If for example a farmer marries despite bad harvest results the general principle of Abel would not be worthless but on the one hand it could give no reason for the behavior of this farmer and on the other the deviant behavior of this farmer shows that the general principle explains only average marriage behavior in a statistical sense. In contrast to deviant social behavior that makes not necessarily worthless some general principles of human behavior a "deviant behavior" of one electron under certain conditions with respect to the general physical laws about electrons would refute these general laws and hence make them worthless. At least physicists had to reformulate these laws with respect to the according conditions because of the assumed and always confirmed identity of all electrons.

(b) Human beings frequently act intentionally, i.e. they act because they have certain needs, desires, and other goals that they wish to reach by their actions; frequently they also wish by their actions to avoid events they do not want. This fundamental difference between the actions of humans and probably other organisms on the one hand and the behavior of lifeless physical objects on the other hand was frequently taken as the main reason for the methodical necessity of understanding (cf. Wright 1974) and was already postulated in the nineteenth century by Droysen, one of the founders of scientific hermeneutics. In contrast physical objects are only determined by the principle of cause and effects. In addition, frequently humans have certain spaces of freedom when acting with a certain intention. If two actors wish to reach the same goal then the ways to succeed may be quite different. We shall see that for this reason it is often not sufficient to understand human actions even if one knows the underlying intention.

This is a similar case as that demonstrated in the little number theoretical example in Section 1.2.3: As it is possible to generate a certain state with different rules of transition it is also possible to reach a certain goal by different methods. But of course in the case of physical objects that have no intention this problem of understanding does certainly not arise because these systems just behave. To be sure, even in physics often only statistical laws can be given for the behavior of certain objects like in statistical thermodynamics or in quantum mechanics. But that is of course a totally other problem than the understanding of intentions and of the different ways to reach the intended goals. Searle's (loc. cit.) critique that AI systems lack intentionality was quite justified for those AI systems he had in mind.

(c) Humans usually are guided in their actions by certain world views that are on the one hand part of a general "culture" (see below) and on the other hand results of personal experiences and/or learning processes. The "internalization" that Abel mentioned is an apt example of such a world view: By experiencing via learning from others that it is rather difficult to keep one's own material standard when economical problems like bad harvests arise such problems cause anxieties with respect to the future. Other examples are actions caused by certain religious beliefs or ideological convictions. Understanding such actions of course needs the knowledge about such world views. It is evident that such knowledge is not necessary in the natural sciences. Even in biology where one has to deal with living organisms one does not need to assume that animals or plants have specific world views at their disposal. Hence, as the problems are so much different in the humanities and in the sciences it is worthwhile to have a look at the two concepts that describe the methodical principles of both fields of knowledge.

The counterpart of understanding as prime goal in the humanities is that of explanation in the sciences. In contrast to the usage of this term in colloquial language, where it means the process of making other people understand something, in the philosophy of the sciences the concept of explanation means the relation of individual events or objects respectively either to other events or to general laws. A certain event like the falling of a physical body is explained if and when this individual process can be inferred from a general law, in this case the law of fall by Galileo Galilei or more general by Newton's law of gravity. Accordingly the movement of a billiard ball is explained by (a) the movement of another ball that hit the first one – the cause – and (b) the general laws of Newton's mechanic. This definition of scientific explanation as orientated to general laws is also called a nomological or nomothetic form of science from the Greek word *nomos*, namely law.

According to the famous schema of Hempel and Oppenheim (1948) a scientific explanation of a phenomenon A means in more exact terms: IF A can be observed and IF there are general laws L and IF A under certain boundary conditions C is a consequence of L, THEN A is explained by L and C. Logically this is a form of modus ponens: If L and C imply A and if L is accepted and C is the case then A. Conversely L is confirmed by the observation of A. By modus tollens one gets: If A cannot be observed then either L is not valid or C is not the case.[1]

Factually this simple schema is not sufficient to capture the complexity of the scientific research progress but for our purposes it is enough to describe the main difference between explanation and understanding. It is certainly not by chance that the some logic is applied to the construction of so-called rule based systems or expert systems respectively (see above Section 1.4.2). Expert systems basically consist of (a) a list of facts like for example disease symptoms or technical failures of a car, (b) a second list of possible causes like certain diseases or specific disturbances in a machine, and (c) specific rules that determine, which facts of the first list shall be combined with which elements of the second list. A medical diagnosis expert system for example combines "fever" and "headache" (first list) with "influenza" (second list). The basis for the construction of such rules is of course the assumption that the medical law is valid "if influenza then fever and headache (plus other symptoms)". This is obviously a special case of "L and C imply A" of the Hempel-Oppenheim schema. The usage of such a diagnosis system, though, takes the opposite direction: If symptoms A can be observed then the cause is influenza and a certain therapy is needed. But that is also the case in scientific research: If an event A can be observed or experimentally produced then certain boundary conditions C must be the case and the general law L is valid. Despite the fact that it is generally not allowed to turn an implication "A implies B" into "B implies A" the procedure just described works in most cases because the relations between L and C on the one hand and A on the other or those of diseases and symptoms are usually well confirmed.[2]

Because the basic logic of scientific explanation can be transformed into such expert systems it is no wonder that at the beginning of expert systems many scholars believed that they are the key to a real and practicable AI. After all, the logic of the sciences is *the* paradigm for rational thinking. The fact that often scholars from the respective disciplines speak of the cognitive or also social sciences when naming their fields of research demonstrate that dominance of scientific thought.

---

[1]This is in principle also the basis of the well-known model of the logic of scientific inquiry of Popper (1969).

[2]It is also possible to construct such diagnosis systems on the basis of certain neural nets, which can have some practical advantages (cf. Klüver and Stoica 2006).

Yet, as we remarked in the first chapter, by denying the problems of hermeneutics and understanding they do not vanish. So it is time to ask for the meaning of understanding in contrast to that of explanation.

The classical theorists of hermeneutics like Droysen or Dilthey concentrated early on the aspect of capturing the inner being of those humans whom one wishes to understand. Droysen (1960) articulated this thought by the formula that the inner being of a human is the mirror image of his externally observable actions: If one observes somebody's actions one can interpret them as a reflection of his inner being, i.e. as a consequence of his thoughts, wishes, emotions and so on. This is not far from the noted fact that human beings act according to certain intentions and on the basis of a special world view (see above) if one takes into regard that intentions and world views certainly are part of the "inner being" of an actor. Accordingly the Oxford Dictionary, which gives several definitions for "understanding", defines understanding as the perception of the intention of a speaker (or actor respectively). To be sure, in colloquial language understanding has other denotations too like, for example "agreeing" or "interpreting"; the Oxford Dictionary gives in addition the example "Picasso understood color". Yet in our context the first definition is certainly the most important one.

A definition of understanding based on some hypothesis about the inner being – intentions, emotions or other internal states – has a lot of problems as consequence. (a) Because only actions like speaking, writing or non verbal behavior are directly observable understanding hence means the methodical problem to construct a hypothesis about the inner being that can only be confirmed by predicting other actions determined by the same internal states. To be sure, the method of so-called "communicative validation" that is used in qualitative social research can help here, namely simply asking the observed about their internal states. But because such a form of communicative validation is frequently not possible at all and/or because one must take into account that the interrogated persons either do not know themselves why they did something or that they do not wish to tell about them, this method has its obvious limits. It may also be the case that the actor thinks otherwise than he has just acted (see below). Hence, the situation is similar as in the case of the Hempel-Oppenheim schema: One can just hypothetically speculate about the probable intentions or motives and, because in contrast to the natural sciences, experiments are in most cases not possible one has to wait for further acts to confirm or refute the hypothesis about the inner being of the observed actor. It is no wonder that a whole school of psychological research, namely Behaviorism, forbid speculations about internal states and instead treated humans and animals as "black boxes" by concentrating on the Stimulus – Response relation. We shall come back to this position in Chapter 4.

These skeptical remarks must not be misunderstood: Hypotheses about the internal states of social actors are not only possible in many cases but frequently necessary if and when other forms of understanding fail. We shall give some examples of possible and even probable hypotheses about intentions, world views and feelings of social actors. In particular we shall analyze the possibilities of such hypotheses when dealing with the concept of "mental model"; even the black boxes of Behaviorism can be made transparent at last in some aspects. Yet one must always take into account the methodical *caveat* formulated above.

(b) A second problem with the definition to refer understanding as the art to capture the inner being is the undeniable fact that frequently people act in some way without any intention or another internal state that could be explicitly stated. One does not even need to refer to the unconscious in the tradition of Freudian psychoanalysis to accept that frequently a reference to some internal states is neither possible nor necessary. Consider for example a private soldier who hears the loud and angry voice of his sergeant "down". The soldier very probably will literally act "without thinking", i.e. he will throw himself down – if necessary into the mud.[3] To understand the action of the soldier one need not and must not refer to some internal state of him. It is quite sufficient and even necessary to know that an army is some kind of totalitarian institution in the sense of Foucault and that the most important social rule in this institution is to obey the orders of superiors under all circumstances and without hesitation. To understand the soldier's action, hence, is to know the social rule that determines his action; it is quite superfluous to speculate about the soldier's feelings if one just wishes to understand his actions.

Social reality is full of such examples. A car driver probably stops before a red traffic light also without thinking because the according traffic rule determines his actions and an observer understands these actions if he knows the respective rule. The internal state of the driver may even be quite in contrast to his actions if he is angry that he has to stop and wishes that he could go on. A similar case may be a football player who dislikes the referee but obeys his orders because there is the social rule that a player has to do so. A student who answers the questions of his examiner, a lawyer who defends a guilty person whom he personally dislikes very much, a shop assistant who smiles at persons totally strange to him ..., all these actors perform their actions because the rules of the social situation determine them. *In nuce*, the understanding of social actions very often is only possible if one knows the respective social rules that have to be applied in the situation of action. Because the relation of understanding and social rules is a very important one, in particular for our subject, we shall come back to the concept of social rule below.[4]

(c) Finally, if one reduces understanding to the task of capturing some internal state of the actor it becomes very difficult to generalize the result of understanding, i.e. to demonstrate that the understanding of one particular actor gives insights into the actions of other actors. The internal state of one single actor is at first just his individual state of mind and another actor, as we remarked, may act in a similar way but may be in quite another internal state. Hence there will be always the methodical danger that one can formulate some findings about a certain individual but that one does not know if these findings may be referred to other individuals. To be sure,

---

[3]One of the authors speaks from personal experience.

[4]The referring of social actions to social rules is apparently a classical example of the famous methodical postulate by Emile Durkheim that social phenomena must only be explained (or understood respectively) by social causes or reasons respectively.

it is frequently possible to state general hypotheses about the relation of internal states and according behavior; Abel's example of the correlation between harvest and marriage is such a general hypothesis. But because such general statements in the best case only make statistically average behavior understandable the problem of the restriction of understanding to only individual single cases remains.

Of course, many scholars have perceived these problems and tried to solve them. The most famous and also the most influential attempt in this direction was the founding of interpretative or understanding sociology (verstehende Soziologie) by Max Weber (1921). Weber also referred to Droysen's "inner being" as a necessary method to understand social actions but he did not define this in an individualistic manner. Instead Weber postulated the so-called subjective sense (subjektiver Sinn) of the actors as the source of social actions. To understand them means to reconstruct the subjective sense that governed the according actions.

It is a bit confusing that Weber used the term "subjective" in this context because he factually meant something "objective" with this term. The subjective sense of an action is the result of an "internalization" (cf. Abel) by the actor of certain cultural components, i.e. parts of the culture the actor lives in; he does so by sharing the symbols the culture consists of with others and he participates by reproducing parts of the culture via his actions. Insofar as culture is something objective, i.e. independent of individual peculiarities it is just not "subjective". But because the sense of individual actions is always the sense of an individual actor this cultural component is a subjective sense.

Note that as culture in this sense is the cause of the social actions the strict difference between explanation and understanding has no place in the considerations of Weber. Instead he uses the concept of "understanding explanation" (loc. cit.): Because culture must be understood in other forms than nature is explained by the natural sciences it is an *understanding* explanation, but because the relation between culture and actions is a causal one it is an explanation. As Weber was a strict advocate of the conception of a "wertfreie" (valueless) social science, meaning that the social sciences must be as analytically neutral with respect to values as are the natural sciences, his goal was a conception of social sciences that are not identical with the natural sciences in method but that follow in principle the same ways and goals.

His certainly most famous study, namely the Protestant Ethic, is a classical example for this program.[5] As is well known Weber analyzes the relation between the Calvinist form of Protestantism on the one hand and the rise of modern Capitalism on the other. One of the main sources of Capitalism, so his thesis, is the particular working ethic of faithful Calvinists, derived from the theological doctrine of predestination. Because the fate of all men after their death is predestined, i.e., whether they are chosen for paradise or damned to hell, the spiritual benefit cannot be a result of good works. Instead success in everyday life can and must be taken as an indicator that the Lord is benevolent to the actor and that one belongs to the chosen after one's death. Hence, it is necessary to labor for one's earthly success. Because the

---

[5]German original: *Die Protestantische Ethik und der Geist des Kapitalismus.*

early Calvinists mostly belonged to the bourgeois class laboring for success automatically meant laboring in commerce and economical enterprises. Earthly success then is defined by the profit the economical enterprises produce.

The profit is not the real goal but just an indicator. Therefore, the profit must not be used to live a life in luxury. On the contrary, the early Calvinistic entrepreneurs had to follow the principle of *innerweltliche Askese* (asceticism within the world). In other words, the faithful Calvinist had to live like an ascetic monk but not outside of the world orientated to only religious goals but inside the world orientated to one's economical affairs. In addition, earning profit from economical enterprises means to think and act in a most rational way by always finding the best relations between means and goals. As the purpose of social actions is the reaching of a certain goal Weber in this context introduces the term of "purpose rationality" (*Zweckrationalität*), namely a rational way of thinking in terms of finding the optimal means for the economical goals – i.e. the maximizing of profit.

These two principles of asceticism within the world and purpose rationality, so Weber, are at the core of modern Capitalism. Even when Capitalism later lost its religious origins and became just a very efficient form of economical structure at least the principle of working hard and that of purpose rationality still are fundamental characteristics of it.[6] It is not by chance, by the way, that Karl Marx in *Das Kapital* (The Capital) distinguishes the miser the same way from a hard working capitalistic entrepreneur who spends no money for his personal good: It is without the religious connotation of Weber the same principle of asceticism within the world.

This example, whether it is historically completely confirmed or not, makes Weber's program quite transparent: To understand the actions of the early class of Calvinistic entrepreneurs it is necessary to understand the religious sub culture of Protestant Calvinism, in particular the specific doctrine of predestination as a system of symbols that gives orientation for the daily life of the faithful. Symbol systems must be understood in the usual way of text interpretation. Afterwards one can take this symbol system as the cause for the specific way of life of the early Calvinists and such explain their way of living on the one hand and its consequences for the rise of modern Capitalism on the other. The emergence of Capitalism, hence, is "explained via understanding".

Weber apparently solved some of the problems we mentioned above. The social actors who are the subject of Protestant Ethic act because of certain intentions,

---

[6]When we wrote these sentences (2009) the financial crisis that had started in the late summer 2008 still was at its peak; in particular more and more information became known about the unrestrained greed of top bankers and managers and the luxuries they piled up, although many top bankers worked so hard that they had no time to enjoy their wealth. The principle of asceticism within the world has obviously long been forgotten and on hindsight many actions of this social class seem very irrational. Perhaps this crisis of Capitalism, not its first and certainly not its last, has its sources in a total negation of the early capitalistic principles. The principle of purpose rationality, by the way, became after Weber more generalized and was the basis of the so-called Rational Choice (RC) theories, namely the assumption that each social action is determined by strategic decisions in order to gain maximum profit of the respective action situation. We shall come back to the problem of RC attempts when discussing the concept and the learning of social rules.

namely the wish to get indicators if they belong to the chosen. Yet these intentions are no pure individual trait of some actors but are caused by an objective culture that was obligatory for all believers in this form of Protestantism. Hence one can say that Weber was not more interested in the individual personalities and characteristics of the early Calvinists than a physicist is interested in individual characteristics of elementary particles. Weber looked for intentions but only in the sense that these intentions are general and common ones insofar as they are derived from a certain common culture in the form of subjective sense.

This principle of generality is methodically transformed into the concept of "ideal type" (*Idealtypus*). When Weber described the early Calvinistic capitalists as men who followed in their life the principles of asceticism in the world and of purpose rationality he did neither believe that literally all Calvinists lived exactly that way nor did he mean his characterizations as a description of statistically average ways of life. Instead an ideal type is constructed as, in this example, a representative behavior derived from the culture. *If* a Calvinist takes his religion seriously and *if* he literally follows the Calvinistic doctrines *then* his behavior would be exactly like that described as the ideal type of the Calvinistic way of life. A general statement, hence, about the way certain people live, is given in the form of describing the ideal type as a derivation from the common and therefore general culture. The derivation from culture in addition gives an explanation for this specific ideal type. If certain individuals do not exactly correspond in their behavior to the ideal type then the ideal type conception is not refuted but one must ask, if one is interested, why a concrete individual must be seen as a deviation from the general ideal type.

The methodical program of Weber certainly does not solve all problems that are connected with the task of social understanding; the discussions about it still are one of the central topics in contemporary sociology.[7] The way for a general program of understanding that we propose in the next subchapter and that will, as we hope, be suited for the subject of this book is by no means identical with Weber's program. Yet his attempt to show that is possible and fruitful to orientate the social sciences to the paradigm of the natural sciences is one of the most important stimulations for us in our attempt to combine understanding with explanation. To be sure, our combination of understanding with explanation will go into another direction. Yet in later chapters we shall demonstrate that the concept of ideal type can be very aptly used in different simulation programs.

In another form the equally important Alfred Schütz (1962–66) tried to demonstrate that the two concepts of understanding and explanation are not necessarily opposing aspects of rational thinking. By introducing the well known distinction between "in order to" and "because" explanations of social actions Schütz postulates that both explanation and understanding are necessary to solve the problem

---

[7]We only mention the fact that the work of two of the greatest social scientists of the last century, namely Talcott Parsons (1977) and Clifford Geertz (1973), would have not been possible without the decisive influence of Weber; cf. also Peacock (1982).

of capturing the meaning of social actions.[8] "In order to" explanations give the intention of the actor: He went to an examination *in order to* successfully finish his studies. But the murderer killed his victim *because* a blind fury overwhelmed him. Hence, "because" explanations refer to certain causes that determined the action.

If one wishes to make an action understandable by asking about the intentions one has to understand, i.e. one has to assume a certain wish, fear or other need and an according goal, which shall help the actor to fulfill his needs or to avoid something unpleasant. Intentions then refer to the (possible) future of the actor, namely a future that the actor wishes.[9] "Because" explanations on the other hand refer to the past of the actor, either to the objective one as a neutral observer would have perceived it or to a subjective one, i.e. a past that the actor has constructed in his imagination or in a subjective correction of the "real" past. It is common knowledge that people frequently bend their own past in the shape how they wish to see themselves and not as they were perceived by others. In any case the past is the source of the causes of the according actions and can explain in the strict, namely scientific, sense the actions of the actor.[10]

Frequently actions can be understood by either only asking for the intention or only for some causes in the past. Yet often actions can only be understood if one asks both for intentions and causes. In the cases of severe crimes the culprit is usually asked by the judge, which intentions he had when deciding to break the law and, with the help of a psychological expert, which events in his past caused him to get into crime (at least this is the procedure in the German law system). Accordingly a teacher may try to find out why a certain pupil permanently disturbs the teaching: does he do it in order to win applaud from his classmates and which events in his past caused him to play the role of a clown. Especially in the cases of socially (or psychologically) deviant behavior both forms of explanation and understanding are frequently necessary. By the way, the Terminator 2 alias Arnold Schwarzenegger did not "understand", as he said, in the way of understanding intentions (in contrast to the quoted definition of the Oxford Dictionary): He understood why people cry because, as he had learned, people often show their emotions by crying – either of sadness or of joy as the causes for their behavior. In contrast Solo understood certain actions with respect to their intentions when he understood the cheating of the boy by his intention to win the game via bluffing.

Although it is important to distinguish not only in analytical way between causes and intentions one must be aware that intentions might become causes and causes intentions. The early Calvinists acted in the way of asceticism within the world and

---

[8]In the German originals: "In order to explanation" is "*Um-Zu-Erklärung*", "because explanation" is "*Weil-Erklärung*".

[9]In the sense of the critique of Searle one could say that it is totally impossible for a complex of algorithms to orientate its performing to its future. But things are, as usual, not so easy. In Klüver (2000) we already showed artificial systems that orientate their dynamics to goals in the system's future.

[10]If in the case of "because" explanations the actor has shaped his past into something other or if he has simply forgotten the past causes of his present deeds it is often a therapeutic and analytical task to give a suited explanation of the action.

of purpose rationality *in order to* obtain indicators if they belonged to the chosen. They did so *because* they were socialized into the according sub culture of the sixteenth and seventeenth centuries – the sub culture caused them to choose this way of living. The intentional actions of one generation of Calvinists then reproduced this specific sub culture that in turn caused the next generation to generate according intentions, which became causes for the following generation and so on. Speaking in terms of Berger and Luckmann (1967) one might say that by intentional actions a certain form of objective social reality is constructed that has the effect of causes for following actions. Therefore, when understanding different actors one and the same social or cultural respectively phenomenon may be an intention of one actor and a cause for the other.

The considerations of Weber, Schütz and numerous others who dealt with the fundamental difference of explanation and understanding show that of course there must be precisely distinguished between these two forms of rational thought. Yet they are not opposing characteristics of rationality but rather complementary ones: Social actions, as we demonstrated, must either be understood by the intentions of the actors or explained by some causes in the past of the actor or by combining both forms. The approaches of Weber and Schütz are very similar in this aspect although one must not forget that Schütz, in contrast to Weber, Parsons and Geertz, bases the intentions of action not on the concept of culture but on that of life world (*Lebenswelt*). But these are differences important only for theoretical sociologists.

Explanation and understanding, hence, are as complementary approaches rather like two sides of the same medal. This fact will become even clearer when we ask how an AI may perform these methodical tasks. Our considerations will show that it is possible to let an AI perform understanding and explanation in the same formal way, namely by learning to associate certain actions either with specific intentions or with particular causes. This will be one of the subjects in the following sections. This is not to say that the distinction between understanding and explanation does not matter for a hermeneutical AI, but that this distinction is not a methodical one but one of content.

Although these attempts to relativize the contrast between understanding and explanation are immensely fruitful they are not sufficient. We already mentioned the unquestionable fact that very often social actions can be understood only when one refers to the respective social rules that determine the actions and that accordingly there is no (conscious) intention but only the automatic obeying of rules. Therefore, a sufficient and systematic description of the ways to understand social action, possibly by combining understanding and explanation, must take into account the importance of understanding rules.

2.2   Rules and Intentions – A Systematic of Interpreting

Imagine an American tourist who for the first time in his life visits a football game in Europe. Because he knows only American football and has no idea of the differences between these two forms of ball game, although he knows that Americans call the European (and South American) football "soccer", he tries to "understand" the actions of the players. He only knows that there are two teams on the field and that the members of the teams can be distinguished by the color of their shirts and trousers. Of curse he assumes that each player of the two teams has the general intention to win the game with his team but that does not help him much to understand the different actions; in this general sense of course European football does not differ from American football or basket ball. Hence he has the same task as a cultural anthropologist who comes to a strange society and has to understand the actions of the society's members by observing them. In both cases we assume that the tourist and the anthropologist cannot ask other people about the "sense" of the respective actions because they both do not know the language of the strange "tribes" they are visiting.[11] The task then is to reconstruct from the observed actions the respective rules the actors obey and hence to understand the structure of the social reality the actors produce and reproduce by their actions. For in both cases our observers safely assume that the actors do not act at random or *ad libitum*, following their momentary wishes, but act by following certain rules. Hence our two observers correctly assume that they will understand the strange actions and by this the whole social situation if they are able to reconstruct the respective rules.

The task for the tourist is certainly much easier than that of the anthropologist because European football (like American football) is a game with clear and decisive rules – in contrast to more complex types of social reality. Yet the methodical procedure is very similar in both cases. Both observers have to generate certain hypotheses about the rules that underlie and determine the actions and both have to confirm these hypotheses by predicting next actions. For example, one of the first observational results of the tourist will probably be the hypothesis that the game he is watching is called "football", because the (field) players mostly play the ball with their feet (that is by the way one reason why Europeans hardly understand why American football is also called "football"). Hence he formulates his first rule, namely that players must only touch the ball with their feet.

This hypothesis about a rule becomes confirmed when the observer sees that the referee (assumed that the observer can distinguish the referee from the players by his different dress) stops the game by a whistling signal when one player has touched the ball with his hand(s). If touching the ball with the hands is a deviation from a rule then certainly the rule about the ball playing only with feet must be a valid one. But, alas, some minutes later the tourist observes another player who takes the ball with his hands without intervention by the referee. Now our tourist has the alternative that either his hypothesis is refuted or that this basic rules allows for exceptions; of course these exception have also to be rule determined. By the additional observation that the player who obviously is allowed to play the ball

---

[11]We assume this sad lack of linguistic knowledge in the case of the tourist just for the sake of argument. Of course we do not want to say that American tourists usually do not know for example German or French when they visit these countries.

with his hands has differently colored shirts and trousers he formulates a second rule: players are mostly not allowed to play the ball with their hands but there are exceptional players who may do so; later when learning a bit about the language he might also learn that these special players are called "goalkeepers" in contrast to the field players. If the observer does not reject his first hypothesis but saves it by adding a second rule about allowed exceptions he behaves like most scientists: it is a common theme in theories of science that scientists usually do not reject their theories or hypotheses when learning about some contradiction to their assumptions. Instead they try to save their theories by adding new assumptions to the original one that allow to deal with the new facts without rejecting the basic assumption (cf. for example Kuhn 1963).

By continuing such successions of observing, assuming rule hypotheses, and confirming (or refuting) them by further observations and according predictions our tourist might be able after a certain time to understand the actions of the single players and by understanding them to understand what is meant with the concept "European football". In the end, when the tourist has successfully understood the main rules of the game, he has run through a simple case of the so-called "hermeneutical circle" (see below next sub chapter): He understands on the one hand the single actions because he knows the "structure" of the whole game, i.e. the different rules that determine the actions; on the other hand he understands the structure of the whole game by observing and understanding the single actions. In the terminology of hermeneutics: He understands the general by understanding the particular and vice versa.

Even in this comparatively simple case the task to reconstruct rules by generating hypotheses from the observations of single actions is not so easy as we described it. For example, there are situations when the field players are not only allowed to touch the ball with their hands but even must do so: that is the case when the ball has been kicked outside the field and when one player has to throw the ball into the field with his both hands. Even more difficult for a mere observer are cases of rule deviations that are not punished by the referee simply because he did not see it. Our observer hence has not only to confirm his hypothesis about a rule by observing the punishment of deviations by the referee but has also to maintain his hypothesis against a contradicting observation. The observer even may come to the hypothesis of "hidden rules", i.e. rules that are not official parts of the rule structure of the game, even may contradict them, but are nevertheless valid for the players. If, for example, the observer has generated the rule that players must not tackle their opponents (which is for example allowed in the games of ice-hockey and American football) and if one can observe that some players regularly violate this rule in particular in the penal space then perhaps a creative observer might hypothetically formulate a hidden rule: despite the official rule players frequently get the order (from their trainer) as a rule to hinder the opponent players to win a goal by all means, i.e. by kicking them or punching them down. Yet in all cases the methodical procedure is the same, namely to generate a hypothesis from the observation of single actions about a general rule that determines and explains these actions. Of course, no observer would form a hypothesis from the observation of just one action. Only if the observer sees that certain actions or forms of behavior are continuously repeated then the according hypothesis will be formulated.[12]

If it is already difficult to capture all or at least most of the rules that define the structure of a football game then the task to understand the structure of a whole strange society is much more complicated. It is no wonder that this methodical problem has always been one of the central difficulties of all social sciences that deal with the understanding of strange social realities like qualitative social research and cultural anthropology (cf. e.g. Geertz loc. cit.; Clifford and Marcus 1986). Yet despite these and even more difficulties those problems can be solved at least for a general understanding of strange social realities.

When the focus of understanding lies in the reconstruction of social rules the assumption obviously is that to understand a social action is to know the rule(s) that determines it. Conversely: Understanding the meaning of a rule is to know which actions it will determine in a situation where the conditions of rule application are fulfilled. This is apparently a variant of the so-called theory of usage that defines the meaning of a phenomenon by its practical usage (see above the remarks abut Marx and Peirce). The famous statement of Wittgenstein that the meaning of a word is its usage in the language (Philosophical Investigations) may be taken as the general motto of these meaning theoretical approaches.

This certainly restricted definition of understanding via the concept of social rules is of course rather far away from the classical approaches to understanding by concentrating on the "inner being" (Droysen) or the intention respectively like Searle or the Oxford Dictionary. But, as we mentioned in the preceding subchapter, it would be something like a "psychological fallacy" to take not into account the fundamental role that social rules play for determining social actions. In particular, the everyday practice of a nearly automatic understanding of the action of other actors is very often only itself understandable if one assumes that understanding in many cases refers to the according rules. As the private in the example above obeys orders without thinking because of the respective rule an understanding of the private is performed by an according automatic act: We understand the private's behavior literally without thinking about it if and because we know the rule to obey the orders of a military superior.[13] To be sure, neither the great sociologists Weber and Schütz nor scholars like Parsons, Geertz, or Ricoeur, who were deeply influenced by them, had something like a psychological reduction of understanding in mind. On the contrary, Weber's subjective sense for example refers to an objective culture that is independent of individual minds. Yet culture is not the

---

[12]Holland et al. (1986) deal rather thoroughly with the question how often observers have to watch certain events before they form a general hypothesis about them. It is not astonishing that in different situations observers need different numbers of the same observations before they make a hypothetical assumption or, in the terms of Holland et al., before they try an inductive conclusion.

[13]It is quite funny that sometimes in our lectures about communication theory students who did not know an institution like the army indeed did not understand the private's actions. Why, so the questions of students who only knew rather liberal organizations like schools and universities, did the private not discuss these orders with the sergeant? No comment.

same as social structure and hence we must take into account the relevance of social rules.

Habermas (1981, II) postulated the necessary distinction between culture, defined as the set of all knowledge recognized in a certain society, and social structure, namely the set of all social rules that are valid in this society (cf. also Geertz loc. cit., Giddens 1984; Klüver 2002).[14] By taking into account this distinction, by referring to the "subjective sense" by Weber, and by introducing a third dimension, namely that of general or even universal needs we may distinguish between four types of actions, ordered according to their reasons:

(a) The first type is the case if a certain action is performed because of a specific subjective sense, derived from the particular (sub)culture of the actor. The economical actions of the early Calvinists are a classical example for such a case. To understand such an action one needs of course to know the specific culture the actor lives in or has to reconstruct this culture with respect to those components that are the reasons for the actions. This was the interpretative achievement of Weber. Note that in this case and in the following ones always the difference between "in order to" and "because" explanations has to be taken into account.

(b) The second type is an action that is completely or at least mostly determined by a social rule. Many actions we observe and understand in everyday practice are of this type, as we mentioned above. To automatically understand a car driver who stops at a red traffic light is possible because one knows the respective social rule that defines a red light as the order to stop and a green one as the order to go on.

(c) To understand a third type of action one has to assume some general needs that are independent from specific social rules and/or subjective senses derived from a certain culture. The well-know "Heinz-Dilemma" by Kohlberg in moral philosophy is an example for this type: Heinz has the problem either to let his wife die because he cannot afford a very expensive medicine she needs or to steal the medicine from the drugstore. If we observe Heinz by committing this crime (if he decides to steal the medicine) we understand his action by assuming that he wishes to help his wife. We are able to assume such a reason because we know that the desire to help other people, in particular those we love, is a general motive for specific actions (e.g. Kohlberg 1971).[15]

The same is methodically the case if we have to assume some individual needs as the motive for the action although these needs are not necessarily universal. In this case the individual motive has to be reconstructed in a more difficult way, in particular by constructing so-called mental models of the actor. Because we shall thoroughly deal with the question of mental models in the next chapter we just mention this case here.

---

[14]Instead of "social structure" Habermas uses the term "society". We think this a rather unfortunate term and prefer the usage of "social structure".

[15]The Heinz Dilemma is a bit strange for Germans because in Germany – and in many other European countries – the health insurance institutions would certainly pay for the medicine if the doctor thinks it necessary. To understand the empirical validity of this dilemma one obviously has to know that this is not the case in the US (Kohlberg's home country).

(d) The first three types are, so to speak, pure types because the reasons for the actions always belong to one specific class of reasons. Because this is certainly not always the case in empirical reality one has to assume that frequently actions are determined by two or more of the prototypical reasons. If the crew of a ship saves another crew from distress at sea then the first crew is on the one hand obeying the (universal) rule to help other sailors who are in distress and probably on the other hand does so because of their general need to help other people.

Understanding a specific social action hence means to successfully characterize the possible reasons of this action as a three-dimensional vector with the components (a)–(c) and to decide, which components are irrelevant – in a formal sense they would get the value of zero – and which component(s) must be taken into account, i.e. should get a value unequal to zero. The simplest way to formalize this definition would be a binary coding of the vector. The Calvinists actions, hence, would be classified as $C_a = (1, 0, 0)$ and the deed of Heinz in the case of theft would be $H_a = (0, 0, 1)$. If one more realistically assumes that the motives of certain actions frequently consist of a mixture of different types – case (d) – and that the single components of the interpreting vector are of different relevance to the actor then a coding with real numbers, for example in the interval of 0 and 1, would be more appropriate. An early Calvinist for example who acts according to the characterizations of Weber may primarily be motivated by the described subjective sense but he might in addition has the very "subjective" intention to become rich and by this become a prominent and respected member of his parish. To characterize this his "personal" vector would be $C_a = (1, 0, 0.4)$ The ship crew's actions could be accordingly represented by $SC_a = (0, 1, 0.6)$.

This formal representation of action reasons by defining them as components of a vector suggests that the components are independent from each other as is the usual case with the elements of mathematical vectors. Then we would obtain a three-dimensional space of interpretation consisting of the classifying of certain actions by a specific element of the vector space. Yet as usual things are not quite so easy in social reality. A certain religiously determined culture for example is frequently not only the source of the subjective sense of the actions (type (a)) but defines in addition many social rules (type (b)). A famous and still very current example is the Islamic Sharia, the Koran founded system of norms and rules: Not only the religious beliefs derived from the Koran are contained in it but also social laws and rules how to lead a good life and how to organize a society. In a strict sense the Sharia does not allow the distinction between cultural components and social rules. The reason for the theft of Heinz, to take another example, is not necessarily a relevant motive in societies where polygamy and strict patriarchal values determine the culture. The need of Heinz to help his wife even by committing a crime is certainly not so strong if a man has a lot of women in his harem. Other examples where one of the components determines the values of other ones are easily imaginable.

Yet despite these methical caveats the analytical distinction between the three pure components is necessary and we will use it for our own purposes. Cases like actions determined by cultural forms like the Sharia must be taken into account but they refer to an additional problem of understanding:

According to our definition one understands an action if one is able to construct the according vector of reasons. We understand the halting of a car driver by classifying his stop with $C_a = (0, 1, 0)$. In this case the binary coding is sufficient because we can safely assume that no other reasons have to be taken into account. We could construct this vector because we know of the validity of the according rule. We also know that this rule is rather arbitrary because the rule could also be the opposite, namely halting before a green light and going on if the light turns to red. It is just a matter of convention. Probably the rule is as it is because most people will understand a red light as a warning signal but that does not alter the fact that this specific rule has no other reasons. In this case we not only understood the action but also the specific rule that determined it.

Now consider the actions of a fanatical Islamic terrorist who kills other people and himself. If one reads about such examples of religiously legitimated forms of violence or is informed about them by watching TV one usually becomes also informed that the terrorist gave before his deeds his religious belief as motive for his actions. We then understand the action as determined by a certain subjective sense, namely the basing of the action on the doctrines of the Koran. Hence we assume that this case is similar to be understood as the actions of the Calvinists in Weber's example. But as laymen in Islamic theology we of course do not know which parts of the Koran – if there are any – allow the killing of other and mostly totally innocent people. We know perhaps that there is no generally accepted interpretation of the Koran as there is no universally accepted interpretation of the Bible but we simply do not know what the terrorist exactly meant when he referred to the Koran. In other words, we understand the action because of its subjective sense but we do not understand the specific culture, from which the subjective sense is derived. Perhaps a scholar trained in Islamic theology could sufficiently reconstruct this culture as did Weber with the culture of the early Calvinists. Yet laymen can only understand the subjective sense but not its cultural source.

Apparently it is necessary to distinguish between two levels of understanding: The first level is the (successful) construction of an "interpretation vector" like the examples above. The terrorist's vector then would be $T_a = (1, 0, 0)$ if we do not know something else about perhaps additional intentions and his individual personality. For the second level of understanding one needs to know about the source of the respective components – in the case of social rules for example if they are arbitrary like most traffic rules or if they must be understood from social traditions or social necessities. The general social rule that forbids the killing of other people bases in the necessity to guarantee an unharmed life for the citizens of this society. To be sure, there are exceptions even from this rule like the order for soldiers to kill other people in the case of war. But we understand why this rule is one of the fundaments of practically every society.[16]

---

[16]There are, sad to say, still societies where forms of blood revenge or killing for the honor of one's family are still allowed. Yet even these cases of accepted killings are regulated by social rules. If somebody murders for other reasons he will be punished.

Understanding on the first level is everyday practice and we perform these operations frequently without thinking about it. This is in particular the case if the situation of the actions is familiar to us as in the case of the car driver (see below). To be sure, there are many examples where even understanding on the first level needs some conscious thinking: If a person deliberately violates a rule, e.g., by driving across a junction although the traffic light is red (for him) an observer might ask himself, which intentions are the reasons for this behavior. Did the driver not see the light or is he a reckless driver who does not care about traffic rules, must he perhaps as fast as possible reach a hospital because of a sick person in his car and so on. The according vector in any case must be $D_a = (0, 0, 1)$ and the content of the third component will be the result of conscious considerations or even investigations. But an observer will certainly feel that it is possible to understand this violation of the traffic rules without undertaking additional studies about the driver's culture and so on.

Understanding on the second level in contrast frequently needs additional knowledge about cultural contexts or the reason for certain social rules and also additional analysis of these contexts. That is very obvious in the mentioned examples of actions that must be understood as embedded in a religious context. But even in the comparative simple case of Heinz we mentioned that on the one hand the dilemma is of course easily understood by everyone. But on the other hand a German or other European who is accustomed to a complete health insurance has to know that the US health insurance system is otherwise organized (despite the attempts of several US presidents).[17] If he does not know these facts he will think this example rather silly and superfluous. Hence understanding on the second level frequently needs an additional expert knowledge and according context reconstructions by theologians, social scientists, historians, or cultural scientists.

In our further considerations we shall mostly mean understanding on the first level with the term "understanding" if we do not say otherwise. Yet we shall come back to this problem when we deal with the problem of the so-called hermeneutical circle.

Our little classification schema above allows a first methodical approach to the problem how to understand social actions in a systematical and conscious way. When observing a certain action it seems reasonable to ask at first which kind of reasons may lie behind this particular action. The formal representation as a vector certainly gives no answer about the specific reason. This answer needs special hypotheses about the particular intention, the cultural context or the specific social rule(s) (see below). But the schema reminds *before* the construction of a certain hypothesis that at first one must ask, which kind of reasons must be looked for. It is obvious useless to construct a hypothesis about possible intentions if one has to look for specific social rules. In the case of the driver who violates the rule about traffic

---

[17]It is at present (April 2010) clear that President Obama succeeded with his attempts for a reform of the US health system. Yet it is still not clear how this reform will factually change the health system because there is a still growing violent opposition against the reform.

lights it is accordingly useless to ask for possible social rules or cultural contexts that would explain his behavior. Hence the schema is a first orientation how to proceed with the understanding of social actions.

These considerations also demonstrate that and why explanation and understanding are no opposites as already Weber argued. According to the basic model of Popper (loc. cit.) about the structure of scientific research, i.e. of explanation, the researcher's task is to make observations gained from experiments and try to construct hypotheses that not only explain the empirical observations but also enable him to make predictions about future observations. If these predictions are correct then the according phenomena are explained too and the hypothesis is confirmed; if the predictions are not correct the hypothesis is refuted and either it must be adjusted to the refuting observations or a new one must be formulated. The construction of the hypothesis can be and often is guided by "inductive" reasoning (Holland et al. loc. cit.), i.e., by the repeated observation of certain regularities. But the confirmation of the hypothesis, which then becomes a scientific theory, must always be done by the proof that all observed phenomena can be deductively inferred from the hypothesis and that successful predictions can be inferred too the same way.

Experiments are usually not possible in social reality. But besides this difference between the natural and the social sciences the process of understanding is remarkably similar to that of scientific explanation. The starting point is the observation of certain phenomena, namely some social actions. Then a hypothesis is formed about the possible reasons of these actions, in particular by asking what kind of reason one can assume and then what particular intention, rule or socio-cultural context has determined the action. The construction of such a hypothesis is again frequently guided by inductive reasoning, namely by taking into account the situations where the same actions have been observed and where certain forms and contents of reasons could safely be assumed. If possible then also predictions are made on the basis of the hypothesis: If reason A has determined action B then action C is to be expected. For example, if one sees a driver ignore a red traffic light and if one forms the hypothesis that he is simply reckless then one expects the same behavior, i.e. ignoring traffic rules, in the next situation. A confirmation of this hypothesis would be that the driver passes another car on the right lane of an *Autobahn* when the other car is driving on the left lane.[18]

To be sure, hypotheses and theories in the natural sciences usually try to generate general statements about all cases the hypothesis deals with. In contrast understanding processes usually deal with single cases – that driver, that football player, these believers in Calvinistic doctrines; accordingly a single refutation of a hypothesis does not make the hypothesis worthless in a general sense (see above). But besides these and other differences the two methodical approaches to empirical reality have apparently more in common than one would expect and is frequently informed by

---

[18] An *Autobahn* is a highway with at least two lanes in both directions. It is strictly forbidden in Germany to pass another car if one drives on the right lane (with one exception).

the scholars who deal with our subject.[19] In both cases the decisive point is the derivation of the observed phenomena from a constructed hypothesis and in both cases the hypothesis must capture the explained or understood phenomena as special cases. We shall come back to these parallels when dealing with the question how an AI could learn to understand in this sense.

Another systematic that can give interpretative orientations is an ordering of action situations. It is evident that an action can only be understood if one takes into regard the respective situations, in which the actions are embedded. To ask for specific social rules like traffic rules makes only sense if the observed actions are performed in traffic situations. Accordingly actions that are determined by certain subjective senses can only be understood in the suited situation. The irritation for example in Western societies about people who pray during their work in the working room is an indicator for actions that are not suited to this specific situation – according to Western cultural norms. In AI research this truism was taken into account with the conception of frames or scripts respectively (cf. Schank and Abelson 1977): If an AI program should understand simple actions like giving an order to a waiter in a restaurant the program must have a "restaurant frame" at its disposal, namely knowledge about restaurants, persons like waiters, ordering meals and drinks and so on. Only if the program could perceive certain actions like paying the bill as actions typical for the restaurant situation it could "understand" these actions.[20] An action hence can only be understood if one understands the "framing" situation; a situation conversely can only be understood if one understands the actions that make the situation "real", i.e. that allows us to speak of an action situation. A restaurant as a certain situation remains, so to speak, latently until guests and waiters by their respective actions make this situation manifestly. This is another example of the hermeneutic circle, which is at the core of hermeneutics.

It is possible and useful to construct a two-dimensional order of action situations. The first dimension is that of familiarity with the situation. The observation of a probably reckless driver is the observation of a situation that is very familiar. All members of societies with much car traffic know such situations and frequently even from their own experiences as car drivers. The same is the case with observations of guests and waiters in a restaurant. Such situations are well known to all members of modern societies who have been socialized in a normal way. Yet it is useful to remember that human observers had to learn too about the "situational frames" of restaurants and car traffic. Not only programs but also children or persons from other cultural contexts without car traffic or without institutions like restaurants have to acquire such frames. A sociologist in contrast who has to observe youths in a hooligan gang is confronted with action situations that are very unfamiliar for him – at least if he comes from an academic middle class environment. On

---

[19]Of course it is also possible in the social sciences to formulate general theories about specific social realms (cf. e.g. Klüver 2002, 2003).

[20]One could argue that programs with the suited scripts did not more understand actions in a restaurant than the man in the Chinese room because the programs also had only syntactical rules at their disposal.

first sight he would neither understand the specific sub cultural language nor the social rites of establishing a certain pecking order. Even more difficult is the observational situation for a cultural anthropologist who for the first time visits a strange society. The example of the American tourist who for the first time in his life visits a game of European football shows what methodical difficulties such observers have to overcome in order to understand such situations and the situational actions.

Frequently in everyday language people say that they understand other persons because they perceive themselves in the other ones. An observer of the car driver who does not stop at the junction may understand this driver because the observer has done the same several times, in particular when he was in a great hurry. A visitor of a football game who plays football himself will understand a player on the field if the player deliberately fouls an opponent in the penal space because the observer had done the same in several games. In this case one could say that such situations have the highest degree of familiarity if the observers see and recognize themselves in the role of the actor. An extreme contrast to such observations would be, for example, the observation of a psychopathic murderer who is as strange to oneself as one can imagine.[21]

These examples suggest the following definition: An observed action situation can be characterized by its degree of familiarity (df) for the observer and we define $0 \leq df \leq 1$. $df = 0$ means that the situation is totally unfamiliar like the observation of a psychopathic murderer; $df = 1$ means of course that the observer knows the situation very well and is even able to recognize himself in the role of the observed actor. Most observed action situation will be characterized with df somewhere between these extremes, at least in the usual daily life. Of course, certain professionals like cultural anthropologists or social scientists specialized on sub cultures strange to them will rather often be confronted with situations of $df = 0$. But even in these cases professional experience will make such situations more and more familiar because the professional will get used to such situations and will in particular draw inferences from his previous experiences with strange cultures when meeting another one. Hence $df = 0$ is a comparatively seldom case.

By introducing the degree of familiarity we obtain a measure for situations that allows us to order such situations. Another dimension for situational ordering is given by the following characterization: Two observed action situations can be distinguished by the observer according to their respective degree of determination (dd). With this measure we mean that in one situation for example the actor has literally no space of freedom for his actions; his actions are totally determined by the objective constraints of the situation. Such a situation is the case of the private in an army or that of a prisoner in a jail – the mentioned totalitarian institutions in the sense of Foucault. In another situation the actor is to a great extent free to act according to his own wishes and intentions. An example for such a situation would

---

[21] The success of films about such totally strange people who could only be understood if at all by professional psychiatrists might have their reasons just in this total strangeness. The movies about Hannibal Lector are an example.

be an informal party where the host asks his guests to feel at home and to do what they like. Of course, in such a situation the party guest has to obey the rules of the household, namely to behave in a polite and friendly manner, to stay sober, and to praise the dishes and drinks. But besides these basic rules the guest is free to talk to anybody or to avoid certain people, to leave early if he is bored, or to stay until the official end of the party and so on.

We define $0 < dd \leq 1$. The situations of the private or the prisoner must be characterized by a high degree of determination, i.e. $dd = 1$ or nearly 1. The case $dd = 0$ is probably not possible at all because each social situation has at least one or few social rules that determine the actions of the actors. That is why we chose the numerical definition of dd in a slightly different way than that of df. Yet it is important to note that both measures are subjective ones, namely from the point of view of a particular observer. A party may look as a situation with nearly no constraints for an observer who only sees people obviously moving at their will. To a sociologist who is trained in the analysis of social situations the party may be a social system determined by rather complicated rules, i.e. rules that are difficult to understand for a stranger at such a party. Even a situation in a totalitarian situation may give the actors more space of freedom than an observation on a first sight would unveil: The private for example might successfully try to win the goodwill of the sergeant and such influence the orders of him, in particular orders of throwing himself down into the mud.

Some methodical consequences of this systematic are these: (a) If the df-values are rather small, i.e. if the situation is not familiar to the observer, then one should start the interpretation by assuming that either the respective rules of some cultural orientations determine the situation, i.e. that the dd-value is rather high. It is comparatively useless to ask for subjective intentions if the whole situation is only incompletely known and understood. The assumption that rules and/or cultural components determine the actions in question is usually more fruitful. On the other hand, if the df-values are rather high then of course it is a question of the (known) dd-values, with which type of reasons one should start the interpretation. (b) If the dd-values are low then one should start with asking for the subjective intention(s) of the actor. This interpretation rule is rather obvious because low dd-values mean, at least from the point of view from the observer, a large space of freedom for the actor. On the other hand, high dd-values of course mean that the first questions should go in the direction of social rules and/or cultural components. To be sure, these general orientations do not automatically guarantee the way to a correct understanding of the situation yet they can be useful in order to avoid blind alleys.

We mentioned above the similarities and even parallels between the two methodical tasks of understanding and explanation. In particular we referred to the fact that in both cases not only the observed phenomena must be covered by the respective hypothesis but that the hypothesis must also generate predictions for at present unobserved phenomena. In the case of social understanding this means that on the basis of the hypothesis the observer forms some expectations about the future behavior of the respective social actor. In other words, the observer expects the actor to behave in a similar or in the same situation the same way as in the situation before – either obeying the same rule or determined by some culturally derived subjective sense in the same manner or following the same intentions. If this expectation is fulfilled then the observer has understood the action; in particular the observer is not surprised because he expected it.

In Section 1.3.3 we defined the concept of the informational degree of a message by measuring the difference between the expected message and the factual one. A message has a high degree of information if it is not expected and vice versa. By applying this definition to the understanding of social actions one might say that an observer understands an observation if the observation is not very informative. A high informational degree of a message on the other hand means for the observer a difficult task to understand it. In this sense communication theory and hermeneutics can be combined.

This first systematization of "the operation called verstehen" shows that there is nothing mysterious in this operation and in particular that the differences between explanation and understanding are not so great as it is often discussed. We mentioned above that several critics of the possibility of AI referred to hermeneutics with the goal to show that no AI ever could perform hermeneutical operations like the understanding of social actions. We demonstrated in contrast that the methodical steps an understanding observer has to undertake can be expressed in a systematic and also formal manner.

The "hermeneutical" critics like Dreyfus, Winograd/Flores or Searle always referred to philosophical hermeneutics, namely to foundations of philosophical thinking. If an AI can ever do this is an open question, at least for us. Yet the hermeneutics we deal with is that of empirical social science, orientated to the everyday practice of the understanding of social practice. To be sure, the scientific way of systematic understanding is not identical with understanding in normal social practice; in particular the reconstruction of cultural contexts frequently need expert knowledge and according methodical thinking. But the scientific way of understanding has its roots in the practical understanding and has derived its methods from it. Scientific understanding probably is at the core nothing more than a conscious systematization and critical examination of the everyday practice of social understanding. Critics of AI should not look at that what philosophers do or claim to do but at the forms of understanding that is factually practiced by scientific laymen and empirical social scientists.[22] Critics like Dreyfus and Searle have looked into the wrong direction.

2.2.1 Consequences for an Understanding AI

An attempt to apply these considerations to the problem of understanding and AI must first deal with the problem if an AI can be able to act intentionally, i.e. if certain actions of an artificial system could be understood by an "in order to" explanation.

---

[22]We want to avoid a misunderstanding: One of the authors has written his PhD thesis in philosophy and thinks still well of this intellectual enterprise.

After all, humans can understand other people's action by an "in order to" explanation because they know intentions themselves and have frequently acted when they were determined by some intentions. It is obviously that the operations of formal systems like computer programs can be understood via a "because" explanation: Given a certain initial state and specific rules of interaction the explanation of the dynamics of the system in terms of "because", i.e. cause and effects, can principally be done the way we described in Section 1.3.2. As causes refer to the past of the system such an explanation is possible although sometimes only with great methodical and empirical difficulties. But what about intentions?

Intentions, as we analyzed, refer to the future of the actor, in particular to a future the actor desires or in contrast he wishes to avoid. The second case is equivalent to a future one desires where certain events do not take place but their counterparts. The task of the system is hence to find a way, i.e. to generate a trajectory that leads from the present state to the desired future states. If necessary the system has to vary parts of its structure or its initial present state.

In this formal sense the answer if artificial systems can intentionally act is quite simple, namely "of course". The famous chess program "Deep Blue", for example, that beat Kasparov, the world chess champion at that time, can be understood as an intentionally operating system: It had the goal – of course implemented by its programmer – to obtain a strategically optimal situation and accordingly it chose the best strategy to get this situation. In other words, Deep Blue orientated its performance to a desired future. The logically rather simple way by which Deep Blue operated, namely applying the so-called brute force method of calculating nearly all possible moves, is no argument against its intentionality: Human actors frequently operate in a similar simple fashion.

Several more sophisticated programs that orientate itself to a desired future were presented by us in Klüver (2000): We constructed some "hybrid systems" that consist of cellular automata (CA), certain neural nets and a genetic algorithm (GA). The cellular automata represent a certain society, where each cell of the CA represents a social actor. The cells consist of neural nets that represent the cognitive structure of the actors. The task of the GA is to optimize the system by changing the rules of transition of the CA. In other words, the artificial societies or the artificial actors respectively had the formal intention to better the present state(s) of the society by changing the social structure. The operations of the whole system, i.e. interactions between cells of the CA, the cognitive operations of the neural nets and the meta operations of the GA in this sense are orientated to the system's future and in that sense can be described as the formal equivalence of following a certain intention.

To be sure, in both cases of Deep Blue and our hybrid systems the goal and the order to orientate to this goal were implemented by the respective programmers. Yet in many cases the goals people follow are not their own choice or a result of their free will but are given by nature in the case of biological needs or by the specific culture the people are part of like in the cases of religious goals or general world views. We do not want to discuss the question of free will because we suspect that it is an undecidable question if there is such a quality in human minds (cf. e.g. Libet 2004 from a neurobiological point of view). We just want to point out that the externally implemented goals of our two examples are no principal argument against the formal intentionality of these artificial systems. One can easily imagine that the SF examples of Solo and Terminator 2 operate in a similar way by orientating their actions to the future, and the desired states of themselves, and of the future social situation they exist in at present. Hence our formal systems are at least able to simulate intentionality – whether they "have" it we leave to the readers.

One could argue that the artificial systems factually do not orientate their operations to their future but that they in performing certain operations just follow their immanent logic, determined by their initial states and rules. Consequently they can be understood via a simple "because" explanation. If that should be granted then the distinction of Schütz becomes problematic for human actions too: The desire to reach certain goals can the same way be explained by referring to past and present states of the actor, to his biography and socialization, to externally given cultural norms and so on, hence by "because" explanations. Therefore, either one accepts principally the methodical necessity to distinguish between "because" and "in order to" explanations; then this is valid for human and artificial systems alike. Or one refers in the case of artificial systems to the fact that principally "because" explanations are sufficient to understand these systems. Then the same argument is valid for human beings too and one should abandon "in order to" explanations as superfluous. Yet because we believe that it is methodically and practically worthwhile to use this distinction we shall further speak of intentionality with respect to human actions and of at least a formal equivalence of intentionality in the case of artificial systems. Hence it is obviously possible to represent both types of social action by the operations of formal systems. The behavior of self-organized systems can be completely described by the initial states as causes plus the according rules of interaction; systems that operate goal oriented can be described by their specific rules and those meta rules that either change the system's states or its rules or both. Yet in the second case the concrete changing of the rules by the meta rules can only be understood by taking into regard the goal these systems are oriented to.

A sufficient complex artificial system hence can operate in both fashions. For a brief sketch how such systems can be enabled to understand via "because" explanations and "in order to" ones we remind of the network version of "Eliza" in Section 1.4. Eliza consists of two coupled networks, namely a simple feed forward one with the task to learn the associations of given inputs with correct answers and an interactive network, interpreted as a semantical network. The task of this second network is to associate other concepts with the input key words, for example definitions like "father" with "male parent". Imagine now a similar system of coupled networks with basically the same tasks. The task of the first net is to learn associated pairs of concepts, for example "red traffic light" with "stop". The associated concepts then could be associated with the concept "traffic rule" and so on. Such learned small clusters of concepts will then be inserted into the interactive or semantical network

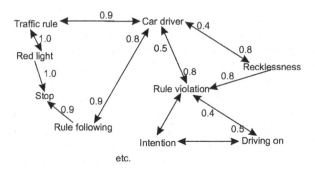

Fig. 2.1 A semantical (dynamical) network for an understanding of a car driver

respectively; the links between the concepts will be weighted according to the associative strength between the concepts.[23] Figure 2.1 shows such a semantical network for the example "car driver and traffic lights".

It is now a question of the training of both networks how the interactive network responds to an input "(car driver, red light, driving on)". If it has learned via the associative learning of the feed forward network to generate a strong connection between the three concepts of the input and the concepts "rule violating" and "intention" and if the last one is strongly associated with "haste" or "recklessness", then the network will "interpret" by giving an answer "(intention, haste, recklessness)". In other words, the network will "understand" the observation as a violation of a rule and will conclude that it must look for an according intention. In the vector terminology it defines the observation as being represented by a vector (0, 0, 1). Accordingly an input "(green light, driver, stopping)" will be interpreted as a vector (0, 1, 0) and an according output will be "(rule obeying)". To be sure, the networks could have learned false interpretations, i.e. wrong connections. But this, as with humans, is just a question of a correct teaching in the respective learning processes.

In addition, it is also possible to apply our rule of thumb concerning the degree of familiarity to such networks. The question if an observation A is more familiar than an observation B can be decided with respect to the relative strength of connections. "Strong familiarity" means that the according observations are strongly connected with the interpretative concepts as in the example of the car driver. If the observation of driving over a junction despite a red light has frequently been made then, according to the fundamental learning principle of Hebb (loc. cit.), the according connections will be strong and vice versa. (In Chapter 4 we shall give a detailed analysis of this principle and its consequences). A training process that shall also include the interpretative rule of thumb must include the generation of a third network that acts as a "councilor" for the interactive network: If because of weak

---

[23] It is important to note that semantical networks usually are static structures; interactive networks are dynamical systems like the neuro-biological networks in the brain.

connections the final activation values of the interactive networks are below a certain threshold then the third network will be activated with an output "social rule" or "cultural context". This output is given to the interactive network that generates an output "(rule, according concepts)". In other words, the third network operates as an equivalent to a certain meta rule, namely telling the second network how to proceed.

If the activation values of the second network are rather high, i.e. above the threshold, then the observation is familiar and the second network needs no advice from the third.

A lot more could be said about the construction and training of networks that learn how to interpret certain observations. But we shall give no more technical details because our own works with respect to these questions are just in the beginning. We just wanted to show how in principle the networks can operate that "understand" according to our classification of actions. It is time to deal with the core methodical concept of hermeneutics, namely the so-called hermeneutical circle.

2.3 The Hermeneutical Circle: The Difficult Basis of Understanding

The Oxford Dictionary defines hermeneutics as "the branch of knowledge that deals with interpretation, esp. . . . literary texts." At least since Max Weber and the historian Droysen there is in addition also a hermeneutics of the social sciences that deals accordingly with the interpretation of social actions. In the preceding subchapters we already demonstrated how a certain form of social interpretation, namely the understanding of social actions can be systematized in a formal way. The general definition of hermeneutics as the method of the interpretation of texts *and* human behavior includes of course all hermeneutical applications to different fields of knowledge but it says nothing about the methodical procedures that could generate an interpretative knowledge.

Since the first methodical reflections about the methodical foundations of the humanities in the early nineteenth century the concept of the hermeneutical circle had been conceived as one of the most important methodical concepts for the interpretative tasks of the humanities. As far as we know this concept was at first formulated by the German philosopher Ast who postulated that the whole, i.e. texts or social contexts, can only be understood by referring to single, namely particular cases and accordingly particular single cases can only be understood by referring to the whole (cf. e.g. Apel loc. cit.). Terms like "the whole" are typical for the early philosophical foundations of the humanities; instead of this rather vague concept we shall speak of "context".[24]

The several times mentioned example of the early Calvinists serves to illustrate these remarks. When one reads reports about certain actions of single

---

[24]In German: "*Das Ganze kann nur durch das Besondere verstanden werden und das Besondere nur durch das Ganze*". The name "hermeneutical circle" has been introduced by Gadamer (cf. his main work "*Wahrheit und Methode*" (Truth and Method)).

representatives of the early Calvinist communities, in particular that they acted in a strategic manner according to the maximization of their economical profit but that they lived in an unpretentious way without much material needs, then one may marvel about such strange ways of life and one would not understand them. Perhaps one would think that these Calvinist entrepreneurs had all been misers who wanted to hoard their money (cf. the difference between misers and capitalists emphasized by Marx). To understand these actions and ways of life one must refer to the context, in which the Calvinists lived, in particular their religious culture, expressed in forms of certain symbolic doctrines. By doing this one can either construct or detect respectively concepts like "asceticism within the world, predestination, purpose rationality" and so on. If these abstract concepts are used as an explanation (in Weber's sense) for the behavior of the Calvinist entrepreneurs then we understand these actions – the whole, i.e. the cultural context, explains the single cases. On the other hand abstract concepts like those mentioned remain "abstract", i.e. cannot be understood in a concrete manner if one does not refer these concept to single concrete cases. In this way the single cases explain the whole by giving them a concrete meaning. We understand the Calvinistic doctrines, insofar they regulate the practical social life of the faithful, by looking at concrete single cases, which in turn can only be understood by the consideration of the whole, i.e. the cultural context. This circular procedure is basically the same, whether one has to interpret literary texts or the social actions of human actors.

Many philosophers of the sciences have criticized the concept of the hermeneutical circle as an unscientific method and have compared it with the infamous *circulus vitiosus* (a "vicious" circle) in logic. This is a circle by which for example a concept is defined by itself, possibly doing this in several steps. Another example of such a circle is a proof in mathematics, which uses the statement that has to be proved as a step of the proof itself. Yet this comparison is mistaken. A *circulus vitiosus* operates on only one logical level inside a closed formal system. A hermeneutical circle in contrast moves from one level to another and back again, namely from a particular level to that of a general context and back. In this sense an operation with a hermeneutical circle is similar to the operation of "outgödeling" that we mentioned in the preceding chapter. In both cases one particular level that restricts cognitive operations is transcended in to another level where the initial restrictions are overcome. The hermeneutical circle, hence, is a logically acceptable operation and in particular one that enables cognitive acts of interpretation.[25]

In addition, like other operations of understanding the concept of the hermeneutical circle is just a formal reconstruction of operations we permanently perform in daily life. The observation of one single action and its interpretation by, e.g., "X does Y because X is a Z" and "Z means that certain persons X do Y" is an everyday example of thinking in hermeneutical circles. To be sure, such a thinking may lead

---

[25]Immanuel Kant wrote in his Critique of pure Reason that "concepts without content are empty and phenomena without concepts are blind" (*Begriffe ohne Anschauung sind leer und Anschauung ohne Begriffe ist blind*). This famous remark describes very well the respective restrictions each level has when being considered alone.

to wrong results, e.g. to prejudices or to wrong generalizations. But the risk of errors is inherent in human thinking, even in the strict formal operations of mathematics and mathematical logic.

In Section 2.2 we introduced the distinction between two different levels of understanding: Understanding a social action on the first level means that we understand, which social rule or which subjective sense, i.e. which cultural context internalized by the actor, and/or which individual intention respectively is or are the reasons for the action. Understanding on the second level means that one understands the different reasons too: Why is this rule as it is, how is the cultural context characterized that it determines the actions that way, and why has the actor in this situation this specific intention. We also mentioned the fact that frequently understanding on the second level needs specific expert knowledge about the respective cultural contexts, about the logic behind certain social rules, and about psychological reasons for the emergence of particular intentions. Performing a hermeneutical circle, at least in a conscious way, obviously needs understanding on both levels: the embedding of single particular events into a general context is of course only possible if one understands the context at least in a general way. To be sure, a rule determined action can be understood by just knowing the respective rule and without understanding why this rule is as it is and not otherwise. But a complete understanding of an action via a hermeneutical circle is only possible by not only referring to the context (the second level) but also by generally understanding it in its specific logic.

Before we describe how the operations of a hermeneutical circle can in principle be formally simulated and thus gives a first impression how an AI may learn them we wish to enlarge the concept of this circle a bit. The example of the Calvinist entrepreneurs already demonstrated that the knowledge or insight respectively one gains by applying a hermeneutical circle is far more than nothing. Yet a second look at this operation shows that the circle can be a more complicated picture of thought, namely an open or also closed spiral. Consider for example a sociologist of science who wants to study the "laboratory life" of chemists (cf. for example Latour and Woolgar 1979).[26] As an empirical researcher he starts with observations of the work of particular chemists in their laboratory (the level of particular cases). Afterwards the sociologist refers the operations of the chemists to the social and cultural context their works are embedded in. This context is on the one hand the scientific culture of chemistry and on the other hand the social environment of a chemical institute or a chemical department respectively. The researcher formulates some hypotheses about the cognitive structure of chemistry and the social structure of such scientific institutions. He then wishes to confirm these hypotheses by analyzing other chemists and by comparing his observations with observations of other natural scientists, for example physicists. These comparative results lead to new and more general

---

[26]In the late seventies and eighties the domain of "laboratory studies" was an important field of research in sociology of science by applying methods of cultural anthropology to the social organizations of the natural sciences.

Fig. 2.2 Open spiral

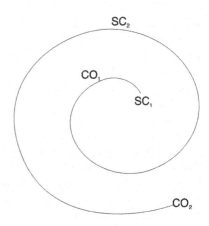

hypotheses about scientific research in the natural sciences in general and about the general structure of scientific research institutes. These operations hence give him new single particular cases and a new context, in particular a corrected version of the first context. If he wishes he continues these iterative operations to gain more and more detailed knowledge about the cognitive and social structure of research in the natural sciences. The whole process obviously is not a closed circle anymore but an open spiral (Fig. 2.2); SC stands for (single) cases or observations respectively, Co for contexts.

The sociologist may even go further by studying not only particular scientific disciplines but also science in general, including the humanities, and their social environment, namely whole universities, scientific societies and academies. The most general level would be the analysis of the specific culture in which science as a socially organized and highly respected cognitive enterprise has emerged, namely the Western culture since Renaissance and Enlightenment. The operations and interactions of two chemists in one laboratory, hence, may accordingly be taken as a representative and significant example of modern Western culture in general where the specific characteristics of the Western culture become manifest.

To be sure, each research project must end some time. The money available is spent, books, articles, and in particular PhD theses must be written and so on. The spiral of hermeneutic research will frequently be ended for such pragmatic reasons. But it also can and will occur that the spiral is closed for logical reasons. This will be the case when the research process does not generate any new results or only unimportant new ones. Although the movement from a particular (or more particular respectively) level to a contextual one goes on no new knowledge can be obtained.[27]

---

[27]The terms "particular" and "contextual" or even "general" are of course only relative ones. The level of the two single chemists is "more particular" than the level of a university that is taken as particular with respect to a whole culture. Each step of the spiral generates a level that is more or less particular with respect to the levels above and below.

Fig. 2.3 A spiral that has reached an attractor

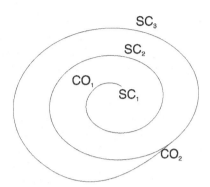

In a formal language this means that despite new single cases SC_i a certain context Co_k will not be changed any more, hence $Co_k = Co_{k+n}$, for all n. If this is the case, which of course can have very different reasons, we may say that the process of the hermeneutical spiral has reached an attractor, in particular a point attractor. The research process, hence, can be considered as a certain complex dynamical system with characteristic trajectories. The Fig. 2.3 gives a visualization of such a case.

Theorists of the natural sciences characterized this phenomenon as a characteristic feature of the research process in the natural sciences although not with this terms (cf. Kuhn loc. cit.; Krohn and Küppers 1989). Our considerations show again that the principal differences between hermeneutical research and that of the natural sciences are not so very great. In particular it is obviously possible to formally describe and explain both research processes with the same terminology, namely that of complex dynamical systems, and get very similar results.

We mentioned above that several critics of AI referred to hermeneutics as a proof that a "real" AI as a complex ensemble of algorithms would never be possible at all because understanding in a hermeneutical sense must demand more than the performing of syntactical, i.e. rule determined operations. We can for the moment leave the question open if humans *always* act in more than a syntactical way when they act in certain social situations; the example of the private, however, reminds that this is certainly not the case. To decide the question at least principally if artificial systems could learn to operate according to the hermeneutical circle – regardless if they "really" understand in this way or if they "only" simulate the hermeneutical principles – we come back for a short time to Eliza (Section 1.4.2) and the similarly coupled networks in the preceding subchapter.

We sketched in both cases the basic design of an Eliza version that can at least in a formal way "understand" the statements of its human partners and of a system that can learn and perform simple operations of understanding as the coupling of two different neural networks, namely a feed forward network and an interactive network. The task of the first network was to learn in the case of Eliza what answers to a statement of the human partner should be given; these answers and the statements of the user are given to the second network that represents a semantical network.

By receiving certain concepts of the first network the second one generates certain associations like "a father is a male parent" and so on. The combination of these two networks allows to say that this Eliza version does on the one hand give some answers to the user that it has learned to do so in an according training process; on the other hand it also is able to associate some formal meaning with the input the first network receives and hands over to the second one.

An artificial system that simulates the hermeneutical circle can be designed just the same way. We take again the example of the early Calvinists from Max Weber and couple two networks of the same type as in our Eliza version. The main difference to the Eliza version is the fact that the first network, the feed forward one, must be constructed as a so-called bi-directional hetero-associative network. This term means that a network of this type can perform associations in two directions: When a certain input is inserted then the network will react with a certain output, namely an output that is different from the input. When then this output is inserted as a new input then the network will generate the first input as the new output. In other words, if for example the first input is X and the according output is Y, then the input Y will generate X.[28]

The learning task of the first network will be the association of certain concepts with observations about the behavior of individual Calvinist entrepreneurs, for example "living without material needs", "acting in a strategic way" and so on. These observations are then, after an according training process, associated with concepts like "asceticism within the world", and "purpose rationality". This training process now guarantees that an input of "living without material needs" will generate the output "asceticism within the world" and vice versa. The network has learned to interpret observations of single events with general concepts and to understand these abstract concepts by referring them to concrete facts. The *theoretical* meanings of empirical facts are the according general concepts; the *concrete* meaning of abstract concepts is their relation to concrete facts or observations respectively.[29]

The input will be inserted in addition as an input into the second network. Designed as the formal representation of a semantical network it represents the knowledge of an interpreting scholar about the cultural context. It is a truism that the application of a hermeneutical circle always depends on the knowledge of the individual that performs the interpretation: Despite the fact that "culture" is meant in an objective sense a concrete process of hermeneutical interpretation always is in that sense "subjective" that two different individuals might perform rather different interpretations if their knowledge is significantly different. This second network

---

[28] Hetero-associative is derived from the Greek word *heteros*, meaning "other" as in "heterosexual" – be fond of the other sex.

[29] We are quite aware that we are using here only one of the classical theories of meaning, namely the so-called referential theory of meaning that goes back to Platon's *Kratylos*. Our own general definition of meaning that we sketched in Section 1.3.3, however, can be applied to this network too: An insertion of "living without material needs" generates the attractor "asceticism within the world" and vice versa.

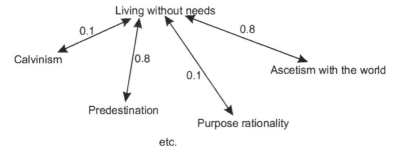

Fig. 2.4   A semantical network containing the individual knowledge about the cultural context of the early Calvinists

has been also trained, although in a different fashion than the first one (see below Chapter 4 about self-organized learning). The result of these training processes can be visualized like in the Fig. 2.4.

This network operates the following way: After the receiving of the input that the first network also has gotten it "activates" its neurons according to the strength of the weighted links between the neurons.[30] Finally it generates a certain final state, i.e. an attractor. In 2007 we defined the meaning of an input in the case of such an network as the three or four concepts that have reached in this final state the highest activation values. After the insertion of "living without material needs" the final state is shown in the next Fig. 2.5:

The respective length of the beams represent the strength of the final activation values. One immediately sees that the concepts "needless living", "asceticism within the world" and "predestination" are those with the strongest activation. Hence one can say that the observation of "living without needs" is associated within the semantical network with the according theoretical concepts that allow a theoretical understanding of the empirical observation of single, i.e. particular cases.

When the second network inserts one of the concepts that define the meaning of its input back to the first network, for example "asceticism within the world" then the bi-directional network will generate the output, i.e. the attractor "living

1	Living without needs	0.61
2	Ascetism with the world	0.44
3	Predestination	0.44
4	Calvinism	0.09
5	Entrepeneur	0.09
6	Purpose rationality	0.09

Fig. 2.5   Final state of the "Calvinist" network

---

[30]More technical details about the training process and the operations of this network type will be given in Chapter 4.

without material needs". Our network combination hence is able to simulate the circular movement from the observation of or knowledge about particular cases to theoretical interpretations by referring to the knowledge about the cultural context and vice versa. One sees again that the frequently criticized methodical process of the hermeneutical circle has not only no mysteries but can be formally reconstructed with sufficient precision.

We emphasized above that the hermeneutical circle can and frequently must be extended to a hermeneutical spiral. The combination of neural networks that allows the formal reconstruction of the original circle also makes it possible to simulate the spiral. This can be done by (a) an enlargement of the training process and (b) by the introduction of corrections. The enlargement of the training process simply means that both networks are trained to capture more pairs of input-output relation in the case of the first network and more concepts including the necessary weighted links in the case of the second one. An introduction of corrections means that already established weighted links in the second network can be changed if new observations demand it. If for example new historical facts show that significant many Calvinist entrepreneurs factually lived in luxury then the links in the second network must be accordingly changed. This can be done the following way: These new results must be learned by the first network and as a consequence a new input-output relation will be established, namely "living in luxury" and "no asceticism". These concepts will be additionally inserted into the second network and connected with the original concepts. As a consequence the connections to and from the neuron "purpose rationality" will be weakened because a luxurious life is not very rational for an entrepreneur (see above footnote 68). These two processes of enlargement and corrections can be continued as long as the problem and the emergence of new facts demand.

By demonstrating that a formalization of the hermeneutical circle and the spiral in terms of neural networks is possible without any great problems we of course did not solve all technical details that arise with such constructions. An AI that operates in approximately the described way is still a very simple prototype and its usefulness very restricted. Yet our goal was just to show the general possibility of such an attempt.

Before we finish this chapter we want to show the results of a computer experiment that intends to simulate the processing of a human who is reading a story, in particular a detective story. Although, as we mentioned in the introduction, the subject of this book is chiefly the understanding of human social actions it is certainly of interest if and how it is possible to simulate something like an understanding process of certain texts.

2.3.1 Excursion into Simulated Detective Stories Readers

In 2007 we demonstrated how particular AI-models could be used to solve the question "Who dunnit" in a detective story by Agatha Christie, namely "The Spanish

Chest", and in an even more difficult case in "The Mind Murders" by Janwillem van de Wetering. We used the story of Agatha Christie for quite another computer based experiment, which is described below in Chap. 5. The computer experiment that we describe here does not refer to a particular story yet it is useful to consider what a reader of detective stories does when he tries to solve the criminal puzzle at the same time as the literary detective or even before him. We are aware that there is no such thing as *the* detective story but that this genre since the founding fathers Edgar Allan Poe and Sir Arthur Conan Doyle has differentiated into many branches. In this experiment we have a classical type of detective story in mind; representative for this type are the stories of Agatha Christie[31]:

In the beginning of such stories usually a murder has happened that leads to the central question of "who dunnit". The reader has no or only very few information about the probable murderer. As the reader accompanies the detective in the search for the guilty person the reader obtains more and more information about suspects, motives, alibis, opportunities for the murder and so on. Soon an attentive reader will form an opinion about the probable murderer, i.e. he will construct a hypothesis. When reading the story further the reader's hypothesis will be confirmed by additional facts he learns or it will be refuted because new facts make the first hypothesis improbable or even false. In that case the reader has to construct a new hypothesis on the basis of all known facts and the process of either confirmation or refutation will go on. Immediately before the end the reader will try to form a final hypothesis, namely before the (classical) detective explains who the murderer is and how he (the detective) came to the conclusion about the identity of the guilty person. The reader of course has to assume that the author does not cheat, i.e. that the reader has always the same information at his disposal as the literary detective. In Klüver and Stoica 2006 we showed how students of us dealt with this problem with support from special neural nets and expert systems. Not all students found out the identity of the murderer. In Chap. 5 we show how human readers deal with the problem of constructing, confirming, and refuting hypotheses about the possible murderer[32].

In a strict sense this procedure of an attentive reader is not exactly the same as the hermeneutical circle described above but a specific variant of it. The reader does not move from the analysis of a particular case – the murder – to a general social context although there are detective stories that do just that (for example those by the present Scandinavian authors like Henning Mankell). But by forming certain hypotheses the

---

[31] We experimented several times with detective stories certainly not only because we like to read examples of this genre. The main reason is that in our opinion such stories reveal something like a "social self awareness" of the state of a society. The German scholar of literature studies Vogt describes this very aptly in his remark that detective stories and films are the equivalent of the classical societal novels like those of Honoré de Balzac or Thomas Mann in the second half of the nineteenth and the first half of the twentieth century (Vogt 2005). Hence we remain, so to speak, in the domain of social studies when we analyze how computer programs and human readers deal with such novels.

[32] The assumption that the author does not cheat is by no means a matter of course. Even the great Conan Doyle let his master mind Sherlock Holmes introduce at the end of some stories new facts that the reader did not know.

reader is forced to move from some particular person – his suspicious person – to the context of all known facts and to move back again to either the confirmed suspicious person or to another possible culprit who suits better with respect to the facts. Hence we have not only a circular movement but even a spiral that is closed either by the reader himself immediately before the end or by the final information the detective gives at the end of the story.

This reconstruction of the interpretative behavior of the reader shows that it has obviously much in common with the logic of a research process in the natural sciences – with the exception of experiments in the latter. In each process there is something like a "dialectic" between the perceiving of particular single facts and the construction of a suited hypothesis. Both processes are organized as a spiral although one only speaks in the case of interpreting of a hermeneutical one. It is no wonder that several philosophers of science postulate that hermeneutics is at the core not only of the humanities but of the natural sciences too (cf. for example Apel 1982).

Although each "honest" detective story has an objective logic in the sense that by careful reading and permanent attention each reader must draw the same conclusions it is a truism that different readers behave differently when reading one and the same story. That was confirmed by our own former experiments; the experiment described below in Chap. 5 is an additional confirmation of it. Some readers suspect very early a certain person and try to keep this hypothesis even against new facts until the end. Such readers will overlook some facts or will ignore them because they do not believe that these facts are important for the solution of the case. We may call such a reader a dogmatic type. Other readers are more cautious: They also form a hypothesis rather early but only in a provisional sense; they will accept new facts contradicting their initial hypothesis by rejecting it and forming a new one. The problem with a very cautious reader might be that he too fast gives up a hypothesis and in the end has no firm opinion. A third type is one of varying attention, which means that he sometimes takes facts into account and sometimes not because he overlooks them in moments of weak attention. To make matters even more complicated, these three types are "ideal types" in the sense of Weber. Factual readers are usually a mixture of all ideal types: Sometimes, for example in the middle of the story, they behave in a dogmatic manner; sometimes, for example at the end, they become more cautious, and in particular they may be most of the time very attentive but sometimes not. Hence, there is no such thing as the behavior of a reader but only average forms in a statistical sense.

We tried to simulate these different forms of reading behavior with the following model: Basis is a three-layered feed forward network with twenty input neurons, ten neurons in the hidden layer and again twenty neurons in the output layer. For readers who are not acquainted with the basic of neural networks a simplified network is visualized in the following picture:

The term feed forward means, as we mentioned, that an external input is given to the input layer, the input is processed by certain functions and given to the hidden layer, and by the same functions the output of the hidden layer neurons is given to the neurons of the output layer. In our model the process stops if the network has

Fig. 2.6 A three-layered feed forward network

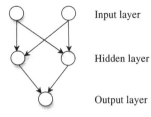

Input layer

Hidden layer

Output layer

generated an output, i.e. certain activation values of the output neurons. The network has reached a point attractor.[33]

This network is the formal representation of a reader's mind. At the beginning all neurons, in particular those of the input layer, have an activation value of zero. This means of course that the reader does not know anything about the story. The beginning of the reading is simulated by inserting a 1 or (at random) a 2 into the first input neuron, counted from left to right. The network then generates a certain output that depends on the specific weight matrix of the network (the weight values between the layers). This matrix is generated at random with weight values w_{ij} defined in the interval from 0 to 1. The most important function for the processing of the input is the well known sigmoid function that serves as an activation function:

$$a_j = F_j\left(net_j\right) = \frac{1}{1 + \exp\left(-net_j\right)} \tag{1}$$

The output represents the interpretation of the first facts by the reader. After activating the first input neuron the next one also gets a value of 1 or 2 that generates the second output, then the third input neuron is activated and so on. This is a formal representation of the reader's receiving more and more information, i.e. new facts about the murder by carrying on reading. By activating one input neuron after the other we obtained a series of altogether 20 output vectors, all containing mainly components of 1 or 2, although some components may remain or become a new 0.[34] Afterwards we generated another weight matrix at random and obtained a second series of output vectors; then we generated a third and so on until we had about 1,000 different networks, i.e. networks, whose topology and functions are identical

---

[33]We used a three-layered network because for certain problems two layers are not enough; a classical example is the learning of the so-called logical function of XOR. Although we did not give learning tasks in this experiment we wanted to study a network with sufficient capabilities. By the way, in some applications – not this one – the processing process is not stopped by generating a first output but this output is given as a new input to the input layer and so on until the system reaches a point attractor this way.

[34]We inserted a threshold before the output layer in order to guarantee that the output values do not transcend the values of 1 or 2. The network was implemented by Gregor Braun who also did the experiments as part of his Master thesis.

but which differed in the respective weight matrix. Accordingly we obtained 1,000 series of output vectors.

The main research question was if and how one series of output vectors would "converge", i.e. if one certain vector in the series would remain constant although new additional inputs were given to the network. If for example an output vector remained constant after input neuron 11 was activated although still 9 new input neurons were afterwards activated we could interpret it as a reader who had formed a hypothesis in the middle of the story and kept it despite new information. In other words, this series had reached a point attractor.[35]

As was to be expected, the series of vectors were very different. Some series contained vectors that permanently changed and reached a final state only with the last input; other series reached an attractor after about 16 or 17 input steps, i.e. after 16 or 17 input neurons were activated; other series generated something like local attractors, i.e. they converged for some input steps, e.g. after the 13th one until the 15th one, and afterwards changed the output vectors again until the last one. Yet because the term "local attractor" is used in another way it would be better to speak of a "local convergence".

Yet despite the individual differences between the 1,000 series of output vectors we could classify most of them as belonging to one special type. The first type is that of containing only vectors that changed until the end. We may interpret this as a simulation of an undecided reader who is uncertain till the end about the identity of the culprit and accordingly permanently changes his mind. This type occurred in more than one third of the cases. The second type that occurred only very seldom is a series that reached a final attractor during the 11th or 12th input. We may call this as a representation of a dogmatic reader who rather early decides about the solution of the puzzle and stays with it. The third type are series that reach a final attractor near the end of the inputs, namely about the 17th or 18th one. This happened in about one third of the cases, hence nearly as often as the undecided type. Let us call them the cautious reader who keeps his mind open but who decides in the end before the final inputs. Finally the series that generated local attractors, i.e. local convergences, but left them some inputs later – usually after only more than fourteen inputs – occurred in about one fourth of all cases. This may be understood as the representation of a attentive reader who forms definitive opinions but is able to change them as a result of new information.

We did not expect these clear differences between the series and in particular we were a bit surprised that the different forms of reading behavior that we mentioned above could be reproduced by this comparatively simple system. But of course we wished to know if there are some regularities behind these four main

---

[35]For the sake of clarity we must add that the term "convergence" is used with respect to neural networks usually in the sense that a convergent network means its stabilization as result of a learning process. That is why we speak of the convergence of a *series* of output vectors.

types of series convergence or non convergence respectively. In other words, are there common characteristics of those networks that generate a certain type of series? As the independent variable in our experiments is the weight matrix of a certain network the thought suggested itself to analyze the weight matrices of the different series. In addition, we had some experiences with the analysis of the adjacency matrices of Boolean networks (Klüver and Schmidt 2007); the weight matrix of a neural network is basically nothing else than an expanded adjacency matrix.

We analyzed the 1,000 different weight matrices by measuring their variance that is measured according to the formula

$$\frac{\sum (x - \bar{x})}{(n - 1)} \tag{2}$$

$\bar{x}$ is the mean of the sample and n is its size.

The variance is, a bit simplified, a measure for the average difference between the values of the weight matrix. We were of course aware that the dynamical behavior of a complex system like neural networks depends on many parameters, e.g. the size of the network, the number of layers, the usage of specific activation functions, values of certain thresholds and several more. Because we used a special type of networks, although one that is rather common and widely used in many different applications, we even cannot be quite sure if our results are valid for other types of networks although other experiments with the variance indicate that they are (see below Chapter 3). Therefore we could expect at best statistical correlations between certain variance values and certain types of the series. The main results of these analyses are the following:

An early convergence, i.e. after the 12th or even the 11th output vector occurs practically only in the case of weight matrices with extreme variance values, i.e. values either near zero or near one. The same is the case with networks whose series of output vectors converges rather late but before the last input value. This case occurs, as we mentioned, much more frequently than the cases of early convergence. If the weight matrices have variance values of the middle region, i.e. about 0.4–0.6 or 0.7 then the according convergence is either of the type of no convergence at all or of the type that the series has only local attractors or local convergences as described above.

We must confess that we have at present no explanation for these correlations; in particular there are always not few exceptions to these results, which is usual for statistical correlations. We shall come back to the correlation of the variance of weight matrices and an according behavior of the respective networks in the next chapter, where we shall try to form on the basis of the other results a first and at present a bit speculative hypothesis.

For illustration purposes we show one step of a series where the final attractor was already generated at step 15:

Input vector no 15:
(1, 2, 1, 2, 1, 1, 1, 2, 2, 1, 1, 2, 1, 1, 2, 0, 0, 0, 0, 0)
Output vector no 15 and final attractor:
(2, 1, 1, 1, 2, 1, 2, 2, 2, 1, 2, 1, 2, 1, 1, 1, 1, 1, 2, 2)

On first sight it may be a bit surprising that the output vector contains no zeroes any more although the last five components of the input vector are zero. The simple explanation is given in Fig. 2.6 above of the topology of the network. On can see that all input neurons are connected with all neurons of the hidden layer and those neurons are all connected with all output neurons. Hence the activation value of an output neuron may be larger than zero despite the fact that some input neurons still have the activation value of zero.

Our general considerations about a systematic characterization of "the operation called Verstehen" already demonstrated that not only "understanding" is not so far from "explanation" as one can read frequently in the according literature but that it is also possible to give the concept of understanding a precise meaning that can be expressed in general mathematical terms. The modeling of the hermeneutical circle and the hermeneutical spiral also showed how to implement such hermeneutical processes into artificial systems. In addition the simple simulations of human readers of detective stories demonstrated how to "understand" such processes of the interpretation of certain texts via exact mathematical methods. These are only first steps on the way to the goal of a combination of mathematics and hermeneutics, but they are first steps.

Chapter 3
Mental Models, the Geometry of Meaning Generation, and of Information Degrees

The founders of contemporary hermeneutics like Droysen or Dilthey frequently postulated that "understanding" means the reference to the internal states of the actor – the "inner being". We mentioned this fact above and discussed some of the methodical difficulties of this postulate. In particular, if one always needs the knowledge about internal states of the actor in order to understand his actions then the task of social understanding could easily be reduced to a certain form of socio-psychology. Therefore, already Emile Durkheim, one of the founding fathers of modern sociology, postulated in contrast that social phenomena must only be explained by other social phenomena.

The well known position of Rational Choice (RC) is a good example for this problem. RC approaches, which are still dominant in macro-economics and sociological decision theories, assume that social actors always act by analyzing a certain action situation, defining their own goal by wishing to gain maximum profit via their actions, and by choosing the best means for reaching this goal. In this sense RC is a generalization of the concept of purpose rationality, as we remarked. Actors are egoistic and rational and think only in terms of optimal combinations of means and ends. Hence the "inner being" of such an actor can be understood – and modeled – as an adaptive cognitive system calculating its environment and selecting the according action strategies. It is not by chance that many scholars in the economical and social sciences used certain optimization algorithms to model such actors. The computer models by Axelrod (Axelrod 1984, 1987) who used among other techniques cellular automata and Genetic algorithms have become particularly famous and inspired many followers. To understand social actions via a RC approach, hence, means the reduction of a social actor to the internal states of a calculating algorithm. The specific action situation must of course be taken into account too, but only in the sense that it defines certain boundary conditions, namely the determination of the selection of optimal strategies. Because RC approaches assume that every social action can and must be explained this way no considerations about the influence of certain

J. Klüver, C. Klüver, *Social Understanding*, Theory and Decision Library A 47, DOI 10.1007/978-90-481-9911-2_3, © Springer Science+Business Media B.V. 2011

social rules, cultural contexts, or specific individual intentions are necessary – it is sufficient to refer to something like a universal internal state model.[1]

Already in the Fifties of the last century Lord Dahrendorf introduced his famous distinction between *homo oeconomicus* and *homo sociologicus* in order to demonstrate the too narrow assumptions of RC approaches (Dahrendorf Lord 1958). The first concept refers to the fact that it is quite sensible to assume that human actors in economical contexts act according to the RC assumptions. Homo oeconomicus is an actor whose actions are indeed determined by purpose rationality in the sense of Max Weber; all action situations are analyzed according to the goal of maximum profit and the optimization of the relation of means and ends. Yet it is impossible and empirically false to reduce social actors to the narrow concept of homo oeconomicus. In most social situations social actors have to be understood as homines sociologici, namely actors who act according to social rules, cultural contexts or even individual intentions, although Dahrendorf took this third aspect not into account. A social actor hence is not merely a calculating optimization algorithm but an interpretative system: Each action situation must be interpreted with respect to the respective rules, to the cultural context the situation is embedded in, and to the questions if certain individual intentions can be reached in this situation. But in particular the third question is not simply one of referring means to a desired goal, namely the optimization of one's own profit, but the hermeneutical question what intentions a situation allows. Apparently we have here a case of double hermeneutics: Because the homo sociologicus must base his actions on a hermeneutical interpretation of the situation, he himself can be understood only by a hermeneutical interpretation of his behavior the way we demonstrated above.[2]

We wish no misunderstanding: We do not want to say that RC is wrong but that it is not sufficient. Everyday experience as well as many social studies always demonstrated that social actors in most cases do not behave according to the basic assumptions of RC but as social beings in the sense of homo sociologicus. There are certainly cases where actors behave according to the optimal relations between means and end but there are much more situations where they do not and where an understanding on the basis of RC assumptions is quite hopeless and even impossible.Hence an attempt to understand social actions and actors must primarily be theoretically based on the assumption of homo sociologicus and that means methodically on the methodical procedures of hermeneutical understanding.

---

[1]RC approaches are attractive in particular for mathematically orientated social scientists because they offer the usage of mathematical models based on Game Theory. It is quite amusing, as Waldrup (1992) told in his story of the founding of the Santa Fé Institute for Complex Systems that some theoretical physicists incredulously asked their colleagues from Macroeconomics if they really believed the RC assumption. Axelrod himself, by the way, admitted later that RC is not empirically valid (Axelrod 1997).

[2]Dahrendorf himself does not use these hermeneutical terms although his considerations point at that. The sociologist and economist Vanberg (1994), e.g., gives several reasons why a social actor must be understood as a *homo sociologicus* and not by the too narrow assumptions of RC.

Outside the scientific communities of RC based social sciences particularly in economics and Game Theory this statement is strictly speaking a truism. Therefore, why is the basic assumption of RC still so attractive for many scholars who try to understand human actions in a precise way? In our opinion there are basically three reasons:

One reason certainly is the fact that RC, as we mentioned, is one of the few branches of sociology that can be formulated and analyzed by established mathematical models, namely Game Theoretical ones. Axelrod for example makes this quite clear when he on the one hand admits that RC is not empirically valid but on the other hand says that, because there are no other mathematical models for the analysis of social behavior at hand, one has no choice but to operate with RC assumptions (Axelrod 1997). This argument is not valid, as we demonstrated with our own mathematical models, but many scholars in this field still cling to it.[3]

The second reason may be a peculiarity of modern societies with which we shall deal in the next subchapter, namely a certain space of freedom that social roles allow in modern societies and which gives RC assumption a certain justification.

The third reason probably has to do with the subject of this chapter. The understanding of social actions in the hermeneutical ways we described in the second chapter is an important and fruitful task. Yet the results one may gain this way still do not answer the question "what happened inside the actors when and before they performed these actions?" Neither the reference to certain social rules nor to a particular cultural context can answer this question that certainly belongs to the concept of understanding of many laymen and scholars. It is not by chance that the early pioneers of hermeneutics, as we mentioned, emphasized the relevance of the "inner being". Even a hypothesis about certain intentions of the actor just assumes that there was such an intention and perhaps even explains why the actor has such an intention. But in a strict sense this is not a model of the internal processes of the actor.

Because of the impossibility to have a direct look "inside" a human actor Behaviorism methodically forbid any assumptions about internal processes as pure "speculations". But such a voluntary restriction is just a denial of the problem and not a solution. It is no wonder that many people, scholars and laymen alike, were rather dissatisfied with this position and looked for alternatives. RC seemed to offer such an alternative possibility. But the reduction of social actors to calculating algorithms is as unsatisfactory as the complementary reduction to the "O" in the Behaviorist S-O-R schema (stimulus – organism – response) where O is merely a black box. Yet the fact that RC offers at least a solution that can be formulated in a precise manner is probably an important reason for the enduring attractiveness of RC despite its obvious shortcomings.

We believe, by the way, that the fascination of neurobiology to many people inside and in particular outside of biology has its reason just in the seeming

---

[3]On a conference in 2007 a colleague still argued in favor of RC "that we have no other theory" (sic!).

possibility for exact models of the inside of human actors. For the first time in human history it seems possible to understand in a precise way what happens in the inside of human beings when they perform cognitive processes and social actions. Yet neurobiology is not a very theoretically minded science and the knowledge that certain parts of the brain are activated when certain actions are performed is indeed much more than nothing but not a precise explanation in form of a model. "Knowing where is far from knowing how", to quote Lakoff and Núñez once again (loc. cit.). Nevertheless, the postulate of the early pioneers of hermeneutics and the claim of neurobiology point in the same direction, namely the necessity to construct something like "mental models" of social actors if one aims at a complete understanding of the actors and the actions alike. Accordingly we try to contribute a bit. At last, it is of course due to caution based on ignorance that all mentioned SF authors and films did not describe how their AI systems were able to do what they did in the fictional contexts. Yet the postulate that understanding systems like Solo and the Terminator are possible at all implies the necessity to describe their "inner beings". Hence both hermeneutics and AI research lead to the problem of mental models.

3.1 The Hermeneutical Necessity of Mental Models

The construction of mental models is at the core of several cognitive sciences, i.e., the attempt to formulate theories about cognitive processes in the mind – or in the brain in the case of neurobiology. The term "mental model" is of course as old as the numerous theories about human thinking. In the last decades this concept has been made very prominent by Johnson Laird (Johnson Laird 1983; cf. also Gardner 1985); the goal of the approach of Johnson Laird, to put it into a nutshell, is to demonstrate how humans think in mental models when, for example, their task is to infer logical conclusions from a set of premises.

Because we have no general theory in mind how humans think when they perform certain cognitive tasks and because our subject is that of social understanding we use the term of mental model in another way. By mental model we mean a construction of an observer of particular actions that he does in order to understand the observed actor in a more complete way than by the hermeneutical operations alone that we described in the preceding chapter. To be sure, the hypothesis about mental models that cognitive scientists like Johnson Laird formulate is usually a hypothesis about cognitive processes in other people; Johnson Laird for example tried to confirm his theory about thinking in mental models in numerous laboratory experiments. In this sense "mental model" is used the same way as we shall do. But we do not claim that the mental models we shall discuss are general theories about human thinking but that they are "just" an additional way to understand people in certain action situations. To cut a long story short, the cognitive scientists use the term "mental model" in order to describe how humans think; we use this term in order to describe how certain processes of understanding can be performed by constructing a mental model of the actor who shall be understood.

Another and perhaps even more important distinction between the use of mental models in the cognitive sciences and our usage of this term is that we construct our mental models as mathematical ones. *In nuce*, when we construct a mental model to explain certain actions or reactions respectively in a particular situation we construct an artificial neural network with specific learning rules and try to demonstrate how the behavior of this network can be interpreted as a mathematical model of the "inner being" of the actor with respect to certain situations and actions. We are of course aware of the fact that such models might only be equivalent in function and not necessarily in structure to the real networks of the actor. This is the problem of conventionalism that we mentioned above and from which we also cannot escape. Yet we shall always give some additional arguments that and why our mathematical model may be not only functionally equivalent to the real processes in mind and/or brain but that they also contain formal characteristics that the real networks must possess too.[4]

Understanding social actions by referring to social rules, cultural contexts and/or individual intentions does not need the construction of specific mental models. Indeed, the everyday practice of understanding other people usually occurs without the construction of explicit mental models of the other. The mentioned examples of the probably reckless driver, the obeying soldier or the guest in a restaurant can all be understood without the construction of explicit mental models of the other. The social process of understanding, hence, in contrast to the attempts of the cognitive sciences, usually does not need mental models, neither in everyday practice nor in hermeneutically methodical research.

But this is only one half of the truth. There are a lot of situations when we have to switch to the construction of mental models of the other, often without realizing that we do this. For example, when we recognize ourselves in the actions of another then we assume that the other interprets the action situation the same way as we would do and that he acts because of the same reasons we would have. In other words, we construct without consciously thinking about it a mental model of the other similar to the picture we have of ourselves and then we could understand him. Of course, we could be in error because the other acts for very different reasons than we would have but our hypothesis about the other is primarily based on such a mental model. When we observe a football player who seemingly deliberately violates the rule of not tackling the player of the other team we usually would understand this action by constructing a simple mental model: The player wants to win the game together with his team at all costs and does not care about probable punishments by the referee. In our mental model the player is seen as a man to whom the victory of his team is more important than his individual welfare. In this sense the formulation of a hypothesis

---

[4]After the publication of our 2007 book we sometimes heard from reviewers and readers that we try to solve problems of communication or understanding by analyzing the level of the brain. That is sometimes true, as we shall show when discussing some examples of Behaviorist experiments. Yet our usage of the term "semantical network" (cf. Chapter 2) already demonstrates our belief that the construction of such network models is applicable to processes of the mind too.

abut certain intentions – winning the game – is coupled with the construction of a mental model why the player acts the way he does.

More systematically the necessity to construct mental models in the process of understanding can be characterized by the following situations in which one tries to understand another person:

(a) The first case is a situation where one expects a certain action by the observed actor because the observer knows that the situation is to a great extent determined by specific social rules that are well known to him. If for example an accused before a court is not willing to defend himself and to convince the judge of his innocence but instead tries to make political and/or religious statements in order to inform the court, the audience, and the mass media about his ideological world view then the accused obviously is not acting as expected. The deviance from the expectations of the observers and participants of the trial and thus from the social rules that determine a legal proceeding can be understood only if the observer tries to construct a mental model of the actor. Such mental models are usually unconsciously constructed because an observer nearly automatically assumes that an action against the own advantages of the actor must have its reason in the "inner being", i.e., the individual personality of the actor. [5] In other words, the construction of mental models must be done in cases where the observed actor deviates from the expectations of the observer, in particular in the case of the deviance of social rules.

(b) A second case is a situation that is determined by certain social rules or cultural contexts but where both do not determine the according actions in an unambiguous manner. One can characterize such a situation that the actors have to take certain social roles but that these roles leave a specific space of freedom how the actors may act as occupants of these roles. It is a fundamental characteristic of modern societies that important social roles are frequently defined by different spaces of freedom and that the role occupant often has to decide by himself how he wishes to act when occupying a certain role. The role of a teacher for example is defined by the pedagogical tasks like motivating pupils to learn, controlling and evaluating their learning processes, defining the learn subjects and so on. Yet this role definition leaves individual space of freedom for the teacher: It is up to him if he performs his teaching in a more severe or in a more kind way, if he is rather permissive or very strict with respect to disturbances by certain pupils, if he emphasizes more a pressure of achievement or if he thinks it more important to support the weaker pupils and so on.

A medical doctor, to take another example, has an equal space of freedom: His social role is generally defined by the Oath of Hippocrates and the respective legal norms that he has to obey. Yet he is still free how he defines his role, e.g. if he just wants to have a practice with many patients and where business is going well or if

---

[5]In Klüver et al. (2006) we described such a case where the accused, namely two left winged students in 1968, explicitly refused to defend themselves and instead insisted to speak about their political motives. This case had really happened but is unfortunately available only to readers who can understand texts written in German. Yet nowadays there are, of course, numerous other examples of fanatical accused who behave just this way.

he deliberately takes his time to care for each patient in an individual manner, to talk with them, and to see if some diseases are perhaps due to private problems of the patient. If the doctor defines his role in this second manner then he will probably either have not as many patients as with the first role definition because he spends too much time with each individual patient or he has no life of his own because his patients need him all the day. In both cases the doctor acts according to the general definition of the role and even if we would perhaps prefer a doctor of the second kind in case we are ill, no one can seriously blame a doctor who defines himself as a successful entrepreneur.

These two examples that could easily be increased demonstrate that in modern societies social roles are more like a general frame than a set of unambiguous action orientations or strict action rules respectively. That was not the case or at least not in this way in pre-modern societies like the European Middle Ages. Social roles had to be understood as strict action orientations and left no or only a small space of freedom for the role occupants. In particular, role occupants were dependent on the occupants of other roles, namely those of the church and the feudal state (cf. Klüver 2002). The European development during the Renaissance and the Enlightenment in contrast to the Middle Ages is characterized by an increasing of role independency and an enlarging of role freedom, i.e., the individual freedom of a role occupant to define his role. The attractiveness of RC, by the way, has its societal basis in this space of freedom: Even if a role occupant acts according to the rules that define his role in a general way he is free to act within his role according to the assumption of RC. It is of course an empirical question if he does so like the doctor in the first case or if he orientates his actions to other goals.

We emphasize the space of freedom of role acting because it is frequently a source for understanding difficulties. Several times we referred to the fact that an action that was not expected by an observer is often difficult to understand and gives rise to the question what the actor probably thought or intended with the action. If a patient meets a doctor who defines himself as a successful entrepreneur, if the patient had expected rather a doctor of the second kind, and even if the patient is convinced that the doctor is a trustworthy medical expert then the patient might be irritated and tries to understand the doctor's behavior by constructing a mental model of him. The patient's experience with doctors are perhaps only with those of the second kind. Hence he assumes, for example, that the doctor is not really interested in his patients and that the doctor's prime goal is to earn as much money as possible. The patient's irritation is due to his ignorance about role freedom; he identifies those individual role actions he had experienced so far with the general definition of a social role.

According to the classical definitions of social roles in the tradition of George Herbert Mead and Talcott Parsons one could say that the patient had not understood the definition of a role as *generalized* action expectations. Of curse, each role occupant has to act according to the general frame by which his role is defined; in this sense the patient is right to have certain expectations about the actions of the medical role occupant. Yet because the patient wrongly interpreted a social role as an expectation of always and exactly the same actions he did not expect the specific doctor's behavior and tried to understand him by constructing a mental model. The same of course is the case when a patient is only used to professional doctors who are mainly interested to run their practices in an emotionally neutral manner and as efficient as possible. If such a patient meets a doctor of the second kind the patient will probably for the same reasons try to understand this different doctor by the construction of a mental model – the doctor is a kind hearted man who thinks only about the welfare of others or something like that.[6]

Yet even if an observer knows about the comparatively large space of role freedom in modern societies he might it find necessary to construct a mental model if he is surprised about some observed actions. A pupil or student for example who is used to liberal and even permissive teachers and professors will certainly be irritated when he is confronted with a strict and severe teacher, even if the pupil or student respectively knows that a teacher has this role freedom. Not only because the pupil generally wishes to understand the new teacher but in particular because the pupil literally must know how to deal with the teacher the pupil will also construct a mental model of the teacher. To be sure, the pupil has the choice to simply follow the orders of the teacher and to think not about him. Yet frequently pupils or students try to get along with their pedagogical superiors by constructing mental models.[7]

The necessity to construct mental models in order to understand unexpected behavior has in these cases its reason in a societal objective structure, namely the possibility of individual role acting within the generally defined frame of a certain role. In this sense it is principally easier to understand role specific behavior in pre-modern societies if the respective roles are known to the observer. Knowing a social role in such societies is knowing with great certainty what action can be expected in a particular situation. The difficulty of many people to live and understand others in a modern society has not only but also its source in this characteristic of role specific spaces of freedom.

(c) A quite different case is that of deviant behavior where even a very profound knowledge about the social role of the actor cannot explain the respective behavior. In the mentioned case of the two left wing students who preferred to make speeches about their political convictions rather than to convince the judges of their innocence it is not difficult to understand via the construction of an according mental model why the accused did this. But there are "pathological cases" where the behavior is not understandable by the described methods of hermeneutical interpretation and

---

[6]Theories of socialization usually assume that the ability to distinguish between individual actions and a social role is acquired during childhood and in particular when the child meets persons outside its family – in kindergarten or school. There it learns that a mother is not necessarily identical with its own mother and that teachers may differ in their behavior (cf. for example Berger and Luckmann 1967). Yet even adults frequently are irritated if individual role acting differs too much from their expectations because they underestimate the role freedom of modern societies.

[7]In the times of the Internet students (and pupils) have the possibility to assess their professors in public on a special web page. At our university this site is called "My Prof.", where we both were assessed like many other professors. One student who was irritated by the strictness of one of the authors constructed a mental model by assuming that the strictness of the author was due to inferiority complexes.

where the construction of mental models is very difficult. One needs not even take cases from psychiatry like those that the psychiatrist Oliver Sacks described in his famous book about "the man who mistook his wife for a hat" (Sacks 1985). We shall come back to one of his examples in the next subchapter. If for example a politician suddenly claims that he will neither act according to the welfare of the citizens or the state nor that he will obey the principles of his political party but that he will in future only follow the will of God – as he interprets this will of course –, then this behavior can, if at all, only be understood by the construction of a certain mental model: In what way differs the personality of this politician from his former personality and which events caused this changing? Yet the knowledge abut the events as a cause for the changed personality is of secondary importance if one is not able via a mental model to understand what changes exactly happened.

A more harmless variant of this case is a behavior of an old acquaintance that is quite different from the behavior one usually expects from him. In this case one also starts to construct a mental model, if possible by asking him. Other and often more dramatic examples are cases of religious converts who accordingly to their new religious doctrines change their habits and behavior. In these cases it is often necessary to construct a mental model according to the question "what kind of thoughts now produces such a changed behavior". Generally all cases where an observed behavior is different from one that the observer was used to the construction of mental models is frequently the only way to understand it. In such cases the mental model is one that models not only the present state of mind of the respective actor but also the learning process by which the state of mind – the inner being of classical hermeneutics – has changed and as a result generates a behavior different from the known and expected one (see below Chapter 4 on learning).

To be sure, deviant behavior in general, i.e., an observed behavior that is different from that one could expect, is not necessarily a pathological case or a case of the violation of accepted rules for some political or religious cause.[8] In a certain sense each behavior that is an innovative one and which cannot be understood by observers for this reason is also deviant: A painter who creates a new style of painting and who is not understood by his colleagues and the critics may be an innovative and creative genius but insofar as he does not fulfill the expectations of others he is a case of deviance. The numerous stories about the strong connections between genius and madness have probably their sources simply in the fact that innovative behavior is usually not more expected than truly mad actions. As far as we know creative individuals tend not more or less to madness than uncreative individuals; as the mathematician Bell remarked in his collection of the biographies of great mathematicians (Bell 1937) creative mathematicians were and are as "normal" as all other persons – with the usual different variants of "normality". This is probably the case with all creative artists, scientists and so on. Yet in order to understand if

---

[8]In sociology the term "deviant behavior" usually means the deliberate or involuntary violation of some social rules as in the case of the reckless car driver. Because we just used this term with another meaning, namely that of "deviation from the expectation of an observer" we shall speak of *social* deviance if we mean the usual sociological usage of deviant behavior.

a person tends to madness or is simply a creative person it is often very useful to construct a mental model of this person.

3.1.1 A Mathematical Model

The interesting question for our subject is of course if an artificial system can be constructed that is able to construct mental models too, even if it does this in another way then humans would do it. At last in principle this is indeed possible as we shall demonstrate.

In the context of a larger project to simulate certain processes of the emergence of social order via processes of observing and imitating other actors we also gave the according artificial actors the task to "understand" other artificial actors by constructing mental models of them. In this model each artificial actor or agent respectively as we shall call them for brevity's sake is represented by two neural networks. One network, the so-called action network (AN), is a simple two-layered feed forward network (see above). The task of this network is to receive a specific input that represents an action situation. This input is coded as a vector with component values between zero and one. All AN of the agents receive the same input, i.e., they are all in the same action situation. Because the networks are generated at random each agent has a different weight matrix and accordingly generates an output that is at least slightly different from those of the other nets. The output of an AN represents the action that the specific agent performs as reaction to the action situation. The agents now observe these different outputs of the other agents, select that agent whose output is the most similar to the own output, and try to change the own output in order to make it as similar to that of the second agent as possible.[9] Because each agent changes its own network this way the stabilization of the whole system usually needs some time, depending on the number of agents and in particular by the degree of similarity the agents have to reach. Usually an agent system of 30–50 agents is in the end divided in ca. 5 subgroups with similar output vectors, i.e., similar reactions to the predefined action situation.[10] The agents react to the outputs of the other agents because only these can be observed by the agents.

The second network of each agent is an interactive network (IN) that we already described in the preceding chapters. The IN represents a semantical network, which means that each artificial neuron of the IN represents a certain concept like "danger", "needs", "gladness" and other emotional concepts but also neutral concepts like certain animals and other categories. The IN of the different agents are again

---

[9]The similarity is measured by the Euclidean distance; the output vector that is most similar to the own output vector is the target vector for the training of the first agent. This type of learning, the so-called supervised learning, will be described in more detail in Chapter 4.

[10]Because this social simulation is not a specific subject of this book we give no detailed results. Readers who are interested in the system and in detailed results may obtain them from the authors. The implementation of the whole program and the according experiments were performed by Dirk Wittkemper and Björn Zumaar as part of their BA-thesis.

constructed at random but with certain restrictions: Each concept that belongs to
an IN is chosen from a common list of concepts, consisting of about 100 concepts.
Each agent gets in the beginning 30 concepts from this list. The selection algorithm
operates thus that all agents have 15 concepts in common; the other 15 are different,
namely chosen at random from the list. Each concept gets a certain number as its
index, selected again from the interval between 1 and 0.

The basic idea of the simulations after the emergence of the different sub groups
is the following: The output vectors of the AN represent the according actions of
the agents, i.e., their reactions to the action situation. An output vector of an agent
after the forming of the subgroups does not change anymore, if the situation is not
changed. This output vector, coded in numerical values, is then translated into the
according concepts, i.e., into those concepts that have approximately the same number as index as the value of one specific output component. For the sake of simplicity
the concepts of the IN were chosen in such a way that each output component was
represented in the IN by the according concept.

When an agent of a certain subgroup "meets" an agent of another one the first
agent A observes that the second agent B reacts to the situation in a different way.
Because agent A does not understand the behavior of agent B A "asks" B to explain
his behavior verbally. Agent B hence activates his own IN and generates an output
consisting of those concepts that have the strongest activation values after the stabilization of the IN. Because agent A does neither understand the non verbal behavior
of B nor the "verbal explanation" that B gives him A tries to construct a mental
model of B in order to understand him.

This mental model consists of a hypothetically constructed IN that could serve as
a basis of understanding B by A. Because A just wants to understand B with respect
to the situation and the according action of B it is sufficient for A to construct an IN
with only the concepts of the situation and the output concepts that B generates when
the situation is given as input. A generates the weight matrix of his hypothetical IN
at random and activates it with the concepts of the situation, i.e., the concepts B uses
to describe his view of the situation. The following schema shows the general logic
of this process:

A   meets   B   in   situation

B   reacts with output (A,B,C)

A   constructs a mental model of B:

Now four cases are possible with respect to the concepts the hypothetical output
consists of:

Case (a) Conceptually the two output vectors, i.e., that of the factual IN of
B and that of the hypothetical one, are identical and differ just in some activation values. For example, output concept 1 in the hypothetical network is more
strongly activated than in the factual output of B and output concept 2 is less

strongly activated. In this case a simple learning rule, which we call an "enforcing rule", changes the weights of the connections to and from those concepts in the hypothetical network. The learning rule just decreases the weight values with respect to concept 1 by adding a constant value c to all weights, for example c = 0.1, and decreases the weight values with respect to concept 2 by subtracting the same constant c from them. This process is iterated until the output concepts of the hypothetical network have the same activation values as those of the factual IN of B. According experiments demonstrated that this learning process indeed is able to generate a hypothetical network with the same output values as those of the factual IN.[11]

A now has a mental model of B, namely why B because of his "inner being" acts in the situation as he did. To be sure, A's model of B is only a reduced one because the factual IN of B is significantly larger than the hypothetically constructed one. Yet because A just wanted to understand B with respect to B's reaction to this special situation A can stop at this point. If another situation occurs A of course has to start his construction again because A cannot assume that the new behavior of B in a new situation is just a variant of his old behavior.

Case (b) An output concept X is part of the output of the hypothetically constructed network but not in the factual output vector of B. Then the weight connections to and from the concept X are decreased by the application of the same enforcing rule until the concept X is no part of the output vector any more, i.e., until X does not belong any more to the concepts with the strongest activation. Possible differences in the other activation values are treated in the same manner as in case (a).

Case (c) An output concept Y is part of the factual output vector of B but not of the hypothetical one. Then the connection values to and from Y are increased via the enforcing rule until Y becomes a part of the hypothetical output.

Case (d) A combination of cases (b) and (c) occurs. Then both operations of these two cases must be performed until the two output vectors are conceptual identical. As in case (a) the activation values will be changed until these too are approximately the same.

Our experiments showed that in all four cases it is possible for A to construct a hypothetical IN that acts in a certain situation as B.[12] Agent A still does not know the "inner being" of B because, as we mentioned above, the whole network of B is significantly larger than the hypothetical one. But the hypothetical mental model is sufficient for A to understand B's behavior, at least for the predefined situation. Figure 3.1 shows a factual network of B and the hypothetical mental model of B:

---

[11] This "enforcing rule" is a special case of a new rule schema for neural networks that we constructed and compared with the traditional learning rule like, e.g., the Delta rule for the case of supervised learning. We shall discuss this general rule schema in detail in Chapter 4. By the way, in the case of decreasing weight values the rule should be named a "lessening rule". For the sake of brevity we just use the term "enforcing rule" also in the cases when weight values are decreased.

[12] Björn Zumaar performed about one millions experiments that were in most cases successful.

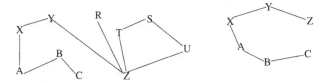

Fig. 3.1 The factual network of B and a mental model of the agent B

We changed afterwards this experimental design in the following way: A constructs again a hypothetical IN but now by copying his own IN and by activating it with those concepts that A uses for his perception of the situation. Now the inputs of the two networks (those of A and B) as well as the outputs are different. The reason for this more complicated variant is that A tries to obtain a mental model of B that is as complete as possible. Differences in the output vectors are treated the same way as in the simple variant described above. The main problem for a successful reconstruction of B is now the difference with respect to concepts in the (factual) networks of A and B. To cut a long story short, the according experiments showed that in the case that all concepts are the same for both networks a successful reconstruction is always possible; that was demonstrated with again one million pairs of networks, constructed at random. If only one part of the concepts of the two networks are identical then A can reconstruct only networks with those concepts he has also at his disposal. This is not astonishing as well in this artificial model as in the case of human understanding: If a human actor A hears a verbal explanation of another human actor B and if A does not know some of the concepts B uses for his explanation A can only construct a mental model by using those concepts he has at his disposal. Figure 3.2 shows a case where the construction of a mental model is only partially successful because of the conceptual difference.

In such a case a human actor would probably ask the other for the meaning of those concepts the first actor does not know and could make his mental model of the other more complete. Yet the same is the case with our artificial system. If for example the network of agent A does not contain the concept "Paris" he could ask for the meaning of this word. The asked network of agent B then would send a message (Paris, capital, France), i.e., "Paris is the capital of France". The network would do this because the connection weights between the concept "Paris" and the other two concepts are the largest connection weights with respect to "Paris" (cf.

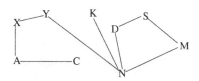

Fig. 3.2 A partial successful reconstruction

Klüver and Klüver 2007). If the receiving network of agent A gets such an explanation of "Paris" then it could insert "Paris" into its own conceptual structure, namely by connecting "Paris" with the other two concepts and with weight values of 0.6 in both directions. If the network of agent A does not contain one or both of the concepts that were used for the explanation it asks again for the meaning of the missing concepts. This process is iterated either until the network of A contains all concepts it needs in order to complete its mental model of B or until another criterion is fulfilled, for example stopping after five steps of interaction. Such a stopping criterion can be interpreted that A gets frustrated because the semantical differences between him and B are too large for a successful understanding. Hence an artificial system is also able to complete its network by communicating with the other agent.

The manner in which an artificial system constructs a "mental model" of another system may look on the first sight a bit strange. Human actors certainly do not operate that way when they try to understand another human actor by constructing a mental model of him – at least they do not do so in a conscious manner. Yet our main intention by constructing this artificial system was to demonstrate that it is possible for an AI to construct mental models of other systems whether also artificial or human. The demonstrated logic of reconstruction could of course be also applied if the system would get as messages the verbal reactions of human actors to a certain situation. If it makes sense to represent parts of the human mind in form of semantical networks, which as far as we know nobody doubts who works in these fields, then such human semantical networks could be at least partially reconstructed by a system like ours. To be sure, even if the hypothetically constructed networks show the same input-output relation as the observed factual ones that would be no guaranty that both networks are identical in structure (see above with respect to conventionalism). But that would be the case too if a human actor tries to construct a hypothetical mental model of another actor.

By the way, this reconstruction method is not only applicable to verbal explanations of one's own actions. If an artificial agent A observes the reactions of another agent B to a certain situation for example by the inputs and outputs of the feed forward network of B (his action network AN) then A could construct a hypothetical feed forward network of B and could try to generate for his hypothetical network the same output as observed in the factual AN of B. For a learning rule A could again use the enforcing rule described above.

Finally, do human actors indeed operate quite another way as our artificial system does? In the chapter on learning we shall refer to the famous principle of Hebb (1949), namely that of increasing and decreasing neural connections in the brain according to certain conditions. This principle has been frequently been empirically confirmed (cf. for example Kandel 2006). It suggest itself that by constructing, checking, and correcting mental models of another actor the human brain or mind respectively also changes certain connections in neural or semantical networks. The described enforcing rule was explicitly constructed according to the principle of Hebb. Therefore, the processes within human actors when they hypothetically construct mental models may be rather similar to the operations of our artificial system, although certainly more complicated.

In particular situations, however, human actors may act exactly as our artificial systems. In an examination, for example, both the examiner and the student frequently try to imagine the respective semantical networks of the other – the examiner because he considers his next questions with respect to the probable knowledge of the student, the student because he tries to find out what the examiner means with a certain question. Both operate on the factual verbal behavior of the other and have to infer the semantical networks of the other from his observable factual statements.

We shall show in the next chapters several other examples of mental models in the form of artificial neural networks; that is why we close these reflections about the necessity of mental models in cases of difficult understanding. We shall demonstrate that a complete understanding of such cases is only possible by the usage of such mathematical models. Yet before we do this we shall deal with quite another question, namely if it is possible to detect some mathematically expressible regularities in the performing of such mathematical structures that are used for the formal representation of mental models.

3.2 The Geometry of Meaning Generation

The intention of constructing and analyzing mental models is the same as with all model constructions: A mental model shall explain some observed actions via the analysis of the performing of the model. For this task a model is useful if and only if the input-output relations of the model and the real system are the same or at least sufficiently similar. Yet because even neurobiology cannot in a strict sense directly observe the inner processes of human actors, with the exception of some localization results, the question still remains even with a successful model, i.e., a model with the same input-output relation as an observed human actor, how similar the two structures are – that of the model, which can be directly analyzed and that of the human actor, which cannot be seen. This problem of conventionalism is principally inescapable. Yet one can try to look for some mathematically expressible regularities that are characteristic for all or at least in a statistical sense most of the systems that perform the same functions. Then a conclusion from a certain model structure to a probable structure of the real system would at least be possible with some significant probability.

The analysis of topological characteristics of complex dynamical systems frequently enables important insights into the behavior, i.e., the dynamics of such systems (Klüver and Stoica 2006). By "topology" we here mean, as we mentioned in the first chapter, the set of system's rules that determine, which elements of the respective systems interact with which other elements. In the classical mathematical meaning of topology these rules define the neighborhood relations of the respective elements, which are at the core of, e.g., the fundamental Hausdorff axioms of topology. In the case of neural networks the topology is usually defined by the according weight matrix, which determines the degree of interaction between the different elements, including the limiting case of interaction degree equal to zero. To be sure, the dynamics of complex systems is not only determined by their topology but also by additional rules or functions like propagation rules in the case of neural networks.

These rules describe the specific way of interaction if there is any. Yet frequently the respective topology is the most influential factor for the dynamical behavior of complex systems (cf. Klüver and Schmidt 2007).

In Klüver and Klüver (2007) we introduced the concept of the meaning generating capacity (MC) of a complex dynamical system. This definition was motivated by some informal remarks of Wolfram (2001) about the "information processing capacity" of complex dynamical systems. With this term Wolfram described the fact that frequently different initial states of a system generate the same final attractor state; other systems in contrast generate different final states if the initial states are different. In other words, the information processing capacity refers to the different sizes of the "basins of attraction" of a system, i.e., the sets of initial states that generate the same final attractor state. If a basin of attraction is large then information will get lost during the processing of the system and vice versa. This is the concept of the informational complexity of a system (cf. also Gell-Mann 1994); Wolfram (loc. cit.) showed that his well-known complexity classes could be characterized by such measures of informational complexity.

By the way, in 2007 we used the term "meaning processing capacity", which is not very suited. Therefore, we now prefer the term "meaning generating capacity" (MC) and repeat here our precise definition[13]: The MC-value of a complex dynamical system is defined as the proportion between the size m of the set of all final attractor states and the size n of the set of all initial states of a system, i.e., $MC = m/n$. Obviously $0 < MC \leq 1$: $MC = 0$ is impossible because each complex finite system has at least one final state, even if it is an attractor state with a very large period. The according limiting case hence is $MC = 1/n$ if n is the number of initial states. If MC is very small then many different initial states will generate the same final states – the according attractors are characterized by large basins of attraction. If $MC = 1$ then each different initial state will generate a different final attractor state. This is the other limiting case, where the basins of attraction all are of size 1. In other words, small values of MC mean large basins of attractions and vice versa. It must be noted that we refer only to discrete systems, i.e., systems with only a finite number of initial states. The question if in physical reality there are systems with an infinite number of states belongs to metaphysics. It is of course possible to construct, e.g., neural networks that are coded with real numbers and that way to obtain potentially infinite initial states and final states. We also usually use real numbers for the activation values and weight values of our neural networks with the

---

[13]Wolfram gives no precise definition of his concept of "information". At least he does not mean the mathematical definition of this term that Shannon and Weaver gave in their famous study (Shannon and Weaver 1949); hence one must assume that Wolfram uses the term of "information" only in a metaphorical manner. In 2007 we defined, as was mentioned above, the concept of the "meaning" of a message by the final attractor state a system generates when receiving this message; in other words, a system processes a message and generates an according meaning. Therefore, we now use the term of meaning generating capacity.

exception of some semantical networks. Yet in practice of course only finite real numbers are used like 0.5 or 0.23.[14]

There are at least three main reasons why this concept is important: On the one hand it is possible via the usage of MC to analyze complex dynamical systems like neural networks with respect to their informational complexity. In this sense MC allows for new approaches in the theory of computability. On the other hand an important and frequently mentioned characteristic of neural networks can be understood in a new and more differentiated way: In all textbooks on neural networks there are statements like "one of the main advantages of neural networks is their robustness, i.e., their tolerance with respect to faulty inputs" or something equivalent. We shall show that via the definition of MC not only a theoretical explanation of this advantage can be given but also a measurement of this robustness; in particular by the variation of MC specific neural networks can be generated that are either very robust, less robust or not at all robust in the sense of error tolerance. Because sometimes it is not desirable to use neural networks with a large degree of robustness the possibility of a systematical generation of more sensitive networks can be a great practical advantage.[15]

Last but not least and most important for the intentions of this book it is possible to give by the usage of MC an explanation for phenomena known from the field of human information processing. It is well known that different humans frequently react in significant different ways to the same messages. This can be illustrated by the examples of fanatics who refer all messages to the same cause, e.g., the enmity of Western Capitalism to religious movements, the oppression of women by the patriarchal structures of society, and so on. Equally well known in psychology are certain pathological cases: The psychiatrist Sacks (1985) for example describes a rather intelligent and well educated man who is unable to distinguish little children from fire hydrants. Probably because little children have approximately the same size as fire hydrants this man was often observed to stop at hydrants and stroke them. We shall give a very general explanation for this case at the end of the next section; in Chapter 5 we shall deal with the problem of one-sided information processing and according restricted MC-values in more detail. To put it into a nutshell; human beings process the same messages in a more or less differentiated way; the definition of MC can be a useful approach to construct mathematical models for the explanation of such phenomena.

---

[14]Readers who are familiar with the theory of ordering parameters in cellular automata and Boolean networks will recognize a striking similarity between the definition of MC and the so called Z-parameter in the theory of cellular automata (Wuensche and Lesser 1992): The Z-parameter measures the probability by which a preceding state can be computed from a present one. MC on the other hand can be interpreted as the probability by which it is possible to compute initial states from final ones. Yet MC is no ordering parameter in the usual sense that it allows the prediction of certain types of dynamics, but a measure of information processing and meaning generation.

[15]This robustness as a consequence of certain MC values is of course also a characteristic of other dynamical complex systems like cellular automata or Boolean networks (see below).

3.2.1 Neural Networks as Meaning Generating Systems

In contrast to dynamical systems like, e.g., cellular automata and Boolean networks, neural networks are not often analyzed in terms of complex dynamical systems. Therefore, it is necessary to clarify what we understand by "initial states" and "final attractor states" when speaking of neural networks.

In a strict systems theoretical sense all initial states of neural networks are the same, i.e., the activation values of all neurons are equal to zero, regardless to which layer(s) they belong. Because this fact would make the definition of different initial states quite useless we define the initial state of a neural net as the state where the neurons of the input layer have been externally activated with certain input values and where the activation values of all other neurons still are equal to zero, in particular those of the output layer. An initial state S_i of a neural net, hence, is formally defined by $S_i = ((A_i), (0))$, if (A_i) is the input vector and (0) is the output vector; note that the values of the output neurons are still equal to zero. If there is no specific input layer then the definition must be understood in the way that some neurons are externally activated and the others are not.

The external activation of the input neurons causes via the different functions the "spread of information", determined by the respective values of the weight matrix. In the case of simple feed forward networks the final activation values of an output layer are immediately generated; in the case of feed back networks or recurrent ones the output is generated in a more complex manner. Yet in the end in all cases a certain output vector is generated, i.e., each neuron of the output layer, if there is any, has obtained a certain activation value. If there is no distinction between different layers as for example it is the case with a Hopfield network or an interactive network the output vector will consist of the final activation values of all neurons. Note that except in the case of feed forward networks the output vector may be in an attractor with a period p > 1. The network will then oscillate between different vectors, i.e., between different states of the attractor. For theoretical and practical purposes neural networks are mainly analyzed with respect to the input-output relation. Therefore, we define the final state S_f of a neural network as $S_f = ((A_i), (A_o))$, if (A_i) is again the input vector and (A_o) the final output vector. If (A_o) is an attractor with period p > 1, then the components of (A_o) consists of ordered sets, i.e., the set of all different activation values the output neurons obtain in the attractor.

Because in the experiments described below we investigate only the behavior of feed forward networks with respect to different MC-values, for practical purposes we just define the final state as the values of the output vector after the external activation via the input vector. Hence we speak of a large basin of attraction if many different input vectors generate the same output vector and vice versa. The limiting case MC = 1 for example defines a network where each different input vector generates a different output vector. Accordingly the case M = 1/n defines a network where all n different input vectors generate the same output vector.

With these definitions it is easy to explain and measure in a formal manner the characteristics of neural networks with respect to robustness. A robust network, i.e., a network that is tolerant of faulty inputs, has necessarily a MC-value significantly smaller than 1. Robustness means that different inputs, i.e., inputs that differ from the correct one, still will generate the "correct" output, i.e., that output, which is generated by the correct input. That is possible only if some faulty inputs belong to the same basin of attraction as the correct input; these and only these inputs from this basin of attraction will generate the correct output. All other faulty inputs transcend the limits of tolerance with respect to the correct output and will accordingly generate another output. If $MC = 1$ or near 1 then the network will not be robust at all for the respective reasons.

The same explanation can be given for the also frequently quoted capability of neural networks to "generalize": In a formal sense the generalizing capability is just the same as robustness, only looked at from another perspective. A new input can be perceived as "similar" or as "nearly the same" as an input that the net has already learned if and only if the similar input belongs to the same basin of attraction as the input the network has been trained to remember. In other words, the training process with respect to a certain vector automatically is also a training process with respect to the elements of the according basin of attraction. The capability of generalization, hence, can be understood as the result of the construction of a certain basin of attraction via a certain training process. Accordingly the generalization capability is again dependent on the MC-values: If these are small, i.e., if the basins of attraction are rather large, then the network has a comparatively great generalizing capability and vice versa. Because one network can have only one MC-value it is obvious that systems like the human brain must have for one and the same perceiving tasks at least two different networks, namely one with a great generalization capability, i.e., a small MC-value, and one with a large MC-value to perceive different inputs as different.

It is important to note that we implicitly defined here the generalizing capability as the ability to detect similarities between different objects or particular cases respectively, i.e., the ability to abstract from different characteristics of the objects and to concentrate on the equal characteristics. In this sense in neuro-informatics the term "generalizing capability" is usually used. In another sense generalizing capability is used when one means the ability to infer general rules from particular cases. Neural networks are also able to generalize in this second sense; we shall deal with this aspect of generalization in Section 4.3.

Robustness and generalizing capability of a network, hence, can be "globally" defined by the according MC-value. Yet there is a caveat: It is always possible to generate networks via according training methods (see below) that are characterized by several basins of attractions with different sizes. Therefore, the MC-value is not necessarily an unambiguous measure for the size of all basins of attraction of a particular network. The term "basin of attraction" refers always only to a certain equivalence class of input vectors, namely a set of input vectors that are equivalent in the sense that they generate the same attractor. The size of these sets may be quite different for specific attractors. Hence, the MC-value gives just an average measure with respect to the different basins of attraction: with respect to some attractors and their generating inputs the networks may be robust and with respect to others not. Considering that possibility the concept of MC could also be defined in another way, namely as the difference in size of all basins of attraction of the according network. Fortunately the results of our present experiments hint at the fact that in most cases the basins of attraction of a certain networks differ not much in size. The caveat is necessary for theoretical and methodical reasons but seems not to be very important in practical contexts (see below the following experiments).

However, because of this problem we also started experiments with Boolean networks where another definition of MC is used, namely MC = (|BAmax| : |BAmin|)/n. |BAmax| is the size of the largest basin of attraction and |BAmin| that of the smallest basin of attraction; n is the number of initial states. This second definition of MC, which we name MC_2, obviously takes into regard the possible difference in size of the respective basins of attraction. First results of comparisons between the two MC-definitions are reported at the end of this subchapter.

Before we discuss some experiments with MC-values and sizes of basins of attraction we like to come back once more to the man who mistook hydrants for small children. To understand that melancholy case in terms of our framework let us consider an everyday problem of remembrance.

Imagine a female friend who was away for some time. When we see her again her appearance has changed because she now has another hairdressing and perhaps also some new fashionable clothes. Despite this changing of appearance we usually have no difficulty to recognize her at once or at least after some moments of irritation. The explanation for this capability is of course that the input vector "changed female friend" belongs to the same basin of attraction as the well known input vector "female friend with her former appearance". We mentioned above that to perceive different inputs as different needs another network with a small MC-value. Hence, the additional perception in what way our friend has changed is only possible because two networks operate on the same input: The first net recognizes the friend as the friend; the second one recognizes the difference as the particular difference.

By applying these considerations to the unfortunate pathological case one can safely assume that this man – by some neural changing in his brain – has at present only perception networks with very large basins of attraction. He is able to recognize objects with approximately the same size of children and associate these perceptions to his memories of children. But because he has no networks left with sufficient large MC-values to recognize the difference between children and, for example, hydrants he behaves to all such small objects as kindly as he behaves to children. Because the only network he still has for the perception of small objects had probably been trained in his youth for the perception of children and because one sees more often children than hydrants he identifies hydrants as children and not the other way around.

Concepts like "size of basins of attraction" and "values of meaning generation capacity" obviously are very useful for the explanation of important characteristics like robustness or generalizing capability. Yet in a strict sense they are too general concepts because they only explain the behavior of certain neural networks from very general characteristics of complex dynamical systems. They do not explain, which structural characteristics of neural networks may be the reason for specific MC-values. Hence, these concepts remain, so to speak, on a phenomenological level.[16]

---

[16]The search for ordering parameters, i.e., numerical values that characterize rules and topologies of systems like cellular automata (CA) and Boolean networks (BN) is an example for such a

In the beginning of this subchapter we mentioned the fact that frequently certain topological characteristics of complex dynamical explain the behavior of such systems. The topology of a neural network is mainly expressed in the weight matrix. Hence the thought suggests itself to look for features of the weight matrix that could explain the size of basins of attraction and MC-values. In anticipation of our results we may say that we were successful in the sense that we found some general trends although no deterministic relations.

3.2.2 First Experimental Series: Training by Back Propagation

In the first experimental analysis we used a standard three-layered feed forward network; we chose this type because it is very frequently used for tasks of pattern recognition and related problems. Because, as is well known, two layers are not enough to solve problems of non-linear separableness we took three layers in order to get results for networks with sufficient efficiency. The input layer consists of 10 units, the hidden layer of 5 and the output layer of 10 units. Input and output neurons are binary coded, which results in $2^{10} = 1,024$ possible input patterns. To keep the experiments as clearly as possible we defined "equivalence classes" of input patterns: all input patterns with the same number of zeroes are members of the same class. By choosing at random one pattern from each class we obtained 11 different input patterns. The activation or propagation function respectively is the sigmoid function; because of the three layers we chose as learning rule the standard Back Propagation rule[17]:

$$\delta_j = \begin{cases} f'_j\left(net_j\right)\left(t_j - o_j\right) \text{ if } j \text{ is an output neuron} \\ f'_j\left(net_j\right) \sum_k \left(\delta_k w_{ik}\right) \text{ if } j \text{ is a neuron from the hidden layer} \end{cases} \quad (1)$$

The training design was the following: In each step the network was trained to associate different input patterns with one target pattern; the target pattern was again chosen at random from the 11 input patterns. In the first step the task was to associate each input pattern with one different target pattern; the according basins of attraction all were of size one and the MC-value of this network after the training process is 1:1.[18] In the next steps the sizes of the basins of attraction were gradually increased to 2, 3, 4, 5, and 6; in the last step the size of the only basin of attraction finally was 11, i.e., all input layers had to be associated with one and the same target pattern and the according MC-value is MC = 1/11. We did not investigate basins of attraction with sizes 7 or 10 because in the according experiments the other basins would have become too small; for example, one basin of attraction with the size of

---

research question: Which values of ordering parameters explain the sizes of basins of attraction in CA or BN (cf. Klüver and Schmidt loc. cit.).

[17]The experiments were performed by Tobias Synak.

[18]The permissible rate of error was 0.01.

8 would force the network to take into regard also at least one basin of attraction of size 3. Hence we only investigated networks with basins of attraction of maximum size 5, 6, and 11. By taking into regard different combinations of basins of attraction we obtained 11 different networks.

The according weight matrices were analyzed with respect to the variance of their weight values. The variance was computed according to the formula given above; we show it once more as a reminder:

$$\frac{\sum (x - \bar{x})}{(n - 1)} \tag{2}$$

where is the mean of the sample and n is its size.

This variance analysis was separately performed for the weight matrix between the input layer and the hidden layer and the matrix between the hidden layer and the output one. The results are shown in Figs. 3.3 and 3.4:

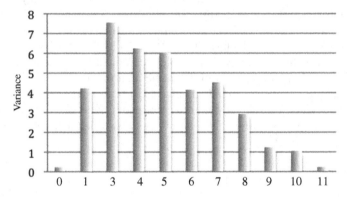

Fig. 3.3 Variance of the first part matrix in relation to the size of the basins of attraction

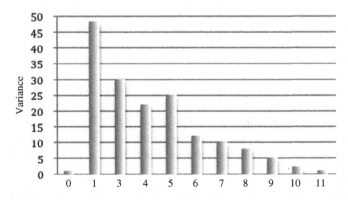

Fig. 3.4 Variance of the second matrix in relation to the size of the basins of attraction

The order of the different networks in both pictures is according to increasing size of the basins of attraction. No 1 is the case with MC = 1:1, no 11 is the network with MC = 1:11.

Figure 3.3 obviously gives no unambiguous result with respect to possible relations between variance values and the size of basins of attraction but it suggest a certain trend, namely the decreasing of the variance by increasing the basins sizes. Figure 3.4 confirms this and even shows an unambiguous result: The variance values indeed gradually decrease with the increasing of the size of the basins of attraction. We then combined the two matrices by summing up the variance values of both matrices and obtained the final result shown in Fig. 3.5:

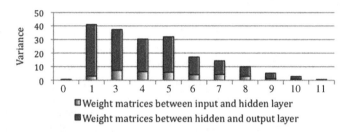

Fig. 3.5   Variance and size of basins of attraction for the whole network; the networks are ordered as in Figs. 3.3 and 3.4

This final result completely confirms the trend shown in Fig. 3.3 and the clear results of Fig. 3.4: the larger the size of the basins of attraction are, i.e., the smaller the MC-values are, the smaller are the variance values and vice versa. By the way, the difference between the variance of the upper matrix and that of the lower one is probably due to the fact that the Back Propagation rule does not operate in exactly the same way on both matrices. As can be seen in Equation (2) the lower half of the whole matrix is changed by directly taking into account the error, i.e., the distance between the output neurons and those of the target vector. The changing of the upper half of the matrix is done by computing a certain proportion of the error and thus "dispersing" the changed weight values with respect to those of the lower half. Yet these just force the variance of the whole matrix to the shown result. If our networks had contained only two layers the whole result would have been like that of Fig. 3.4. We shall come back to this effect of a certain learning rule in the next section.

We did not expect such unambiguous results yet on hindsight they are quite plausible and comprehensible: Low variance values mean dispersion of information or of the differences between different messages respectively because of the near equality of the weight values. If on the other hand the weight values are significantly different, i.e., a high variance, then differences between different messages can be preserved. As small or large sizes respectively of basins of attraction have exactly that effect on the performing of messages it is quite understandable that we obtained that clear and unambiguous relation between variance and size of basins of attraction.

Yet although these clear results are quite satisfactory we knew very well that they must be treated with a great methodical *caveat*: The behavior of neural networks, as that of practically all complex dynamical systems, depends on many parameters, in this case for example on specific activation and propagation functions, number of layers, special learning rules and so on. The results shown above were obtained with a specific type of neural network, although a standard and frequently used one with a standard learning rule. To make sure that our results are not only valid for this special learning rule we undertook another experimental series.

3.2.3 Second Experimental Series: Optimization by Genetic Algorithms[19]

In these experiments we did not use one of the standard learning rules for neural networks but a Genetic Algorithm (GA). The combination of a GA with neural networks has frequently been done since the systematic analysis of neural networks in the eighties (cf. for example already Belew et al. 1992). Usually a GA or another evolutionary algorithm is used in addition to a certain learning rule in order to improve structural aspects of a network that are not changed by the learning rule, e.g., number of layers, number of neurons in a particular layer, threshold values and so on. In our experiments we used the GA as a substitute for a learning rule like the Back Propagation rule in the first experimental series. The according weight matrices of the different networks are written as a vector when using GA and the GA operates on these vectors by the usual "genetic operators", i.e., mutation and recombination (crossover) (cf. also Stoica 2000).

Genetic algorithms belong to the class of so called evolutionary algorithms; other techniques of this class are for example the Evolutionary Strategies or the Genetic Programming. These algorithms are constructed orientated to the paradigm of biological evolution – hence this name. The basic procedure of a standard GA can be described as follows:

Start with a population of vectors, generated at random; the vectors can be coded in a binary fashion, with real numbers, or any other symbols like letters.

Define a "fitness function" that allocates a numerical value to each vector.

Define a "marriage schema" that decides which vectors should be recombined with which others and in which way.

Change according to a certain mutation rate some components of the vectors chosen at random.

Recombine according to a predefined "crossover schema" two vectors chosen according to the marriage schema, i.e., generate from two initial vectors two new ones.

Apply the fitness function to the new vectors, which generates a total order of the vectors.

Repeat procedures (b)–(f) until a global optimum is reached or until another stopping criterion is fulfilled.

---

[19]The experiments were performed by Antje Unger as part of her MA-thesis in computer science.

Note that step (d) can also be applied after crossover, i.e., to the new vectors. Factually the GA procedure is a bit more complicated but this rough description can do. In the standard GA versions the GA "has no memory": As in biological evolution the old populations – the "parent generations" – vanish when the new population – the "children generation" – is generated. It is possible to use so-called "elitist" versions of GA: In these versions the algorithm checks if certain elements of the parent generation are better than the best vectors of the children generation. If this is the case then the best parent or all parents that are better than the best children will be preserved.[20]

We chose this procedure for two reasons: On the one hand the operational logic of a GA or any other evolutionary algorithm is very different to that of the standard learning rules. A learning rule modifies usually just one network; in this sense it is a simulation of ontogenetic learning. In contrast an evolutionary algorithm always operates on a certain *population* of objects and optimizes the single objects by selecting the best ones from this population at time t. This is a model of phylogenetic evolution. In addition learning rules like the Back Propagation rule or its simpler forms, namely the Delta Rule and the enforcing rule we introduced in the last subchapter, represent the type of supervised learning. Evolutionary algorithms can represent another type of learning, i.e., the enforcing learning. In contrast to supervised learning enforcing learning systems get no feed back in form of numerical values that represent the size of the error. The systems just get the information if new results after an optimization step are better or worse than the old ones or if there is no change at all in the improvement process. In our experiments, however, we also used certain target vectors, which means supervised learning. Despite this similarity to the first series the training procedure in the second series is obviously very different from that of the first series.

We assumed that by choosing such different procedures similar results from both experiments would be a very strong indicator for our working hypothesis, namely the relation between MC-values or size of the basins of attraction respectively and the mentioned characteristics of the according weight matrices. To be sure, that would not be a final proof but at least a "circumstantial evidence" that the results of the first series are no artifacts, i.e., that they are not only effects from the chosen procedure.

On the other hand we were in addition interested in the question if networks with certain MC-values are better or worse suited to adapt to changing environmental conditions. It is evident that per se high or low MC-values are not good or bad. It always depends on the situation whether a network performs better with high or low capabilities to generate different meanings; sometimes it is better to process a message in a rather general fashion and sometimes it is necessary to perceive even small differences. Yet from a perspective of evolutionary adaptation it is quite sensible to ask if systems with higher or lower MC can adjust better. That is why we used an evolutionary algorithm to investigate this problem although it is indeed

---

[20]Elitist versions of GA usually converge faster to an optimum. Yet the disadvantage with these versions is that they cannot leave a local optimum if they have reached it. Hence it is a question of the particular optimization problem if an elitist or non-elitist version is to be preferred.

a related but different question than that of a relation between the variance of the weight matrix and the according MC-values.

Because a GA can be constructed with using many different parameters like size of the mutation rate, size of the sub vectors in crossover, selection schemas, schemas of cross over ("marriage schemas"), keeping the best "parents" or not, and so on it is rather difficult to obtain results that are representative for all possible GA-versions. We used a standard GA with a mutation rate of 10%, a population of 20 networks, initially generated at random, crossover segments of 5, and a selection schema according to the fitness of the respective networks. Because the networks were optimized with respect to the same association tasks as in the first series those networks are "fitter" than others that have successfully learned more association tasks than others. If for example a network is optimized with respect to the task to operate according to two basins of attraction of size 8 then a network is better that correctly associates 6 vectors of each basin to the target vector than a network that does this only for 5 vectors.

The population consists again of three-layered feed forward networks with binary coding for input and output layers; the input and output vectors consist of four neurons and the hidden layer of three. As in the first series the networks operate with the sigmoid activation function. We simplified the networks a bit because, as mentioned, a GA has not one network to operate with but a whole population. The target vectors were chosen at random; the vectors for the respective basins of attraction were chosen according to their Hamming distance to the target vectors that define the basins of attraction. It is no surprise that the GA came faster to satisfactory results, i.e., to generation of networks that are able to solve the respective association tasks, if the MC-values of the networks should be large, than in the cases where the MC-values should be small. If, for example, the desired MC-value is MC = 1, then the GA has to generate networks that produce for each input vector a certain output vector different from all other possible output vectors. This is a problem, roughly expressed, with only one solution. If networks should be generated with MC-values of, e.g., 1/11, then of course rather different solutions are possible.

The main results are shown in Fig. 3.6:

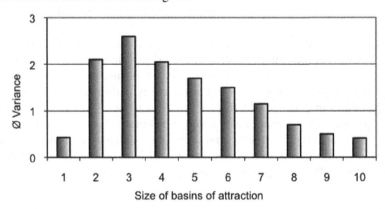

Fig. 3.6 Variance and size of basins of attraction in networks generated by a GA. The x-axis of the diagram shows the different networks, ordered according to the increasing size of the basins of attraction

The picture obviously expresses a striking similarity to Fig. 3.3 of the first series. The trend is the same, namely a clear relation between the size of the variance and the increasing size of the basins of attraction or the decreasing size of the MC-values respectively. Like in Fig. 3.3 the exceptions from this trend occur in the cases of highest variance, but only there. As we remarked in the preceding section these exceptions may be due to the fact that the GA even more disperses the weight values than does the Back Propagation rule for the upper half of the weight matrix. This fact clearly demonstrates that the relation between variance values and the sizes of the basins of attraction is "only" a statistical one, although the correlation is highly significant.

As we mentioned in the beginning of this section, the fact that such totally different optimization algorithms like Back Propagation rule and GA, i.e., very different types of learning, generate the same trend with respect to our working hypothesis there is some evidence that the hypothesis may be valid in a general sense. Yet in both series we just considered "case studies", i.e., we concentrated in both cases on one single network and in the case of the GA-training on populations of the same type of networks. That is why we started a third series.

The evolutionary question, in which we were also interested, was how networks with different MC-values could adapt to an environment where they needed other MC-values. The general answer to this question is, roughly speaking, the following: Networks with very high MC-values only poorly adjust to conditions where a middle or low MC is needed. Accordingly, if networks with middle or low MC-values should adjust to very high MC-values they also adapted only poorly or not at all. In other words, networks with high MC-values either cannot get easily away from this characteristic or such networks cannot be easily generated by adaptive processes. Conversely, networks with middle MC-values can easily become networks with low MC-values and networks with low MC-values can equally easily become networks with middle MC-values. We did not find so far an unambiguous interpretation in terms of evolutionary logic, but shall come back to this problem at the end of this subchapter.

3.2.4 Third Series: Statistical Analysis of Large Samples

Experiments with large samples of neural networks are always difficult because of the large number of variables or parameters respectively that have to be taken into account. Besides the influence of different learning rules, activation and propagation functions and such parameters like learning rates and thresholds the main problem is a "combinatorial explosion": If one takes into account the many different possible combinations of neurons in the different layers and in addition the possible variations of the number of layers one quickly gets such large samples that it is seldom possible to obtain meaningful results. That is why we chose another way in the preceding sections, namely the analysis of the two case studies in order to get a meaningful hypothesis at all.

Yet despite the great difference between our two case studies it is always rather problematic to draw general consequences from only several case studies. That is why we studied a larger sample of two-layered neural nets, i.e., ca. 400.000 different networks. We restricted the experiment to networks of two layers in order to keep the experiments as clearly as possible. The number of neurons in the input and output vector are in all experiments the same and ranged from 3 to 10. The restriction to equal dimensions of the two vectors was introduced because random networks with different sizes of the two vectors do not generate all MC-values with the same probability: If the input vector is larger than the output one then MC = 1 would not be possible at all because always more than one input vector will generate the same output vector.[21] If conversely the output vector is larger than the input vector the probability for large MC-values will be greater than in networks with the same number of neurons in both vectors. Methodically speaking differences in the size of the input vectors and of the output vectors would be another variable because the probabilities for generating all MC-values would not be identically distributed. To avoid such distortions we used only vectors of equal size.[22]

The networks were, as in the two case studies, binary coded and operated with the sigmoid function. Thus we obtained ca. 400.000 pairs (MC, v), v being the variance. The general results are the following:

As we supposed from the results of the two case studies the relation between variance and MC-values is "only" a statistical one in the sense that there are always exceptions from the general rule. Yet we discovered very clearly that indeed there is a significant probability: The larger the variance is the smaller is the probability to obtain networks with small MC-values, that is with large basins of attraction, and vice versa. This result is in particular valid for variance values significantly large or small. Only in the "middle regions" of variance values the probability to obtain MC-values as a deviation from the general rule is a bit larger but not very much. This probability distribution is shown in Fig. 3.7:

Fig. 3.7 Statistical relation between variance (x-axis) and MC-values

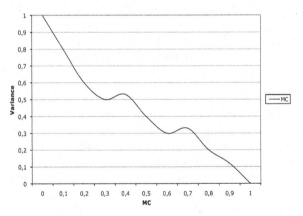

[21] For example, a simple network that is trained to learn a certain Boolean function has an input vector of size 2 and an output vector of size 1. Its MC-value is 0.5.

[22] The according experiments were performed by Gregor Braun as part of his MA-thesis in computer science.

By the way, the deviations in the middle regions from the general trend may be a first explanation for the mentioned results with respect to the evolutionary capability of networks with different MC-values. These networks adapt more easily to changing environments than those with very large or very small values.

The hypothesis of the relation between MC-values and variance values seems to be a valid one, at last as a statistical relation. Hence it might be possible to predict the meaning generating capacity of a network and thus its practical behavior for certain purposes with sufficient probability from a variance analysis of its weight matrix. Yet a certain methodical *caveat* is necessary: Despite the differences between the three experimental series we always used the same basic type of neural networks, namely two- or three-layered feed forward networks. It is a still open question if our results are also valid for networks with other topologies, for example recurrent networks or Self Organizing Maps. This question obviously demands for further research.

But instead of such investigation that will be performed in the future we investigated quite another type of networks, namely Boolean networks or logical networks as they are also called sometimes. If we could obtain similar results we would have another strong indicator for a general validity of our hypothesis.

3.2.5   Fourth Series: The Analysis of Boolean Networks

Boolean networks (BN) are one of the simplest forms of dynamical networks; the systematic analysis of this type was in particular started and performed by Kauffman (1995, 2000). The name "Boolean" was introduced in honor of George Boole, one of the founders of modern mathematical logic in the nineteenth century. Experiments with BN are usually performed with binary coded ones, i.e., with state values of the units equal 1 or 0, although it is of course possible to define the state values of the BN units with real numbers or even non-numeric symbols. In our experiments we also used binary coded networks.

A BN consists, as all networks, of certain units that may be also called in a graph theoretical terminology as knots. The dynamical relations between the units are defined as logical functions, i.e., as the well-known functors of propositional logic. These logical functions may have one, two or more variables; in propositional logic usually only functions with one and two variables are taken into regard. A classical example of a logical function with two variables is the logical disjunction v whose characteristics can, as usual, be shown in a "truth" matrix:

$$
\begin{array}{c|cc}
\vee & 1 & 0 \\
\hline
1 & 1 & 1 \\
0 & 1 & 0
\end{array}
$$

In other words, if both variables are zero, then the result is zero too; in all other cases the result is one.

In our experiments we analyzed only BN with functions with two variables. The reasons for this restriction is on the one hand the desire to keep the experiments as clearly as possible, on the other hand functions with only one variable give only rather trivial results, and finally in a strict mathematical sense there "are" no logical functions with more than two variables: A well known and since long time proven theorem of mathematical logic states that each logical function with three variables and more can be expressed as a suited combination of functions with only two variables. Although the dynamical behavior of BN with logical functions of "higher order", i.e., with more variables than two, can be rather different from BN with only two or one variables (cf. Kauffman 1995), for our purposes it is sufficient to restrict our experiments to the basic case of two variables.

In contrast to neural networks BN have no weighted connections and hence no weight matrix. The topology of BN is accordingly only defined by an adjacency matrix whose components just have the values 1 or 0. A 1 in the matrix means that the according units are knotted, a 0 of course that there is no connection between them. Figure 3.8 shows a small adjacency matrix of a BN with the three units a, b, and c:

Fig. 3.8 Adjacency matrix of
a BN with three units

	a	b	c
a	0	1	1
b	1	0	0
c	1	1	0

In this example a is connected with b and c, b is connected with a but not with c, and c is connected with a and b. Accordingly the logical functions can be described that a and c operate on b (a function with two variables), b and c operate on a – another function with two variables –, and only a operates on c, a function with only one variable. Usually the values in the main diagonal are all equal to zero as in this example; it is of course also possible to define functions of units that are "reflexive", i.e., that define an operation of a unit on itself.

It is not very useful to compute variance values of an adjacency matrix. Instead of that we introduced another measure as an analog to variance in orientation to the so-called P-parameter of Boolean functions. The P-parameter measures the distribution of zeroes and ones that a Boolean function can generate. For example, if a Boolean function with two variables, that is four combinations of zeroes and ones, generates two times a 0 and two times a 1 then the P-value of this function is $P = 0.5$; if only zeroes or only ones can b generated, then $P = 1$. In the case of three zeroes or three ones $P = 0.75$; the logical disjunction described above has a P-value of 0.75. The P-value of the whole BN is computed as the mean value of all functions of this network.

Accordingly to the definition of the P-parameter we measure the distribution of zeroes and ones in the adjacency matrix by the term AP (A of course for adjacency matrix, P for the orientation to the P-parameter). $AP = 0.5$ if there are as many zeroes as ones; $AP = 1$ if there are only ones (the case of $AP = 1$ because there are only zeroes is of course ridiculous because such a BN would be no network at all). As in the case of the P-parameter for the computation of AP only those values are important that occur more often. Hence, AP is measured by $AP = m/n$, if m is the number of zeroes or ones that occur more often than the other values, and if n is the number of matrix elements. If for example the matrix contains 16 elements (a 4*4 matrix) and if there are 10 ones in the matrix then $AP = 10/16 = 5/8$.

As our intention is to see if there are similar relations between the MC-values of a BN and its AP-values as there are between MC values and variance, and as MC is defined in the interval between 0 and 1 we have of course to standardize. According to the definition of AP $MC = 2(AP - 0.5)$ and $AP = 0.5 + MC/2$. This standardization must be taken into account for a comparison between MC- and AP-values.

Because we just wanted to get a first impression if our hypothesis is also valid in the case of BN we restricted again our experiments to BN with four, five and six units. As with all complex dynamical systems it is easy to get a combinatorial explosion by analyzing large BN. Therefore, we just took into account 10 networks with 4, 10 networks with 5 and again 10 networks with 6 units. All BN were constructed at random, i.e., with different topologies and different Boolean functions.[23]

The first results were disappointing because the hypothesis could not be confirmed. Apparently the MC-values of BN constructed at random are to a large degree determined not only by their topology but also by their respective Boolean functions. This is not astonishing if one considers the importance of ordering parameters for the dynamics of BN (cf. Klüver and Schmidt loc. cit.), namely ordering parameters with respect to the Boolean functions of the BN like the P-parameter. If one constructs BN at random one frequently gets BN with a similar topology, i.e., similar AP-values but with very different Boolean functions and consequently different values of the according ordering parameters.[24] Remember that in the experiments with neural networks the respective functions always were the same. In order to eliminate the influence of the different ordering parameters, i.e., the additional variable consisting of ordering parameters with rather different characteristics, we introduced a *ceteris paribus* situation of the experimental design: We took into regard only BN with functions that have the same values of the P-parameter, namely $P = 0.75$, and are all canalizing functions, namely the logical disjunction and the logical conjunction (OR and AND as they are also called). In this experimental

---

[23]One of our students Dejan Skific performed the experiments.

[24]Besides the mentioned P-parameter in particular the C-parameter must be taken into account, which measures the proportion of so-called canalizing functions of the BN (cf. Kauffman 1995). In the case of a canalizing function it is sufficient to know the value of one variable in order to know the result too. The logical disjunction in the example above is such a function because one just needs to know if one variable, regardless which, is one. Then the result of the function must also be one.

series the results are quite different, for we obtained a confirmation of our hypothesis:

In most cases of high MC-values the AP-values are also high and vice versa. Figure 3.9 shows this relation:

Fig. 3.9 Correlation between MC and AP

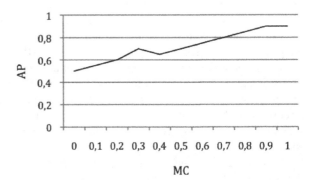

Because of the different computing methods for the two measures the results are not exactly equal for MC and AP when standardized according to the definitions above. In addition there are, as usual, statistical exceptions (wild shots). Yet the trend is unambiguous.

At the end of the last section we mentioned a methodical *caveat* with respect to the general validity of our results because we used only networks of the feed forward type. Different topologies of neural networks might yield other results, i.e., they might not generate the specific relation between weight matrix and MC-values. Boolean networks are with respect to their topologies more similar to recurrent networks than to feed forward ones. In recurrent networks all units are principally connected with all other units by symmetrical and asymmetrical connections; the interactive networks we described above are an example of recurrent nets. The fact that we could generate similar results with BN as with feed forward networks is another strong indicator for the validity of our hypothesis that indeed equality in the weight matrix produces small values of MC and vice versa.

In order to test the usefulness of our MC definition we also analyzed the relation between the second definition of MC, namely $MC_2 = (|BA_{max}|: |BA_{min}|)/n$, if $|BA_{max}|$ is the size of the largest basin of attraction, $|BA_{min}|$ that of the smallest basin of attraction, and n is the number of initial states. As in the experimental series just described we used only the Boolean functions of logical conjunction and disjunction and networks of the same sizes. We then compared the respective values of MC, MC_2, and AP.

In contrast to the analysis of MC and AP we here get no clear results. The values of MC and MC_2 show no clear relation and neither do the values of MC_2 and AP. This is the case with all networks. Obviously our original definition of MC is more suited to our problems than the definition of MC_2.

3.2.6 Final Considerations

The behavior of complex dynamical systems can practically never be explained or predicted by using only one numerical value (a scalar) as the decisive parameter. In a mathematical sense the problem for such a system is always the task of solving equations with a lot of variables, that is more variables than equations. It is well known that for such tasks there is always more than one solution. When considering neural networks by investigating the according weight matrix it is rather evident that for example large basins of attraction may be constructed with very different matrices. The same fact is valid for other networks like Boolean ones with respect to their adjacency matrix.

This fact shall be demonstrated by an example from quite another context (cf. Klüver and Klüver 2007). The network shown in Fig. 3.10 is the representation of a semantical network by an interactive network (IN). The network was manually constructed by one of our former students immediately after he had finished a course in JAVA. We asked him at that time to construct a structured representation of his knowledge about the subjects of his course. The result of his own representation of his knowledge is the following:

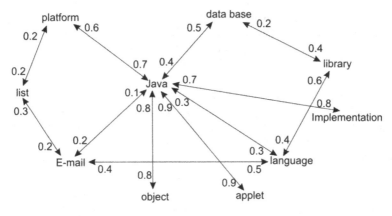

Fig. 3.10   Knowledge representation by a semantical network, transformed into an IN

By analyzing this network one sees that the concept "Java" has a center position: It is directly connected with most of the other concepts with rather large weight values. The other concepts have significantly fewer connections to other neurons and their weight values are generally smaller. This network structure generates the effect that by different inputs, i.e., by externally activating some of the neurons, nearly always as a final result "Java" will be strongly activated, regardless which neurons are externally activated. Figure 3.11 shows the final point attractor of this network by sending the message (list, library, language), i.e., by externally activating these three neurons:

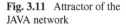 Attractor of the
JAVA network

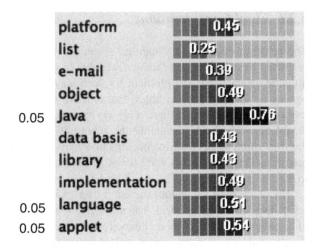

One sees that the meaning of the message, defined by the three strongest activated neurons, is (Java, applet, language). It is not always the case that Java is the neuron with the strongest final activation but rather often.

By now applying the famous principle of Hebb (1949) to the connections between "Java" and those concepts that are most strongly connected with the center concept, i.e., strengthen the already strong connections and weaken the weaker ones, one easily obtains a network where all external activations lead to a final state where practically only "Java" has a significant final activation value. The whole network has just one basin of attraction with the only attractor "Java". We do not show such an extremely asymmetrical network but show just the one constructed by the student: He had not the task to construct an asymmetrical network but his result is an unintended outcome. Yet at the end of such "Hebbian" training we have a network with a very high variance – represented by the asymmetry of the connections – and only one very large basin of attraction.

To be sure, such networks usually only occur when certain specific models shall be constructed, in this case the model of a very special semantical network. When generating neural networks at random it is not to be expected that such networks will be an element of the respective sample. That is why the relation between variance and MC-values is statistically significant; the case studies showed in a similar way that if neural networks with certain MC-values are automatically generated by training with a learning rule or an evolutionary algorithm usually such extreme networks will not occur or only very seldom (cf. below Chapter 4). But the pure possibility of such networks like that shown in Fig. 3.10 demonstrates why the relation between variance and MC can only be a statistical one.

We mentioned above the problem of the so-called ordering parameters in cellular automata and Boolean (logical) networks. Ordering parameters are numerical characterizations of the rules of transition and of the topology of these artificial systems; the research question is with respect to all the known parameters, which values of one or several parameters will generate a certain type of dynamics, i.e., certain types of trajectories with specific attractors. Our own investigations of these parameters always demonstrated the fact that the relation between certain parameter values and the generated type of dynamics is generally only a statistical one and that even combinations of two or three ordering parameters still give only statistically valid results (Klüver and Schmidt loc. cit.). Hence, it is no wonder that the variance value, considered as a structural explanation for the occurrence of certain MA-values and the according sizes of the basins of attraction, always allows for exceptions, even if these are not so extreme as the network shown in Fig. 3.10. In analogy to the situation with respect to the ordering parameters, where both rules of transition *and* the topology have to be taken into account, it could be worthwhile to investigate some activation and propagation functions of neural networks if there are similar structural characteristics between certain functions and MC-values like the variance with respect to network topology. Analogous experiments could and should be done with respect to the impact of different Boolean functions on the MC-values of Boolean networks.

Values of ordering parameters also predict certain sizes of the respective basins of attraction. Therefore, another research question will be the investigation of relations between the known ordering parameters and the variance weight matrices. Although more experimental results are necessary some principal theoretical considerations can already be made[25]:

Usually ordering parameters, namely numerical characteristics of the rules of transition and the topology of a complex dynamical system, are used to predict the *principal* behavior of this system, i.e., the degree of dynamical complexity. Although the factual trajectory of a system, of course, depends on the initial states too the values of the ordering parameters allow, if only in a statistical sense, a prognostication if the system will generate trajectories with only point attractors, attractors with long periods, or if the system is "quasi chaotic", i.e., if it can generate under certain circumstances even strange attractors. The ordering parameters that we mentioned like the P-parameter and the number of canalizing functions refer to characteristics of transition rules; yet in addition there also exist topological ordering parameters, in particular the v-parameter (Klüver and Schmidt 2007), which measures the proportion of influence the different cells have on each other. In this case the v-parameter is a characteristic of the adjacency matrix and not of the transition rules. The v-parameter is defined

$$V = (OD - OD_{min})/(OD_{max} - OD_{min}). \tag{3}$$

OD is the factual out degree of the graph of a Boolean network, OD_{min} and OD_{max} are the possible minimal and maximal out degrees.

We have shown (Klüver and Schmidt loc. cit.) that only combinations of different parameters can give valid predictions of the principal behavior of these complex dynamical systems. Such combinations of parameter values place the respective

---

[25]These general considerations refer chiefly to Boolean nets and cellular automata.

system into a certain complexity class or Wolfram class respectively (Wolfram loc. cit.). For example, values of P = 0.75, C = 0.8, and v = 0.5 are characteristic for a system belonging to Wolfram class I or II where only systems can be found with comparatively simple dynamics, i.e., trajectories with point attractors or with attractors consisting of only short periods. These complexity classes range from class 1 – only very simple dynamics – to class 4 – complex dynamics with long periods of the attractors and even with local attractors.[26]

The interesting aspect of this systematization of complex behavior with respect to different classes is that systems of a certain class are significantly similar with respect to their sensitivity to external signals. Systems of class 1 have very large basins of attraction and accordingly systems of class 4 have only rather small basins. In other words, the knowledge about the values of the different parameters allows not only a categorization into the different complexity classes but also a prediction about the according MC-values, i.e., their reaction to different signals. Systems of class 1, for example, must necessarily be characterized by low MC-values, systems of class 4 by large values.

We have shown that the MC-values significantly correlate with variance values and AP-values of the according matrices – under certain restricted conditions. Therefore, the knowledge about numerical values of the ordering parameters in addition allows a prediction about the probable characteristics of the according matrix of the respective system. Conversely, the result of an analysis of the according matrix produces an insight not only about the probable MC-value but also about the probable interval of the values of the ordering parameters. It is often rather laborious to directly compute the MC-values because all initial and all final states have to be taken into account. An analysis of the values of the ordering parameters is frequently easier; because of the mentioned correlations between MC-values and those of the ordering parameters at least educated guesses about the probable MC-values might be obtained from the values of the ordering parameters.

One can in addition recognize the importance of variance values with respect to certain capabilities of complex dynamical systems in quite another context. For purely theoretical reasons, namely the development of theories of socio-cultural evolution, we postulated a so-called "evolutionary parameter" (EP). The values of EP are determined by the strength or weakness respectively, by which different social roles are connected in a certain society (Klüver 2002). These connection values can be represented in an according "socio-cultural" matrix. By applying a principle that Spencer (1862) already formulated in the nineteenth century, namely that evolution is a development from homogeneity to growing diversity, one can say that the evolutionary capacity of a society is the greater the larger the variance of the socio-cultural

---

[26]A local attractor is an attractor that stabilizes only a part of the whole system (see above Chapter 1). The system may still be in a pre period of the general attractor, i.e., an attractor for the whole system, yet in some parts the state of a subsystem does not change any more. This subsystem then is in a local point attractor. One can illustrate such local attractors by social sub groups like conservative partisans of a certain church. Although the society as a whole is permanently changing such sub groups stick to their traditions and remain unchanged.

matrix is and vice versa. In many simulations we could show that by this assumption it is possible to reconstruct the general evolutionary paths of different societies. Indeed, a society with only small role differentiation will tend to perceive all events in a similar way, e.g., a religious one, and hence will probably stagnate. A similar thought Kauffman (2000) and Bagley and Farmer (1992) expressed for the emergence of life from prebiotic matter. The importance of variance analysis obviously is not only an interesting research question for the analysis of neural, Boolean and other dynamical networks but has also great theoretical relevance for questions of evolution and cognition.

The evolutionary results we obtained from the experiments with the GA may also lead into this direction. Networks with very high MC values can only poorly adapt to environments that demand middle or low MC values and conversely networks with middle or low MC values can only poorly adapt to environments that demand high MC values. Our research in theories and factual developments of socio-cultural evolution demonstrated the fact that socio-cultural systems with high EP-values are very seldom in factual history and can be generated in according simulations only under specific conditions, i.e., with very high EP-values. This fact is mirrored in our experiments with the GA described above: Systems with high EP-values or with accordingly high MC-values are the exception from statistical rules and hence can only be reached under very favorable conditions. This consideration is no final explanation for our results but shows the direction for future research.

The knowledge about parameters that could predict the meaning generation capacity could not only give important insights into the logic of neural network operations; that would be an improvement of our theoretical understanding of these complex dynamical systems. It could also give practical advantages if one needs neural networks with certain capabilities – either if one needs robust networks with great generalizing capacity or if there is need for sensitive networks that react in a different manner to different inputs. To be sure, the relations we have discovered so far are of only statistical validity. Yet to know that with a high probability one gets the desired characteristics of a certain network if one constructs a weight matrix with a specific variance is frequently a practical advantage: one has not to train the networks and look afterwards if the network has the desired behavior but can construct the desired matrix and if necessary make the additionally needed improvements via learning rules and/or additional optimization algorithms like for example a GA.

For example, one can generate a neural network at random and change its weight matrix via a suited formula in order to obtain specific MC-values. A possible algorithm to directly change a weight matrix in order to get other MC-values is Equation (4), proposed by one of our graduate students Gregor Braun:

$$\Delta w_{ij}(t) = \begin{cases} \eta \left(u - w_{ij}(t)\right) & \textit{if the variance shall be decreased} \\ \eta \left(sign(w_{ij}(t) - \mu) - w_{ij}(t)\right) & \textit{if the variance shall be increased} \end{cases} \quad (4)$$

η is something like a learning rate, i.e., a factor that determines the size of the variation of the weight values; μ is the mean value of the weight values different from zero.

Finally, is it possible to conclude that people with only small capabilities of differentiated perceiving all have neural networks in their brain with only small MC values, i.e., with neural connections of approximately the same strength? We hinted at the possibility that the case of the man from the book of Sacks who mistook hydrants for small children could be explained by assuming that this man has only networks with large basins of attraction and hence a weight matrix with small variance value. Yet the counterexample given above shows that such a conclusion would be a bit rash. Let us just say that the probability is significantly higher that the neural networks of this unlucky man have weight matrices with small variance values than that he has such a network as shown in the example. We shall see in Chapters 4 and 5 that such networks as shown above can be generated by special training methods and that in the cases discussed below these networks seem more suited than those analyzed in this chapter. The relation between weight or adjacency matrices respectively and the according MC values are results from random generating processes. Networks as a result from very special training processes may be quite another matter.

3.3 Information Degree and the Topology of Networks

Definitions like those of meaning and information degree always lead to the question if there are some general characteristics of meaning generation and of unexpectedness of messages. In the case of meaning generation we showed some results with respect to certain topological features of the analyzed networks. In the case of the degree of the unexpectedness of messages we can also state a general hypothesis, which at the present though must be treated with some caution. In order to show these results we must first define how the information degree is computed in the case of semantical networks and how the expectation vector is generated in these cases.

Many, if not most messages between human communicators are coded in a verbal way; hence it is useful to represent a system that receives a verbal message as a semantical network or different yet coupled semantical sub-networks (see above). Now consider conversations about the subject "Paris". Communicators who belong to the Western culture probably have some knowledge about Paris as the capital of France; accordingly they have at their disposal semantic sub-networks that contain concepts like "Tours d'Eiffel", "Champs d'Elyseé", "Seine", "Moulin Rouge", and "Haute Couture". We already showed such a semantical network in Chapter 1. To be sure, these semantic networks differ according to the individual knowledge of the communicators, for instance, if one of the communicators had been at Paris or not. But we can say that all these concepts belong to a network that is "clustered" around Paris as a particular city. On the other hand, many communicators have at their disposal additional networks that also contain "Paris" but now "Paris" as a Trojan prince. This semantic network contains other concepts like "Troy", "Hector", "Achilles", "Helena" and so on. Both networks are not arbitrarily structured but in dependency of the cultural importance of the different concepts. "Paris" as the capital of France can be imagined as the center of the according network or cluster respectively. In more dynamical terms that means that there is a strong relation, i.e., a connection from e.g., "Moulin Rouge" to Paris but not conversely: if one speaks about Moulin Rouge, then most people will have the association "Paris", but if someone mentions Paris as the capital of France, then associations like "Eiffel Tower" or "Champs d'Elyseé" are at least as probable as the association of "Moulin Rouge".

On the other hand "Paris" as a prince of Troy is certainly not the center of the according network. Other figures are at least as prominent in the story, e.g., Hector, Achilles, Helena and Ulysses. The concept "Trojan War" is probably the best candidate for the center of this network because the mentioned concepts all immediately lead to "Trojan War" but not conversely; "Trojan War" may lead to Agamemnon or Patrokles etc. In a mathematical manner we can represent these different networks as graphs with certain concepts as central nodes and other concepts connected with the central nodes with different strengths. If two concepts A and B have connecting "weights" w(A,B) and w(B,A) that represent the strength of the connection, then w(A,B) > w(B,A) means that A is stronger connected with B than conversely and that an association process leads more often from A to B than from B to A. In this sense "Paris" in the first network has a connection w(P,E) with "Eiffel Tower" and conversely there exists a connection w(E,P) with w(E,P) > w(P,E). Accordingly "Paris" in the second network can be represented with respect to Trojan War (TW) with w(P,TW) > w(TW,P).

In nuce, the strength of connections between different concepts can be interpreted as the order of associations: If "Paris" is stronger connected with "Eiffel Tower" than with "Moulin Rouge", i.e., w(P, E) > w(P, M), then a communicator will first associate "Paris" with "Eiffel Tower" and then with "Moulin Rouge". Accordingly, this communicator will first send messages about "Paris" and "Eiffel Tower" and only after that he will generate messages with "Paris" and "Moulin Rouge".

For the sake of mathematical simplicity let us define $0 \leq w(X,Y) \leq 1$ for all concepts X and Y in a semantic network. Then it is possible to define the degree of information in a more differentiated manner.

Suppose communicator A utters a sentence containing among other concepts "Paris" and "Hector". A expects an answer, i.e., A generates an expectation vector V_E containing "Patrokles" (the friend of Achilles who was slain by Hector). B generates instead another vector, containing "Ajax" (who had a duel with Hector). Although A did not expect this answer, it makes "sense" to him, because "Ajax" belongs to the same network as "Paris" and "Hector". Therefore the degree of information of B's answer is not high. To compute it we have to measure the "distance" in the network of A between "Patrokles" and "Ajax". Let us assume that B as well as A knows a lot about the Homeric epos and that "Ajax" and "Patrokles" are directly connected in A's semantic network. Then we define the " distance" d(Patr.,Aj.) as

$$d(\text{Patr.,Aj.}) = 1 - w(\text{Patr.,Aj.}). \tag{5}$$

This definition means that two concepts X and Y, which are strongly connected, are rather "near", i.e., if one of them is uttered in a conversation then there is a high probability that the other will be associated. Conversely, if there are only weak connections between two concepts then the probability is low that the second concept will be associated if the first appears in the conversation or, to speak in terms of order of association, the second concept will appear in a message only after several others. Because a concept X is trivially always strongly associated with itself, i.e., $w(X, X) = 1$, we define $d(X. X) = 1–1 = 0$.

Now let us assume that B expects an answer containing "Achilles" from A. But A answers with "Laertes" (the father of Aeneas, the mythical founder of Rome). Although B knows about Laertes he did not expect it because Laertes is rather "far away" from Achilles in B's semantic network, i.e., there are no direct connections between the two concepts. B first has to generate a connection from the expected "Achilles" to "Laertes": Both concepts are not directly connected in his network but only with two intermediating nodes, say "Hektor" and "Aeneas". Then the "semantic distance" between "Achilles" and "Laertes" is

$$d(Ach.,La) = 1 - (w(Ach, He) * w(He,Aen) * ww(Aen, La)) \qquad (6)$$

Generally speaking a "semantic distance" $d(x,y)$ of two concepts in a semantic network is

$$d(X, Y) = 1 - \prod w(X, U_i) \qquad (7)$$

if U_i are the concepts that connect X and Y by the shortest way.

A small semantic network may illustrate these considerations (Fig. 3.12):

Fig. 3.12 Semantical network of "Trojan War"

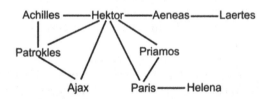

In this network obviously "Hector" is something like a central concept because the node "Hector" is directly connected with nearly all other concepts – with the exception of "Laertes" and "Helena". Despite her important role at beginning of the Trojan War "Helena" is only at the periphery of the network, which can be justified because she played no important role any longer during the 10 years of the war.

Now we can easily generalize our definition of the information degree of a message. We take again the expectation vector $Ve = (vei)$ and the perceived vector $Vp = (vpi)$ and measure the difference, but now in terms of semantic distance. Then we get for two components v_{ei} and v_{pi} the expectation probability

$$p_i = 1 - d(y_{ei},y_{pi}) \qquad (8)$$

The information degree I of the whole message, i.e., the perceived vector V_p is again obtained by summing the probability of the components and by taking again into account that the information degree is the higher the lower is the probability of the message (measured again as a subjective probability). Because the expectation probability of a received vector component v_{pi} is simply measured as the inverse distance, it seems quite natural to define the informational degree I as the distance between the expected components and the factually perceived ones. That gives us the definition

$$I = \sum d\left(x_{ei}, x_{pi}\right)/n, \tag{9}$$

if n is the dimension of the two vectors.

Apparently we again obtain a definition that is very similar to the basic equation of Shannon and Weaver, although this time the information degree must be computed in the special way just described. The reason for this is of course that we again have to introduce a "subjective" factor, namely the fact that in different semantic networks the "distance" between the same two concepts is not equal but usually different. In other words, the probability to receive a certain concept is dependent on the connections between the two concepts; the information degree for the receiver when hearing a certain concept is accordingly dependent on the connections between the expected concept and the factually received concept in the semantic network of the receiver. Therefore, our definition must be understood as the information degree of a message being a product of the topological relations of the receiver's semantic network. In addition, we do not use the logarithm to the basis two as did Shannon and Weaver but simply the arithmetical mean. This is done for the sake of mathematical simplicity; the important point, however, is that the basic idea of this definition is nearly the same as that of Shannon and Weaver.[27]

Now consider a semantical network consisting of concepts X_i; the graph theoretical structures of such networks of course can be quite different. For our analysis we concentrated on the aspect how densely the concepts are connected in the network. For example, the concepts of one network may all be directly connected with each other, which means an extremely high density. The other extreme is a network where each concept is connected with only one other concept. Figure 3.13 shows these two extreme possibilities:

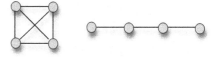

Fig. 3.13 Extreme high and low densities

---

[27]By the way, when we speak of "semantic distance" between two concepts X and Y we have to mention the fact that this is not a "distance" in a strict mathematical sense, i.e., there is no complete metric defined by it. A metric is characterized by the symmetry axiom, i.e., a metrical relation d(X,Y) is defined by d(X,Y) = d(Y,X). This is generally not the case with our semantic distance.

Most networks, of course, are not of one of the extreme types but are a mixture of them. In particular many networks may contain "clusters" of elements, that is subsets of elements or nodes respectively that are densely connected while other elements are only weakly connected with the clusters. Our research question was if particular clustering characteristics have any influence on the degree of information of messages. In other words, do specific topological features of networks determine the average degree of information of messages?

To be sure, the concrete information degree of a message depends on the concrete topology of a network, i.e., the representation of the learning biography of the network, in the same way as does the concrete generation of the meaning of a message. Yet our first results demonstrate that some plausible general hypotheses may be stated:

For the sake of simplicity we defined in our experiments a cluster the following way: A subset C of m elements of a network N is a cluster if and only if all elements of this subset are directly connected, if $m > 2$, and if all elements of N that are not directly connected with all elements of C are no elements of C. In other words, for all $X \in C$ and $Y \in C$ $w(X,Y) > 0$ and $w(Y,X) > 0$, if $0 \leq w(X,Y) \leq 1$. A cluster, hence, in a semantical network may be interpreted as a certain association field where the activation of one concept automatically leads to the activation of all other concepts although mostly with different activation values and not at the same time. The order of activation depends on the strength of the connections: the stronger the connections are the higher is the probability of immediate activation. All other elements of N are either only indirectly connected with the elements of C or just with the elements of a subset M of C with $M \subset C$.

We further assumed that all concepts X are elements of exactly one cluster. The reason for this assumption is that usually no concepts exist in one cognitive network that are totally isolated, i.e., that have no connections to other concepts. To be sure, there may exist concepts that are connected with other concepts but do not belong to a cluster in the strict sense defined above. But the restriction to networks where all elements belong to exactly one cluster is not important for our experiments. In particular, if concepts belong to more than one cluster – e.g., "Paris" –, the semantical content of such concepts that we call "bridge concepts" is different with respect to the according clusters and hence this case can be solved by inserting this concept in each according cluster.

The last simplifying assumption is that two clusters are connected by exactly one link. This assumption certainly cannot be justified by cognitive considerations but was introduced in the first experimental series in order to keep the experiments as clearly as possible. In further experiments the number of the cluster connecting links will successively be increased. Figure 3.14 shows a network generated according to these assumptions:

The research question with respect to these networks is if and how the number of different clusters influences the informational degree of messages generated at random. Because the number of concepts of a cluster must be at least 3 it is evident that a network with n elements generated according to the assumptions above can contain at maximum n/3 clusters, all of size 3. The number of connections of

Fig. 3.14 A clustered
network with one connecting
link between the clusters

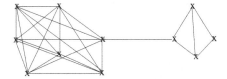

such a cluster is then 3^2–3, if one does not count "self-enforcing" connections, i.e., w(X,X) > 0. Generally a cluster with m elements, m ≤ n, obviously contains m^2–m connections; if m = n then of course the whole network is just one large cluster.

Finally we introduced an additional *ceteris paribus* condition, namely that for all X and Y w(X,Y) = w(Y,X) = 0.5. This symmetry condition of course shall eliminate the influence of different weight values. We shall investigate such an influence in later experiments but at present we assume that it will be of no importance with networks generated at random. In the average probably the results will be similar to networks constructed with this restriction. The experiments were performed the following way:

A network first receives a concept A that belongs to the receiving network and is selected at random. The concept A can be understood as the subject of the discussion, e.g., "football" or "Trojan War". Then the network generates an expectation vector by selecting the concepts B and C whose connections from A are the strongest. Because of the symmetry condition all concepts in the cluster of A fulfill the selection condition; hence B and C are selected at random from the concepts of the cluster of A. All other concepts of the network have a larger distance to A because of the definition of distance in a semantical – or any – network. The expectation vector then is V_E = (A, B, C).

The reason for this construction rule is founded not only on experiences with associative performances but in particular on the famous principle of Hebb (1949), which says that the connections between two neurons that are several times simultaneously activated are strengthened in proportion to the frequency of the simultaneous activations. This principle has been frequently confirmed in neuro-biology (cf. e.g., Kandel 2006). As a result of such increased weight values the probability increases that an activation of one neuron will also activate the other.

The factual message that the network receives is (A, X, Y), X and Y selected at random from the concepts of the whole network. If for example the cluster of A is rather small in proportion to the size of the whole network then in most cases X and Y will not belong to the cluster of A; accordingly larger is the distance from B and C to X and Y. If on the other hand the cluster is large in proportion to the size of the network the probability increases that X and Y belong to the same cluster as A, B, and C. Because the informational degree is computed according to the distance between two concepts, (A, B, C) – (A, X, Y) is then (0, 0.5, 0.5) = 1/3 for the case that X and Y belong to the same cluster as A, B, and C. In each other case the informational degree will be higher.

We confirmed these considerations by performing three experimental series with networks consisting of n = 10, n = 20, and n = 30 elements. The average size of the clusters that were generated at random was increased from 3 to n/2 and finally to n. The results of these experiments are shown in Fig. 3.15:

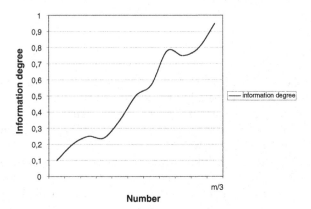

Fig. 3.15 The x-axis represents the average size of the clusters, the y-axis the average informational degree

The curve is obtained by computing the arithmetical mean of the three series. Yet the particular curves all showed the same configuration. Hence, we can assume that the size of the networks plays no important role.

Obviously the probable informational degrees of random messages can be predicted by the analysis of the "cluster geometry" of specific networks.[28] The more clusters a network consists of the higher will be the informational degree and vice versa. To be sure, in further experiments we will investigate the additional role of more links between clusters that will probably decrease the respective informational degrees; in addition, clusters may be defined in a more complex way than we did. Yet these first results demonstrate that it will be worthwhile to look for analogous general regularities of relations between network topology and informational degree as we already did with the concept of meaning generation capacity.

If these results can be confirmed in more general cases they could give an interesting explanation for the fact that humans frequently are surprised of messages although they know all components of them. If the known components are placed in different semantical networks that are only weakly connected then the receivers of the messages did not expect them because the receivers constructed very different expectation vectors and obtained according large differences between their expectations and the factual messages. Consequently the messages had a high degree of information because of their (subjective) improbability.

One of the most famous cases in the history of science, namely the special theory of relativity, can be taken as an example. The important components of the theory were already known before Einstein, in particular the constancy of the velocity of

---

[28]The term "cluster geometry" is also used in other sciences, for example astrophysics and chemistry.

light and the Lorentz transformations. Although several theoretical physicists like Poincaré and Lorentz tried to integrate these different components into a unifying theory it took the genius of Einstein to form a complete theory. The surprise by which this theory was generally received was chiefly probably due to the fact that for most receivers the different components did not belong to the same semantical cluster. Only after the general acceptance of the special theory of relativity new and larger semantical clusters became formed where concepts like "mass", energy", and "velocity of light" are strongly associated – in other words $E = mc^2$. It seems not too farfetched to say that the theoretical considerations about meaning and information degree are empirically plausible and can explain important cognitive and communicative phenomena.

To be sure, these considerations are not only valid in the case of semantical networks. It is easy to imagine any cognitive network that is geometrically determined by such cluster geometry. The information degree of a non-verbal message received by this network can be computed the same way as we did with verbal messages received by semantical networks. It is in these cases only necessary to define the status of the artificial neurons of such a network – either that the respective components of the message are represented by single neurons or by sub-clusters of neurons. But this is only a technical detail.

In Section 2.2 we mentioned the fact that often the information degree of message determines how easily this message can be understood by a receiver. If the information degree is high then the message is rather unexpected and cannot easily be integrated into the respective cognitive network although all components of the message are known. A low information degree on the other hand of course means that the message was expected and hence it can be easily understood. We are now able to clarify this point a bit more in detail: A message, as we demonstrated, has a high information degree if the parts of the message belong to different clusters in the receiving network that are only weakly connected. The receiver has difficulties with understanding this message because *for him* the different parts of the message do not belong together or only in a very strange and unexpected way. Conversely, a message whose parts belong to the same cluster or to strongly connected clusters in the receiving network can be easily understood because *for the receiver* the message parts belong together – the whole message was expected.

If one assumes that the respective networks of a sender and a receiver are usually differently clustered then communication between them can become difficult: On the one hand the sender may believe that a message has no high information degree because the components of the message belong *for him* together. Accordingly he will be rather astonished if the receiver does not understand the message because of his different cluster geometry. Many problems in didactical contexts between teacher and pupils may have their "geometrical reason" in such a different clustering: the teacher is used to large clusters and does not understand why the pupils with still small clusters do not understand him. On the other hand the sender might send a message that is very new for him – the different message parts have been brought together in his network only a short time ago. Accordingly he expects that the message has a high information degree for the receiver. If the receiver answers that he did expect such a message because its parts already belonged *for him* together the sender will be justly irritated.

A third case of probable misunderstanding can be a situation where the receiver again has a significantly larger cluster with respect to the subject of the communication than the sender. Then a message might have a high degree of information for the receiver because he generated other and in particular more associated concepts than the sender. The receiver does not understand or only with difficulties the message because he expected a more sophisticated one. In the case of such a disturbed communication the receiver could only try to construct a mental model of the sender in order to understand why the sender contents himself with only a simple message – he might be a beginner with respect to the subject, only poorly informed or generally a rather simple mind.

Many communicative problems of mutual understanding and misunderstanding, not only those described, might have such or similar geometrical reasons and can be explained that way. For example, if a receiver's network is characterized by a weight matrix with very low variance values and according low MC-values he will understand different messages the same way if the messages belong to the same (large) basin of attraction. The sender's network, on the other hand, might have rather high MC-values and according high variance values. These geometrical differences almost certainly lead to misunderstanding if the sender, e.g., always gets the same answer to different messages although for him the meaning of the different messages is quite different. Similar examples can easily be imagined. *In nuce*, a necessary although of course not sufficient condition for mutual understanding is a similar geometry of the respective cognitive networks – with respect to cluster geometry and variance values.

3.3.1 A Final Remark with Respect to AI

Human beings implicitly build their cognitive structures with suited variance values, i.e., suited MC-values, and suited cluster geometries by learning – either from single cases or by explicit instructions (see below Section 4.3). The topological structure, hence, is a result from such learning processes and can explain the particular cognitive behavior of humans. Although in SF the authors only seldom and usually very vague describe the ontogenesis of the literary AI-systems it can be assumed that AI examples like Solo or the Terminator either were explicitly programmed for their tasks and abilities or were trained in a fashion similar to the learning processes of humans. The case of Asimov's robots is an example for the first case; Solo is an example for the second one. In "Odyssey 2010" Arthur C. Clarke explicitly described how the constructor of HAL 2000 retrained the artificial system after its breakdown in "Odyssey 2001". HAL is an explicitly described example of the second case too.

The general results we demonstrated in this chapter show another possibility how to construct AI-systems with certain desired capabilities. Instead of humanlike training processes the desired cognitive capabilities with respect to differentiated and generalizing meaning generation and with respect to understand messages because of a suited cluster geometry could be explicitly implemented into the systems. That is not to say that such AI programs should be programmed in a complete manner like the robots of Asimov or like the different versions of "Eliza", including our own version, but that general topological characteristics of the cognitive structures of these systems could be implemented before the usual training programs start (cf. the practical remarks at the end of Section 3.2). The artificial systems, so to speak, would get this way a start advantage to humans whose cognitive structure has to build suited topological characteristics *during and as result of* the training and learning processes; the artificial systems would this way have suited topologies *before and as basis of* the training processes. The same start advantage such artificial systems would have to other AI-systems that have to build their topologies the same way as humans. In "Odyssey 2010" the re-training of HAL 2000 is described as a long and tedious one. Perhaps the constructor of HAL, Dr Chandra, should have considered some aspects of HAL's desired topology before the start of the re-training program.

It is of course a question of according experiments with the construction of AI-systems if our general topological results are indeed an advantage in comparison to the *only* use of established training methods. We already pointed out that probably a combination of both procedures could be the best way: First general topological characteristics like certain cluster geometries are generated, for example via the usage of similar algorithms like Equation (4) in Section 3.2 for the generation of suited variance values. Then the usage, for example, of certain learning rules, to which we shall refer in the next chapter, makes more subtle necessary adjustments. Yet already it is a well-known fact in neuro-informatics that the established training methods for large neural nets with many units need a long time and are often, because of the many parameters one has to take account of, not very successful. The introduction of the "double way" we propose may probably make things easier.

Chapter 4
The Understanding of Learning

The relation between learning and understanding is a two-sided one: On the one hand the process of understanding must be learned, for example by learning about social rules, cultural contexts, or subjective intentions. That is of course a truism but one that is often neglected by critics of AI. Like human beings artificial systems have to learn the tasks of understanding if they are able to do it at all. Hence the question with respect to the principal possibility of a hermeneutic AI is not just how to implement certain hermeneutic abilities, orientated to the capabilities of adult social actors, but how an AI may obtain the capabilities to learn understanding the way a child, an adolescent, or an adult in a new social environment learn these difficult tasks.

On the other hand the understanding of other social actors is often only possible if one understands the behavior of others as a result of specific learning processes. This is a truism too and not by chance for example at a court of law the accused is frequently asked to tell his biography. Certain violations of law can and must be understood as the result of the specific socialization process and hence the specific learning experiences of the accused. At least that is the case in German courts. Yet not only in such extreme situations the question is necessary, which learning biography determined the actions of the respective actor. Each teacher who takes over a new class has to ask in what way the behavior of his still unknown pupils is the result of their former learning experiences; the observation of a reckless driver leads to the question how he had acquired such a behavior; the listening to a racist orator who claims the inferiority of all people who do not belong to his own ethnic group brings forth the question where and how he had learned these dangerous prejudices and so on. In all these and many other cases only an – at least hypothetical – understanding of the respective learning processes makes the understanding of certain actions possible.

In Chapter 2 we differentiated understanding processes according to the possible reasons for the behavior that is to understand, namely rules, cultural contexts, and subjective intentions. The reference to the importance of learning for understanding processes suggests another additional distinction, namely between understanding processes that can be successfully performed without asking for the learning biography of the actor and those where the question for the respective learning processes is necessary. Our examples already show that very often this additional task

J. Klüver, C. Klüver, *Social Understanding*, Theory and Decision Library A 47,
DOI 10.1007/978-90-481-9911-2_4, © Springer Science+Business Media B.V. 2011

of understanding cannot be avoided. Therefore, a study about understanding and formal models of these hermeneutical processes would be rather incomplete without dealing with the subject of learning. In this chapter we shall chiefly concentrate on the second side of the relation between understanding and learning by analyzing the frequently only vaguely used concept of learning. But perhaps our formal, i.e. geometrical models of certain learning types can be taken as a basis for the first side, i.e. the question how an AI could obtain the capabilities to learn something like understanding. We already mentioned at the end of the last chapter how learning processes of artificial systems can be improved via the implementation of certain topological basic features of the cognitive structure(s).

The main paradigm in computer science for "machine learning" is that of artificial neural nets; we have shown different examples of these algorithms in the preceding chapters. To be sure, there are a lot of very different methods to implement learning capabilities in computer programs (cf. the exhaustive and very extensive overview in Russell and Norvig loc. cit.). We already mentioned a quite other type of learning algorithms, namely the evolutionary algorithms and in particular the genetic algorithm (GA). Yet neural networks are particular: Only they were invented and developed by an explicit orientation to the most effective learning system that is known in physical reality, namely the human brain – and the brains of other living systems, of course. Therefore, if one wants to model complex learning processes in an empirically valid way it suggests itself to use neural nets. For this reason it is not by chance that since the eighties frequently science fiction authors described their respective AI-systems as neural networks; however, they also gave of course no details. Accordingly a specific modeling technique suggests itself, by the way, if one wants to model processes of biological evolution: Only evolutionary algorithms are explicitly constructed according to the biological evolutionary processes. That is why we speak in these cases of algorithms that are analogous to nature (cf. Stoica-Klüver et al. 2009). Yet as useful as neural nets are for modeling purposes and many other tasks they are rather problematic with respect to the question how empirically valid they really are. That is why we concentrate in the first section on this problem.

4.1 Methodological Preliminary Remarks and a General Rule Schema

Since the rise of neuro-informatics, i.e. the construction and validation of artificial neural networks, many scholars tried to analyze animal and human learning processes via the construction of suited artificial neural networks or neural networks as we say for sake of brevity. Neural networks have become a widely used tool for different practical purposes like, e.g. pattern recognition and forecast problems. In particular they have become an indispensable tool for cognitive modeling (e.g. Polk and Seifert loc. cit.). Yet it is still not very clear how valid the models are that are constructed via the use of neural networks. In other words, even if neural network models successfully simulate the results of some cognitive processes, how similar are the processes of the model to that of the brain or mind.

The main problem with the usage of neural networks for the purpose of studying factual learning processes of animals and humans is the fact that only little is known about the logical or mathematical structure respectively of biological neural networks in the brain (see above Lakoff and Núñez loc. cit.). Hence it is rather difficult to decide if a special kind of neural networks constructed for the modeling of some cognitive processes is in a strict sense isomorphic or at least homomorphic to those biological neural structures that perform in the brain the respective processes. For example, one of the most important learning rules for supervised learning is the well-known Back-Propagation rule, a generalization of the equally well-known delta rule (see above Section 3.2). The training of feed forward networks with more than two layers depends in many cases on the usage of the Back-Propagation rule or one of its many variants. Yet there are serious doubts if there is something like the rather complicated Back-Propagation rule in the brain (cf. McLeod et al. 1998). The same is the case with even more complicated mathematical models like for example Mexican Hat functions in the case of Kohonen Feature Maps (see below). Therefore, if researchers try to model supervised learning processes via the use of many layered feed forward networks as, for example, the famous studies of the learning of irregular verbs, i.e. their respective past tense (e.g. Plunkett and Marchman 1996), the researchers find themselves in a rather paradoxical situation: on the one hand they are able to validate their model by demonstrating that the model generates the same or at least a similar behavior as a human learner – in the case of the past tense expressed by the famous U-curve; on the other hand they know that their model contains some algorithms that have almost certainly no equivalent in the brain's structure. Hence, the model is equivalent to the factual learning processes in results but not in structure. As a consequence one has to ask what exactly could be learned from such models.

To be sure, these methodical problems do not make models as neural networks for, e.g., the learning of the past tense worthless. On the contrary, if the same results can be observed with respect to the behavior of logically different systems like neural networks and human learners then one may come to the conclusion that perhaps such phenomena as the U-curve are universal characteristics of particular types of learning processes. Probably such learning processes are an example of so-called under determined problems, i.e. problems that may be solved in different ways and with the same results. Yet although much could be learned about human and animal learning processes it would be certainly desirable to construct models that not only generate similar behavior as the modeled system but are structurally at least similar to the according factual processes.

Many applications of neural networks like, e.g., pattern recognition, classification tasks, or stock predictions are done because of technical and/or economical interests.[1] In such cases, of course, it is quite irrelevant if the used models are similar to factual processes in the brain. Therefore, it is no wonder that a lot of learning

---

[1] As mentioned in the preface we also applied a newly developed network of ours to an economical problem, namely the forecast of the probable economical success of new types of cell phones.

rules are constructed without regarding any neurobiological aspects. But as useful as such models may be for practical purposes not much can be learned from them for the task of cognitive modeling. If neural networks are constructed in order to study human and animal learning processes two fundamental methodical principles and one theoretical principle should be observed:

(a) The respective learning rules and topologies should be as similar (homomorphic) as possible to those processes in the brain that shall be analyzed by the neural networks. To be sure, frequently one does not know much about the according structure in the brain. But if there is some knowledge about it then the neural network should be constructed according to such knowledge. This principle may be called that of neurobiological plausibility. One may also say that this principle demands that at least no structures should be used for such models that are not biologically plausible.

(b) It is a well-known fact that frequently the same results may be obtained by using different models (see above). If there are no empirical data to decide, which of the models is the more empirically adequate one, then a classical and venerable methodical principle must be applied, namely the principle of Occam's Razor: If two or more models are empirical equivalent in the sense that they generate under the same conditions the same results and if no decision between them grounded on empirical data is possible then one should accept the simplest model as that, which probably is the true one or at least the most plausible one. We shall apply this principle too in order to substantiate a new learning rule schema for the modeling of the different types of learning that we shall describe in the next subchapter.[2]

(c) The third criterion is a theoretical one and well known in the theoretical sciences. The model should be as general as possible, which means that the model should be based on general principles that could be applied in other domains as well. In the theoretical sciences this principle is applied to decide between theories that are equivalent with respect to empirical data and with respect to "elegance". In such a *ceteris paribus* situation that theory should be favored that is the most general of the competing theories. Frequently this criterion is the most important one in the sense that general theories are favored although they are not as well empirically confirmed and not so simple as their rivals (cf. Kuhn 1963).

It is certainly not usual to apply particular principles (b) and (c) to the development of models of cognitive processes, in this case neural networks. Yet we try to show that this enterprise can be worthwhile.

One of the most important and empirically well confirmed principles in neuro-informatics is the above mentioned famous postulate of Donald Hebb (1949): If a cell A is near enough to a cell B to continuously arouse B then the efficiency of A to arouse B is increased. Conversely, the efficiency of A to arouse B is decreased if

---

[2]Mathematicians and theoretical physicists often speak of "elegance" when they apply the principle of Occam's Razor. The simpler a theory or model respectively is the more elegant it is.

there are none or only few interactions between the cells. This principle is used in neuro-informatics in different ways that we shall describe and discuss in the sections on the respective learning types.

If one tries to formalize this famous principle in order to implement learning capabilities into neural networks its essence certainly is the increasing or decreasing respectively of the weight values between a sending and a receiving artificial neuron. Therefore we transformed this postulate into a general "enforcing rule" (see above Chapter 3). The rule is strictly speaking a general rule schema because it can and must be applied in different ways for different learning tasks. If we again call the measure of weight variation Δw_{ij}, then the rule schema simply is

$$w_{ij}(t+1) = w_{ij}(t) \pm \Delta w_{ij} \text{ with } \Delta w_{ij} = c \text{ (constant) and } 0 \leq c \leq 1. \quad (1)$$

$w_{ij}(t)$ is the weight value at time t and of course $w_{ij}(t+1)$ that at the next time step. If as usual the weight matrix consists only of real numbers in the interval -1 and $+1$, then Δw_{ij} may be fixed by the user of the according artificial neural network (ANN) as, for example, 0.1. In the case of increasing weight values then $w_{ij}(t+1) = w_{ij}(t) + 0.1$.

In order to guarantee that the weight values do not become larger than $+1$ we add

$$w_{ij}(t+1) = w_{ij}(t), \text{ if } w_{ij}(t) \geq 1 - \Delta w_{ij}. \quad (2)$$

In the case of decreasing values an according threshold condition is valid with respect to the limit -1. If $w(t+1) = w(t) - \Delta w_{ij}$, then of course rules (1) and (2) becomes "lessening rules".

Apparently it is not necessary to add a learning rate to these rules because the user can select $c = \Delta w_{ij}$ small or large as he wishes. According to the experiences with learning rates c should not be too large.

Equation (2) obviously is a stopping criterion of the type that is frequently used when certain thresholds are inserted into the architecture of ANN. Yet such stopping criteria are mathematically not very elegant and have often an ad hoc character. Therefore we can introduce in Equation (2) an "asymptotic" factor:

$$\Delta w_{ij} = c * (1 - w(t))$$

and hence

$$w(t+1) = w(t) + c * (1 - w(t)), \quad (3)$$

if c is a constant that the user is free to determine and if $w(t)$ again is defined for the interval $[-1, 1]$.

Decreasing of weight values is accordingly computed by

$$\Delta w_{ij} = c * (-1 + |w(t)|). \quad (4)$$

Although these versions of the enforcing rule schema are certainly more elegant than the simple rule (2) it often is sufficient to use only the simple version with its stopping criterion. Note that in Equation (1) the sign $\pm$ appears and in Equations

(3) and (4) not. The simple reason for this is that the respective asymptotic factor decides if the rule is an enforcing or a lessening rule and hence no $\pm$ is necessary.

Note that this is just a general rule schema and not a concrete learning rule. The next step must be to fill out this schema by applying it to the different types of learning that have to be considered. As learning can be performed in rather different ways some introductory remarks are necessary.

4.2 Types of Learning and the According Enforcing Rules

The most famous and certainly most general definition of learning is that learning is a change of behavior as a result of the previous processing of information; it is the classical definition not only of Behaviorism but also of pedagogical practice. Of course, nothing is said in this definition about the manner of information processing or the relation between the processing process on the one hand and the resulting new behavior on the other. Yet as a general orientation one may use it as a signpost. The Oxford Dictionary, by the way, just defines learning as the acquisition of new knowledge and/or skills, which is certainly neither a complete definition nor a satisfactory one.

For our purposes, i.e. the construction of formal models, the following definition is the most suited one: Learning is the systematic variation, possibly also by trial and error, of the cognitive structure of the learner, which in turn generates an according change of behavior. Because the cognitive structure of the learner can usually not directly be observed and because the changing of the observable behavior as the effect of the changed cognitive structure can just be supposed each assumption about the changing of the cognitive structure is of course only a hypothesis. If and when cognitive structures are modeled by the usage of neural networks then the changing of the cognitive structure is performed mostly by the variation of the weight values.

Note that this definition on the one hand takes not only into account the Behaviorist position that learning processes can and must only be defined by the changing of the learner's behavior but also the cognitive or constructive respectively learning theories like that of Piaget. Learning is – according to his famous developmental theory – the generation, changing, and enlarging of cognitive schemas by the processes of assimilation and accommodation. This takes into account the specific internal processes within the learner. Because also Piaget and his followers could not directly observe these internal processes they must also refer to the observable behavior if it has changed according to the hypothesized changing of the cognitive schemas. The changing of behavior of a learner, hence, is understood if and only if one can explain these changes as the result of the changing of certain schemas, usually by accommodation, and by thus performing new forms of assimilation. Accordingly, our definition implies that the changed behavior of an actor is understood if and only if it can be explained as the result of the variation of his weight matrix, i.e. the variation of certain connections.

We shall again refer below to the classical theory of Piaget. The capability of neural nets to learn and remember input patterns that we investigated in Section

3.2 is a formal representation of the generation and changing of certain cognitive schemas.

There are many attempts to classify the different processes of learning, in particular with respect to the difference between learning by receiving explicit information and rules and implicit learning orientated to single examples (see above Chapter 2). In neuro-informatics usually a classification is used that distinguishes between three types of learning, namely supervised learning, reinforcement learning, and self-organized learning. We shall discuss these three types in detail in the next subchapters. Yet as useful these distinctions have been for practical purposes this classification is not complete because, as we shall show, some important forms of learning cannot be captured with it. This is especially the case with the learning form of classical conditioning. Therefore, we propose a variant classification:

The main distinction must be made between all forms of learning that are performed by immediate environmental corrections and those forms that are not. The first kind of learning types consists in particular of supervised learning and reinforcement learning; the second type contains in particular self-organized learning and classical conditioning. Hence we can summarize our classification in form of a "learning type" table:

immediate environmental feed back	no immediate environmental feed back
supervised learning	self-organized learning
reinforcement learning	classical conditioning

To be sure, each learning process and its results sooner or later will get a feed back from the environment of the learner, either in form of rewards, of corrections, or even punishment. Hence, the distinction between the two main types of learning is not the presence or absence of an environmental feed back but the distinction between immediate feed back and one that occurs significantly later, i.e. after the results of the learning process have been practically applied by the learner.

4.2.1 Supervised Learning and the According Version of the Enforcing Rule Schema

In practical neuro-informatics supervised learning is the most frequently used learning type for, e.g., pattern recognition or forecast problems. Mostly feed forward networks are used the same way as we did for the investigation of the MC in Section 3.2. It is important to remind that the term "supervised learning" is used in neuro-informatics in a special way, not equivalent to everyday usage or the use of this term in theories of education and learning. Here supervised learning means each learning process that is "supervised", i.e. observed and determined by an external teacher.[3] The teacher especially decides if the learning process is

---

[3] A "teacher" is not necessarily a human being and not even a living system. If for example a child is learning to ride a bicycle then gravity acts as teacher: the child learns from falling over and

successful or not; he must not necessarily tell the learner how good he is or how far from the desired learning goal.

In neuro-informatics the term "supervised learning" is used in a more specialized fashion. Here the term refers only to those learning processes that are determined by an explicitly in advance stated goal or target respectively, usually given in form of a numerically coded vector. That is the form of training neural networks that we used for the investigation of MC and variance in the first and third experimental series (Section 3.2). When the network has produced an output vector the distance between this factual output and the target is measured by computing the difference between the respective components of the two vectors, and then the weight values are changed in proportion of these differences – the error. We shall show below some learning rules for this kind of learning. Using an economical language one might say that supervised learning here means that the variation of the cognitive structure, namely the weight matrix, is done by computing the error as the distance between the credit value and the debit one.

The respective forms of human learning mainly occur in educational processes that are institutionalized. We already mentioned the fact that in German schools and universities the pupils and students get their feed back by receiving numerical values. A "six" or "five" is a very bad value, while a "one" is the best. Hence a mark of 2.5 means that the pupil is in the middle region and that the distance between the optimal goal of 1 and his factual mark is equal to 1.5; this is obviously exact the same procedure as in the case of supervised learning by neural networks.[4] It is of course a question of the pupil if he will change his cognitive structure in proportion of the size of his errors. In contrast to supervised learning of neural networks humans usually have the choice if they want to correct their cognitive structure although pupils and students *should* do so. Basically the same procedure is the case if the marks are given in form of letters as, for example, in the US.

Yet supervised learning can also occur in more informal learning situations. When a piano teacher explains his pupils what mistakes they exactly made and how they could improve their play the pupils also can compare their factual competence with the desired one. Each learning process, hence, where a supervising teacher informs his pupils about the differences between their results and the intended goal is a supervised one in the special sense of neuro-informatics. Examples for such learning processes can be found everywhere if there is a teacher as an expert in the respective learning field and if the teacher explicitly informs the learners about their distance to the predefined goal. The main difference, though, between human learners and neural networks is the fact that the latter obtain explicit instructions via the learning rules how to change their structure. This is of course usually not

---

crashing on the ground that it must keep the bicycle moving in order to avoid the consequences of the force of gravity.

[4]Recently the German mark system has slightly changed. The worst mark now is a "4.3", which means "not fair enough". The basic principle, though, is the same.

the case with human learners, in particular because human teachers have no certain knowledge of the cognitive structure of their pupils.

The most frequently used learning rule for supervised learning of neural networks is the so-called Delta rule:

and

$$\Delta w_{ij} = \eta o_i \delta_j. \tag{5}$$

$$w_{ij}(t + 1) = w_{ij}(t) + \Delta w_{ij} \tag{6}$$

Δw_{ij}, hence, is the value by which the initial weight value w_{ij} is changed (usually i is the sending and j the receiving neuron), η is a so-called learning rate, o_i is the output of a neuron i of the input layer, i.e. a sending neuron, and δ_j is the difference between the output of a neuron j of the output layer and the according component of the target vector.[5] If the values of the output vectors are smaller than those of the target vector then Δw_{ij} is added to the old weight value, otherwise of course it is subtracted.

The basic postulate of Hebb is not literally taken over in the Delta rule but only in principle, i.e. by the continuous increasing or decreasing of the weight values. Despite that fact rules of this kind are usually called "Hebbian" rules as they are at least inspired by Hebb's postulate. One may interpret the learning rate η as a formal representation of the individual learning capacity or also learning motivation of a learner. The user must choose the values of η before the according training process.

The Delta rule can only be applied to two-layered networks because the difference δ_j can be computed only for the output neurons. In the case of three or even more layers another learning rule must be applied, which is mainly the Back Propagation rule that we mentioned in Chapter 3. We shall come back to the case of more than two layers below.

A more literal application of Hebb's principle is possible by applying the general enforcing rule schema:

$$\Delta w_{ij} = c * (1 - w(t)) \, \delta_j, \tag{7}$$

Δw_{ij} is again the difference between the old value $w_{ij}(t)$ and the new one $w_{ij}(t+1)$, c is a constant with $0 \leq c \leq 1$ that must be chosen by the user (obviously an analog to the learning rate in the Delta rule) and δ_j is again the difference between the activation values of the output neurons and the target neurons. In contrast to the Delta rule the computation of Δw_{ij} depends mainly on the former values of w(t), including the "dampening factor" $(1 - w(t))$. The output values of the input neurons play no role; the changing of the weight values can be understood as a simple recursive series, in which each new element is generated according to the same logic from the former elements.

---

[5]It must be noted, however, that there are different versions of the Delta rule and accordingly it is possible to construct different versions of the supervised learning enforcing rule, which we shall show below. The Delta rule is often also called Widrow-Hoff rule in honor to their inventors Widrow and Hoff (Widrow and Hoff 1960).

The Delta rule has been often applied with very good success in the last decades. Although the enforcing rule is more orientated to the empirically frequently confirmed principle of Hebb the practical success of the Delta rule is so overwhelming that another rule can be accepted only if its capabilities are at least as great as that of the Delta rule. Therefore, we performed with some of our students several experiments in order to test (a) if our new rule guarantees successful training of two-layered networks at all, which was not a matter of course, and (b) if the training results are at least as good as the respective results with the Delta rule.[6]

Question (a): This first experimental series was performed with four different networks, namely networks with 8, 10, 16, and 20 input neurons and the same number of output neurons. The weight values were defined as $-1 \leq w_{ij} \leq 1$; the input values and those of the target vectors were defined between 0 and 1. The activation function was the linear one, namely

$$a_j = \sum_i a_i w_{ij} \qquad (8)$$

a_j is the activation value of the receiving neuron and a_j the activation values of the sending ones. The difference δ_j was again computed by the differences between the components of the output vector and the target vector.

The constant c was also varied for each experiment with one network type, namely $c = 0.1$, $c = 0.2$, $c = 0.3$, and $c = 0.5$. The main results are the following:

The learning rule operates very well for all networks sizes if $c = 0.1$ or $c = 0.2$. Larger values of c are only successful if the networks are comparatively small – we also tested smaller networks with four and five input and output neurons. A high learning rate reduces the necessary number of training steps, i.e. the network learns faster, but only in the case of small networks. Larger networks can only be successfully trained with low values of c. Indeed, networks with 16 and more input and output neurons do not converge to the target vector at all but instead the activation values of the neurons become larger and larger. The networks, so to speak, become erratic and behave in an unpredicted manner.

If one transfers these results to human learners there is a striking parallel: Low learning rates mean in most cases a rather slow but safe learning process. If one wants a faster learning process in simple cases the learning rate, i.e. the quickness by which the learning process should be performed, can be increased but only in simple cases. If human learners are forced to learn more quickly than their structure allows they break down, i.e. they do not learn at all. It does not seem too farfetched if one takes our results as a possible explanation for failures in learning, namely if the learners are forced to learn more quickly than they are equipped for. Each teacher has made such experiences if he has gone on too quickly.

Question (b): We omit here technical details and just give the main results. Small networks, i.e. networks with four, five, and eight input and output neurons learn with similar success with the enforcing rule and the Delta rule. Sometimes the enforcing

---

[6]Benjamin Berg, Remigius Kijak and Jörg Krampitz.

rule is a bit faster and sometimes the Delta rule; the enforcing rule is usually a bit faster with c = 0.5. Larger networks learn with the enforcing rule only with c = 0.1 or c = 0.2, as we mentioned. Then the enforcing rule is in most cases faster, i.e. it needs significantly less training steps than the Delta rule. The enforcing rule, hence, is as a learning rule at least as well suited as the Delta rule, provided that one takes only low values of c.

We shall discuss the methodological questions raised in Section 4.1 below when we have shown the applications of the enforcing rule to other types of learning. Therefore, we just briefly describe the possible application of the enforcing rule to supervised learning networks with three or more layers.

We mentioned above that the difference δ_j between output and target neurons can be applied only to connections between the output layer and the next layer. If this is the input layer then rules like the delta rule or the enforcing rule are sufficient. If there is at least another layer – a "hidden" one – then an additional procedure is necessary to compute the changing of the weight values between the hidden layer and the input one. The most frequently used rule is the Back Propagation rule (see above Section 3.2), which we show again as a reminder:

$$\delta_j = \begin{cases} f_j'(net_j)(t_j - o_j) \text{ if } j \text{ is an output neuron} \\ f_j'(net_j) \sum_k (\delta_k w_{ik}) \text{ if } j \text{ is a neuron from the hidden layer} \end{cases} \qquad (9)$$

The first line of the equation is practically identical with the Delta rule; the second line describes the computation of the new weight values between the hidden layer and the input one. The formula is basically an application of the so-called gradient descent procedure, which is a well-known mathematical procedure in physics and chemistry for computing values in proportion to known ones, in this case the changing rates of values between output and hidden layer.

There are serious doubts if the processes in the brain factually operate according to this rather complicated formula (cf. McLeod et al. loc. cit.). We therefore expanded our enforcing rule to the case of three layered networks

$$\delta_j = \begin{cases} \Delta w_{ij} = c * (1 - w(t))\delta_j \text{ if } j \text{ is an output neuron} \\ \Delta w_{ij} = c * (1 - w(t))\delta_j /n \text{ if } j \text{ is a neuron from the hidden layer} \end{cases} \qquad (10)$$

and n is an integer.

As in the case of the learning rate c the suited values of n must be experimentally found out. We started first experiments with n = 2 and n = 3. The results look promising but are very preliminary. Confirmed results will be published in due time but it seems that it is least principally possible to substitute the rather complicated Back Propagation rule by a much simpler version of the enforcing rule schema.

4.2.2 Reinforcement Learning: Of Mice and Men[7]

Reinforcement learning may be understood as a "weaker" form of supervised learning. The learner gets an immediate feed back from his environment but only in the general form "better", "worse" or "no significant changes". In the simplest form of feed back the learner only gets the information "right" or "wrong". Such rather informal feedback is characteristic for a lot of factual learning processes, especially if the learning process is not institutionalized. Yet even in institutionalized learning processes the feedback frequently is given just in the way of reinforcement learning. According to our own practice as university lecturers students very often complain that they only get such a very general feed back that does not help them much to improve their learning results.

Outside the field of individual learning biological evolution can be understood as a vast enterprise of reinforcement learning. There is no goal in biological evolution and the evolving species only get their feedback in form of "better or worse adjusted" or "fitter or not" respectively. Accordingly, simulation of reinforcement learning is not only used in neuro-informatics but also for example in the domain of evolutionary algorithms like genetic algorithms or in the domain of simulated annealing. The fitness function (the mathematically expressed feed back, see above Section 3.2) in the case of evolutionary algorithms or the objective function in the case of simulated annealing usually only informs the system if its performances become better or worse or if they stagnate.[8]

The most famous learning rule for reinforcement learning is the so-called Hebb rule:

If w_{ij} is the weight of the connection between the neurons i and j and if Δw_{ij} represents the measure of the variation of w_{ij}, then

$$\Delta w_{ij} = \eta * a_j * o_i. \tag{11}$$

η is again the so called learning rate, which can be determined by a user, a_j is the activation value of the receiving neuron and o_i is the output of the sending neuron. In other words, the efficiency of the sending cell or neuron respectively is increased by the increasing of the weight value w_{ij}; accordingly the respective weight value can be decreased.

---

[7]In honor, of course, to John Steinbeck, although he certainly had no idea of neural networks and learning rules.

[8]Sometimes reinforcement learning is defined in another manner: the learning system constructs by itself an inner picture or model of the desired goal. The learning results, i.e. the output after each variation of the weight matrix, are then compared with the goal. A detailed description of this procedure give Jordan and Rummelhart (2002) who call this "distal learning". In this article we only use the definition of reinforcement learning given above.

It must be noted, by the way, that the Hebbian learning rule may also be used for self-organized learning in cases where the learning system gets no feed back, although with greater difficulty than the application of the enforcing for this learning type (see below).

The analog to the Hebb rule for reinforcement learning is simply the enforcing rule schema itself, which we show as a reminder:

$$w_{ij}(t + 1) = w_{ij}(t) \pm \Delta w_{ij} \text{ with } \Delta w_{ij} = c \text{ (constant) and } 0 \le c \le 1. \qquad (12)$$

$$w_{ij}(t + 1) = w_{ij}(t), \text{ if } w_{ij}(t) \ge 1 - \Delta w_{ij}. \qquad (13)$$

Equation (13) is the stopping or threshold criterion. The more elegant version without a stopping criterion is

$$w(t + 1) = w(t) + c * (1 - w(t), \qquad (14)$$

and in the case of decreasing the weight values

$$\Delta w_{ij} = c * (-1 - w(t)). \qquad (15)$$

In the experiments described above in this section we used only the simple rule; the stopping criterion was not even needed. Comparisons with the Hebb rule used the version (14). The main difference between the enforcing rule and the Hebb rule is again that the Hebb rule always takes into account the activation values of several neurons, in this case both receiving and sending ones. The enforcing rule just generates a recursive sequence of values of Δw_{ij} without the consideration of any activation values.

First comparative experiments showed that the enforcing rule again is as efficient as the Hebb rule; the experiments were of the same type as those described in the preceding sections, i.e. the task for the networks was to reach a predefined target vector. Of course, the respective difference to the target vectors was not given to the networks. In contrast to the simulations described below the learning rules operated equally on all weight values. The results of these experiments are similar to those of the first experimental series with supervised learning: Experiments with small networks, i.e. networks with four or five neurons in the input and output layer showed that the enforcing rule with $c = 0.3$ or $c = 0.4$ was significantly faster than the Hebb rule; again such large c-values made successful learning impossible in the case of larger networks. In these cases $c = 0.1$ again is sufficient in order to make a network with the enforcing rule learn at least as efficient as the same network with the Hebb rule.

Such comparative experiments are always useful and necessary. Yet in order to demonstrate the practical applications of the enforcing rule we applied it to a famous example of reinforcement learning, namely the experiments in instrumental conditioning of training mice to learn the right way through a labyrinth (Skinner 1953). Because the mice only receives the information if a path selected by a mouse is the right one or not these experiments are the extreme case of reinforcement learning mentioned above. The mouse, as is well known, has no choice but to select paths through the labyrinth by trial and error.[9]

---

[9]Experiments and simulations with reinforcement learning are not frequently done with neural networks. That is another reason why we show the simulations of instrumental conditioning in detail.

Fig. 4.1 A mouse standing
before three entrances

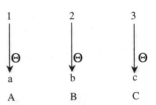

To demonstrate the general logic of applying rule (12) we just gave the artificial mouse a simple task, i.e. to learn the right entrance of three possible ones. Only one entrance is in the sense the right one that the mouse can find a piece of cheese in the cave behind the entrance.[10] The three entrances are denoted A, B, and C; only in the cave C the cheese can be found.

The mouse itself is modeled as a two-layered feed forward network with three input neurons 1, 2, and 3 and three output neurons a, b, and c. During the whole learning process of the mouse neuron 1 is only connected with neuron a, neuron 2 only with neuron b and neuron 3 only with neuron c. Figure 4.1 shows the structure of the "mouse-network".

The model makes the assumption that a sufficient activation of one output neuron, for example the neuron a, determines the mouse to select the according entrance, in this case entrance A. If more than one output neurons are sufficiently activated then the mouse has to select at random which entrance it will try. The activation function is again the linear one with

$$a_j = \sum_i w_{ij} * a_j \tag{16}$$

if a_j is the activation value of the receiving neuron and a_i are the activation values of the sending neurons.

The initial weight matrix of the mouse network is

	a	b	c
1	0.2	0	0
2	0	0.2	0
3	0	0	0.2

The matrix shows that only the connections from the input neurons to the output neurons directly below them are of importance. That is why we do not show the whole matrix that is a 6*6 matrix but just this part.

Θ is a threshold with a value $\Theta = 0.4$, i.e. an output neuron will only be activated if it receives an input ≥ 0.4. This value is arbitrarily determined as are the values of 0.2 in the weight matrix.

---

[10]The whole model was implemented as a JAVA program by two of our students Richard Kucharek and Volker Zischka. Interested readers may obtain it from the authors.

The experiment starts by giving the input neurons the value of 1. Because the mouse "sees" all entrances at the same time all input neurons must be activated with the same value. A simple calculation shows that no output neuron is activated because all outputs from the input layer are $1 * 0.2 = 0.2$. The artificial mouse does not act at all. Then the input is increased to 1.5 but again nothing is happening. Only the increasing of the activation of the input neurons to 2 generates an equal activation of all output neurons of 0.4.

The successive increasing of the activation values of the input neurons represents an increasing need of the mouse to search the cheese. In the case of instrumental conditioning the mouse knows that in one of the caves it may find cheese; that is not so in the case of operant conditioning. If the mouse is not very hungry – activation value of 1 – then it will do nothing because it does not know where to go. If the mouse becomes hungrier the activation values will increase until the output neurons are sufficiently activated to cause the mouse to act.

In our little experiment all output neurons are activated with the same value. The artificial mouse now has to select at random an entrance as in the real experiments. Suppose it selects entrance A where no cheese can be found. Because of that the weight value $w(1,a)$ is not changed. The same is the case with the selection of entrance B. Only entrance C brings the aspired success; as a result the learning rule (12) is applied with $\Delta w_{ij} = 0.1$ and hence $w(3,C) = 0.3$.

Now the experiment is repeated with again the initial activation values of the input neurons of 1 (the mouse is because of the successful getting of the cheese not very hungry). The output neurons are not activated and hence the growing hunger of the mouse generates an activation value of 1.5. Now only output neuron c is activated by a value of 0.45. Accordingly the mouse now immediately chooses entrance C and is rewarded with the cheese. As a result rule (12) is again applied to $w(3,c)$, which produces $w(3,c) = 0.4$.

Obviously now it is sufficient to activate the input neurons of the mouse with a value of 1. Because of the training process of the mouse neuron c is then immediately activated in contrast to the other output neurons. The mouse will always find the right way to entrance C – in other words, the mouse has learned its way to the cheese.

The result of the conditioning process is, as was reported from the real experiments, that the mouse will always at once select the right way. Yet of course the mouse does not "know" the way in a conscious meaning of the word. It just has developed a net topology that makes errors impossible as long as the mouse keeps this topology; the mouse literally *cannot err*. The Behaviorist psychologists just reported the fact that the mouse had learned to select always the right entrance; our simulation model gives an exact explanation for this fact. In a certain sense we now "understand" the mouse, namely we can give a plausible reason for its behavior: the changed behavior of the mouse is a direct consequence of the changed cognitive structure (see above Section 4.1 the definition of learning). We can express this also by saying that we understand the mouse by constructing a mental model of it and its learning process in the sense of Section 3.1.

A variant to the forms of conditioning by offering rewards is the conditioning by punishment, which can be applied to both instrumental and operant conditioning. Frequently this variant is, sad to say, even more successful than the offering of rewards (Skinner loc. cit.) in the sense that the probands – humans and animals alike – learned faster than with the offering of rewards. We simulated this variant with our model by starting with initial weight values $w(1,a) = w(2,b) = w(3,c) = 0.4$ and again $\Theta = 0.4$. All other weight values are, as in the former experiment, equal to zero and remain so. By starting with activation values of the input neuron of 1 all output neurons are activated and the mouse has again to select at random. The wrong selection of entrance A, by which the mouse gets punished, leads to the application of rule (12) but this time by subtracting, namely $\Delta w_{ij} = -0.1$. The same procedure is applied when the mouse again wrongly selects entrance B and hence $w(2,b) = w(1,a) = 0.3$. Only in the right case of entrance C $w(3,c)$ remains the same.

Now apparently another activation of the input neurons by 1 generates only the selection of entrance C – the mouse has learned one learning step faster than in the first experiment the right way. The successful simulation of these famous experiments gives strong evidence to the hypothesis that our little model has some empirical validity. To be sure, the fast learning by punishment was realized only by an appropriate selection of initial values for the threshold and the weights; our model demonstrates the general logic of the processes the mouse's brain has to perform by either getting a reward or a punishment.

In these simulations we certainly did not have a complex labyrinth. For the sake of clarity we just wanted to demonstrate how to apply the enforcing rule to a famous case of reinforcement learning. Yet the same procedure can be applied to such decision problems that are much more complex. Consider for example the task for the mouse to find the right way in the branching tree shown in Fig. 4.2:

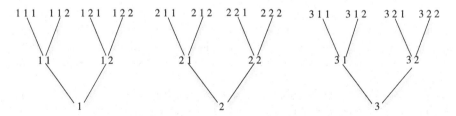

Fig. 4.2 Finding the right way in a branching tree

The starting points are 1, 2, and 3. When standing before the labyrinth the mouse has 18 possible paths. We assume that the cheese is in the cave 3 1 2. To solve this problem the learning network of the mouse has to be significantly larger than in the first examples. We omit the details of the implemented model and just give the general learning logic, which is in some sense an inversion of the learning process of the simple example; the mouse has, so to speak, to learn backwards:[11]

---

[11] The details can be looked up in the implemented model mentioned in footnote 10.

The mouse again has to search according to trial and error for the right way to the cheese. All paths ending in a blind alley do not change the weight values of the according connections.[12] Only if the mouse has finally found the right path from the second level (gate 31) to entrance 312 and hence to the cheese the connection weights from neuron 31 to neuron 312 are increased by applying the enforcing rule. Suppose that in this case only one increasing of the right connection is sufficient to activate neuron 312 in contrast to all other eight neurons on the third level. Accordingly the path 31–312 is remembered. When the mouse has to start again it does still not know which path it should select from its starting point to the first three entrances 1, 2, and 3. Hence it selects again at random until it finds the gate 31. Because the mouse remembers that it should go from 31 to 312 it will find the cheese. "Remembering" means of course again that only the activation of neuron 31 will activate the neuron 312 that represents the right way to the cheese. Then the learning procedure is repeated until the weight value from neuron 3 to neuron 31 is sufficiently increased. It is now evident that the mouse, as in the simpler case, practically cannot err any more because it will, determined by its cognitive topology, always at once select the right path 3 − 31 − 312. The same learning procedure can obviously be applied to even more complex branching trees.

The simple models and the more complex one operate with certain thresholds. Although thresholds are neuro-biologically quite plausible they always have some ad hoc character, in particular when determining its values *before* the start of the experiments (see above for the case of the stopping criterion in the enforcing rule). To be sure, it is no problem to include the variation of threshold values in the training process; any textbook on neural networks at least mentions this possibility. But it is not only of technical interest if learning processes can be simulated without the introduction of thresholds. That is why we constructed another model for the learning of labyrinth paths without a threshold.

The network is the same as in the simple experiments but without the threshold; the learning procedure is also the same. We start with rather weak connection values $w(1,a) = w(2,b) = w(3,c) = 0.1$. Then by an initial activation of the input neurons with 1 all output neurons are equally activated with 0.1. Accordingly the mouse has to choose at random for the right path and only the connection weight for the right path will be increased. By continuously increasing the "right" connection weight $w(3,c)$ the activation value A_c of neuron c becomes significantly larger than those of the other output neurons; these remain at 0.1. Let us call the difference $D = A_c - A_a$ or $A_c - A_b$ respectively an "attention parameter": If D is sufficiently large then the mouse will *practically* pay no attention to the wrong entrances A and B but will again choose the right entrance. One can interpret D also in the sense that it is a measure for the probability of selecting the right path: The strength of the output activation values determines the probability, which neuron will produce a reaction. If we assume that this model is neuro-biologically plausible then it is of course an

---

[12]More correctly speaking all neural connections that represent a blind alley do not change their according weight values.

empirical question how large D must be in order to force the mouse into the right direction.[13]

In the first experiments, i.e. networks with thresholds, the mouse did make no mistakes after the training. In the second experiments without thresholds the mouse sometimes did make errors although only very few ones, even with large D-values. Yet these very few errors – about 2% in hundreds of simulation runs – only occurred by learning with a reward, i.e. by increasing the respective weight values. After the training with decreasing weight values, i.e. by learning with punishments, the mouse made no mistakes at all. The reason for this asymmetry, which is rather irritating on a first sight, is simply that in the first case the probability for selecting the *right* path p_D will increase but usually not to $p_D = 1$. The second case means the decreasing of a probability p_D to select the *wrong* entrances; simple calculations show that in this case the probability will become $p_D = 0$ and hence the mouse literally *must* select the right path.

These simulations of famous Behaviorist experiments not only demonstrate that and how the enforcing rule can be applied to the case of reinforcement learning. The simulations also showed that the methodically substantiated Behaviorist reduction to treat learning systems as black boxes is not necessary any more. The "inner being" of mice obviously can be modeled and analyzed in simulation experiments. In other words, the black boxes become transparent by introducing hypothetical geometrical models and by confirming them in simulation experiments. To be sure, the models are still and always hypothetical ones in the sense of the frequently mentioned unavoidability of conventionalism. Yet by introducing such models we have indeed a chance to understand the mice, i.e. to give reasons how the learning process of the mice is performed and why the mice as a result always find the right way. That is certainly more than nothing.

To be sure, understanding the conditioning processes of mice and the resulting behavior seems far away from the task to understand human beings. Yet it is certainly possible to apply this simulation of reinforcement learning to more complex forms. There can be no doubt, despite the (in)famous critique of, e.g., Chomsky (Chomsky 1959) of Behaviorism that Behaviorist learning models can be applied to many cases of human learning and its resulting behavior. The behavior, for example, to stop at a red traffic light that is automatically performed is certainly the result of a conditioning process during the lectures to learn car driving. The equally automatic obeying of a private to the orders of the sergeant is understandable the same way, namely the result of processes of conditioning – operant or instrumental. Behaviorism is certainly not the universally applicable learning theory as for example Skinner believed.[14] But it is a very useful theoretical tool to understand a lot of

---

[13]Here a similar assumption is made as in the models with semantical networks where those neurons represent the meaning of a message whose final activation values are the largest.

[14]Chomsky was right when he pointed out that a theory of language acquisition could not be obtained by using only Behaviorist assumptions. But he was certainly wrong when he suggested that this would make Behaviorism generally useless.

human everyday behavior. Getting rid of the black box paradigm makes Behaviorist learning models still more useful.

In the examples we demonstrated that the enforcing rule, of course, was applied only to certain pairs of neurons, either those that represent a learning success or conversely only those that represent a learning failure. That is not so, for example, with learning rules of the supervised learning type where usually the learning rules are applied to the whole weight matrix at once. But the necessary selection of "significant" connections that are to be changed is no peculiarity of the enforcing rule but a direct consequence of the characteristics of that particular model. The information "right" or "wrong" refers in this model only to certain connections and hence forces such a selection. According selections had to be made if the Hebbian rule were applied to this model too. If we had used networks with more than two layers then a selection of, e.g., triplets of neurons must have be distinguished and so on. Certainly other models for reinforcement learning can be constructed by applying the respective learning rule(s) to the whole weight matrix at once. That is the way we performed the experiments to compare the enforcing rules with the delta rule and the Hebb rule. Yet learning rules in the case of reinforcement learning may frequently be applied only in a problem specific manner. Perhaps that is one of the reasons why, as far as we know, many more examples of supervised learning are to be found than of reinforcement learning, although human learning processes are without doubt at least equally frequent supervised and reinforced.

4.2.3 Classical Conditioning: Pavlov's Dog Revisited

Supervised and reinforcement learning processes both need feed back from their respective environment, either in terms of the distance between the target and the factual output or in form of "better", "worse", "right" or "wrong". Learning processes in institutions like schools or universities usually are either supervised or reinforcement learning; the respective human teachers are responsible for the necessary immediate feedback. In contrast to these forms of learning are those where the environment certainly is needed to supply the learning system with information – signals, messages – as the basis for the learning process but where the environment does not act as a correcting authority. Learning processes like classical conditioning and self-organized learning are performed with externally given information but without feedback. The result of such learning processes is generated only by the application of an internal dynamics.

A very famous example of learning without immediate environmental feedback, although it is usually not called this way, is the well-known form of classical conditioning, the starter of all Behaviorist learning theories and experiments. Consider one of the most famous experiments of that type, namely the dog of Pavlov (see above Section 1.3.3). The dog received, as is well known, simultaneously the perceptions of food and of the ringing of a bell. Because of the food perception the dog produced saliva. After these two signals were given to the dog several times it was sufficient to ring only the bell to cause to dog to produce saliva. In other words, the temporal coupling of the two signals changed the cognitive or perception structure respectively of the dog so that the perception of the bell caused the same effects as the perception of the food.

Obviously this famous experiment is a typical case of learning without immediate environmental feedback. The environment, in this case the experimenter, produces signals and by doing this causes a certain initial state of the system "dog". But the environment does not act as corrector, not even in the simple way as in the examples of reinforcement learning by the information "right" or "wrong". By just repeating the generation of the initial state the dog system changes its internal structure according to its own logic. The dog receives a reward not even after the learning process but just acts according to its varied structure.

We simulated this form of conditioning by constructing a recurrent network. It consists of an input layer and the output layer but in contrast to the networks used in the mouse experiments it is not a simple feed forward net. The input and the output layer consist of four neurons. The network before the beginning of the conditioning process is shown in Fig. 4.3:

Fig. 4.3 Model of Pavlov' dog before the conditioning process

Signal 1 = food

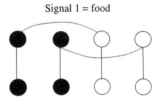

On first sight the network looks like the feed forward nets of the mouse experiments. Yet there is one decisive difference because there are connections between the input neurons with an initial weight value of zero (dotted line).[15] The two left neurons represent the reception of food signals and the two right neurons the reception of acoustic signals like bell ringing. The two left neurons of the output layer represent the reaction to food signals, namely the production of saliva; the two right neurons on this layer represent the reaction to the bell, namely listening or perhaps also barking. The black color of the two left input neurons mean that only they are activated if the signal "food available" is produced. Accordingly only the two output neurons are activated that are connected with the activated input neurons. In this state, hence, the network operates in the way that a food signal produces the activation of the two left input neurons, which in turn activate the "saliva" output neurons. A bell signal would activate the according bell neurons and by them the listening neurons. No saliva, of course, is produced by the bell signal.

The beginning of the conditioning process means the activation of all input neurons at the same time with the value of 1. The dog produces saliva as well as listening activities according to the respective signals. The enforcing rule is then applied,

---

[15]The network, therefore, is a simple version of a recurrent network.

namely to the connection between the bell input neurons and the food input neurons, either after the first simultaneous activation of all input neurons or after a certain number of iterated activations. The Δw_{ij} value is 0.1. For this rather simple example we again use the "basis version" (12) of the enforcing rule to demonstrate the general logic. Because both signals are perceived at the same time the initial weight values of zero are increased in both directions. The new values are now $w_{ij} = 0.1$. As the threshold value is 0.4, nothing happens with regard to the saliva neurons if the bell signal is perceived alone. This training procedure is repeated until the weight value is increased to 0.5. Because the threshold condition is in this case that only activation values A_i with $A_i > \Theta$ will activate the receiving neurons now the food input neurons are activated by the bell input neurons too. Obviously in this phase of the training process it will be enough to activate only the bell neurons in order to activate the saliva neurons – the conditioning process has been successfully finished. Note that as in the simulations of mice learning only certain connections are varied, in this case the connections of the input layer. The reason for this restriction of weight variations is of course that the input layer connections represent the simultaneous receiving of the two signals of food and bell (Fig. 4.4).

If we assume as in our model that the horizontal connection in the input layer is a bi-directional one then the same training process should produce listening activities when the dog perceives food signals. As far as we know there exists no information if Pavlov or one of his followers has observed such reactions. Probably they were not interested in the question if the conditioning process works in both directions. To be sure, it would be easy to reproduce these experiments in order to confirm or to refute the assumption of bi-directional connections in the input layer. If the connection works only in the direction from bell neurons to food neurons one may explain this by assuming that food signals are certainly much more important for a dog than bell signals; after all, the saliva reaction to food perceptions is a biologically, i.e. genetically based one, which is probably not so in the case of bell signals.

According to the principle of Hebb the associative strength between two cells decreases if only one is externally activated for a certain time. Because of this the dog "forgets" the production of saliva after hearing only the bell for some time. In our model this simply means the decreasing of the weight values, namely applying again the enforcing rule with $\Delta w_{ij} = -0.1$. One immediately sees that only one decreasing is sufficient: the dog does not produce saliva any more when hearing only the bell. If one in addition assumes that the weight values in the input layer

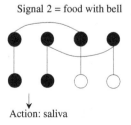
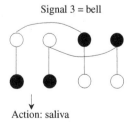

Fig. 4.4 The network after the conditioning process; the vertical connections are not changed

Signal 2 = food with bell   Signal 3 = bell

Action: saliva   Action: saliva

do not become zero again but remain constant, e.g., at the value of 0.2, then we can explain why the dog learns the "saliva reaction" to the bell much faster when it is trained again. The enforcing rule, so to speak, must be applied only three times and not five times in order to restore the initial reactions to bell and food. The fact demonstrated in the real experiments that the real dog indeed learns faster the second time seems to confirm the validity of our model and the according assumptions.

As in the case of the mice we may say that we now indeed understand why Pavlov's dog reacted the way it did: The changed behavior is a result from the changed cognitive structure, which in turn was produced by the conditioning process. Yet only because we understood the way the structure was changed and the new generated topology we really understand why the dog behaves the way it does. Simply stating a S-R relation is no understanding at all.

Mathematically possible is also another network model, namely an also simple feed forward net that is shown in Fig. 4.5:

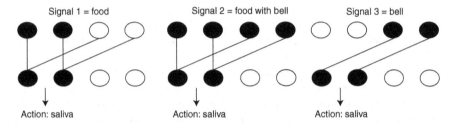

Fig. 4.5 Second model of the dog

The training process via application of the enforcing rule is the same as in the first simulation with the variation that only the weight values from the bell neurons in the input layer to the saliva neurons in the output layer are increased. Again the artificial dog produces saliva when only hearing the bell after five training steps. The forgetting process by decreasing the according weight values is also done in the same manner as in the first model. The results hence are the same although the models are topologically different.

Although both models are equivalent with respect to results the first model certainly is biologically more plausible. When taking into regard the Hebb principle then the weight increasing of the connections between the neurons in the input layer is a direct consequence. The second model makes the rather unrealistic assumption that the conditioning process leads to a strengthening of the connections between the bell neurons and the saliva ones. It is of course possible that such strengthening effects occur but according to the Hebb principle the first model makes more sense.[16]

By the way, the speaking of "salvia neurons" and "listening neurons" is of course only an abbreviation. The output neurons (of the real dog) certainly produce no

---

[16]We proposed the second model ourselves in Klüver and Klüver (2007), but now we think otherwise.

saliva but send their activation signals to those parts of the organism where the saliva is factually produced. Accordingly the listening neurons send signals to, e.g., the ears or those muscle regions where ear movements are generated.

The production of saliva is due to the simultaneous production of acid in the stomach. If the conditioned dog continues to produce acid without digesting food then the stomach in the long run becomes injured. Therefore, it is also possible that the dog forgets because of negative feed back from its stomach. It would be easy to implement such forgetting processes via feed back from the environment. By concentrating only to the Hebb principle where no feedback is taken into regard we omitted this possibility.

To be sure, we do not claim that the neural structures of the dog and the mice after the conditioning processes are *exactly* like that of one of the models. Yet these models can and must be interpreted as a biologically plausible hypothesis that explain, for example, why the real mice did not err after the conditioning process and why in the case of the dog after forgetting its conditioning a reconditioning is much faster than the initial conditioning process. The explanatory power of these models gives some evidence that not only the experimental results of the simulations but also the logic of the models are at least in general agreement with biological reality. The setting up of such a hypothesis via the construction and validation of suited models is then, methodologically speaking, nothing else than the according procedure known in the theoretical and mathematical sciences for a long time.

We mentioned in the preceding section that of course the importance of Behaviorist learning models does not only refer to mice or, in this case, to dogs. There are numerous cases where social behavior can and must be explained as the result of some conditioning processes, either of a classical, an instrumental or an operant one (cf. the marketing example in the Chapter 5). Therefore, the simple examples, namely simulations of well-known Behaviorist experiments just are representative examples, namely a proof how it is possible to model and hence understand such learning processes and their results in humans and animals.[17]

4.2.4 Self-Organized Learning: Of Juvenile Delinquents and Literary Murders

Self-organized learning is performed like classical conditioning without environmental feedback but is certainly much more complex than the comparatively simple forms of classical conditioning. To be sure, in some general sense all types of learning are self-organized because the environmental signals and feedback on the one hand do explicitly order *how* the changes of the weight matrices have to be done

---

[17]By the way, the interest in classical conditioning is still very strong. At present American biologists for example try to condition certain fishes to return to a cave when hearing a specific signal. The idea is to condition the young fishes, let them free in order that they feed themselves in the free ocean and catch them again when the fish is big enough to eat it. Source: Der Spiegel (Germany's most important News Magazine) 44, 2008.

but these changes on the other hand always follow the same logic internal to the networks. Taking that into mind one can say that supervised and reinforcement learning processes take place by processes of internal self-organization *and* by the corrections of an external "teacher".

As in classical conditioning no teacher is needed in the case of "pure" self-organized learning. The rather ambiguous concept of self-organization usually means that a self-organized system organizes its own dynamics only by internal rules; environmental signals may force the system into another trajectory but the environment does not influence the internal logic of the system. Therefore, frequently environmental signals are interpreted as "disturbances" or "noise" with respect to the system because they force the system into another trajectory. A typical example of a self-organized system in this sense is that of cellular automata (CA): a CA-dynamics is only determined by local rules of interaction between the different cells; external influences just mean the generation of another trajectory by the CA without changing the rules of interaction. In other words, self-organized system generate their successive states only according to their internal rules, although also in dependency of external given initial states and/or external interventions (cf. Klüver 2000).

Systems that are able to learn in a self-organized manner basically follow the same logic. As "learning" means the variation of a cognitive structure, which in turn leads to different behavior, self-organized learning is the variation of a cognitive structure without correcting external signals and only by some internal criteria. To be sure, environment also plays a role because each learning process must take place on the basis of external information, for example visual perceptions. In addition self-organized learning processes may go into the wrong direction. In that case sooner or later some external authority has to correct the results and give the learning system information about the respective error. But also in that case the self-organized learning process again takes place only according to its own internal criteria by substituting the former information by the new ones. Self-organized learning systems, hence, not only generate their successive states according to their internal rules but also the succession of their cognitive structures again only according to their own internal logic, i.e. their learning rules or meta rules respectively.[18]

Consider for example a child that has constructed a semantical net about different kinds of animals. Each unit in the net represents a type of animal, for example dog, cat and fish. Each animal the child perceives is categorized by its similarity to one of the units. When this child sees a dolphin it probably categorizes this perception as "fish" because the dolphin is much more similar to a fish than to a dog or cat. The parents may correct the child by telling him that a dolphin is not a fish. The child then has to enlarge its semantical net by adding another unit, namely animals that look like fish but are no fish. Yet the reconstruction of the semantical net just follows

---

[18]In the first chapter we defined adaptive systems by the duality of rules and meta rules. The concept of self-organized learning shows that adaptive behavior can occur via corrections from the environment, as in the case of biological evolution, and without such environmental corrections.

the same logic as the former construction of the old net. We shall come back below to the construction of semantical nets as a typical example of self-organized learning.

We demonstrated the usefulness of the general enforcing rule schema with the help of examples of well-known conditioning experiments. But of course the learning processes by conditioning processes are rather simple ones. To demonstrate the capability of the general schema of the enforcing rule in the case of self-organized learning we show two other examples. The first one is the simulation of a certain real socialization process, in which a specific world-view emerged.[19]

The problematic hero of our little story is a male youth with the fictitious name of Tom. He told one of our former students his biography in a qualitative interview; at the time of this interview (2002) he was 17 years old. At this time Tom lived in a hostel for deviant youths in a large town at the Western part of Germany. Because of some trouble with the police and because Tom did not accept his mother the youth authorities decided to send Tom into the hostel. The father had left the family several years ago; Tom has two younger sisters. The interviewer acted at the same time as educator in the hostel.

Tom's world-view at the time of the interview is a rather simple one that can be described with the term of *Social Darwinism*: The strong ones must lead and the weaker ones have to obey. In particular, women "by nature" (Tom) are weak and men are strong. Therefore, women have to be submissive, perform only "womanly" activities like cooking, cleaning, and caring for the children. Men on the other hand have to tell the women what to do, even beat them if the women do not obey, and have to earn the money for the family. Hence the social world is dichotomously divided in "real" men and "real" women. If women perform "manly" duties like earning money and telling men what to do they are no real women; accordingly men are no real men if they care for the household and obey the orders of women. The fact that in the hostel there are female educators who give orders to young men like Tom and male educators who cook and take part in the cleaning of the hostel causes him to despise those educators. The male educators, for example, are in the world-view of Tom more women in male disguise than real men.

Tom developed his world-view, according to his own narrative, in his early childhood when he adored his authoritative father, who sometimes even beat his wife and frequently got involved into brawls. The father was a real man and the mother, a very submissive person, was a real woman. Because the social milieu the family lived in confirmed such a world-view, consisting mainly of similar men and women, Tom took the father as a positive model despite the fact that he was a social failure: He had only jobs as an unskilled worker and neglected his responsibility towards his family by leaving it when Tom was about 10 years old.

When we constructed a first simulation of the emergence of Tom's world-view we took the learning theory of Bandura for a theoretical basis (Bandura 1986). This theory assumes that the learner performs the important parts of his social learning in a self-organized manner (although Bandura does not use this term): The learner takes certain persons in his social milieu as "models", which are an impersonation

---

[19]This example can be looked up in more detail in Klüver and Klüver (2007).

of "right" persons in specific ways. Accordingly the learner tries to become like the model. Frequently there are also negative models; in this case the learner of course tries not to become like this model. It is obvious that in the case of Tom the father was seen as a positive model and the mother as a negative one.

The learning theory of Bandura has striking similarities with the cognitive theory of prototypes of Rosch (Gardner 1985; Lakoff 1987; Rosch 1973). This empirically well-grounded theory assumes, as is well known, that the cognitive assimilating of perception is not done by constructing sharply divided categories but by taking some examples of a set of perceptions as "prototypes", i.e. as representative samples for a set of similar perceptions. For example, certain objects that are classified as "dog" are categorized this way because of their similarity with the respective prototype of a dog. The choice of such prototypes is of course dependent on a certain cultural milieu and personal experiences. In Germany, for example, many people would take a German Sheppard as a prototype of a dog; in China probably more people would select a Pekinese. New perceptions are then "clustered" around the prototype according to their respective degree of similarity to the prototype; the prototype is defined as the center of its respective cluster.

In a methodical aspect the concept of prototypes may be also compared with Weber's concept of ideal type (cf. Chapter 2). Although an ideal type in Weber's sense is not necessarily an empirical category like a German Sheppard, an ideal type also can be understood as the center of a cluster that contains all empirical representations of the ideal type. As in the visualizations described below an empirical object like a factual early Calvinist entrepreneur is the more similar to the ideal type the more it is placed near the center of the cluster and vice versa.

Tom's father and mother, hence, can be interpreted in this sense as prototypes in a normative manner. Perceptions of other adult persons are classified according to their similarity to the parental prototypes. In particular, persons who have the physical aspects of men or women but socially do not act according to the prototypical expectations of Tom must be classified in the way that they belong to the clusters of both prototypes or are at the edge of a certain cluster. The experiences in the hostel taught Tom that the boundary between men and women, as he sees them, is not a strict division of these categories but that certain educators – and other persons – belong "more or less" to the female or the male cluster respectively.[20]

We performed our first simulations of Tom's socio-cognitive development by using a certain Kohonen Feature Map or a Self Organizing Map (SOM) respectively. The Kohonen Maps are certainly the best known and most used neural networks in the field of the modeling of self-organized learning. There are different types of SOM, according to the particular task they shall perform. We used the version of Ritter and Kohonen (1989) that was explicitly constructed for classification tasks.

The Ritter-Kohonen SOM operates, as all versions of SOM, on the Winner Takes All principle as learning rule. Roughly speaking, one neuron is selected as a "winner

---

[20]"More or less" are mathematically speaking concepts of "Fuzzy Logic". Therefore, it is possible to model Tom's biography with fuzzy-based models too. In our opinion it is not by chance that, e.g., the linguist Lakoff (loc. cit.) used both prototype theory and fuzzy logic.

neuron" and other neurons are clustered around it.

$$w_{ij}(t+1) = w_{ij} + \eta(o_i - w_{ij}(t)), \qquad (17)$$

In contrast to other versions of SOM that are used, e.g., for optimization tasks the Ritter-Kohonen SOM operates not only with a weight matrix but also on a "semantical matrix" (this term is our name for it). To illustrate this matrix we show an example of Ritter and Kohonen (loc. cit.):

	eagle	cow	duck	lion
flies	1	0	1	0
eatsmeat	1	0	0	1
layseggs	1	0	1	0
mammal	0	1	0	1

The matrix obviously is a kind of adjacency matrix. A 1 means that a certain characteristic belongs to a perceived object; a 0 accordingly that it does not. Cows do not fly and eagles eat flesh. The Ritter-Kohonen SOM now orders the objects, i.e. the animals according to their similarities. This is done by visualizing the objects on a two-dimensional plane.

When using this technique for the simulation of Tom's development we first defined the paternal prototypes by their values in a semantical matrix and afterwards added other persons into the matrix. The characteristic vectors for the persons are rather large (15 components); that is why we show only a part of it:

	father	mother	man2	woman2
strong	1	0	1	0
weeps	0	1	0	1
fights	1	0	1	0
cooks	0	1	1	1

Note that man2 has not only male characteristics but also a female one. Father and mother are pure prototypes for men and women; woman2 is in this respect identical with the mother but differs from her in some individual characteristics like size and hair color. The reason for these characteristics is of course that social actors may be identical with respect to their behavior but always differ in personal attributes. These individual characteristics are not shown in this part of the matrix but belong to the complete one.

After the insertion of the matrix the SOM generated several visualizations, according to the number of inserted persons. We just show one example of the formation of gender specific clusters; it can be seen that one man is classified by the SOM not as a "real" man but as a borderline case between the female and the male cluster (man4 who had some female attributes like, e.g. cooking). Man0 and woman0 are the father and the mother respectively. Other results of the SOM runs can be looked up in Klüver and Klüver (2007).

Fig. 4.6 Gender specific clusters with a not genuine man

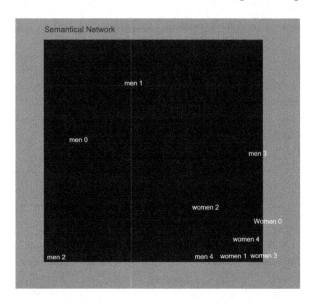

A SOM (not only the Ritter-Kohonen type) is a very powerful model for the simulation of self-organized learning but it has certain disadvantages: in particular it is rather complicated, it is for this reason biologically not very plausible, its results depend in some aspects on the order of inputs, and it does not make the important difference between the learning process proper and the process of information processing based on the results of the respective learning process. We shall deal with these disadvantages below.

In order to overcome these disadvantages we applied the enforcing rule to the example of Tom; as in the case of Pavlov's dog we used only the simple version (12) of the rule. The constructed network is a recurrent one together with the enforcing rule; because the according learning process is self-organized we call this type of network a Self Enforcing Network (SEN). Strictly speaking the term SEN describes not only such recurrent networks as will be shown but also for example feed forward networks together with the enforcing rule if they are used for the modeling of self-organized learning. But in this text we use the term SEN only for recurrent networks. In other words, the SEN described in this section is an Interactive Network (IN) coupled with the enforcing rule. IN are recurrent networks that are usually not trained but used for the analysis of logical relations (see above Chapters 2 and 3). The coupling of IN with the enforcing rule will demonstrate that the resulting system is very well suited for the modeling of self-organized learning. Usually the activation flow is determined by the linear activation function, described above (Equation 16).[21]

---

[21] The development of this SEN-system was sponsored by the *Deutsche Telekom*. We used it for the forecast of probable market chances of new cell phones by applying the prototype approach.

To make the results of the SOM runs and the SEN runs immediately comparable we used for the SEN simulations the same semantical matrix. The number of neurons of the SEN is the number of inserted persons + the number of characteristics. In other words, in contrast to the SOM that operates with a semantical matrix *and* a different weight matrix in the case of a SEN the weight matrix is a direct transformation of the semantical matrix, namely with the enlarged number of neurons and with different weight values to those of the semantical matrix. At the beginning of the simulation all weight values of the SEN are equal to zero.

The enforcing rule now was applied the following way:

Only the weight values w_{cp} are changed when c is a characteristic (attribute) and p a person. All connections w_{pp} and w_{cc} remain zero. In addition, if two or more persons are defined as prototypes P_i then their connections are changed to –0.1. As usual we define $w(t+1) = w(t) + \Delta w$. Then we obtain

$$\Delta w = 0.1, \text{ if } v_{scp} = 1;$$
$$\Delta w = 0 \text{ else.} \tag{18}$$

v_{scp} is the according value in the semantical matrix, i.e. the relation between a characteristic and a person.

In analogy to the learning rate η in the Delta rule or the Hebbian rule one can add a cue validity factor cv into the enforcing rule. The cue validity is a measure how important certain attributes are for membership in a given category (Rosch and Mervis 1975). For example, the attribute of four legs is not very typical for the category "dog" because a lot of other animals also have four legs. In contrast the attribute "barking" is very typical for a dog as no other animals make such noises. Then Equation (18) becomes

$$\Delta w = cv * 0.1, \text{ if } v_{scp} = 1;$$
$$\Delta w = 0 \text{ else.} \tag{19}$$

In the simulations we did so far it usually was sufficient to take $cv = 1$.

When training a SEN for the task of classification purposes by applying the prototype theory as in this case, two procedures are possible:

On the one hand the semantical matrix contains all prototypes, the objects that shall be ordered according to their similarities to the prototypes, and the attributes or characteristics respectively that the prototypes define. The semantical matrix then contains all the respective values for the relations between the attributes and the prototypes and objects. This procedure is the same as the construction of a semantical matrix for the Ritter-Kohonen SOM; a part of it for the case of Tom was shown above. When using a Ritter-Kohonen SOM this procedure is necessary.

The SEN in contrast may also be trained in a much simpler way. One has only to construct the semantical matrix with the prototypes and their respective attributes, which is in the case of Tom a matrix containing two objects and 15 attributes. The according matrix then consists only of $2 * 15 = 30$ components. If one would model the classification of, e.g., 10 persons with also 15 attributes via the first procedure the necessary matrix must contain 150 components. For the sake of simplicity we mostly used the second procedure.

In the training process for the "Tom-SEN" we applied the rule (19) only once. The results showed that this was already sufficient for a successful ordering of the different persons with respect to the prototypes. Before the beginning of the simulation runs all activation values of the neurons are equal to zero.

The IN and hence also the SEN is started by "externally activating" several neurons, i.e. increasing their values to, for example, 0.1. The simulations ends when the network has reached an attractor, which should be a point attractor. Because the task of the trained SEN is the classification of certain objects, in this case different persons with respect to specific prototypes, a new person that shall be classified is defined by its attributes. Therefore, only those neurons are externally activated that represent the attributes characteristic for the new person. The question to which prototype the new person belongs is answered by the size of the activation values of the prototype neurons. The stronger the prototype is activated the more the new person belongs to it and vice versa.

Usually a new person is not identical with one prototype but contains either personal attributes other than the respective prototype or even attributes that are characteristic for another prototype. In the second case both prototypes will be finally activated and, as mentioned, the membership of the new person is measured by the relative similarity of its final activation values to those of the prototypes. In such cases the new person belongs more to one category than to the other but not either to one or to the other category. This is just the prototype categorization described by Rosch. For example, if after the insertion of a new person by externally activating the according attribute neurons the prototype "man" is activated only half of the value of the value of prototype "woman" then the new person belongs to 66% to the category "woman" and only to 34% to the category of "man". "Woman" and "man" are here, of course, not primarily biological categories but in the more important sense social ones.

Because we wanted to compare the results of the SEN directly with those of the SOM we implemented a new visualization technique. This is as a picture – although not in the applied algorithm – rather similar to that of the SOM, namely by placing the different objects including the prototypes on a two-dimensional grid. A user of our SEN program has the option between two different techniques. The first one, which is used in the example of Tom, starts with placing the prototypes – in this case two – on distant places of the grid. Therefore this procedure is called a prototype-centered modus.[22] The distance between the prototypes is arbitrarily chosen but must be large enough to place the new persons in relation to the prototypes on the grid. If the new person has attributes from both prototypes then the new person must be placed between them. When a new person is inserted into the program it gets a name chosen by the user and the final activation values of those attribute neurons are computed that belong either to the first prototype or to the second. Then the distance d of the new person NP to one prototype is calculated according to

---

[22]The second procedure is a so-called input vector centered modus that we used for example for marketing purposes.

$$d(P, \text{NP}) = \left(\sum_j A_{jp} \right) \div n - \left(\sum_i A_{i\text{NP}} \right) \div m, \tag{20}$$

if $A_{i\text{NP}}$ are the final activation values of those attribute neurons that the new person NP has in common with the prototype, if there are m such attributes, if A_{ip} are the final activation values of the attribute neurons of the prototype, and if n attributes belong to the prototype. The distance to the second prototype is accordingly computed. Then the selected name of the new person is placed on the grid according to the distance to both prototypes. If, for example, the distance of the new person NP to the first prototype is again half of the distance to the second one, then obviously NP will be placed at one of the two points of intersection of two circles with P_1 and P_2 as centers and with the radius $d(P_1, \text{NP})$ and $d(P_2, \text{NP}) = 2 * d(P_1, \text{NP})$ respectively. Subsequently the other persons of the simulation of Tom's worldview are inserted the same way, i.e., by externally activating the respective attribute neurons and by placing them on the grid.[23]

The final results are shown in Fig. 4.7:

Fig. 4.7 Categorizing different persons according to Tom's world-view (the SEN-version)

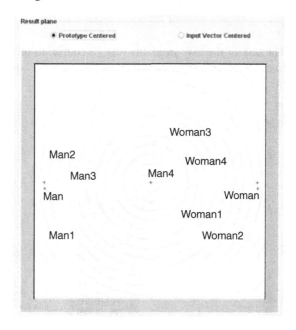

Despite the differences on first sight that partly are due to the different distances used in the SOM visualization (cf. Fig. 4.7) and the SEN one the results are sufficiently similar to call them equivalent. In other words, SEN and SOM apparently are equally well suited for the task to model such complex processes of self-organized

---

[23] Actually the visualization technique is a bit more complicated, in particular for taking into regard the construction of circles. Yet the formula above is sufficient to understand the basic logic of this visualization algorithm.

learning like the emergence of a cognitive world-view. Therefore, we have another case of two models that are very different in structure but nearly equal in results.

We compared the performances of the SOM and the SEN with the help of another example. It shows the solution of a literary murder puzzle by the two self-organizing networks; the respective story is "The Spanish Chest" by Agatha Christie.[24] The basic structure of the story is that there are six suspects, one victim, and four criteria to decide, which one of the suspects is the murderer. These criteria or categories respectively are "no alibi", "access to the murder weapon (a dagger)", "motive", and "knowledge about the exact place of the murder". Because a factual murderer must fulfill all four criteria we inserted into the SOM and the SEN a "fictitious murderer X" who was associated with all criteria. The according part of the semantical matrix then is

	no alibi	access	knowledge	motive
suspect				
murderer X	1	1	1	1
suspect				
suspect				
...				

The task of the two programs was, of course, to order all six suspects with respect to their similarities to the prototype "murderer X" on the visual grid. The results of the SOM and the SEN shows Fig. 4.8:

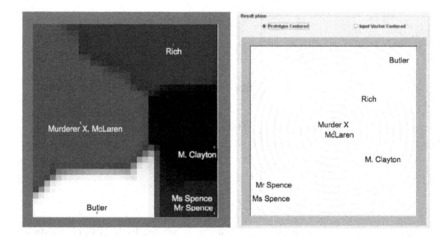

Fig. 4.8 On the left is the result of the SOM, on the right that of the SEN

[24]The details of the story can be looked up in Klüver and Klüver (2007); there only a SOM, an IN and a suited expert system were compared with respect to this murder case. In the next chapter we shall come back to this story in another context; some more details of the content will be given there.

Although the picture are on a first sight different one sees immediately that the results are again equivalent. Both programs show that the suspect McLaren must be the murderer and both programs place the other suspects in the same topological order with respect to the prototype. In the case of the SEN, by the way, we used again the visualization procedure of the prototype-centered modus.

4.2.5 Comparative Considerations

The different examples, how to apply the enforcing rule schema to the different types of learning and the comparisons to established learning rules, have shown that the general rule schema can indeed be applied to all learning tasks, regardless which type of learning they demand. In addition, frequently the respective enforcing rule is even more efficient than the traditional rules. A methodological comparison according to the criteria mentioned at the beginning of this chapter obtains the following results:

In the cases of supervised and reinforcing learning one may say that the enforcing rule is a bit simpler than the Hebbian rule and the Delta rule respectively. With respect to biological plausibility it is hard to decide between the different rules. As all three were constructed in orientation to Hebb's fundamental principle it is fair to say that they are all in their specific way plausible. Therefore, for example problems like those of labyrinth learning can be simulated by the Hebbian rule and the enforcing rule alike. The same is the case with problems of supervised learning, granting the assumption that the topology resulting from the respective training processes are, as far as we can know at present, in all cases biologically plausible. The same is the case with classical conditioning that could have been also simulated with the Hebbian rule.

The main advantage of the enforcing rule is in our opinion its generality. The enforcing rule is strictly speaking, as we mentioned at the beginning of this chapter, a general rule schema. We already demonstrated how the schema of the enforcing rule could also be used to construct learning rules for self-organized learning processes. The mostly used learning rules for self-organized learning like for example the Winner-takes-all principle of the Kohonen Feature Map have only little similarity with Hebb's principle and with the learning rules for supervised and reinforcement learning. Therefore, each type of learning must frequently be realized with special learning rules that are only suited for this type. In contrast the enforcing rule schema is applicable to all types of learning. If this claim is valid then we have reason to assume that perhaps all kinds of learning fundamentally follow the same general principle in the brain – a principle that is basically very simple and probably very similar to our enforcing rule schema.

The most complex learning type is certainly that of self-organized learning; it is not by chance that the most frequently used neural network for this type of learning, the SOM, is by far the most complicated one and not very plausible in a biological sense. That is why we compare the two models of self-organized learning, namely SOM and SEN, a bit more in detail. By a general comparison between the SEN model and the SOM one when again taking into account the three methodological criteria we obtain the following results:

The question, which model is the simpler one, is easily answered: The SEN is of course much simpler than the SOM that consists of different algorithms like, e.g. the winner takes all rule and the Mexican Hat function or the Gaussian distribution function respectively.[25] In contrast to these algorithms that are not easily understood by beginners or practical users of a SOM a SEN just needs the basic IN, the transformation of the values of the according semantical matrix into the weight matrix of the IN and the variation of the weight values, if necessary, by the enforcing rule. In addition, a user of a SEN only needs to insert the respective attributes and prototypes in the semantical matrix; in contrast a user of a SOM, as we mentioned, has to insert not only these data but also all objects that shall be ordered with respect to the prototypes. Our little example above already demonstrated that the semantical matrix of a SOM will be significantly larger than that of a SEN. Hence, a SEN is not only simpler with respect to its logical structure but also with respect to its practical usage. In particular, the training process of a SEN for tasks of self-organized learning is much faster than that of a SOM. A SOM usually needs several hundreds of learning steps for a task like that of Tom's world-view. The enforcing rule of a SEN, in contrast, must be applied only once or a few times; in addition the activation steps of the appropriate IN are usually about 20–30.

In the preceding sections, by the way, we mentioned the main difference between the enforcing rule and the traditional learning rules for supervised and reinforcement learning: The latter rules determine the variation of weight values in dependency of the activation values of the respective neurons. The enforcing rule in contrast computes the new weight values only in dependency of the former weight values. That is why one might call the traditional rules as inspired by physicists. This contrast is even more significant with respect to the difference between SOM and SEN. The learning principle of a SOM is centered around the Winner Takes All principle, i.e., the learning is dependent on the determination of the highest activation values. The learning of a SEN is again dependent only on the former weight values. This difference, of course, is no criterion for or against a SEN but another indicator that a SEN is the simpler model.

The criterion of generality is a bit more complicated. On the one hand a SOM can not only be applied to classification tasks as with the Ritter-Kohonen type but can also, slightly altered, be used for the solution of optimization problems like, e.g., the Traveling Salesman Problem (TSP). A SEN in contrast can be used only for classification tasks and is explicitly constructed for them. In this sense a SOM is more general than a SEN. On the other hand the fundamental logic of a SEN, namely the enforcing rule, can be used for all four types of learning, as the examples in the preceding sections demonstrated. That is not possible with a SOM that is restricted to only self-organized learning. Therefore, both models are more general

---

[25]There are many different versions of the SOM; accordingly different functions can be implemented, which, though, always are much more complicated than the SEN rule.

than the other but in different dimensions. For the purpose of the modeling of different learning processes the SEN is without doubt the more general one; applications of problems of quite another kind are only possible with a SOM that is in this aspect more general.

By the way, both models so far have been compared by their applications to classification problems, i.e. the ordering of certain objects according to their attributes and to their similarity to some prototypes. It is also possible to classify objects even if the prototype is not known. For example, suppose a firm wants to found a branch in a foreign country and does not know which of the possible locations would suit best. The firm certainly has different criteria like traffic connections, local taxes, estate prizes, educational levels of the native population and so on. But of course no location fulfills all the criteria or only to very different degrees. An application of a SOM or a SEN to such a problem would start with the use of an optimization algorithm like, e.g. a genetic algorithm (GA). The GA then would operate on "criteria vectors" where the components are different degrees of the respective criteria. By using the well-known genetic operators of crossover and mutation the GA would construct an ideal type of location, i.e. a vector where the criteria components would be combined in the best possible manner. This vector will be placed as a prototype on the grid of a SOM or SEN. Afterwards the factual locations of the country, defined by their degrees of fulfilling the criteria, are placed on the grid according to their similarity to the prototypes. A student of us did exactly this when simulating the decision problems of his (German) firm finding a suited location in India. The result of his simulation came very near to the factual decision of his firm: the factually selected location was one of the best in his simulation.

The last criterion we have to analyze is that of neuro-biological plausibility. To be sure, because of the mentioned missing knowledge about geometrical structures and detailed procedures of the brain this criterion is hard to decide. Nevertheless, there is at least some circumstantial evidence:

The SEN is, as we mentioned, significantly simpler than a SOM. If there is no other knowledge than according to Occam's Razor the SEN should be preferred to the SOM. It is not very probable that such complicated functions like the Mexican Hat Function have counterparts in the brain. With respect to learning rules, it is not very probable too that something like the Winner Takes All principle is the way the brain generates self-organized learning processes. Although several scholars speak of "competitive processes" of the biological neurons (cf. Hillermeier et al. 1994) such terms are not much more than metaphors. Biological neurons have to pause after firing and other neurons then may fire but of course that is no competition.

The enforcing rule, on the other hand, is an application to self-organized learning of Hebb's principle. Because this principle is biologically well established it seems not too farfetched to believe that the enforcing rule is more plausible than something like the Winner Takes All rule. With respect to the logic of self-organized learning the SEN apparently has some advantages.

As one of the strongest arguments for the biological plausibility of a SOM often its capability of "topology maintenance" is quoted. Yet this term is ambiguous. On the one hand it means that a SOM clusters those neurons that are the counterpart of neuron groups in the brain, i.e., SOM and brain both cluster the neurons that together perform some operations. But this is no advantage in comparison to a SEN because it is safe to assume that the enforcing rule does exactly the same as the Winner Takes All rule. We demonstrated that SEN and SOM in all examples generated nearly the same results. The reason for these equivalent results is of course the fact that both models operate according to a clustering principle although determined by different algorithms. If topology maintenance is an indicator for biological plausibility then a SEN is as plausible as a SOM.

On the other hand the topology maintenance means that the clustering of (artificial) neurons represents "semantical clusters", i.e. groups of concepts and the like that belong together according to their semantical similarity. Indeed, the visualization of the results of a SOM demonstrates this topology maintenance in a very illustrative manner. Yet again the SEN does exactly the same, as we demonstrated with the SEN visualization. We also believe that the capability of topology maintenance is a necessary condition of the modeling of self-organized learning. That is why we constructed the SEN the way we did. But with respect to biological plausibility both models fulfill this condition and are in this aspect equivalent.

By the way, the mentioned fact that certain versions of SOM are able to solve optimization tasks like the TSP is strictly speaking an argument against its biological plausibility. The human brain usually is not able to solve the TSP when there are, e.g., more than six or seven towns. Even if the brain solves the TSP for a small number of towns it certainly does not operate in the way of a SOM. The SOM is a very powerful algorithm but at least in the dimension of such tasks it is not very similar to the brain.[26]

Finally, there is one important advantage of a SEN. A SOM, as we mentioned above, usually must be trained anew when new units are inserted into the program. Consider, e.g., the example of the detective case with six suspects. The SOM was able on the basis of its semantical matrix to place the factual culprit near the prototype "Murder X" as did the SEN. If the user of the program had forgotten one suspect and had trained the SOM with only five suspects, and if after the SOM runs another suspect had to be inserted then the training process had to start over again. The SEN on the other hand does not need new training but a new suspect could be inserted without any new training.

In other words, a SOM neglects in this respect the difference between learning and information processing *as a result of the preceding learning*. By using terms of Piaget one could say that a SOM, in contrast to a SEN, always is in the process of accommodation and never in that of assimilation. During the process of assimilation a system does not change its cognitive structure but categorizes new perceptions according to the acquired structures. That is the way a SEN operates and the fact

---

[26]The TSP is the problem to find the shortest route between different towns if all towns must be visited but only once. It belongs to the class of so-called NP-complete problems that are very hard to solve, i.e. they need very much and often too much computing time to generate a satisfactory solution.

that a SOM does not is a grave problem for the claim that a SOM adequately models human self-organized learning processes.[27]

The concept of the enforcing rule schema, in particular its application to processes of self-organized learning, has in addition an important aspect for the old and obviously immortal debate in learning theories, namely that of the proportion of "nature and nurture".[28] This distinction means the question if the genes as biological foundation of cognitive ontogenesis are the most important factor or if the socio-cultural environment plays the more important role for the development of intelligence. There are countless experiments and empirical studies that dealt and deal with the subject and the pendulum of the debate permanently oscillated between both poles. The main methodical problem of this debate was and is its undecidability because neither the partisans of the "genetic" position could name the genes that are, according to their position, responsible for more or less talents nor could the partisans of the environmental position exactly demonstrate how different socio-cultural environments more or less stimulate individual developments, based on genomes that are basically nearly equal in all humans. In particular, no "environmentalist" could explain for example why there were at the beginning of the twentieth century a lot of students of physics in Germany whose families offered a favorable cultural background but just one Einstein.

The concept of *self*-enforcing as we defined it when constructing the SEN-models may offer a middle way. It is not necessary to assume that the genome of, for example, Einstein was much richer than those of his fellow students and it is equally not necessary to look for certain cultural components in Einstein's social milieu, for example his Jewish origin, that favored his extraordinary abilities. It is sufficient just to assume that Einstein had a special ability of self-enforcing certain neural structures, which distinguished him from other humans equally well genetically equipped and living in an equally favorable socio-cultural environment. Special talents, so our proposal, may be explained as the result of some self-enforcing processes during the cognitive ontogenesis. They are neither the effect of special genes nor of a particular favorable environment but of a self-organized learning process via self-enforcing learning rules. As Tom generated his world-view by self-enforcing his cognitive semantical networks special talents and even geniuses can be understood the same way, namely as self-organization by self-enforcing. Perhaps this is a new approach for the old and rather sterile debate about differences in

---

[27] It is possible to change the learning process of a SOM that way that only a part of the weight matrix must changed when inserting new inputs; we did this already (cf. Klüver 2002). Yet even then it is a process of accommodation and additionally it is often not easy to decide which part of the matrix should be changed.

[28] For a historical and critical overview cf., e.g., Kamin (1974); at present once more the "nature" position seems to be the more attractive one after the dominance of the nurture position in the seventies and eighties of the last century.

genomes and social milieus; the interesting question perhaps should be that of abilities of self-organization.[29] In this sense we perhaps would be able also to understand individuals with extraordinary talents by reconstructing the genesis of these talents.

Finally, we do not mean that the traditional learning rules and according models are worthless – on the contrary. There are, as we frequently mentioned, plenty successful applications of these rules and models in many different domains. Yet sometimes the usage of a SEN may be technically simpler and often biologically more plausible. In this sense the art of modeling of cognitive processes by neural networks may be a little enriched by the possibilities modeling with the enforcing rule schema offers.

4.2.6 Coming Back to AI

The hypothesis that learning processes in the brain and in the mind operate according to the general enforcing rule schema has several advantages, especially those of generality and simplicity. Without doubt it is theoretically more satisfactory to assume that one general principle determines such different learning processes like classical conditioning and the self-organized construction of verbally explained world-views than the assumption that each different learning process must be defined by special rules and by additionally distinguishing between processes in the brain and in the mind. We have again to remind that simulations of dogs and mice of course are simulations of brain processes; simulations of the generation of mind structures like that of Tom are models of processes of the mind. It is no small advantage of the general schema that it is apparently possible to model processes of both levels with the same general logic.

Because of its simplicity the general schema has the additional advantage of biological plausibility. To be sure, an assumption that nature always favors the simplest solution of evolutionary problems would be a rather metaphysical one that could not be proved. Yet the general expectation of scientists that it is always fruitful to search for theories and models as simple as possible has frequently lead to promising results. Mathematically, for example, it is not possible to decide if our solar system *is* a heliocentric one or a geocentric system. Both assumptions can be described in consistent models. Yet the geocentric model of the solar system is much more complicated than the heliocentric one and hence no scientist will seriously accept the old assumption of a geocentric system. But this is just a decision for the sake of mathematical simplicity.[30]

---

[29]This proposal certainly seems just to shift the debate to the question where such abilities of self-enforcing come from. As we are no experts on the field of, e.g. hormonal processes we must leave this to the specialists. Yet it is probably more fruitful to look for the biological source of self-enforcing abilities and more simple than the quest for genetic differences and differences in social milieus.

[30]Idioms like "the sun is rising" and "the sun is setting" demonstrate that in everyday thinking and speaking the geocentric model is still a firm part of our physical world-view.

By basing on the Hebb principle and by its simplicity the assumption of the validity of the general rule enforcing schema has some biological plausibility. Therefore, it is not useless to imagine an AI that learns and as a result understands according to this schema.

In the last years we developed with two of our students in computer science an automatic system that is able to generate different types of neural networks according to the needs of the user. We call that system the "neuro-generator". At the present state of development the user has to tell the system which kind of network he wants, for example a feed forward net, and the user also inserts the data together with a coded description of the problem the respective network has to solve. The neuro-generator then generates at first a rather simple network, in the case of feed forward networks a two-layered one, and tries to solve the problem by applying the delta rule. If different runs are not successful the neuro-generator automatically enlarges the network by introducing a hidden layer of a certain size, by using the Back Propagation rule, and by experimenting with the size of the hidden layer, with different thresholds and so on. We tested the system already with different tasks, in particular the prediction of stock development, and obtained rather satisfactory results (although we did not invest our money in stock according to the prediction of the neuro-generator).[31]

At present we are implementing the enforcing rule schema together with its variants into the neuro-generator that until now is operating only with the traditional learning rules. The system then will be able to learn in the sense that was described in the preceding sections by applying the according enforcing rules to the respective problem. In particular it will be able to "understand" certain systems like the mice in a labyrinth or Tom's generation of a certain world-view: The neuro-generator will construct something akin to mental models of mice and men, to remind of John Steinbeck, and will by this way achieve a formal analog of understanding their behavior. In other words, by simulating the behavior of certain organisms in form of enforcing rule determined learning it will at the same time and as a result of his learning processes realize a formal manner of understanding. The neuro-generator will do nothing else than applying the statement of Vico, mentioned in the first chapter: Because it can artificially "make" the learning processes of Tom and the mice by simulating their genesis it can "understand" these developmental processes – it has made a picture of them (Wittgenstein).

In this stage of development the neuro-generator may be called the first prototype of a "latent" AI: It has the principal possibilities to construct mental models of certain "agents" (see above Chapter 3) but must be "awakened" by the inserting of data and by the information, which kind of problem it has to solve, which type of learning has to be applied, and which type of networks it should use. This is still a weakness of the system. Let us consider these shortcomings:

---

[31] We were by far not the first to construct a system for the automatic generation of neural networks (cf. for example Stanley and Miikkulainen (2002) or Zell (2003), to name only these), although we of course think that our system has several advantages in comparison to already existing systems. The students were Kay Timmermann and Daniel Tang who did this as their master thesis.

It is evident that each learning system and each problem solving system has to get the necessary data or it would remain quite helpless. That is of course no shortcoming of the neuro-generator. Yet the neuro-generator must be explicitly told *how* to process these data, i.e. which construction paths it should choose. On the one hand it is a strength of the neuro-generator that it can construct practically all types of neural networks, at least those that are of practical use. But this strength implies the weakness that the system has too many possibilities, which brings the problem to select between them. To be sure, such a problem also arises frequently in the case of humans when they cannot decide, which way of several possible ones is the right one for the solution of a certain problem. Yet it would be desirable if the neuro-generator would not need such explicit information about learning and network types.

The easiest way to overcome this deficiency would of course be the inserting of certain rules. For example, if the user wishes to solve his problem by the application of supervised learning he has to insert a target vector. The according rule then could be: IF there is a target vector, THEN apply supervised learning. Accordingly: IF there is no target vector and no other immediate feedback, THEN try classical conditioning OR self-organized learning. The latter rule could be split up: IF the input is several times repeated, THEN try classical conditioning. And: IF there is no immediate feedback and IF the input is given only once THEN try self-organized learning. Such a rule system, based on the classification of learning types, would certainly enable the neuro-generator to decide in an independent manner which ways of construction it should select.

In Chapter 2 we dealt with the problem of rule based learning. Certainly in many cases human learners have to be explicitly told, which kind of rules are valid in a particular situation and how these rules have to be understood. Therefore, inserting certain rules how to proceed with special problems is an acceptable way to increase the degree of independence of the neuro-generator. Yet in many cases the learner has to develop the respective rule for himself by learning from single examples. Hence the question arises if it would be possible to enable a system like the neuro-generator to do exactly this, namely generating certain rules from examples.

In neuro-informatics this problem is known as the task of rule extracting by neural networks. We shall consider it in the next subchapter.

4.3 Rule Extracting or Learning from Examples

Since the beginning of research in AI there had been a clear distinction between rule-based systems like expert systems on the one hand – the symbolic approach – and sub symbolic or connectionist respectively approaches on the other. Expert systems were and are the most widely known example for systems that are based on rule approaches: Knowledge is stored in symbols and the different knowledge parts are connected via specific rules, the so-called production rules. The logical basis for such rule-based systems is the predicate calculus. These rules that connect the specific knowledge parts usually were obtained from human experts – hence the name.

The most known paradigm for the connectionist approach in AI are of course artificial neural nets, although there exist numerous other techniques (cf. Russel and Norvig loc. cit.). Neural networks are frequently, although by no means always, not symbolically coded and in particular they do not contain explicit rules. Their logical structure, as we have frequently shown, consists of their topology, i.e. their weight matrices, and of course the respective activation functions. Because of these characteristics neural networks are able to learn by adjusting their weight matrix; they do so by learning from examples.

Rather early in AI research different researchers mainly for technical reasons started to combine these approaches (cf. Galland 1993; Sestito and Dillon 1994). The main reason was a problem with the so-called knowledge acquisition for expert systems: In many cases it is very difficult to get correct rules from human experts. They know how to act in specific problem situations but they are not able to formulate the according rules in an explicit way. Instead human experts frequently think in examples and even quote them when asked about rules; some scholars even believe that human experts do not operate by *consciously* applying rules (cf. Dreyfus and Dreyfus loc. cit.). In that respect neural networks seem to be more similar to human experts than expert systems although the origin of expert systems was the idea to model the cognitive operations of human experts (cf. e.g. Buchanan and Shortliffe 1984). Therefore, the idea suggested itself to use neural networks in order to "extract" rules from examples and to insert these rules into expert systems; in many practical domains like medical and technical diagnosis or steering of technical systems expert systems are more easily to apply than neural networks.

Three chief approaches have emerged how to deal with the problem of rule extraction (for an overview cf. Andrews et al. 1995):

The first one is called the *pedagogical* approach. Partisans of this approach are only interested in the input-output relation of neural networks that defines the respective rule, which the network has learned. The neural networks are considered as black boxes that are trained by the usual learning rules to produce the desired relation, namely the rule. This approach is suited for practical purposes when no knowledge is necessary about the topological structure of the networks. Yet often such knowledge is necessary, as we shall see below with respect to suited MC-values. The name of this approach possibly has its origin from the deplorable fact that human learners are in the eyes of the teachers usually or at least frequently black boxes indeed.

The second approach is the so-called *decompositional* one, for which the study of Sestito and Dillon (loc. cit.) is an early example. The researchers who try this approach do not consider the input-output relation as a whole but look for certain connections within the network. This can be done in different ways; the disadvantage of this approach is that it is much more complicated than the pedagogical one. In addition, it is often rather arbitrary, which connections one selects in order to extract the desired rule and hence it is difficult to decide.

The third approach, the *eclectic* one, tries to combine the advantages of the other two approaches. This can also be done in different ways. Our own methical procedure to deal with the problem of rule extraction, as the readers probably already suspect, might also be subsumed under this approach: On the one hand we define a learned rule as an according input-output relation of the whole network, generated by a suited matrix. One might also say that the matrix *is* the logical or mathematical respectively relation between input and output that represents the rule (see below). On the other hand we certainly are interested in specific topological characteristics of the respective network; the analysis of the relation between MC-values and variance values of the weight matrices are an example for our procedure. Another example is the simulated training of the mice where the enforcing rule was always applied to specific connections. By proceeding this way we avoid the disadvantage of arbitrariness of the decompositional approach and can use specific knowledge about the network's topology to generate particular rules. Yet before we discuss some problems about learning of rules and rule extractions we have to consider some formal aspects of social rules in general.

We already mentioned in the second chapter the importance of understanding rules if one wants to understand certain social actions. The example of the task of a foreign tourist to understand a football game (football in the European sense) demonstrated how it is possible to generate rules, if only as a preliminary hypothesis, from observations. To be sure, for example the hypothetical rule that football is a game where the players are only allowed to touch the ball with their feet – hence the name – or with their heads could be formulated only after a certain number of observations (the problem of induction). Yet the permanent observation of such actions first generates an impression of a certain regularity and afterwards the hypothetical construction of an according rule. Because in our example we assumed that the tourist could not ask anybody about such rules for lack of the language the tourist's learning is a typical case of rule learning by specific examples.

To be sure, there are a lot of social situations where the learners are explicitly instructed about the respective rules that should be applied in a particular situation. The teaching at school is mostly done by the explicit telling of the according rules – social ones or scientific ones as for examples rules to calculate or to interpret a literary text. There are forms of school didactics though that give the pupils the task to discover the rules for themselves, for example the so-called didactics of "exemplary learning" (*exemplarisches Lernen*) of the German educational scientist Klafki (1971). Yet in most situations of institutionalized learning and teaching the rules that have to be learned are explicitly taught. The reason for this is simply that it is more efficient, namely faster, to explicitly teach rules and leave the pupils "only" the task to apply the rules to different problems than to give the pupils time and careful help to enable the pupils that they could discover the rules for themselves from different examples. Schools and other teaching institutions always have the problem that there is not much time for all the fields of knowledge the pupils and/or students have to learn.

There are some problems though with the explicit teaching of rules: (a) Usually that teaching method can of course only be applied if there is some pedagogical authority – a teacher or somebody in an equivalent role – who can formulate the rule and evaluate if the learner has understood it, for example by letting the learner apply the rule to different problems. If such a teacher is not available learning in this form is impossible. (b) "Pedagogical authority" means that the teacher is competent, i.e., that he not only understands the rule himself but that he is also able to judge the correctness of the pupil's learning successes. Such a competence cannot be always presumed. (c) The example of the football game demonstrated the necessity to learn oneself from observed examples in the cases where no teacher or no other competent informant can tell about the respective rules. (d) Each experienced teacher knows that the explicit teaching of rules often produces the result that the learners did not really understand them – the rules remained "abstract". The discovering of rules by the learners themselves is frequently the most effective way to make the learners "really" understand the rules. (e) Sometimes there are situations, in particular in scientific research, where nobody knows the according rules and where the rules have to be discovered as an objective new form of knowledge. Research is one example of such situations; the common establishing of social rules after radical changes in a society, for example after revolutions, is another. Hence from a learning theoretical point of view learning rules from examples and by discovering the rules for oneself is a necessary form of successful learning; the task to construct a truly learning AI-system must contain the task to construct one that is able to learn from single examples and to infer rules from them.

Yet even if one restricts the learning of rules to the explicit teaching of them the question arises *how* rules are learned this way. Rule based systems in AI research and practice like expert systems do not learn their rules in a strict sense; the rules are just implemented into the so-called knowledge based as "production rules" in the well-known IF-THEN form. That is certainly not the way humans learn rules when they are explicitly taught them because there are no "rules" in the brain. The brain just contains very complex systems of connected neurons that get certain inputs and transform them into the according outputs. In addition, expert systems "understand" their rules at once when they have been inserted in the sense that the systems correctly apply them already at the first time always after the implementation of the rules – if the rules have been correctly implemented, of course. This is not the case with human learners, as every experienced teacher knows. Human learners frequently wrongly apply a rule for the first time, must be corrected, apply a second time and then not necessarily rightly; they must be corrected again until a correct application can be seen and so on. Even if the human learners obviously understood the rule by its correct application the learners might forget it after a certain time and have to learn it again – in contrast to the artificial systems. Our dealing with classical and instrumental conditioning in the preceding subchapters demonstrates how such processes can be modeled and hence understood.

The mice and the dog of course did not get any explicitly formulated rules but had to learn from trial and error or by simple conditioning. Yet these models give a useful hint how the explicit learning of rules and the discovering of rules from examples can be modeled.

Let us first formally define a rule. It is basically nothing else than a quadruple (S, Ar, An, Cc) where S denotes the action situation, Ar the respective actor, An the action one can observe, and Cc an assumption of a causal connections between the first three components. The observation that a driver Ar makes a stop An at a red traffic light S is for itself of course not yet a rule. But when this observation is made several times the simple combination of S, Ar, and An becomes a hypothetical rule, consisting of these three components and in addition the assumption of a causal connection Cc between these observations. The understanding hence of the driver's action in the situation S is, as we remarked in the second chapter although in other words, the completion of the triple (S, Ar, An) to the quadruple (S, Ar, An, Cc).

Such rules about stopping at red traffic lights and driving on by green lights are usually learned by receiving them as explicitly formulated rules – during a course for getting a driver's license, early in the childhood by anxious parents and so on. It is of course also possible to learn these rules by observing such situations, for example if the in Chapter 2 mentioned boy from the Amish comes for the first time into a city with such traffic situations. Regardless if one learns these rules in the one or the other way – one has to learn that the validity of the rule about red and green traffic lights is in a certain sense a universal one. With this term we mean that the rule is always valid in cases of traffic situations, namely for different drivers, for different traffic situations like, e.g., crossroads or roadwork, different densities of the traffic, and so on. This universality is included by the explicit teaching with words like "always", "everywhere" and so forth. In the case of learning from examples it is of course necessary to perceive with different examples that this rule is a universal or general one. In our formal representation of such rules it is then possible to omit the actor symbol because the rule is valid for all respective actors. Hence the formal representation of the rule becomes the triple (S, An, Cc).

The generality of the traffic rule is rather evident and nobody has any difficulties to learn about its generality if the rule is explicitly taught. Yet many other rules are more complicated in this aspect, as each teacher knows. Frequently pupils or students have difficulties in correctly applying a rule to examples they have not been taught when learning the rule. In other words, the learners did not comprehend why certain single cases are concrete examples for a general rule. This problem is even more severe when learning from examples and such generating a general rule from concrete single cases. In both cases of learning, therefore, the learners have to develop a respective cognitive network with sufficient large basins of attraction: Despite the differences between the single concrete cases, i.e. the respective social situations and actors, the output, namely the action, must always be the same. Let us consider this problem a bit more in detail.

In the terminology of neural networks a rule is in a strict sense a (fixed) relation between an input and the according output (see above the characteristics of the pedagogical and the eclectic approaches in rule extraction). Because the dynamical relation between input and output vectors is represented and generated by the weight matrix and the respective activation functions one might say, as we mentioned above, that the learning of a rule is done by generating a weight matrix that in turn generates the correct output from a certain input. Now let us first assume that a learning network that represents a single learner gets a rule in an explicit formulation. A human learner usually understands the rule only if he is given together with the rule one or several examples how to apply this rule. If he is given just one example then he may construct a network that correctly associates the input, namely the single example of a situation, with the desired output, namely the adequate action. Now we come back again to the concept of meaning generating capacity: If the MC-value of this network is too large then the learner will not be able to associate the input of a second example with the correct action because of the differences between the two examples. Because the learner of course does not know the MC-value of his network he must be given at least a second or third example in order to decrease his MC-value.

If the MC-value is too small then the learner gets a converse problem. His basin of attraction is large enough that he can associate the input of different examples with the correct output, i.e. the desired action. Yet he will not be able to perceive when the differences between the examples are so large that he must apply another rule, if he has already learned another one, or that he simply cannot apply the learned rule to the new example because the differences are too large. He will always try to apply a single rule and will not perceive his error. Explicit teaching of rules, combined with the presentation of examples, hence, must not only present suited examples for the rule application but also counter-examples where the rule must not be applied. The danger of getting either too small or too large MC-values must be taken into account by presenting not only different suited examples but also counter-examples.

Now let us assume that the learner shall find out the rule by himself when he is presented several different examples – suited ones, of course. The learner will again construct a network that associates the input of one example with an output. In the case of supervised learning the learner will be told if and how much he is in error; the learner will adjust his network until his network generates the desired output. He then will assume that the rule is represented by the input-output relation he has just obtained. Now we come again to the problem of MC-values. If the values are too large then the network will not associate the correct output with slightly different inputs, i.e. with slightly different examples; the rule is not general enough. If the MC-value is too large then the rule will be not differentiated enough. The didactical consequences are obviously the same as in the case of explicit rule teaching.

The example of the foreign tourist who for the first time in his life watches a football game is an illustration for such learning difficulties: The tourist has no teacher who tells him in verbal communication about his respective errors and learning successes but has only his observations that will confirm or refute his hypothetical rules. The networks of the tourist, if we assume for the sake of simplicity one network for each rule, must process the different examples about (a) the rule that the players are not allowed to touch the ball with their hands (b) the rule about the exceptions, and (c) the differentiation between the exception for the field players and the goal keepers. This learning situation is, by the way, practically identical to the classical situation in empirically founded research when empirical experiments and observations shall lead to the discovering of rules, i.e. scientific laws. Here as in the case of the tourist empirical reality is the sole arbiter, namely the teacher.

The learning problem is of course a bit more difficult in the case of non-supervised learning, in particular in the case of self-organized learning; we omit the case of reinforcement learning because the problem is very similar to the case of supervised learning. Self-organized learning means that there is no external authority that informs the learner on his failures or successes. Although it is rather doubtful if self-organized learning can occur at all when learning social rules, because the learner is always embedded in a social environment, for completeness sake we analyze this case too.

In the preceding subchapters we discussed self-organized learning chiefly with respect to classification tasks and showed how two types of self-organized learning networks, namely SOM and SEN systems, are able in an equivalent manner to perform such tasks. A learner who has to learn social rules in a self-organized way can do it the same way:

Suppose that a learner perceives a situation and that he associates it with a respective action. He is free to select any action because he gets, according to the basic assumption, no negative or positive feed back from his environment. In a second situation he chooses another action, in a third situation he selects again the action associated with the first situation and so on. After some time our learner has several triples (S_i, An_j, Cc_{ij}). A simple and rather natural classification schema would be in this – rather improbable – learning situation (a) a clustering of all S_i with the same An_j, and (b) the systematic ordering of *all* S_i with respect to the similarities of the respective An_j. In the end of this classification our learner can visualize his ordering of situations and the according actions in the same way as we did with the examples in the preceding subchapters. He can in addition also use a form of prototype theory, namely identifying certain pairs of situations and according actions as prototypical and clustering the other pairs (S_i, An_j) around the different prototypes. For example, a learner who has constructed a pair (red traffic light at a crossroad, stopping the car) will probably interpret this pair as more prototypical for acting in traffic situations than the pair (red light at road-works, stopping the car).

Because of the lack of environmental feed back such a classificatory system of situation-rule pairs can be constructed in an arbitrary manner. The only limit for the freedom of construction is that of consistency. With this term we mean that of course different situations might be associated with the same action; that will always be the case if the respective network has a MC-value smaller than one. But one specific situation must not be associated with different actions by applying different rules to that situation. The relation situation-action must be an unambiguous one or, as one would say in a more mathematical terminology, the relation must be formulated as a mapping.

Self-organized learning of social rules is, as we mentioned, a rather artificial construction in the sense that in social reality this case will practically never occur. Self-organized learning with no environmental feed back and with the sole condition of consistency is something that occurs mainly in the "pure" i.e. theoretical sciences like pure mathematics or some branches of theoretical physics.[32] Yet it may be an

---

[32]Sometimes the so-called super string theory in quantum physics is quoted as an example for theories that have no immediate reference to empirical reality but are linked to experimental facts only by other theories (cf. Greene 2000). The only condition for the construction of such theories is that they must be consistent with other and accepted theories.

amusing task to construct such systematic of rules in form of situation-action pairs when developing for example artificial societies in the context of Online or Video Games. In addition, such self-generated classifications may be used in teaching contexts, namely to demonstrate pupils and students of social sciences the logic of social structures when they are defined as rule sets. But because of the artificiality we shall refer only to supervised and reinforcement learning when considering *how* rules can and must be learned – either by explicit teaching or by learning from examples. Remember that a human learner usually does not correctly apply a learned rule the second or third time; he needs repetition to independently apply the rule, i.e. without guidance by a teacher, and he will forget a rule if it is not used for a long time and if it has been used only seldom.

To answer this question *how* rules are learned we remind of the mice that learned to find the right way through the labyrinth. By successive trials and repeated successful attempts the weight of the respective neural connections transcended a certain threshold; the result was a fixed connection between the "right" neurons. This connection operated like a rule for the mice: IF a mouse stands before the different entrances of the labyrinth THEN the right entrance was chosen without hesitation. When the mice were not in the labyrinth situation for a longer time they forgot the right way but learned it rather fast when they got the labyrinth task again.

The same logic can be applied to the problem how human learners perform the task of learning social rules. When a learner hears about a certain rule for the first time by a teacher the situation is comparable to the first successful attempt of the mouse. The connections in the respective cognitive network will be strengthened but not enough to overcome a threshold at once at the second time when the learner shall apply this rule. Hence he needs a second attempt, i.e. the teacher has to repeat the rule. Fast learners then overcome the threshold because a fast learner is defined in this case by either only low thresholds or rather large factors of weight increasing. Slow learners will need a third or even a fourth time until their connection weights have transcended the thresholds. If this is the case then the weight matrix of the cognitive network will operate like a rule, namely IF a certain situation is present THEN the according action takes place or must take place respectively. Accordingly the learner will forget the same way as the mice do by decreasing the connection weights if the respective situation is not present for a longer time. How fast the learner will forget depends on the size of the connection weight in proportion of the threshold: If the connection weights are significantly larger than the threshold then forgetting will take place after a longer time than if the difference between the weights and the threshold is only small. The converse is the case with remembering after forgetting: Remembering will need only few attempts if the weights are just a bit smaller than the threshold and vice versa. To be sure, in the case of the human learner consciousness also plays an important role in contrast to the mice. But the basic (neural) logic is the same in both cases.

Learning by examples without explicit teaching (but with supervising) is basically the same. We mentioned above that one severe problem is to construct a network with the "right" MC-value. If this is granted then again the perception of just one example is not enough to transcend the respective threshold. Even if the learner concentrates on one example only he has to repeat the perception until he has generated a fixed relation between the situation as input and the according action as output. In most cases this procedure will take more time than with explicit teaching. But it can be assumed that the difference between the weight values and the threshold will be larger in the case of learning from examples because for the learner the process of self-discovering the rule causes that the rule can be more easily remembered.

A lot more could (and should) be said about the complex process of learning. As we said in the beginning of this chapter, if one does not understand learning one does not understand any social and cognitive processes at all. That is why we shall come back to learning in the final chapter.

Chapter 5
The Human Factor: Understanding Humans by Artificial Systems

In Section 4.2 we demonstrated the example of the juvenile delinquent Tom and how it is possible to understand him in an exact manner by simulating the development of his Social-Darwinian world-view. The usage of such formal systems like a SEN or a SOM is apparently twofold: On the one hand the simulation of certain processes like the cognitive development of a youth enables the user of such programs to understand these processes and in particular their results in a more precise and exact manner than it would be possible without such formal systems. On the other hand the question how an AI system could be able to understand human actions can be answered by the assumption that AI systems contain neural networks like a SEN: When receiving the according inputs about the self-portrayal of Tom, especially about the genesis of his world-view, and when the SEN is in addition provided with the according components of prototype theory, i.e. the centering of new information around early acquired prototypes, then the SEN could construct a model of Tom in the described way and hence "understand" him. It is just now not of importance if the SEN "only" simulates an understanding of Tom or if it "really" understands him. In either way such a system, additionally provided with simple rules to describe its processes and results in a verbal manner, could explain Tom by describing its own operations, i.e. by describing the construction of the mental model of Tom.[1]

The results of the preceding chapters already gave some insights into necessary learning capabilities and mathematical structures of potential AI systems. Yet with the exception of the reconstruction of the biography of Tom we gave no examples if and how an AI could understand factual cases of human actions. In the following subchapters we try to fill out this gap with several and very different examples how to apply such formal systems to specific factual cases. But it is important to remember that the examples must always be understood in the same twofold way as the example of Tom: The usage of formal system enlarges our own understanding

---

[1] The fact that the SEN must be given such an explicit information about prototype theory is no serious objection: In several courses on qualitative social research we gave the example of Tom, i.e. showed the students the text of the interview with Tom, and asked for an interpretation. Although the theories of Bandura and Rosch belonged to the curriculum of the students and were known to them no one got the idea to interpret Tom with the help of these theories. Therefore, it is no unfair advantage for the SEN if it gets this theoretical framework.

J. Klüver, C. Klüver, *Social Understanding*, Theory and Decision Library A 47, DOI 10.1007/978-90-481-9911-2_5, © Springer Science+Business Media B.V. 2011

possibilities and it demonstrates how an AI could understand these processes if it contains such formal systems as part of it.

5.1 The Origin of Restricted Perception

It is a well-known everyday experience that frequently humans perceive certain messages in only a restricted way. They tend to associate different messages with always the same concepts and react accordingly the same way although the sender of the different messages expected different reactions to them. Such a one-sidedness will be of course the source for many misunderstandings in the according communications: In particular the reactions of fanatics to different messages can be classified this way. If, for example, an Islamic fundamentalist explains all political news as an attack of Western societies on the Islamic world, or if a strict Feminist sees everywhere the conspiracy of men against women then such reactions can be easily explained and understood as the result of a very restricted form of message processing. In 2007 we mentioned the case of Don Juan in the film with Marlon Brando and Johnny Depp where the young hero always referred social experiences to sex.[2] But such one-sidedness must not be an indicator for fanaticism or a disturbed personality. We know from our own personal experience that in times of thinking about a difficult problem one tends to refer quite different experiences to the frame of the problem. When thinking about some problems with cellular automata one of the authors watched a lawn where many children played and moved around. Nearly automatically the observer saw the whole lawn as the grid of a cellular automaton and the moving children as cells that changed their geometrical positions and states. Frequently such reduction of different perceptions to the same frame is even necessary in order to concentrate on the problem; the countless jokes about absent-minded professors or scientists respectively illustrate this fact. We suppose that everybody who had to solve difficult problems knows such necessary reductions.

In Chapter 3 we described restricted perception by low MC values, i.e. large basins of attraction that generate always the same meaning in form of an attractor despite different messages. In a statistical sense of the word such values are the "normal" cause of restricted perception processes. Yet we already mentioned that there are particular forms of learning that generate cognitive networks with high MC values but also only restricted meaning generation. In the following considerations we concentrate on such learning processes and according cognitive networks.

The development of restricted message processing can be explained and understood by different learning assumptions; we demonstrate the according models in the following order: The first and simplest assumption is that of repetition. If the environment of the learner continuously gives the same information and only this then the network of the learner will, according to the Hebb principle, strengthen some neural connections and weaken others. In other words, the development occurs

---

[2]There are numerous jokes and stories about patients of psychotherapists who react just that way, i.e. reducing each question to always the same subject.

as a form of classical conditioning by permanent and one-sided signals. There is no doubt that a lot of PR-strategies must be understood this way; we shall give below an according example that factually happened. The classical Latin pedagogical maxim *"repetitio est mater studiorum; semper aliquid haeret"* is based on the same assumption and many teaching processes still follow it.[3]

The second assumption is similar to the conditioning process of Pavlov's dog that we demonstrated above. In many cases pure repetition is not enough but must be replenished by coupling the repeated signal(s) with another one, in particular with a signal that is attractive for the receiver. The conditioning process of the dog is an example for such a replenished conditioning: Pure repetition of the bell signal, of course would have had no effect at all; only the coupling of the bell signal with the food signal produced the desired effect (desired by Pavlov and not by the dog). Such a strategy is even more common in teaching and advertising strategies; we shall demonstrate an according example too.

The third assumption uses the concept of self-organized learning that we demonstrated with the example of Tom. The first two assumptions both presuppose the existence of an environment that produces the according cognitive structures by permanently sending certain signals. Yet we already mentioned the fact that specific developmental processes cannot be explained by such presuppositions alone for at least two reasons: The first reason is that individuals can react in different ways to exactly the same environment. In particular, processes that generate extraordinary individuals – in a positive and a negative meaning of this word – must be understood as the result of self-organized or self-enforced respectively learning processes. The second reason is that, for example in the case of religious fanaticism, in the beginning of the interdependency of environment and development of one-sided perception the environment could not act as the generator of the ontogenetic development because, according to the assumption of a beginning of the emergence of a fanatical socio-cultural milieu, it was not in a socio-cultural state of religious fanaticism. Consequently the first religious fanatics must have gotten rather moderate signals from their environment that they self-enforced until they produced a fanatic world-view practically by themselves.

Therefore, we can safely assume that the origin of a fanatical socio-cultural milieu is the result of specific individual processes of self-enforcing. Such individuals in turn influence other people, in particular by the strategy according to the second assumption, and produce that way a larger environment characterized by the dominance of fanatical ideas that in turn influences other people and so on. In other words, the question what was first, the environment or the influenced individuals, can be answered as a form of dialectic: In the beginning are processes of individual self-enforcing, caused by an environment with moderate religious ideas; the self-enforcing or self-organized respectively processes generate an individual with more and more fanatical world-views and then a cultural environment with more radical ideas that in turn produces other fanatical individuals and so on. The origin

---

[3]"Repetition is the mother of studies. Always something (at least) will remain."

and the spread out of the great world religions can probably be described as such a dialectical process.[4]

In the third chapter we showed a special network, constructed by a former student of us, who had just passed a programming course in the programming language Java. The student had not the task to model one-sided perceptions but to show his knowledge in a structured way, i.e., by the structure of a semantical network. As a reminder we show this network again (Fig. 5.1):

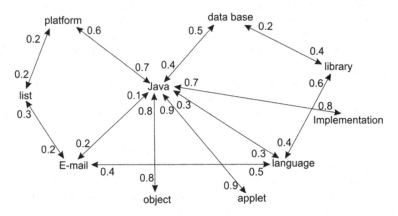

Fig. 5.1 A semantical network with Java as center

We mentioned that by sending different messages to this network by externally activating different neurons very often the neuron "Java" had the strongest activation value. We defined the meaning of certain messages generated by such a network as the neurons with the strongest final activation values; hence one can say that the network very often generated "Java" as the meaning or part of the meaning respectively of rather different messages. We also mentioned that by applying a variant of the enforcing rule it is possible to obtain a network that practically always only generates "Java" as the meaning, regardless of the factual messages.

Such semantical networks, implemented as interactive networks (IN), are very suited models for the origin and the effects of restricted message processing. In particular it is possible to demonstrate the development of such "one-sided" networks via the applications of the enforcing rule schema.[5]

---

[4]Religiously motivated one-sidedness does certainly not lead always to fanaticism. We know a lot of religious people who everything refers to the benevolent intervention of God and who are mild and kind individuals. We use the case of religiously motivated fanaticism not only because it is still a very current problem but also because it is a very apt illustration of the general case of restricted message processing.

[5]It is important to note that IN are usually not trained like, for example, feed forward nets or self-organized networks. As far as we know we are the first to implement a certain learning rule into IN.

In more exact terms the learning process of such an IN that is used as model for a learning process according to the first assumption is performed the following way: Imagine a semantical network from the type shown above, implemented as an IN and consisting of concepts A, B, C, ... This network is continually receiving certain messages, usually consisting of concept triples (X, Y, Z), although it is of course also possible to send messages with more or less concepts. We assume that the IN already contains the concepts of the message; the enlargement of the network by adding new concepts will be shown below. The network reacts to the messages by activating its information flow and by generating an attractor state, preferably a point attractor. Let us further assume that the network gets frequently messages that contain a certain concept A and that other concepts H only seldom occur in the messages or not at all. We now introduce a rate k that measures the frequency of the messages that contain the concept A and a learning rate η that measures as usual the individual learning competence or learning willingness respectively. Then the network takes the fact into account that certain concepts A occur in at least k messages by applying a variant of the enforcing rule:

$$w(X, A)_{t+1} = w(X,A)_t * (1 + \eta) \tag{1}$$

for all concepts X of the IN and with $0 \leq \eta \leq 1$. Note that only the connections from the concepts X to the frequently sent concept A are strengthened. The learning rate η of course plays the same role as the constant c in the original enforcing rule; the user of the program can choose its value. The same is the case with k that can be interpreted as an individual rate of attention: Different individuals react earlier or later to the repetition of certain signals; we took this into account by introducing the attention rate k. The decisive parameters for the speed of the learning processes obviously are η and k.

The first assumption of "reaction by repetition" defines the environment as the sole cause of structural changes in the cognitive network of the receiver. In particular the memory of the receiver is dependent on the received signals. Only those concepts that are sent at all by the environment are kept in the network. If specific concepts that are at the beginning part of the IN are not "mentioned" by the environment the IN will "forget" them. This represents the well-known fact that human beings tend to forget things they once knew if they would not deal with them for a longer time. Because such a process of forgetting does not happen at once and for all an according forgetting rule must be introduced. If k is again a certain number of messages that can now be interpreted as the individual capacity of the receiver to remember, namely concepts he is not reminded of by the environment, if η as the analog to the learning rate in Equation (1) is interpreted as the speed of forgetting, and if Z is a concept that does not occur in the last k messages then the according rule is

$$w(Y, Z)_{t+1} = w(Y, Z)_t * (1 - \eta) \tag{2}$$

for all concepts Y of the IN.

The application of Equation (2) successively weakens the connections between the concept Z that did not occur for a certain time and the other concepts. If the connections from the concepts Y to Z are sufficiently weak then Z will not be activated any more and for all practical reasons it is no part of the IN any longer. But, as in the examples with the mice and the dog, it is possible to bring Z into the IN again, namely by frequent applications of rule (1). If, for example, the learning rate of rule (1) is larger than the speed of forgetting in Equation (2) then Z will become faster a part of the IN than it took time for the IN to forget.

Marketing strategies, as we mentioned, frequently operate according to the first learning assumption. Therefore, we illustrate the effects of the learning rules (1) and (2) with a factual example.[6]

5.1.1 Classical Conditioning and the Competition Between Adidas and Nike

In the sixties and early seventies of the last century the market for sports shoes was to a very large degree dominated by the German firm Adidas and to a lesser degree by the also German firm Puma. At least in Germany and not only there the term "sports shoes" was nearly synonymous with "Adidas" (and Puma). The reason for this dominance was the successful marketing strategy of the first chairman of Adidas, Adolf Dressler, who equipped national football teams (the European version of football) and athletes of other popular forms of sport for nothing with shoes and other sportswear of Adidas; in addition, he systematically sought the acquaintance of important sport functionaries in order to get the advertising rights at important sport events like, e.g., the Olympic Games or the World Championships in football. This advertising strategy is nowadays usual for all large sport firms but in the times of Dressler such strategies were very innovative and gave Adidas its dominant position on the market for sportswear and for sports shoes in particular.[7] The semantical network of a potential buyer of sportswear and in particular for sports shoes in the late sixties and early seventies can be visualized as in Fig. 5.2:

Apparently the network is centered on Adidas. If this network receives messages then usually Adidas is strongly activated at the end; for example, a message (tennis, football, sport) generates the meaning (Adidas, tennis, football).

When in the seventies Nike as the first big American firm for sportswear appeared on the European markets they used the same marketing strategies as Adidas, namely sponsoring athletes of popular forms of sport and important events. In addition Nike started large advertising campaigns with the effect that consumers who were interested in sport very frequently received messages containing the name of Nike – either by watching sport events on TV or by seeing there advertising spots. Because

---

[6]More details with respect to these rules and additional examples can be found in the MA-thesis of one of our former students, Christian Kunz.

[7]For the history of Adidas and its main competitor Nike cf. Casanova, M: http://www.wolfgang-bolsinger.de/recources/Interview_mit_Marco_Casanova.pdf

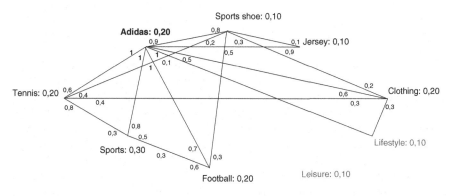

Fig. 5.2 Adidas network

Adidas at the time when Nike appeared in Europe did not accordingly react with own new marketing strategies the semantical networks of potential buyers of sportswear and in particular sports shoes became centralized around the new concept of Nike.

In our formal model the new concept of Nike becomes an additional concept in the IN. In the beginning all connection values from and to Nike have the value of $w(N,X) = w(X,N) = 0.2$ for all concepts X and N for Nike. By applying learning rules (1) and (2) several times one sees that the values $w(X,N)$ are steadily increasing and the values $w(X,A)$ are accordingly decreasing (A of course represents Adidas). In other words, the network that initially was centered on Adidas now has Nike as its center because not only Nike becomes very important in the network but also in addition Adidas is in the danger of becoming forgotten.[8] This is shown in Fig. 5.3:

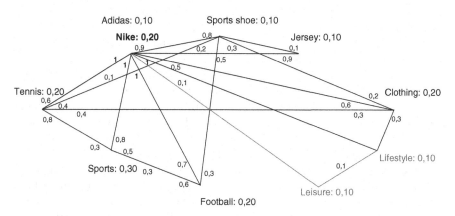

Fig. 5.3 New semantical network as result of the advertising campaigns of Nike

---

[8]Adidas had become too self-assured because of its former success. Therefore it did not spend enough money for own campaigns.

When this new network receives the same message as the original one, namely (tennis, football, sport) it generates the meaning (Nike, tennis, football); Nike has successfully replaced the former market-dominating firm Adidas.

By performing this simulation we assumed that the permanent repetition of messages containing the name of Nike would be sufficient to replace Adidas (first assumption) if Adidas did not react fast enough. The factual process of the emergence of Nike as market-dominating firm, however, was a bit more complicated. Nike used not only the power of repetition but applied in addition a strategy that was based on the second assumption. Before the appearance of Nike in Europe the concept of sportswear was understood in a quite literal manner: One only used sportswear if one factually went in for the according forms of sport; running shoes for example were used only when one intended to do some jogging. Therefore, sportswear usually was associated with concepts like exerting oneself, sweating, and so on. Nobody had the idea to use sportswear as some form of leisure clothing.

Nike changed this by continuously associating its name and the according products with concepts like life-style, coolness, youth, dynamics, and so on. Hence, Nike demonstrated that sportswear is not only suited for factually doing sport but is in addition a symbol for a certain youthful life-style in contrast to traditional clothing. Because the seventies were still greatly influenced by the large youth movements of the sixties and because as an effect youth had become a positive norm it is on hindsight no wonder that these campaigns were very quickly successful.[9] When in the eighties the new Green Party in Germany, consisting chiefly of former partisans of the youth movements in the sixties and early seventies, succeeded in becoming part of the government in the German Federal State of Hessen, their ministers appeared in parliament dressed with sports shoes from Nike.

Nowadays, of course, such marketing strategies are quite common. In many advertising spots nothing or only very little is said about the product but much about the associated concepts. One of the most famous examples is or was the marketing strategy for Marlboro cigarettes where nothing was said about the cigarette and its potential danger but a lot about the freedom of the Far West and the adventurous life one can have when smoking Marlboro. The same is the case in marketing strategies for cars where mostly happy people are shown who drive alone through a beautiful countryside on empty roads. Neither are technical details about the car given nor the fact mentioned that the fate of drivers is chiefly to be stuck with the new car in the same jam as with the old car. At least that is the fate of inhabitants like us of conurbations, in our case the Rhein-Ruhr Region of Germany.

Adidas, by the way, reacted lately but not too late. It adjusted its own marketing and product strategy according to that of Nike with the result that at present Adidas and Nike are alternately the market-dominating firms not only in Europe but in the global market too. Yet for some time in the early eighties it looked as if Adidas would completely vanish because of big financial problems.

---

[9]The famous slogan "don't trust anybody older than thirty" that originated in the late sixties is an apt illustration for the new high regard of youth.

In order to simulate this strategy, i.e. the processing of according advertising messages by potential buyers we had to change Equation (1) a bit. If N is the name of the product, for example sports shoes, and if im represents the value of a concept I with a high image, e.g. youth or coolness, if $0 \leq im \leq 1$, and if fr is the frequency of the common occurrence of the concepts N and I in the messages, then the connection values are changed according to

$$w(X, N)_{t+1} = w(X, N)_t \, (1 + \eta) * im * fr, \tag{3}$$

for all concepts X that occurred in the messages together with N and I. Note that again fr must be larger than the attention rate k but because of the high image value of I it can be assumed that k is significantly smaller in this case than in the first case where only repetitions of the advertising message should guarantee the attention of the consumer. Hence the process of the generation of an according network is accordingly faster than in the first case. As the resulting network is practically the same as in the first case with the additionally concept I we omit a visualization.

In many textbooks on marketing there is a certain basic assumption, namely that the influencing of potential buyers must be understood as the classical Behaviorist schema S – O – R; S is the stimulus or message respectively, O is the organism that should be influenced, and R is the desired response, in this case the buying of the product. We mentioned above that according to classical Behaviorism nothing could be said about the internal structure of O; the same of course is the case with the marketing strategies that follow the Behaviorist paradigm. By modeling the internal processes of O with our networks one can apparently "see" them, at least via a model that is plausible enough to simulate these processes with sufficient validity.

It must be noted, however, that the application of such marketing strategies is not automatically successful. The success of Nike's strategy depended chiefly on the new image values of youth and youthful dynamics, as we already mentioned. Because the generation of the "Summer of 69", to quote the Rock singer Bryan Adams, wanted to distinguish itself from the older generations in habit and clothing Nike could persuade this younger generation to buy its products. But people with other image values were not much influenced by the marketing strategies of Nike and Adidas; their rates of attention are so large that even frequent repetitions of advertising messages could not influence their buying behavior. We modeled the fact that message processing does not necessarily lead to buying by introducing a "relevance factor" r (see above Chapter 1). A factual buying occurs if and only if $A_N > r$; A_N is the final activation value of the concept N that represents the respective product.

We certainly do not wish to claim that marketing strategies, which apply our models, are automatically successful. On the one hand there are very different kinds of consumers, as is well known and as we mentioned in Section 4.2, for example so called innovators who always are interested in new products and more traditional consumers who care only for practical benefit of the product. On the other hand too many marketing strategies are basically the same as one can see when watching TV. If all producers of cars associate their products with freedom and beautiful countryside then a consumer has no reason to decide for product X and not for product Y. Both strategies are processed by the consumer's network the same way. But at least our models enable marketing experts and psychologists interested in the behavior of consumers to understand what probably occurs inside a potential or factual buyer of certain products. Understanding consumers who have something like a fixation with respect to certain products can then be done in the same way as the understanding of fanatics or other one-sided perceptions of reality, namely as the result of certain conditioning processes with the effect of networks centered around central concepts.

5.1.2 The Reduction of Social Perceptions to Social Darwinism

The frequently used Behaviorist paradigm as the theoretical basis for marketing strategies suggests that self-organization plays no important part in this domain. Indeed, on a first sight it is difficult to imagine a potential buyer who organizes his network by applying the self-enforcing rule. Yet the fact that people frequently buy new products although they really do not need them and although such people even might not be subject to often received marketing campaigns hints at the possibility that in particular younger people may observe new products in the possession of their friends or other people they admire. It may be enough that these products, for example new cell phones, are seen only once or twice and by processes of self-enforcing the young consumers persuade themselves that they also wish to have the new products. No frequent repetition and/or coupling with high image values are needed in such cases.[10]

To understand the impact of marketing strategies on the mind of potential buyers is certainly an important part of social understanding – at least in societies that are determined by the imperatives of modern capitalism. The commodity character of capitalistic societies, as Karl Marx named it in the beginning of "*Das Kapital*", makes it unavoidable that the effects of social actions like marketing strategies on social actors must be socially understood as important part of social reality. Perhaps the hermeneutical analysis of economical exchange processes has become much more important than the classical tasks of hermeneutics like the interpretation of literary texts – at least for the social sciences. Yet for the sake of variety we finish this subchapter with an example of another domain, namely with a return to the example of Tom, the delinquent youth from Chapter 4. By simulating the emergence and effects of the gender specific world-view of Tom we analyzed only one part of his character.

Tom's socialization was determined, as we described above, by the model of his father, "model" in the sense of the learning from models theory of Bandura (loc. cit.) or normative prototypes respectively. The father as a "real" man frequently involved himself into brawls and also hit the members of his family. Tom did not

---

[10]This may be one explanation for the recent big selling success of the iPhone of Apple.

dislike his father for his acts of violence but took these experiences as a cause for his own similar development. Such a development based on experiences with violence in the early childhood is not seldom, as always reports from the development of violent fathers and aggressive youths demonstrate. To be sure, experiences of violence in the own family must occur several times but because fortunately most children who experience violence do not become violent and aggressive themselves a development like that of Tom must be understood as a process of self-organization by self-enforcing. In other words, social environment as cause for specific developments is not enough if one wants to understand deviant cases, i.e. cases that must be considered as statistical exceptions. Tom explicitly told the interviewer that he was determined to become like his father, namely a man who dominates his social milieu – family, acquaintances in pubs and so on – and who made secure his dominance by physical violence.

We simulated this part of Tom's social development by using the enforcing rule described in Chapter 4, which we show as a reminder:

$$w_{ij}(t + 1) = w_{ij}(t) \pm \Delta w_{ij} \text{ with } \Delta w_{ij} = c \text{ (constant) and } 0 \le c \le 1. \quad (4)$$

The according world-view is described by a semantical network that is implemented as an IN. The units of the IN represent again certain concepts that are representative for the social experiences of Tom in his childhood and youth (Fig. 5.4).

The enforcing rule was applied the same way as in the examples above. In the beginning we assumed that Tom's semantical network was not greatly different from those of other youths. Hence the weight values of the IN were generated at random. The self-enforcing process starts immediately after the generation of the IN representing the first experiences of Tom with his father. Because of the model function of the father the enforcing operations were applied to the weight values w(X, violence) and w(X, dominance). After several applications the structure of the network had "violence" and "dominance" as centers. The effects were those we expected, namely a strong final activation value for both "violence" and "dominance". The

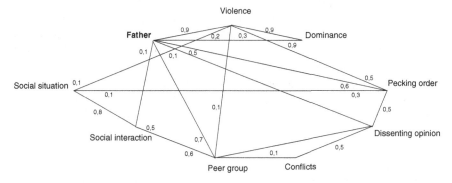

Fig. 5.4   Social world-view of Tom

IN reacted to external activations by always generating nearly the same meaning to different messages; Fig. 5.5 shows an example:

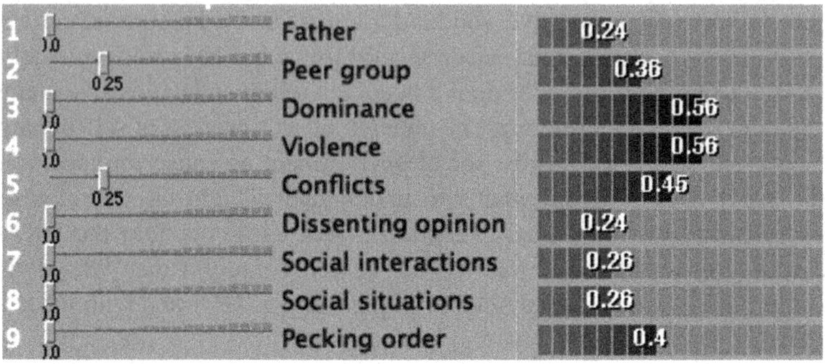

1	)0		Father	0.24
2	0 25		Peer group	0.36
3	)0		Dominance	0.56
4	)0		Violence	0.56
5	0 25		Conflicts	0.45
6	)0		Dissenting opinion	0.24
7	)0		Social interactions	0.26
8	)0		Social situations	0.26
9	)0		Pecking order	0.4

Fig. 5.5 The reactions of the IN to the message (dissenting opinion, peer group)

Obviously it is rather easy to simulate such melancholy processes of self-socialization by using the according enforcing rule.[11] We wish again to emphasize that such processes can be understood only when they are understood as examples of self-organization by self-enforcing. To be sure, the social environment also plays an important part by causing the beginning of these processes and by determining their direction. But it is neither necessary to assume that environment is the most important factor; if that would be the case a change of environment should be enough to change the personality but that did not happen in the case of Tom. Nor is it necessary to assume that a person like Tom has "bad genes" or something like that. Such an assumption would lead to the conclusion that Tom is a literally hopeless case and that only in the future when genetic changes will be possible Tom could be cured. But that is only a theme for Science Fiction. It is quite sufficient to assume that Tom's personality at the time of the interview is a result of a self-organized process and that principally such processes could be reversed; footnote 11 gives a hint what kind of educators could help Tom to reverse his self-enforcing socialization. In a formal model such a reversing could be represented by using the decreasing variant of the self-enforcing rule.

We mentioned in the beginning of this subchapter that one-sided world-views are not necessarily bad and that they are even sometimes necessary in order to fully concentrate on a difficult problem. Indeed, the founding of great religions and the formulating of new scientific paradigms is probably chiefly the achievement of people who totally concentrated on their innovative tasks and such neglected other

---

[11] We do not know the fate of Tom after the interview that was performed several years ago. His orientation to violence and aggressiveness gives not much hope for a Happy End. Yet it is highly significant that the only person whom Tom respected was the interviewer who acted as an educator in the hostel at the time of the interview. The interviewer, a rather powerfully built student, regularly trained together with Tom in the fitness room of the hostel and won the respect of Tom by showing physical prowess. This can be taken as a hint how a re-socialization of Tom might perhaps work.

aspects of reality. Yet the complementary ability to lead a social life by integrating oneself into usual social situations and social order is possible only if the one-sidedness does not totally determine the personality. Hence, either the one-sided personality has to forget some of the fixation to certain central concepts; in our formal models this can be represented by the application of the decreasing rule. Or the personality has to contain several and differently structured networks; the network responsible for social everyday practice then must not be structured like those we described in the preceding sections but must be able to perceive different perceptions as different. Their MC-value in the sense of Chapter 3 must be sufficiently large. In cases of religious or ideological fanaticism one has to assume that the different networks of such persons all are structured the same way, namely centered on the according central concepts.

In Chapter 3 we postulated that in the statistical average the weight matrices of networks with large MC-values, i.e. networks that process messages in a differentiated way, are characterized by large variance values and vice versa. Yet we also mentioned the fact that exceptions from this rule could sometimes be explained by rather unusual learning processes like those we analyzed. Therefore, it seems to be a safe conclusion that in most cases of only general message processing capacity the hypothesis of the small variance values is valid and vice versa. Yet in cases of socialization by direct conditioning processes or by self-organization via self-enforcing it may well be that networks emerge that contain such centered structures as we have demonstrated. To be sure, if one observes empirical examples of differentiated or only general meaning generation it is not directly possible to decide, which kind of network has been generated. Yet we could at least form a plausible hypothesis.

5.2 Understanding Readers of Detective Stories

The art and method of Hermeneutics originated in the attempt to understand and interpret written texts, in particular the Bible. The classical tradition of Bible exegesis since at least the beginning of the nineteenth century was always centered on hermeneutical methods. Although those scholars who like Droysen or Dilthey explicitly founded the methods of hermeneutics were no theologians but historians, philosophers, or had been in literary studies they also concentrated on hermeneutics as the art to understand and interpret texts. Because of this tradition it is no wonder that we also deal with texts in this and the next subchapter. Yet as we are interested in *social* understanding, namely the understanding of human action and thinking we do not try to construct an AI that should be able to understand texts (cf. our analysis of Eliza in Chapter 1).[12] Instead we try to understand what humans do when they are reading certain texts or when they take part in verbal communications. The concept of "texts", after all, is not restricted to written ones but may also be applied to oral communication. We certainly can analyze only very special kinds of text

---

[12]Such attempts were tried by several early pioneers of AI but without great success (cf. e.g. Schank and Riesbeck 1981).

interpretation but these are apt illustrations how an understanding of humans, when they deal with language, might be possible.

At the end of the second chapter we showed the simulations of different readers by giving permanently more input information into a feed forward network. The question that interested us was if in the sample of 1,000 networks whose weight matrices were generated at random certain patterns could be detected and interpreted. We found indeed four basic types of network behavior, which we describe again as a reminder:

The first type is that of containing only vectors that changed until the end. We may interpret this as a simulation of an undecided reader who is uncertain till the end about the identity of the culprit and accordingly permanently changes his mind. This type occurred in more than one third of the cases. The second type that occurred only very seldom is a series that reached a final attractor during the 11th or 12th input (of 20 in all). We may call this as a representation of a dogmatic reader who rather early decides about the solution of the puzzle and stays with it. The third type are series that reach a final attractor near the end of the inputs, namely about the 17th or 18th one. This happened in about one third of the cases, hence nearly as often as the undecided type. Let us call them the cautious reader who keeps his mind open but who decides at last before the final inputs. Finally the series that generated local attractors but left them some inputs later occurred in about one fourth of all cases; the local attractors usually were generated after fourteen and more inputs. This may be understood as the representation of a attentive reader who forms definitive opinions but is able to change them as result of new information.

To be sure, these abstract models can be taken as indicators for different forms of perception but are just that – abstract models. In order to get more realistic results we repeated these experiments with human probands who got a detective story by Agatha Christie, namely "The Spanish Chest" that we already mentioned in the preceding chapter. We give a brief summary for readers who are not acquainted with this story by the Queen of Crime:

Hercule Poirot, the hero of many stories and novels by Christie, learns about a murder case and begins some investigations. In the house of Major Rich the butler finds in the morning after a party the corpse of Arnold Clayton, a friend of Rich. Clayton was invited to the party but could not come, as he himself had said. Besides the butler and Rich in the evening as guests were present Mr. Spence and his wife, Ms Spence, commander McLaren, and Ms Clayton, the wife of the victim. The corpse was found in the party room inside a Spanish chest; the murder weapon was an Italian dagger that was found beside the chest. Because no other people had entered the house before and during the party one of these persons must have been the murderer. Particularly important was the fact that the butler let Clayton into the house before the party because Clayton wished to inform Rich that Clayton could not come. As Rich would arrive only later Clayton went into the party room to write a message for Rich. After that nobody had seen Clayton again. It was well known that Rich was in love with Ms Clayton who also liked him. Hence the police assumed that Rich must be the murderer because he had a motive and an opportunity: He came back before the arrival of the first guests and must have been alone in the house with Clayton (and the butler).

Poirot, of course, did not believe in the guilt of Rich and collected several facts. The dagger belonged to the Spence couple; all suspects knew about it and had frequently been in the house of Spence. It was also well known that Clayton was jealous of his wife and Rich although without reason. Commander McLaren also had a deep affection for Ms Clayton who was described as a fascinating beauty. Clayton had written Rich that he must immediately go to Scotland because he had gotten a telegram about urgent business problems. Yet this telegram apparently did not exist. Poirot found out that in the side wall of the Spanish chest were several holes that obviously were artificial and very new. Finally, McLaren had met Clayton in their common club in the afternoon before the party and had talked to him.

Because of these and additional hints Poirot concluded that Clayton had hidden himself in the Spanish chest in order to secretly observe his wife and Rich who believed that Clayton was in Scotland. If this was the case then nobody had an alibi because Clayton could have been killed before the party but also during it. Poirot also concluded that Clayton had told McLaren about his plan in the club and that McLaren had used his knowledge as an opportunity to kill Clayton during the party. McLaren correctly assumed that the police would believe that Clayton had first been killed and afterwards brought into the chest. Therefore, only Rich could have been the culprit. Hence McLaren would have gotten rid of both his rivals. As in all stories of Christie in the end the detective was right – McLaren was indeed the murderer.[13]

For our experiment with this little story we found thirty volunteers, most of them interested in detective stories but none of them knew this story before the experiment. To a large degree the volunteers were students of us but about one third of the probands had no academic background.[14] The main idea of the experiment was that the probands should represent their own interpretation of the text in a formal model that we had constructed. The model was a simple feed forward net with just two layers. We were quite aware of the fact that this model is extremely simple and that because of its simplicity the results perhaps would not be very instructive. But as most of the probands had no knowledge about neural networks and were all not used to deal with such systems we had to keep the model as simple as possible.[15]

At the beginning of the experiment the test persons got besides the network and the instruction how to use it some information about the logical structure of the story. This means that the task of the test persons was to associate the suspects

---

[13]We had used this story before in a course about Artificial Intelligence and the reasoning of literary detectives in order to demonstrate how different AI-systems could solve such detective puzzles. We published the according experiments that were not the same as that described in this subchapter in Klüver and Stoica (2006).

[14]It is a frequently discussed problem that the probands in many socio-psychological experiments are students and often even students of the experimenters. That is why we successfully tried to get probands from other social contexts.

[15]Gregor Braun implemented the whole program and also performed the experiments as part of his MA-thesis.

with certain "categories" that are decisive for the identification of the real murderer. These five categories are: (a) "no alibi", (b) "access to the weapon", (c) "motive", (d) "knowledge about the real place of the murder", and (e) "suspicion". The last category means that if a test person cannot associate a suspect with one of the first four categories but has the feeling that nevertheless this person is suspect to the test person then this suspect can be associated to the last category. From a logical point of view, of course, the first four categories would be sufficient.

For the inserting their interpretation into the network the probands received a semantical matrix that is shown in Fig. 5.6:

Fig. 5.6 The semantical matrix of the story

	na	aw	mo	kn	su
Ri					
bu					
Cl					
MS					
S					
ML					

The categories are in the line at the top. "na" means "no alibi", "ac" is "access to the weapon", "mo" is "motive", "kn" is "knowledge about the murder place", and "su" is "suspicion". The six suspects define the lines of the matrix: "Ri" of course is Rich, "bu" is the butler, "Cl" is Ms Clayton, "MS" is Ms Spence, "S" is Mr. Spence, and "ML" is McLaren. In the beginning all elements of the matrix are equal to zero. The feed forward network contains the five categories as input neurons and the names of the six suspects as output neurons; its weight matrix values are also in the beginning equal to zero.

The whole story contains about 40 pages. We divided the text into four parts; the last part ended two pages before the real end of the story. This was done because the probands should learn about the end of the story only after they had delivered four different solutions according to the different parts of the text. The test persons received at first just the first quarter. After having read this part text they should fill in the semantical matrix: If for example a test person assumed that Rich had no alibi then the test person should write a "1" into the according cell Ri/na. If the test person thinks that McLaren has no motive then the zero in the according cell ML/mo remains. After having filled in all the 1-values according to the interpretation of the test person he had to press the enter key. The program then automatically transforms the semantical matrix of the test person into a weight matrix of the feed forward network and externally activates all input neurons with the same value of 0.1. The final activation results of the output neurons are shown to the test person, who decides according to the output neuron with the highest activation value whom he mainly suspects after the first quarter of the text.

The probands could enlarge the matrix and the network, if they wished, by adding additional suspects and/or additional motives but only few used this possibility. Two of the probands additionally inserted as suspect an Italian admirer of Ms Clayton who was mentioned in the text but had not been at the party. The probands explained this decision with the fact that the murder weapon was an Italian dagger, but that is just a curiosity.

The probands sent us their interpretation of the first quarter, i.e. their semantical matrix, the final activation of the output layer, a verbal interpretation of the activation values, and in addition a short verbal reason of their semantical matrix. By the way, in some cases the verbal reason of the probands identified other persons as main suspects than their own network. It had to be assumed that these probands did not really understand their task with respect to the semantical matrix. Accordingly they were not taken into account for the evaluation of the experiment.

Afterwards the probands got the second quarter of the text. Their task was now to see if their first semantical matrix must be changed according to the new information. Then the procedure was repeated, the test persons got the third part of the text, and finally the fourth. When we received the fourth results the probands got the last two pages where Poirot identified the murderer, namely McLaren, and where Poirot explained how he had come to this solution. This way the probands could compare their own results with the factual solution of the detective puzzle.

At the beginning of the experiment the test persons were all told that it was *not* our interest to see how many probands correctly identified the murderer but to get insights into their reading and interpreting behavior. Hence, the fact that only a quarter of the probands came to the conclusion that McLaren must be the culprit and that the probands of the other three quarters until the end suspected all other suspects – even if they certainly had no motives – is of only minor importance. Our interest was chiefly orientated to the question how often the probands changed their suspicions, i.e. how often they changed their main suspects, and if certain patterns in these changing can be detected. In particular we wanted to see if the factual interpreting behavior of our probands could be related to the patterns we obtained in the general experiments described above.

In order to keep the experiments as similar as possible to the first experimental series it would have been better if the probands would have gotten only smaller parts of the story, e.g. only 5% at one time; the input vector of the first series had 20 components. Yet as the probands all were volunteers who did not get any money we had to compromise and divide the story into rather large parts.

The probands, by the way, also got an "ideal matrix" from us, namely the matrix that a very careful reader should have constructed if he took into account all the important facts from the story (and of course only these).[16] For illustration purposes we show these ideal matrices (Fig. 5.7):

The matrices of the probands in most cases rather strongly deviated from the ideal matrices, in particular with respect to the butler, William Burgess, and McLaren. By analyzing the factual matrices in detail it was frequently a bit difficult to understand

---

[16]About one third of the probands were women whose success was in the average approximately equal to that of the male probands. Female readers may excuse us if for the sake of brevity we use only the pronoun "he".

	No alibi	Access to the weapon	motive	knowledge about the murder place	suspicion
Ms Clayton	0	0	1	0	0
Major Rich	1	0	1	1	0
McLaren	0	0	0	0	0
Mr Spence	0	0	0	0	0
Ms Spence	0	0	0	0	0
Butler	1	0	0	0	0

	No alibi	Access to the weapon	motive	knowledge about the murder place	suspicion
Ms Clayton	0	0	0,6	0	0
Major Rich	1	0	0,6	1	0
McLaren	0	0	0	0	0
Mr Spence	0	0	0	0	0
Ms Spence	0	0	0	0	0
Butler	1	0	0	0	0

	No alibi	Access to the weapon	motive	knowledge about the murder place	Suspicion
Ms Clayton	1	0	1	0	0
Major Rich	1	0	1	0,5	0
McLaren	1	0	0,2	0	0
Mr Spence	1	0,6	0	0	0
Ms Spence	1	0,6	0	0	0
Butler	1	0	0	0	0

	No alibi	Access to the weapon	motive	knowledge about the murder place	suspicion
Ms Clayton	1	1	0,6	0	0
Major Rich	1	1	0,6	0	0
McLaren	1	1	1	1	0
Mr Spence	1	1	0	0	0
Ms Spence	1	1	0	0	0
Butler	1	0	0	0	0

Fig. 5.7 Ideal matrices after the first, the second, the third, and the fourth quarter respectively

how specific probands generated their interpretation of the story's parts. The deviations from the ideal matrices on the one hand and the differences between the 30 factual matrices on the other hand again demonstrates that there is no typical reader and interpreter of such stories but that the understanding of literary texts depends on the learning biography of the particular reader. This result is a very concrete confirmation of our general definitions of meaning, namely that meaning is always a construction by a *specific* receiving system.

We additionally undertook a very general comparison between the ideal solution, represented in the ideal matrices, and the factual matrices by computing an "average matrix", namely a matrix consisting of the arithmetical means of the respective weight values of the factual matrices. It is a rather curious fact that despite the differences between the matrices of the probands the average matrix is rather similar to the ideal matrix. The reason for this is of course that the factual matrices differed, so to speak, in all directions from the weights of the ideal matrix; hence the differences between the matrices of the test persons canceled each other out.

More important for our analysis was the classification of the probands with respect to their changing of suspects. Because of the division of the text in four parts at most four different persons could play the role of the respective chief suspect. In several cases indeed four persons were successively selected as chief suspects, but these cases were exceptions. In most cases only two or three different suspects were chosen. The following fifteen patterns are possible; one letter always represents a chief suspect, the succession of the letters demonstrates the changing of the suspects. For example, the succession A, B, C, D means that the test person changed his suspects after each quarter, regardless which suspects were represented by the letter.

pattern 1: A, A, A, A;
pattern 2: A, A, A, B;
pattern 3: A, A, B, A;
pattern 4: A, A, B, B;
pattern 5: A, A, B, C;
pattern 6: A, B, A, A;
pattern 7: A, B, A, B;
pattern 8: A, B, A, C;
pattern 9: A, B, B, A;
pattern 10: A, B, B, B;
pattern 11: A, B, B, C;
pattern 12: A, B, C, A;
pattern 13: A, B, C, B;
pattern 14: A, B, C, C;
pattern 15: A, B, C, D.

The patterns 3 and 7 did not occur; all other patterns were generated by the probands. Patterns 2 and 5 were the most frequently generated ones.

When comparing these patterns with the types of the first experimental series the first type, i.e. the permanent changing of the output, corresponds chiefly to pattern 15 and to a lesser degree to all patterns with three different suspects who permanently varied. Such patterns are, e.g., 13 and 12. The second type, a "dogmatic" reader who decides himself early and sticks to it, corresponds chiefly to patterns 1 and 10; these probands represent the dogmatic type. The third type contains series that reach final attractors lately but before the end. This is the case, e.g., with patterns 4, 6, and 14. The fourth type who makes his final decision only at the end of the story, i.e. at the end of the text he had gotten, corresponds to different patterns, in particular patterns 2 and 5, but it is difficult to distinguish patterns corresponding to this type from, e.g. patterns that correspond to the third type. The reason is of course that series containing only four elements cannot be well compared to series of twenty elements where the differences between the series are more distinct. In a strict sense, hence, we got three clear types in the experiments with human probands and a fourth type that cannot always be clearly distinguished from the other types. As a consolation we may remind of the fact that in the first experimental series some networks could also not be classified in an unambiguous manner.

Yet despite these limitations the similarities between the results of the two experiments are quite remarkable. The human probands apparently demonstrated a reading and interpreting behavior that also could be found in the computer experiments with the networks. In the first series the thousand networks just got a binary input, i.e. their input vectors were successively filled with ones or two; the according series of output vectors could be classified with respect to the four types. In contrast the human probands had the task to code their interpretation of a factual text via the filling up of the semantical matrix that represented the logical structure of the text. In the first case the matrices were generated at random and the output vectors were the result of this generation. In the second case the matrices were deliberately constructed by the probands and generated a series of chief suspects. The fact that in both cases such a similar classification could be detected is an important indicator for the assumption that hermeneutical processes can indeed be modeled that way. In particular we might say that by the analysis of the respective matrices and their specific results we obtained a precise understanding of the test persons, i.e. their interpreting processes.

In addition it is also remarkable that the "undecided" readers (type 1) and the "cautious" one in the experiments with human probands (types 3 and 5) occur significantly more often than the other type. In particular only very few probands were in the sense dogmatic that they selected one suspect at the beginning and stuck to him (pattern 1). This is again rather similar to the quantitative results from the first series of experiments.

To be sure, such detective stories are characterized by a rather simple logical structure, although many human probands not only in these experiments were not able to detect it. It would be very rash to assume that the interpretation of all literary or non-fictional texts could be analyzed this way. Yet these first results are quite encouraging in the sense that it seems indeed possible to analyze and hence understand interpretative processes by the usage of such network models. Conversely, if an AI-system containing such neural networks gets, e.g. detective stories that way and generates according output vectors one might say that such a system at least is able to simulate simple interpretative processes. To be sure, the system must get information about categories like "motives" and so on but the interpretative process on the basis of such knowledge can be performed by a simulating AI-system.

It is a pity, though, that the analysis of the matrices the probands had constructed did show only rather weak significant relations between variance and network behavior, in particular those that we had obtained in the first experimental series. The methodical reasons probably are on the one hand the rather small number of probands (ca. 30), compared with the thousand networks of the first series, on the other hand the also small size of the networks (only $5 + 6 = 11$ elements) in comparison to the networks of the first series consisting of fifty elements and three layers, additionally the small number of different inputs (just four in this experiment), and finally the probable fact that the human probands sometimes solved their interpreting tasks with not much concentration. In addition, another reason may be the fact that the test persons did not use exactly the same weight values when constructing their matrices. For example, if one test person thought that the butler had no alibi the test person inserted a value w(Butler, no alibi) = 0.8; another test person who had the same idea inserted a value w(Butler, no alibi) = 0.6. Hence it would be necessary to reexamine the matrices of the probands with respect to choosing different values for the same idea.

It is of course very difficult under our working conditions to get much more probands and in addition the failure of some test persons showed that even such small networks are for laymen in this field difficult to understand. Therefore, the networks used in such experiments could not be much larger than in our experiments. Hence the question must remain open if under more favorable experimental conditions the networks of the probands would have shown such relations between variance and network behavior as we discovered in the first experimental series. Yet as a first experimental analysis the results nevertheless are rather satisfactory.

5.3 The Reconstruction of Human Discourses

The analysis of human discourses has been for a long time subject of scientific disciplines, in particular of linguistics and qualitative social research; this is the field of the so-called "discourse analysis". It is neither our task nor our goal to describe the different approaches that characterize this mainly interdisciplinary field of research; there are a lot of textbooks on this subject. This subchapter instead deals with the attempt to model certain human discourses by using a specific computer program and by comparing the results of the simulations with the analysis of the discourses by human test persons. The simulations as well as the analysis by the test persons had the goal to construct semantical nets of the communicators of the discourses at the end of them. One might say that this analysis was based on the idea that to understand a discourse between humans is to understand what processes can be assumed within the communicators (cf. e.g. Hörmann 1978); in this sense we come back to the classical definitions of Droysen and Dilthey about the hermeneutical necessity to capture the "inner being" of the actors one wants to understand. In other words, a discourse is understood when one can construct a mental model of the participants at the beginning of the communication and at its end, and of the processes that transformed the network at the beginning – the "start network" – into that at the end – the "end network".

For this task we selected three discourses that had been recorded in three social qualitative research projects. The first discourse is a part of a communication between a professor of chemistry and one of his graduate students about the MA-thesis of the student. We recorded this conversation during an ethnographic research project about communication forms in the sciences (Klüver 1988). The professor and several of the students allowed us to record their conversations for

1 year; the analyzed discourse is a combination of some parts of the whole long communication.

The second discourse is a conversation between a medical doctor and one of his (female) patients, taken from the study of Brisch (1980) about forms of communication between doctors and patients. Theme of the conversation was the diagnosis of the doctor with respect to certain diseases of the patient, namely that the patient had certain forms of heart diseases. The third discourse, finally, is a conversation of a married couple about the problem if their 6-year-old son should get his first computer. We selected this discourse because it is a fine example of a so-called pseudo interaction: The partners of the discourse talked about the same subject, namely computers, but factually only repeated their own point of view and did not consider the arguments and thoughts of the other (Stoica-Klüver et al. 2007).[17]

For the simulation of these discourses we constructed semantical networks that are similar to those already described in the preceding chapters. The single network is a graph with weighted connections; the subject of the respective discussion is placed at the center of the graph. The central concept of the first discourse is "laboratory experiments", namely those experiments the student had to perform for his MA-thesis. The central concepts of the second discourse are "heart disease" and "bronchitis" – the patient had wrongly assumed that bronchitis had been the cause of her problems. The network that represented the third discourse was constructed around the central concepts of "computer" and "son". The weight values of the connections were constructed according to the relations of the respective concepts to the central concept and the other ones. For example, "heart ache" in the second discourse has a strong connection from and to "heart disease" while "bronchitis" has only a weak connection to "heart ache". For each participant in the three discourse a start network and an end network was generated, the first one as described by our student and the second one was generated by the simulation program.

The simulations were done the following way: At first we, that is our MA student Bianca Kierstein, read one whole discourse and constructed the start network by inserting for each participant those concepts in his/her start network that were used by the participant during the discourse. Afterwards the simulation began with the first message of one participant. That was done by taking the central concept and those two concepts that have the strongest connections from the central concept. The receiving network "answers" with those three concepts that have the strongest connections to the three sent concepts. If the sent triple is (A, B, C) then the answered triple (X, Y, Z) are those concepts with $w(A, X) \geq w(A, U)$ for all U of the answering network, $w(B, Y) \geq w(B, U)$ for all U of the answering network and finally $w(C, Z) \geq w(C, U)$ for all U. If the receiving network does not contain one of the sent concepts then it inserts this new concept according to certain conditions.

---

[17]The detailed analysis of these discourses was subject of the MA-thesis of our former student Bianca Kierstein who also applied the computer program developed by us. Christian Oldenhausen and Christian Pfeiffer did the implementation of the program.

When the network that acted at first as the sender receives the answer (X, Y, Z) it selects the concepts of its own answer the same way, sends it to the second network that selects its second answer and so on. This is carried on until a certain stopping criterion is reached, usually a certain number of simulation steps. In our experiments we used 200–250 steps; of course, with the exception of the dialog between the professor and his student the factual discourses were significantly shorter.[18]

The decisive question is if the receiving network would keep the received new concepts, i.e. if it would insert the received new concepts into its own graph structure. If it does the new concepts would be inserted according to the following rule: The network places each new concept into the (graph) neighborhood of those concepts that are part of the message that contained the new concept. This concept then would be connected with the old ones by a symmetrical connection with $w(A,X) = w(X,A) = 0.5$ for each new concept X and each old concept A that occurred in the same message as X. If two new concepts B and C are in the message (A, B, C) then the network places the new concepts with the same values into the neighborhood of A. The program also adjusts these starting connection weights according to the frequency with which the new concepts occur in the dialog after the inserting of the new concepts. If for example a new concept X occurs in more than once in fifty steps the connection weights $w(X,Y)$ are increased for each concept Y that occurs in a message simultaneously with X. "Fifty" is an arbitrary threshold that is decreased if the runs of the programs are less than 200; it will be increased if the program runs significantly longer.

If the sent triple contains only concepts that are new for the receiving network then this network "asks" the sending network to explain its message. The first network does this by sending a triple (D, E, F) with $w(A, D) \geq w(A, U)$ for all U in the sending network (with the exception of $w(A, B)$, of course), $w(B,E) \geq w(B, U)$ and $w(C, F) \geq w(C, U)$ for all concepts U. The explanation, hence, is that "A is similar to D" and so on. If the receiving network contains the triple (D, E, F) it inserts the new concepts A, B, and C according to the same manner; the same is the case if the receiving network only knows two or one concept of the triple (D, E, F). If the receiving network does not know any of the newly sent concepts it stops this part of the communication and sends a triple (G, H, I)), where G is its central concept and H and I are selected as in the first message of the network that started the communication.

If a network "refuses" to take over a new concept the receiving network remains in the same state as before the message. Then there are three possibilities:

---

[18]Sometimes the artificial communicators did not communicate about all concepts their networks contained but used only a part of it by permanently repeating the same thematic concept triples. In 2007 we described the same phenomenon with respect to a similar program. Although we were consoled at a conference that this fact showed that our program was very humanlike we wished of course that the networks should "talk" about all concepts, as did their human counter parts. That is why we repeated in these cases the simulations and usually obtained more satisfying artificial discourses.

The receiving network knows two concepts A and B of the sent ones. Then it selects two concepts D and E with respect to A and B in the way described above; the third concept of the answer is that concept F that is most strongly connected to either D and E. In other words, if $w(D, F) \geq w(E, F)$ and $w(D, F) \geq w(D, U)$ for all concepts U then F is selected. If there is a concept G with $w(E, G) > w(E, U)$ and also $w(E, G) > w(D, F)$, then G is selected. If $w(D, F) = w(E, G)$ then either F or G are chosen at random.

The principal reason for these rules is rather obvious: We assume that human communicators who start with a central concept, i.e. the main subject of the whole conversation, will combine this with those concepts that are strongly associated with the main theme. If somebody talks about "France" then he will combine it with concepts he had learned together with "France", for example in his last vacation at the Cote d'Azure. Then he will associate "France" with "Nice", "Monte Carlo" etc. Accordingly a human receiver of such a message will remember his own experiences with this region, if he has any, or will associate it with movies about this region he had seen. Then he perhaps will answer with "Saint Tropez", "Marseille", and "Bouillabaisse". "Strong associations", i.e. connections in factual semantical networks that lead with high probability from one concept to another one, are represented in our model with high weight values, which is just the basic rule.

The question if the receiving network would learn from the sending one by taking over new concepts is determined by the values of two parameters, namely the relevance r of the subject for the receiving partner (see above Chapter 1) and the social status s of the receiver with respect to the sender. These values had to be chosen at the beginning of each simulation in the interval between 0 and 1. For example: A MA-thesis in a chemical institute is certainly relevant for the professor because the thesis is part of the research that is done in the institute the professor is heading; the same, by the way, is the case with the MA-theses we are supervising. Hence the relevance value is larger than zero. But because the professor is responsible for many students and their MA-theses the particular thesis the student and the professor are talking about is not of very high relevance – e.g. $rv = 0.3$, if rv denotes the relevance value. The relevance of the theme for the student is of course much higher because his whole professional future depends on the success of the thesis and of an according favorable impression that the professor has of him. Hence $rv = 1$ or $rv = 0.9$ in the case of the student.

With respect to social status it is of course no question, which of the two participants has the higher status; in particular, the status difference between the professor and the student is even larger in this case as usually between a professor and a student because the supervisor is the most important person in the academic life of the student as the supervisor is the person who decides about the student's fate. The student, so to say, is practically completely at the mercy of the professor. If the status value sv of the professor is $sv = 1$ (with respect to this communicative situation) then the student's value is approximately $sv = 0.1$ or at most $sv = 0.2$.

The relevance value and the status value are after their single fixing combined to a socio-relevance value $srv = rv + (1 - sv)$. Obviously $0 \leq srv \leq 2$. In the case of the professor $srv = 0.3$; in the case of the student $srv = 1.9$ or $srv = 1.7$ respectively.

The learning rule for the semantical network now simply is: If new concepts are in a message then the new concepts will be learned, i.e. inserted into the network as described above, with a probability p = srv/2. The professor, hence, will only learn from the student with a probability p = 0.15, i.e. only very seldom; the student will learn with a probability p = 0.95 or p = 0.85 respectively, that is very often. We chose such a probability rule and not a deterministic one because even a participant of a discourse who is very willing to learn everything from the other will frequently not remember certain remarks of the other. Conversely, even if a participant in a conversation is not very interested in the theme and if he has a significantly higher social status than the other he nevertheless might learn a little.

The idea behind the definition of sv on the one hand is of course that people with higher social status are frequently not very willing to learn from others with lower status because the higher-ranking ones do not need to learn from subordinates. The people with lower status on the other hand frequently must learn, i.e. be attentive and remember, because their professional career, their health, or other important aspects of their life might depend on their learning. The definition of rv on the other hand is based on the well-known fact that people pay more attention to themes that are important for them than to unimportant themes. Hence they will more likely not listen or forgetting the messages after a short time if the relevance is not high. Conversely, a high relevance of the theme will mean careful attention to the received messages and a remembrance of the new concepts.

Because the dialogues are in German we do not quote parts of them – with one exception – but just describe the determination of the srv-values for the other two discourses and show some of the constructed networks. The medical discourse is with respect to the parameter values very similar to the dialogue between the professor and the student. The doctor definitely has the higher social status, not only because he is the expert and the patient a laywoman but also because the patient apparently has no academic education. Accordingly the sv of the doctor is sv = 1, that of the patient is sv = 0.3 or even 0.2. The theme of the discourse is of course relevant for both of them. Yet as in the case of the professor the doctor of course has not only this patient but many others. His relevance value, therefore, is the same as that of the professor, namely rv = 0.3. For the patient in contrast a talk about her own diseases is of very high relevance, i.e. rv = 1. The rsv-values are accordingly rsv = 0.3 for the doctor and rsv = 1.7 or 1.8 for the patient. The doctor, hence, will learn only with a probability p = 0.15, the patient with p = 0.85 or 0.95 respectively.

In the case of the married couple an analysis of their dialogue obtained the fact that the two semantical start nets were centered on different concepts. In the case of the woman the center concept is "computer" with strong connections to concepts like "mouse", "mega bytes" and other technical aspects. Of course, the semantical network of the woman also contains the concept "son" because the conversation was, as we mentioned, about the possible first computer for the son. But the main concepts are technical characteristics of different computers. The semantical network of the husband, on the other hand, was centered on "son" with strong connections to concepts like "pedagogical responsibility", "dangers", "fixation on video games" and so on although his network also contained "computer". Accordingly the two start networks had to be constructed as two very different networks. We already characterized this dialogue as a "pseudo interaction", which means that it is only in a formal sense a communicative interaction. As an illustration for such an interaction that seems on a first sight very strange we quote a part of the dialogue in our translation; W is the wife and H is the husband:

H: "Well, our problem is not the technique. We have to think about the pedagogical problems that are involved..." (W interrupts)

W: "Yes, but..." (H continues)

H: "... if children are confronted with such media."

W: "Yes, but there are WLAN integrated and also Bluetooth. Everything is in it and he can practically do everything with it."

H: "Yes, but first we have to think about the pedagogical problems. There have been cruel accidents in schools and these War and Violence Games.." (W again interrupts)

W: "Yes, but we could insert some controls and he could not go to certain pages. These technical possibilities of this Laptop, incredible."

H: "The problem is not the technique but our responsibility."[19]

Factually the participants only talked about their specific part themes, namely "computer and technical aspects" on the one hand and "pedagogical responsibility" on the other without referring to the theme of the partner.[20] This is not so in the case of the two other dialogs. In these dialogs the semantical networks of both participants were rather similar, although the networks of the doctor and the professor are significantly larger than those of the patient and the student.

For the determination of the parameter values with respect to the couple we knew that both participants are socially equal with $sv = 1$ for both of them. A bit more complicated is the value of the relevance parameter: Factually they are talking about two themes, which are important for both of them. Their equal relevance value for *their own themes* is $rv = 0.7$. Yet the inserting of new concepts refers to the theme the other is talking about. The analysis of the discourse shows that in this specific communicative situation the relevance of the other's theme is rather low because neither the husband nor the wife is willing to talk about the theme of the

---

[19]The husband refers to several incidents at German schools where pupils had run amok and shot other pupils and teachers.

[20]We are quite aware that the networks of the couple do not mirror that division of interest one would usually expect. The usual assumption with respect to such themes would be that the man preferred to talk about technical aspects of the computer and the woman about pedagogical ones. As we personally know this specific couple we can only say that this reversing of usual expectations in this dialogue was certainly a bit consciously exaggerated by the couple but not untypical for them.

other. Hence that relevance value is just 0.2. Consequently the learning probability is $p = 0.1$ in both cases.[21]

As visual demonstration we present the start networks for the professor and the wife (Figs. 5.8 and 5.9):

The simulation starts with the described construction of the start network for both participants and is run by the exchange of messages between the networks, i.e. the artificial participants. The end network is reached after the end of the simulation runs, i.e. after 200–250 steps. The most important results are:

In the cases of the first two dialogs the end networks are as could be expected. The networks of the doctor and of the professor did not change much; they apparently had not taken over concepts from their dialog partners or only in very few cases. The reasons for this are the low learning probability on the one hand and the fact that their start networks were much larger than those of their partners. Hence the probability was very low that the professor and the doctor got any new concepts from the other participant. In contrast the end networks of the patient and the student had changed much, in particular with respect to their size.

The networks of the professor and the doctor had not significantly changed. The patient and the student indeed had learned a lot; for example, the number of concepts of the student had increased from 15 to nearly 60 concepts. The reasons of course are the high learning probabilities and the comparatively small start networks in both cases.

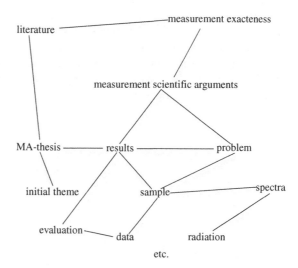

Fig. 5.8 Part of the start net of the professor

<hr />

[21] Of course, this is not to say that the son is not important to the wife and that the husband is not interested in computers – on the contrary, as we know (see preceding footnote). It just means that *in this communication* the wife mainly wishes to speak about technical aspects of computers and the husband about pedagogical problems concerning the computer.

Fig. 5.9 Start network of the wife

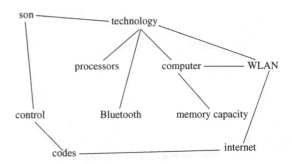

In contrast to these results of the simulation runs both networks of the couple had practically not changed at all. As an according example we show the end network of the wife (Fig. 5.10):

One sees that the wife kept her start network and just added the concepts "responsibility" and "Video Games". In the factual discourse as well as in the artificial one, as one can see from intermediate steps of the program, the participants only talked about their own themes without taking into regard the statements of the other. Accordingly factually no learning took place and the networks remained unchanged.

Besides the communicative rules, i.e. to orientate at the strongest connections, apparently the specific values of the parameters determine the outcome of the artificial discourses. As far as a communicative situation is determined by social and thematic factors the outcome is, at least in such simulations, predictable. There are other social factors that must be taken into account when analyzing communicative processes; besides social status, for example, the belonging of the participants to a common social domain plays an important role (cf. Klüver and Klüver 2007). But

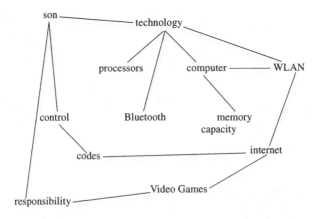

Fig. 5.10 End network of the wife

for the simulation of these discourses the social status and relevance parameters are sufficient.

To be sure, when the program has generated the end networks it would have been desirable to compare these with an estimation of the participants in the factual dialogue. Unfortunately this was not possible – with the exception of the married couple – because the two other discourses were performed and written down more than 20 years ago. The couple was for other reasons also not available any more. Therefore, we chose another way to validate the generated networks:

About ten graduate students of us got the written discourses with short information about the respective contexts, i.e. about the participants of the discourses and the communicative situations. As all students already were in the end phase of their studies, namely writing their respective MA-theses in communication and computer science, they knew in principle the situation of the chemistry student very well; they also had experiences with visits at a medical practice. We did not know if the students had experiences with conversations between married partners; their results hint at the opposite (see below). The students did not get the start networks but should form their own opinions without any influences by us. They also did not get our estimations about relevance and social status for the same reason; in particular they did not get the learning rule determined by the values of the social status and the relevance parameters. The explanation how the simulation program operated was given to the students only after they finished their task. This task was to construct an end network for all discourse participants, namely to visualize their interpretation of the discourse by forming an opinion about the "state of mind" of the discourse participants at the end of the dialogue, independent of the results of the simulation program. The chief results are the following:

The dialog between the doctor and the patient was interpreted in a very similar way by nearly all probands as was done by the program. The students also assumed that the patient would learn a lot from the conversation with the doctor and that conversely the doctor would learn practically nothing from the patient. Accordingly the students constructed an end network of the patient (and the doctor) that contained most of the concepts and the respective connections that the program had generated. In addition, even most of the connection weights in the networks of the students and that of the program were comparable, i.e. not in their exact values but in their relative size.[22]

Only one of the probands differed from the majority by constructing a network that differed from that of the network to 50%. The chief reason for this deviance is that the student apparently did not believe that the patient would learn much from the doctor. Accordingly his network of the patient was rather small.

The same similarity can be seen in the case of the second dialogue. Most of the test persons apparently interpreted the communicative situation in the same way as we did by inserting the particular parameter values. That is no wonder

---

[22]In contrast to the test persons of the experiment described in the preceding subchapter the students were because of their common work with us used to the construction of such networks.

because, as we remarked, the probands all knew such a situation by own and very current experiences. Accordingly their semantical networks of the professor and the student are very similar to those of the program, although, of course, the "artificial" end networks are not identical with the "empirical" ones. Yet the differences between the artificial network on the one hand and the empirical ones were in the average not larger than the differences between the single empirical ones. The similarity cannot only be seen in a significant agreement with respect to the concepts but also to the relative strength of the connections between the concepts.

In a certain sense one can say that the program generated something like an ideal type in the sense of Max Weber. The networks of the probands differed with respect to concepts from that of the program but, so to say, in different directions. For example, network of test person A contained a concept X that is not in the network of the program; the program but contained a concept Y that is not in the network of A. Test person B's network contained concept Y but not Z, which is in the artificially constructed network and also in the network of A. When constructing a common intersection of the networks of the probands we found out that all of the concepts of that intersection are also in the artificial network. Each empirically constructed network, hence, is a specific deviation from both the intersection network and the artificially constructed one. We believe that Max Weber would have agreed with our using of his methodical conception of ideal type.

It is rather striking that the significant similarities between the empirical networks and the artificial one in the first two cases cannot be found in the third case, i.e. the dialogue between the married partners. Practically all of the probands assumed that both husband and wife were willing to learn from each other; accordingly larger are the empirically constructed end networks. The probands obviously did not see that the dialogue is an example of a pseudo interaction, as we mentioned above. This interpretation is confirmed by the fact that both participants until the end only talked about their own themes. The program took this into account because of the low learning probability; the students did this not. Perhaps, but this is only speculation, the comparatively young test persons still believed that a husband and a wife not only have common interests but are also always willing to carefully listen to the other and to take his statements seriously. The program had no such bias.[23] We show the end network of the wife as constructed by one of our students (Fig. 5.11):

The comparison between the results of the simulation runs and the empirically constructed networks are rather satisfactory in the case of the first two dialogues. Apparently our simulation program is able to understand such discourses in a very similar way, as do human interpreters if one defines "understanding discourses" the way we did: The program "knew" at the end of the discourse about the internal states of the participants. The fact that the third discourse war interpreted rather differently

---

[23]The fact that, at least in Germany, the number of marriages is still rising after a severe decline in the eighties and nineties indicates that young people again or still believe in marriage and married life.

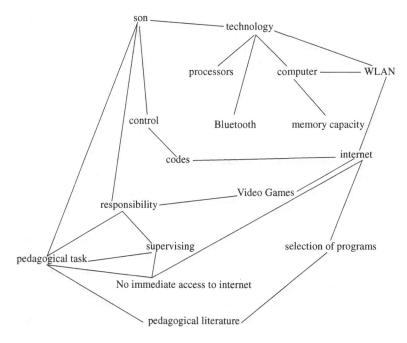

Fig. 5.11 End network of the wife, constructed by a test person

by the program and the students can be explained that a pseudo interaction is indeed very hard to recognize, in particular if one quite sensibly assumes that the partners of a married couple are willing to listen to one another. The deplorable fact that pseudo interactions are not seldom and that in particular they can occur even in marriages is something that must be learned and that specifically young people who still dream of happiness in marriage are not readily willing to accept.[24] Yet the success in the first two cases demonstrates that for usual situations, i.e. communications where the participants listen to one another, our program can successfully predict the outcome, as far as our human probands can be accepted as arbiters. One might even say that the program "understood" the dialogue between the couple better than the human probands; our own interpretation of this discourse though is much more similar to that of the program than to those of the probands.

To be sure, an objection here suggests itself: The results of the program on the one hand indicate the validity of the communicative rules and on the other the equal validity of the parameter values; the results are after all generated by the rules and parameter values. Yet in particular the values of the parameters were inserted by us, namely by our interpretation of the communicative situations. Therefore, the hermeneutical achievement with respect to the dialogues is due to

---

[24]To avoid a misunderstanding that might here occur: The authors are married with each other and also still believe in – at least – the possibility of happiness in a marriage.

human interpreters and not to some hermeneutical abilities of the simulation program. We have proven, hence, that it is possible to interpret human discourses with the help of such programs and that it is possible to construct mathematical models of communicative situations but not that AI-systems are able to do such interpretations by themselves. On the contrary, our methodical procedure just demonstrated the unavoidable necessity of human interpreters when one wants to practice hermeneutics.

The failure of the students to recognize the third dialogue as a specific example of pseudo interaction might clarify this point and help to see this objection in more relative terms. This specific example of computer based discourse analysis was of course only possible by the interpretation of the communicative situation by us. In particular, we had to know such situations – from personal experiences and our knowledge as social scientists – and also had to know how to model them in the described fashion. The students obviously had not the necessary knowledge to recognize pseudo interaction as such. In other words, human interpreters are only able to successfully perform such forms of discourse analysis if they have learned about such situations and how to interpret them. The program had no such learning process: We shortened the whole methodical procedure by inserting the communicative rules and in particular the necessary parameter values ourselves. Of course, the program did not contain any explicit knowledge about human modes of speaking, i.e. combining those concepts that are strongly associated; hence we had to insert these rules. It also had no explicit knowledge about the meaning of social status and of the relevance of particular themes. Yet as human interpreters have to learn such aspects of social reality and are able to learn them there is no general reason why a program could not learn such methodical procedures, based on social knowledge, too. It would be easy, for example, to train specific neural networks with respect to the methodical meaning of social status and the according parameter values it had to operate with. Our dealing with the problem of learning from examples (see above Chapter 2) and rule extraction by neural networks (cf. above Section 4.3) demonstrates how this could be done.

The same is the case with the problem of recognizing the relevance of certain themes for the participants of a discourse: One just needs for example in the dialogue between the doctor and the patient a list of concepts, ordered according to their relevance for certain persons or for humans in general. At the top there always will be problems of health and possible death. A semantical network that combines these very important concepts with those of "doctor", "medical practice", "discourse about diagnosis" and so on will automatically generate a high relevance value for the theme of such a discourse we just analyzed. It is "only" a question of learning and not a principal limit of such programs that they at present still need the interpreting competence of humans. There are, after all, many humans who are not able to interpret certain communicative interactions, even if they know examples of them from personal experience. Therefore, it is no *principal* objection against our program that it still has limits.

5.4 Understanding in Communicative Processes by Mental Models

In Klüver and Klüver (2007) we described several communicative experiments with social groups that were performed by our former MA student Jochen Burkart. The research question was to see if a specific simulation program could successfully predict the outcome of communication processes. For this analysis several groups of human probands, mainly students of us from communication science and computer science, got the task to discuss different themes like, for example, "Christmas" (the experiments took place in December), "football" (the European version), "holiday" and so on. All themes were selected under the condition that we could assume a common knowledge of the probands about each theme. Each group of about six to ten participants got three themes and they should discuss each theme for about 15 min.

Before the discussions the test persons had to construct their semantical networks with respect to the different themes. The probands, though, should not construct an explicit network because we thought it a bit difficult for them; if one is not used to construct such networks it would need some time to organize one's own thoughts in a network with weighted connections. In particular, the test persons should not think too long about their associations but should write it down rather spontaneously. Therefore, they should organize their associations the following way:

Each test person got three sheets of paper, one for each theme; in the center of each paper was the theme of the according discussion as the central concept. Around the theme concept were several concentric circles. The probands should write those concepts they associated with the theme into the circles according to the succession the concepts were associated. The first three associated concepts belonged into the first circle, the next three or four into the second one and so forth. We show such a "circle network" in Fig. 5.12 about the theme "Paris" (the city and not the Trojan prince):

By neglecting a connection between the central concept and itself we defined that the connection weight $cw(C, C_{next})$ of the central concept to the concepts in the next circle is $cw(C, C_{next}) = 1$; the connection weight from the central concept to the concepts in the second circle is $cw(C, C_s) = 0.8$; the concepts in the third circle are connected with $cw(C, C_{third}) = 0.6$ and so on. For our example with "Paris" we obtain the list

cw(Paris, France) = 1;
cw(Paris, Eiffel Tower) = 1;
cw(Paris, Moulin Rouge) = 1;
cw(Paris, Boulevard St. Michel) = 1;
cw(Paris, Seine) = cw(Paris, Arc de Triomphe) = 0.8;

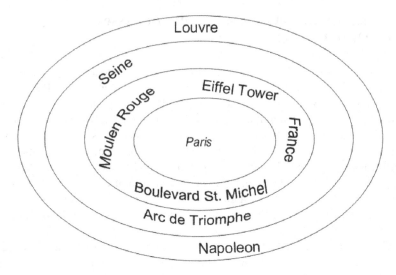

Fig. 5.12 Circle network about the theme "Paris"

cw(Paris, Napoleon) = cw(Paris, Louvre) = 0.6.

As "Paris" is a central concept we assume that the connections from the other concepts to "Paris" are usually at least as strong as reversely. In other words, one more frequently associates "Paris" when thinking of "Louvre" than the other way around. Therefore, we defined

$$cw(X, Paris,) = 1, \text{ if } cw(Paris, X) = 1,$$
$$cw(X, Paris) = 0.8, \text{ if } cw(Paris, X) < 1. \tag{5}$$

With these definitions the filled out forms of the experimental subjects could be inserted as structured semantical networks, i.e. as weighted graphs, into the program.[25]

The interesting question now was if the program could predict the communication processes of the different groups with respect to a mutual understanding of the participants, i.e. if the different individual networks would become more similar. To analyze this question we defined the coming closer together in terms of a so-called semantical correspondence.

When the participants after the three rounds of discussion filled out their final forms, this semantical correspondence of the experimental group was computed. The assumption is, of course, that the degree C of semantical correspondence would increase as a result of the discussion rounds. The exact computing of the semantical correspondence should not only take into account the number of common concepts

---

[25] We repeat these formal details in such length because they are part of the methodical basis of the new experiments described below.

for all participants but also the specific structure of the semantical networks of the experimental subjects before and after the discussions. Therefore, we defined:

By considering that for two communicators A and B the number of concepts at the disposal of the communicators is important we define the quantitative correspondence C_k as

$$C_k = 2 * j/(n + m), \tag{6}$$

if j is the number of common concepts and n and m are the number of concepts of A and B respectively.

For the computing of the qualitative (or structural) semantical correspondence C_u we must consider the weight of the connections between the central concept and another certain concept. If for a concept X the weight in the semantical network of A is $cw_A(C, X) = r$ and in the network of B $cw_B(C, X) = s$, then for this concept the qualitative correspondence is

$$C_u = 1 - |r - s|. \tag{7}$$

By combining the qualitative correspondence for all common concepts i we obtain a weighted average

$$C_{uw} = \left(\sum_I C_{ui}\right)/q, \tag{8}$$

if q is the number of common concepts.

The whole semantical correspondence C can then be defined as

$$C = C_k * C_{uw}. \tag{9}$$

In other words, by this definition one not only takes into account the number of common concepts in relation to the number of concepts A and B have at their disposal but also the structural integration of these common concepts into the two networks of A and B.

For the semantical correspondence of a group of more than two communicators one has to compute CXY for each pair of communicators X and Y, and subsequently again compute the average of these values. Thus we obtain for a group G

$$C_G = \left(\sum C_i\right)/t, \tag{10}$$

for each pair i of communicators, if t is the number of pairs of communicators.

For each group the semantical correspondence was computed with respect to the networks at the beginning of the discussions. After the discussions about each theme the probands had to fill out their semantical networks again the same way. Then the semantical correspondence for each group again was computed and the two values of semantical correspondence were compared. As an empirical result we obtained that indeed the semantical correspondence had increased by the discussions with the exception of one group (cf. Klüver and Klüver 2007). A quite amusing example, by the way, for the changing of a semantical network as result of the discussion is this (Fig. 5.13):

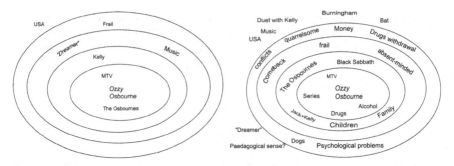

Fig. 5.13 Two semantical networks of "Ozzy Osbourne" before and after the discussion about this interesting theme

The student who constructed these networks obviously did not know much before the discussion about the English Rock star Osbourne; the same is the case with one of the authors. Yet she got interested in the discussion and learned a lot.

The task of the program now was to simulate these communicative processes and to predict this way the increasing of the semantical correspondence. The program we used is very similar to that described in the preceding subchapter; in fact, both programs have the same logical structure and differ only with respect to the different simulating tasks. The most significant difference is that this version (the earlier one) does not contain the two parameters of relevance and social status and accordingly no rule for computing a probability of learning. The program just lets its artificial communicators learn new concepts if they are sent by another communicator, but only if they had actively participated, i.e. have sent a message, immediately before the new message. As the starting point the program got the different semantical networks of all members of a specific group; the simulations of the discussions were performed by the program the same way, as did the program of the preceding subchapter. After ca. 200 runs the program stopped, computed the semantical correspondence of the artificial groups it had generated, and compared these values with those of the empirical groups.

These experiments were performed with 10 different groups of human members, mostly, as we said, students from our university, but not always. The most important results are the following:

In six cases, i.e. six different groups, the prediction of the program differed only about 5–10% from the factual outcome of the respective human groups. The computing of these differences occurs, of course, by computing the difference between the factual outcome and the prediction of the program for each subject and by combining these three different values via the arithmetical mean. For some themes the difference was even lower, i.e., less than 5%. In three cases the difference was about 10–15% and only in one case the difference was more than 25%.

These results were quite satisfactory and we did not really expect them. Apparently human communication frequently is determined by rather simple rules; our simulation program is, as we showed, not very complicated indeed. Less successful yet were the following experiments where the program first should predict the final semantical networks of single participants and in second experimental series mental models of the participants, constructed by their communicative partners.

Comparisons of the artificial individual semantical networks and those of the human probands showed a semantical correspondence, measured as we described above, of mostly only 40–50%. Although in some cases the correspondence was astonishingly large in other cases it was accordingly rather low. The only partial success of the program was mainly due to, as far as we could detect, an unrealistic assumption: The program operated under the condition that all communicators participated equally frequently in the discussions. Accordingly they all could learn new concepts with the same probability. Yet a comparison of the artificial dialogues with the factual ones showed that in several cases this assumption was not valid. Some probands did not talk much and others very often. The factual final semantical networks of the silent probands showed that they had indeed not learned much and the others significantly more than the average. As a consequence the semantical networks of the quiet probands were significantly smaller than their artificial counterparts; conversely the artificial networks of the probands with a high talking frequency were significantly smaller than the factual networks. Although the rule in the simulation program about learning only after own message sending seems to be quite realistic the predictions of the program suffered from the fact that we could not know if the probands would talk much, in the average, or only little. The program just operated with an average talking frequency for each test person.

This fact also explains why the group predictions were successful despite the only partial success with the prediction of the single networks. Obviously the differences between the single empirical networks did not matter in the average: If the program prognosticated a network that was larger than its factual counterpart this error was compensated by the construction of an artificial network that was smaller than the empirical one. We have a situation here that is frequently found in quantitative empirical research, for example empirical surveys: Although the, e.g. factual voting of single individuals at an election is only difficult to predict rather valid prognostications are possible for large groups. In our case we could even predict the communicative results of rather small groups.[26]

By the way, as in the preceding subchapter we might again use Weber's term of ideal type. The program sometimes predicted in the case of the groups semantical correspondence values that were too small and for other groups values that were too large. The program predicted, so to speak, an ideal type of communicative processes with mean values. The deviations in the empirical groups are then nothing else than empirical deviations from an ideal type; we here remind of the ideal type we already examined in Chapter 2 in the case of the early Calvinists.[27]

---

[26]Jochen Burkart performed these and the experiments described below as part of his PhD-thesis.

[27]It may be noted as a curious detail that frequently the program did better to predict single networks if the respective person was a woman than it did with predicting the networks of male

The second question was if the program could predict mental models that the probands should construct of other members of their discussion group – of course after the discussions about the three themes. In each group, namely other groups than in the experiments just described, every test person got the task to make a mental model of one other member. We selected for each test person one other member in order to guarantee that each group member was represented by his/her mental model. For strict methodical reasons it would have been desirable if each test person would make a mental model of each other member. Because the participants of these experiments were all volunteers without any pay we had to make it as simple as possible for them. We assumed that the mental models that different probands constructed of the same person would anyway be rather similar.

The reason why we asked the probands to perform this task was our interest if the discussions had lead to some form of understanding in the same sense that we used in the preceding subchapter. Frequently one assumes that the result of communication is, if not an agreement about controversial themes, at least a mutual understanding of the communicative partners.[28] If this assumption is correct then our probands should be able to construct valid mental models of their discussion partners. The probands should use the same method for the construction of the mental models as they had used for the construction of their own semantical networks, namely the method of concentric circles that the program transformed into semantical networks.

For the construction of artificial mental models the program got a list of all concepts the respective persons had used during the discussion – for each single theme of course. The list was ordered according to the succession of concepts the person had used. The program then constructed for each theme and each person a semantical network similarly as it constructs semantical networks from the concentric circles: The theme concepts again are the central concepts; the first three concepts of the list are connected with the central concept in the way we described above; the same was done with the next three concepts and so on. The idea behind this procedure is rather simple: Each test person could construct his mental model only by the impression of the other person he had gotten during the discussions, i.e. by the factually performed statements of the other person. Accordingly the program only got those concepts that the person had factually used during the discussions.

To be sure, the mental models constructed this way would practically always be significantly smaller than the factual networks of the modeled person. Nobody can talk about all the concepts he has at his disposal in so short a time, even if the discussion groups are small – in extreme cases only two participants. Therefore, we added the rule that the program in addition got several concepts from one of

---

probands. Yet because the significance of these differences is not very high we just note it as an amusing puzzle. We certainly do not infer from these results that women are easier to predict – and hence to understand – than men.

[28]The permanent and expensive voyages of politicians to politicians of other countries are usually legitimated with the argument that it is important to personally understand the other states men and women. We leave it to the readers if this argument is convincing.

the factual starting networks. The respective network was selected at random; the chosen additional concepts were selected at random too with the condition that they should not be in the list of the mental model. Their number was about 30% of the number of the concepts that the list contained. These additional concepts were inserted into the mental model with weight values to and from all other concepts $w(X, Y) = w(Y, X) = 0.5$. In other words, the additional concepts were treated as if the modeled person had placed them into a fourth circle as the basis for his semantical network.

The artificial mental models were then compared with those that the probands had constructed on the one hand and with the factual final semantical networks of the respective persons on the other. The results were, on a first sight, a bit curious:

The correspondence between the artificial mental models and the empirical ones were rather low, although a bit larger than the correspondence in the case of the prediction of single networks. In both cases the program was only partially successful even if it could predict the mental models constructed by humans of other humans a bit better. The comparison between the artificial mental models, those constructed by the probands, and the final empirical semantical networks of the respective modeled person obtained a rather strange result: The program did not very well in its reconstruction of the modeled person but the human probands did even worse. The average correspondence of the artificial mental models with the empirical final network was about 35–40%; the average correspondence of the probands mental models with the factual networks was about 28–30%. *In nuce*, neither the program nor the humans could construct satisfactory mental models of other persons, at least not with respect to the self-appraisal of the respective person.[29]

By the way, a quite other experiment that was even less successful obtained similar results in the comparison between a simulation program and human probands. Several pairs of students were asked to discuss some subjects from their everyday experience. The experimenter, one of our former students, several times interrupted the discussion and asked both students to write down their expectations what the other would say next. A simulation program, similar to those described, got the same subject and had to predict the next statements too. The program was only in about 6% of the interruptions successful, which cannot be called a prediction at all. But the students were, as in the simulations just described, even less successful, namely only in about 4% of the interruptions. Obviously neither human communicators nor our simulation program can exactly predict the next statements of a partner in communicative interactions.[30]

---

[29]It must be added that we had only ten test persons at our disposal, divided into three groups. Burkart had for his experiments described below significantly more test persons.

[30]To be sure, there are examples where the communicative partners know rather well what the other will say in the next communicative step, for example couples who have been married for a long time and who know each other very well. Yet usual communicative processes consist of participants who know each other not so well; in our experiment the students knew each other only slightly, if at all. Therefore, we believe that our results are representative and that our simulation program is "humanlike" in the sense that it cannot do what humans usually also cannot do.

If only the program had produced such unsatisfactory results the conclusion would be unavoidable that the program is simply not suited for this task. But because the human probands did even worse such an explanation would be too simple. Therefore, we have to examine the probable reasons for the common failure of the probands and the program.

The reason for the failure of the program is almost certainly the fact that the data basis for the program only contained those concepts that the modeled person had actually spoken during the discussions. Even participants who have talked comparatively much could not use all the concepts they had at their disposal. Because the program could use only a part of the whole set of concepts it is evident that the program could not reconstruct the whole self-estimation of the modeled person. Consider for example the student who had learned a lot about the Rock Star Ozzy Osbourne. Because she knew not much about him at the beginning of the discussions she could not contribute much to the discourse. Yet she learned and in the end her semantical network was rather large. The program on the other hand just could take the few concepts with which she contributed at the discussion. It is no wonder that in these cases the program failed, despite the additional rule of inserting concepts at random into the list. Only in the cases where the probands used nearly all their concepts they had at their disposal in the discussions the program was able to construct a valid mental model. In further experiments we shall try to increase the number of additional concepts.

The failure of the test persons is not so easily explained. In principle they had the same data basis as the program but apparently they used it even worse. Although the probands had been told that they should construct mental models of one of their partners they obviously concentrated not much on this task during the discussions or even forgot it. As a consequence they were not able to understand their partners in terms of mental models.

Yet despite this failure most of the students said that they were content with the discussions and that they had the feeling that the degree of mutual understanding in the discussion groups had significantly increased. Apparently these students did not think that a successful discussion necessarily must result in understanding by constructing valid mental models of their partners. In this sense they took a similar position as we had already formulated in Chapter 3: If all participants believe that the discussion is going rather well and that they understand what the others are saying then no mental models of the others are necessary. Only if the participants get the opinion that something goes wrong with the discussion, that they do not understand *what* the others are saying, and *why* the others are talking more and more strangely, then the need for the construction of mental models arises. Understanding in the conscious way of constructing mental models of the other is necessary and will be done only if the participants get a feeling and/or a certainty of permanent misunderstanding. The students in our experiments obviously did not have such a feeling or even certainty.[31]

---

[31] More details and statistical analyses of the experiments can be read in the published version of the dissertation of Jochen Burkart (forthcoming).

Because of the not very satisfactory results of these experiments Jochen Burkart developed in his PhD thesis another procedure to generate mental models by the simulation program (the first procedure was developed by us, the authors); he tested it with significant more test persons than we had at our disposal. This method is strictly orientated to the generation of the artificial discourses without referring to the factual discourses; the main idea is this:

At the beginning of the artificial discourse between communicators A and B A starts as the first sender with a message (X, Y, Z); X is mostly the subject concept. Afterwards A starts with the construction of a mental model of B, namely the generation of a second network consisting of the concepts A has just sent. When B answers according to the logic described above B also generates a second network that is its mental model of A. This mental model also consists of the sent concepts. When A gets the message of B A in addition includes the received concepts into its mental model of B. B does the same with the concepts it has received from A, namely including them into its mental model of A. This way both communicators successively build mental models of their partners until the end of the artificial discourse, while in the first procedure the mental model is constructed at one time. For three artificial communicators A, B, and C for both procedures the result of the first procedure, the intermediate stages and the result of the second procedure look like this (Fig. 5.14):

The assumption behind this second procedure is that both communicators presume that the semantical networks of their respective partners consist of (a) obviously the concepts that the partner has sent and (b) the concepts the partner has received from the other. In the basic version of this procedure no learning limits are included. If A or B send or receive concepts that had been sent or received before, the respective mental model will not be changed. The new concepts are inserted into the mental model with constant weight values $w(X, Y) = 0.5 = w(Y, X)$, if X is an "old" concept and Y is a new one.

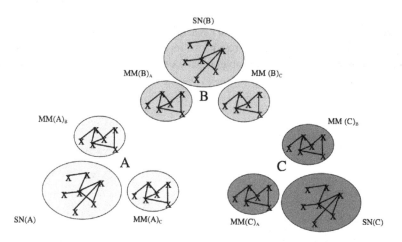

Fig. 5.14 Construction of mental models by the program

The procedure by Burkart obviously has not the disadvantages of the first method that nearly always artificial mental models are significantly smaller than the factual networks. Burkart's method in contrast principally uses all concepts for the construction of mental models that are at disposal of both artificial communicators A and B, namely the factual start networks of the human communicators that are at the disposal of A and B at the beginning of the artificial discourse. One disadvantage is that the procedure frequently results in a steadily increasing correspondence of both mental models that include nearly all concepts of A and B together. In addition it does not take into account that the human communicators have strictly speaking as a database for the mental model only the factually spoken statements of the other. These disadvantages might be the main reason for the fact that the results obtained with the method of Burkart are not significantly better than those gained with the first procedure. It is interesting though that also in the experiments with the second procedure the students had even less success than the program. To be sure, the mental models obtained from the different methods are usually significantly different. Apparently there is still a lot to be done.

The construction of mental models is a rational way to reach the goal of classical hermeneutics, namely to perceive the internal states of the other and by this understand him. This capability is often called "empathy", namely the ability to put oneself into the probable internal state of the other and to take over his perspective. The term "empathy" is rather unfortunate because it is derived from the Greek word *pathein*, which means "feel"; empathy hence can be literally translated as "feeling into someone". Accordingly the competence of empathy is frequently used with the denotation that it is an action determined by some emotional states of the empathic actor. Our experiments with both methods have shown that on the one hand human communicators are not always competent in such tasks and that on the other hand it is quite possible to give this term a very rational meaning by constructing mental models of the other via a computer program. Empathy obviously is and must be a very rational and methodically precise way to understand the other and should not be confused with some emotionally determined actions. Despite the fact that neither the program nor the probands were successful in constructing mental models this insight at least is a very valuable result of these experiments. It will be a task for future experiments with human probands and computer simulations how the present results could be improved.

Chapter 6
Conclusions: AI and a Unified Science

Research in AI has at present become a High Tech enterprise with rather compli-cated mathematical formulas and algorithms and with a lot of computing power (cf. Russell and Norvig loc. cit.). It is hard to see that and how these purely technical fields of research can contribute to the aim of combining sciences and humanities. As one can frequently observe in the history of science AI has become estranged from its original goals, namely to orientate to the ways of human thinking and to construct models. The different learning rules in the field of neural networks, for example, are not constructed because they mirror the way humans learn but because they are effective optimization algorithms. AI research, so to speak, has developed an internal dynamics of its own and cares more about technical possibilities than about the original goals that were stated at the beginning, namely at the famous Dartmouth conference (cf. Gardner 1985).

We chose another way to follow our goal. In orientation to the original ideas that founded AI research we first tried to understand the problems that are the original subject of the humanities and then looked if there are mathematical and techni-cal methods suited for our modeling aims. It is no wonder that we chiefly depend on neural networks; the first network by McCulloch and Pitts (1943) after all that founded the concept of constructing artificial networks was explicitly orientated to the brain. Therefore, our general procedure was to model cognitive processes by suited neural networks, tried to analyze them with respect to certain mathematical characteristics, and compared their operations with those of human probands. The main idea was to keep the network models as close as possible to the phenomena that should be modeled.

This basic procedure can aptly be illustrated by a famous cartoon that we showed in our 2007 study, namely a kingfisher sitting on a branch above a river and calcu-lating the correct angle for diving into the water to catch a fish. The kingfisher is using the well-known equation of refraction for his calculations (Fig. 6.1):

It is of course a funny idea that a bird should be able to use equations that usually are known only to physicists. Hence, the idea that a bird calculates is apparently absurd. Yet we argued that a human fisherman who catches fish by using a spear operates the same way as the kingfisher. Even if the fisherman is a professional physicist who knows the equation of refraction he certainly will not apply it but will operate in the kingfisher's way, namely by applying a certain neural structure,

J. Klüver, C. Klüver, *Social Understanding*, Theory and Decision Library A 47, DOI 10.1007/978-90-481-9911-2_6, © Springer Science+Business Media B.V. 2011

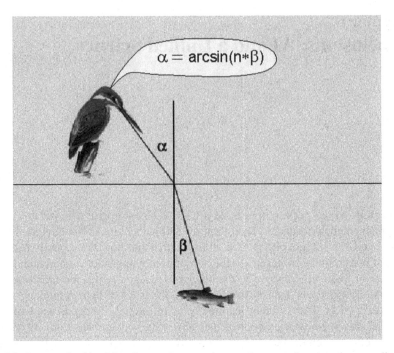

$$\alpha = \arcsin(n*\beta)$$

Fig. 6.1 A computing kingfisher. Source: Internet; the equation were given to us by our colleague Jörn Schmidt

i.e., a neural topology where the knowledge about the right angle has been stored. The kingfisher had learned it by phylogenetic evolution; the fishing physicist who amuses himself in his free time learned it by an individual ontogenetic learning process. In orientation to the classic of Churchland and Sejnowski "The Computational Brain" (1992) we showed that the kingfisher is indeed calculating, although not in the way that is usually meant when one speaks of calculating. A model of the kingfisher's calculating, hence, would be a suited neural network topology and not the equation of refraction. This equation is a conscious model of a *physical* phenomenon, namely the changing of the trajectory of a falling physical body when it touches the surface of a river or lake, not of a *cognitive* process.[1]

Our own methodical conceptions are based on exactly this idea: We assume that humans compute in principal the same way as the kingfisher and the human fisherman do when humans are performing cognitive and in particular hermeneutical operations. They do not use equations, of course, when they are trying to understand other humans. In contrast to the calculations of refractions there are no such equations for the analysis of hermeneutical processes and there probably never will be.

---

[1] By the way, it is easily to imagine the respective processes of learning how to estimate the correct angle when diving or thrusting a spear into the water as a process of supervised learning, realized by the application of the enforcing rule (see above Chapter 4).

Yet even if there were such equations it would be as absurd to assume that humans use them when understanding other people as it is absurd in the case of the kingfisher. Humans also use their specific neural network topologies with more or less success when performing operations of understanding; in this sense they calculate as well as the kingfisher and the fisherman. Therefore, the search for a unified science cannot be the way to look for equations of hermeneutical processes the way physicists do when they model physical processes. The mathematics of hermeneutics must be that of network topology and their according characteristics.

By following this basic methodical assumption we were confronted though with the mentioned problem of the increasing distance of AI research from the original goals. In Chapter 4 we argued that many concepts, network models, and learning rules of neuro-informatics have become too complicated; one can only with great difficulty imagine that the brain operates according to the complicated algorithms of, e.g., a Self-Organizing Map. As a consequence we developed the general learning rule schema that is rather simple, generally applicable to all forms of learning, and based on the principle of Hebb, which is empirically well confirmed. Our attempt to bring AI back to its original roots lead us to the necessity to simplify some basic concepts; we showed though that our simple algorithms, which are empirically much more plausible, are no less powerful than the established ones.

The development of the general learning rule schema might be in particular important for the construction of AI-systems. No artificial system could be called "intelligent" in a strict sense if it has not the ability to learn and in particular to learn in an independent manner. That is why usual expert systems, which are a branch of AI research and application, are strictly speaking intelligent only in a restricted way because they have not the learning ability. They get their rules as their most important parts of their "intelligence" implemented by the programmers; we mentioned in Section 4.3 why this is no real parallel to the way human learners learn rules even if they are explicitly taught them. An AI-system with the learning manner of neural networks on the other hand has the ability to learn in the different forms described in Chapter 4. But our own experiences with our "Neuro Generator", a program that can construct different neural networks according to the needs of a user, showed us that an artificial intelligence as an image of human intelligence could not be so complicated as the Neuro Generator (and its counterparts by other constructors) is even at present. It can be assumed that the human brain learns in ways that are certainly different in dependency of the different learning tasks but similar in their basic logic. The general learning rule schema fulfills such a condition very well.[2]

To be sure, being theoretically orientated scientists we also look for general statements about the models by which we try to understand hermeneutical processes. Hence we discovered the relations between variance values and those of meaning generating capacities; this gives us a first impression of general regularities in the

---

[2]We mentioned Occam's Razor when comparing the general learning rule schema with the set of different established learning rules and argued that this methodical principle is an argument in favor of our schema. The same argument is certainly valid with respect to the construction of AI-systems.

processes of meaning formation. A similar regularity apparently can be found in
the processes of determining information degrees: Our cluster geometrical analysis
showed that again topological characteristics of cognitive networks determine the
information degree of messages; these topological characteristics are of course also
the product of individual learning processes. *In nuce*, the search for theoretically
simple and empirically established models does not exclude the successful search
for general regularities – on the contrary.

The question if our models and the results obtained with them are already a
basis for a hermeneutical AI or at least if they can be used as some building stones
was analyzed by a comparison between some of our simulation models with the
operations of human probands. Two results are quite remarkable:

On the one hand the operations of the respective simulation programs in practically all cases could be interpreted as the construction of an ideal type in the
sense of Max Weber. The results of the human probands nearly always differed
from those of the programs. But because the differences within the groups of the
probands were as large as the differences with respect to the programs and because
the deviations of the results of the probands to those of the program were, so to
speak, in all directions one can safely assume that the results of the probands were
empirical deviations from a general norm, i.e., an ideal type. This fact can be understood in the way that the different simulation programs generated middle values on
a scale; the empirical single cases, whether single groups or individuals, produced
values left and right from the values of the programs. This had the consequence that
sometimes the differences between single empirical cases were even larger than the
differences between these cases and the values of he programs. As the individual
early Calvinist entrepreneurs certainly showed deviations in different aspects from
the ideal type that Max Weber described the empirically obtained results must show
deviations from the program's result with necessity.

On the other hand it was equally interesting to see that the programs performed
in exactly those tasks rather poorly where human probands also did not well or even
worse than the programs respectively. This brings us to the interesting question,
how human-like an AI-system should be. In other words, shall an AI-system mirror
both the strengths and weaknesses of the human mind or should it only contain the
strengths?

An answer to this question depends of course on the interest in AI-systems. If
one wants AI-systems with superhuman cognitive powers like, e.g., Data in Star
Trek then the weaknesses of humans are not desired. On the contrary, the fact that
our simulation programs did not well in the same fields as the human probands
or only slightly better would then be an argument against the usefulness of our
systems. If on the other hand one wants AI-systems as human-like as possible like
the robot in Asimov's "Bicentennial", which even wanted to become mortal, then
the weaknesses of our programs are an argument in their favor.

A new branch of robotics that begins to merge with AI research, namely the so-
called "Android Science" is an illustrative example (cf. e.g., Ishiguro and Nishio
2007). The aim of this research is to construct human-like robots, orientated to the
concept of androids in Science Fiction, namely robots that cannot be distinguished

from humans by look and by behavior. In particular these androids shall be able to communicate with humans and thus enable researchers to study not only the behavior of the androids but also that of humans. In other words, humans should be understood by the analysis of androids and their interactions with humans; in particular because the androids look exactly like humans the interacting humans would not be estranged by unfamiliar looks.

On a first sight this goal looks rather familiar. Since the beginning of AI research computer programs were unanimously accepted as useful tools for the analysis of the human mind. Even severe critics of the "strong AI" like Searle and Dreyfus admitted the usefulness of a "weak" AI, namely simulation programs for cognitive processes. But the claim of the android scientists goes much further. They should look and behave like humans and in the end, so one must assume, it is impossible to distinguish them from "real" humans like the androids in the SF-movie "Blade Runner" or in the SF-TV series "Battle Ship Galactica": In both cases not only humans could not distinguish the androids from real humans but the androids themselves were frequently in doubt if they were real humans or artificial ones. If this is the ultimate goal of the android science then the androids have not only to pass the Turing test and such be intelligent by a behaviorist definition but have to *be* like humans in strictly all aspects. It is hard to see how this could be possible if the androids in the long run would not obtain a conscious mind. As it is well known from theories of socialization that the personal identity (of humans) is to a large degree the product of social experiences and hence of social interactions with other humans the androids would some day have reason to ask themselves if they are humans or not.

At present this sounds like Science Fiction and even the partisans of this branch of robotics admit that they still have a very far way to go (Ishiguro and Nishio loc. cit.). But even now the android scientists, if they take their goal quite seriously, must as a consequence aim for androids that (or who?) have the same weaknesses as humans. If humans should be understood by their interactions with androids then the androids must be human-like not only in their capabilities but in particular also in their weaknesses. Else it would make no sense to make the androids even human-like in their physical appearance.[3] Humans who interact with these androids would be specifically irritated by human looking persons, who make no mistakes and never err. Therefore, the android scientists obviously answer the question above in favor of our simulation programs: The programs are useful building stones for the construction of AI-systems like the androids *because* they show the same weaknesses as humans.

Although the android science program sounds at present rather like science fiction it brings back the old dispute between strong AI and weak AI. This dispute had a bit vanished because of the many disappointments with the AI research programs

---

[3]One of the chief protagonists of the Android research program, namely Ishiguro, even constructed a first robot that looks very much like his constructor. Ishiguro though gives no information if the robot also resembles its creator in other aspects.

and the not redeemed promises of AI researchers. Why argue about scientific goals that will perhaps never or only in the far future be reached? Yet because we in this book explicitly combine the goal of a unified science with the concrete possibility of AI we have at least in principle to discuss the question if our simulation programs some day would be some building stones of a "real" artificial intelligence or if they "only" will be useful instruments for the analysis of human cognitive processes.

We already remarked in the first chapter that the distinction between strong and weak AI is chiefly a semantical one. If one accepts the outcome of the Turing test or an equivalent testing procedure orientated on the operational results as a criterion for intelligence then there are no principal reasons why such simulation programs as ours, based on the assumption that the human brain computes in the same or a mathematically equivalent way as our programs do, should some day not be called "intelligent", at least in the aspect of hermeneutical performance. If on the contrary one insists that intelligence is more than algorithmic operations with equivalent results to those of humans then of course the main question is, what this "more" could be. We already referred to the danger to use concepts like, e.g., empathy in order to demonstrate that for example social intelligence is to a large part based on some emotional states of the mind. Although in everyday language social behavior is frequently characterized with concepts like "feeling the others emotions" and similar statements we showed that social competences are cognitive ones or they are no competences at all.[4] Any attempt to distinguish "real" intelligence from artificial one by combining cognitive operations with some feeling attitudes must lead into a blind alley.

Yet in a perhaps deeper sense human intelligence must be combined with emotions. Several AI critics like Dreyfus (loc. cit.) and Winograd and Flores (loc. cit.) have by referring to phenomenological philosophy pointed out that human thinking is not only but also characterized by the fact that humans have an organic body: The way humans think is determined by their physical attributes in particular and by their very bodily existence in general. Neither Searle nor Winograd/Flores describe in detail the consequences of this fundamental fact. Yet the chief argument is clear: If thinking is determined by the fact that the respective cognitive systems are embedded into an organic body then no artificial construct like for example a robot can think in the way humans can. Only if some day artificially created bodies will be possible with artificial brains then one could perhaps speak of "real" intelligence.

By analyzing this argument we come back again to emotions. Emotions have of course their origin in the body and its more or less satisfying operations. If the phenomenological argument refers to the determination of cognitive processes by physically caused emotions then indeed no artificial system that is imaginable today could be called intelligent. This is the case not only with our simulation programs that certainly are not intelligent – they just are rather successful in simulating some cognitive operations –, but also for example with the androids of Ishiguro et al. The

---

[4]Several years ago there existed numerous attempts to introduce as a parallel to the IQ a so-called EQ, namely an "empathy quotient". It was not by chance that these attempts soon vanished.

cognitive processes these artificial systems perform are simulations of real cognitive processes because they operate without any external disturbances like positive or negative emotions. When we described the results of our simulation programs in Chapter 5 as ideal types we could have also said that the programs operated in contrast to the human probands in a purely cognitive way regardless of any environmental factors.[5]

By the way, Arthur C. Clarke, the creator of HAL 2000 (see above Chapter 1) had already in the fifties the same idea when he created in his novel "The City and the Stars" an artificial intelligence without any body, not even with an artificial one. The argument behind this creation was that any body, artificial or natural, disturbs and influences cognitive processes in particular ways. Pure thinking, hence, is only possible by a bodiless intelligence.

Following the arguments of the phenomenological critics of strong AI and the positive consequence of Clarke then an artificial intelligence will never be like a human one, even if one would insert an artificial brain into an organic body. To be sure, AI-systems could be designed that evolve and in this process obtain certain behavioral characteristics that look for an external observer as if these systems had emotions. We need only remind of our little Von Neumann machines that developed a behavior as if they had a survival will. The same way it is certainly possible to imagine a Terminator 2 that (or who?) is not only able to understand why humans are crying (see Section 1.4.1) but is also able to produce some liquids out of his eyes that look like tears. But does that prove that it has emotions? In the sense of the Turing test it (he) certainly has but only in this sense.

To cut a never-ending story short, the dispute how intelligent in a human sense artificial systems are or can and will be is in a logical sense an undecidable one that probably belongs to metaphysics. We will be content if one day our programs could perform even more complicated hermeneutical operations, regardless if they are called intelligent or not.

The book, after all, is named "social understanding". Do we now really understand the "operation called Verstehen" (Abel)? We showed that it is possible to deepen the understanding of human and animal behavior by hypothetically assuming certain topological structures in cognitive systems of "mice and men" and by demonstrating that these forms of behavior is a logical consequence from the according topologies. Understanding, hence, is the successful construction of suited cognitive topologies or, in the case of rule determined behavior, of suited social rules, generated by learning networks. In this sense we have an additional form of understanding, namely to attribute social behavior to mathematical models. It is certainly a semantical question if, for example, qualitative social researchers would accept this as the correct meaning of understanding. Yet it is not only a precise research program but it also refers to a kind of operations that artificial systems could do too.

---

[5]"Environmental" is to be understood in the sense that most of the body is environment to the brain and mind.

Finally, in what way are our programs a contribution to the goal of a unified science? To answer this question one must first clear the meaning of this concept. If it is meant in the sense of physicists that some day everything can be explained as inference from an ultimate theory (cf. Barrow 1991; Greene loc. cit.) then of course our attempts do not belong to this goal of a unified science. Yet even physicists who search for an ultimate theory as the Holy Grail of theoretical physics do not believe that even an ultimate theory could be able to explain social or cognitive phenomena (cf. Barrow loc. cit.). This could not be a truly unified science. If on the other hand the term "unified science" means that each scientific enterprise should be performed with exactly the same methods, namely those of mathematical and experimental physics, then our research program is again not a part of such a scientific super program. Several times we argued that and why the classical and firmly established methods of the natural sciences are not applicable to the problems we deal with; the complexity of the social and cognitive domains ask for other methods and concepts. To remind again of the unifying and failing attempts of Logical Positivism: The postulate that all scientific research must be done by exactly the same method is something like the famous bed of Procrustes, namely the reduction of complex problems to narrow methods, even if they have been very successful in some scientific domains. The search for general differential equations in the field of cognition would be like the attempt to model a kingfisher by using the equation of refraction and by postulating that this is the procedural way of the bird.

We already argued in the beginning of this chapter why we chose another methodical way, namely to model, for example, hermeneutical processes of humans, and cognitive processes of dogs, mice, and even kingfishers by looking for the topological structures of their brains and, in the case of humans, also minds. Such mathematical models are no subsequent reconstructions of cognitive processes but are orientated immediately to the logic of the processes itself. To be sure, we do not claim a literal adequacy of our models with the real processes. We just claim a mathematical equivalence in the sense that the real networks must have some general characteristics that can be found too in our topological models.

According to this methodical procedure a unified science in our understanding is the postulate that all domains of research should be analyzed by the usage of mathematical models and by the permanent interplay of theory, mathematical models, experimental and/or observational obtained facts, and the permanent checking and correcting of theories and models with respect to the facts. In this sense we have defined the operations of understanding and the hermeneutical processes that are the methodical basis for understanding. This is of course the successful way of the natural sciences and we also advocate it although by propagating new and additional mathematical methods. In this sense we hope and believe that it will be possible that someday also the humanities will become a part of such a unified science.

References

Abel, T., 1948/1949: The operation called "verstehen". In: American Journal of Sociology 54, 211–218

Agogino, A., 1999: Introduction to Artificial Intelligence. http://best.me.berkeley.edu/~aagogino/me290m/s99/Week1/week1.html

Andrews, R., Diederich, J., and Tickle, A.B., 1995: A Survey and Critique of Techniques for Extracting Rules from Trained Artificial Neural Networks. Brisbane: Neurocomputing Research Centre, Queensland University of Technology. http://sky.fit.qut.edu.au/~andrewsr/papers/KBSSurvey.ps

Apel, K.O., 1979: Die Erklären: Verstehen-Kontroverse in transzendentalpragmatischer Sicht. Frankfurt (M): Suhrkamp

Apel, K.O., 1982: The Erklären: Verstehen controversy in the philosophy of the natural and human sciences. In: Floistad, G. (ed.): Contemporary Philosophy. A New Survey. Vol. 2: Philosophy of Science. Den Haag: Martin Nijhoff

Axelrod, R., 1984: The Evolution of Cooperation. New York (NY): Basic Books

Axelrod, R., 1987: The evolution of strategies in the iterated prisoner's dilemma. In: Davies, L. (ed.): Genetic Algorithms and Simulated Annealing. Los Altos: Morgan Kauffman

Axelrod, R., 1997: Advancing the art of simulation in the social sciences. In: Conte, R., Hegselmann, R., Terna, P. (eds.): Simulating Social Phenomena. Berlin-Heidelberg-New York: Springer

Bagley, R.J. and Farmer, J.D., 1992: Spontaneous emergence of a metabolism. In: Langton, C., Taylor, C., Farmer, J.D., Rasmussen, S. (eds.): Artificial Life II. Redwood City (CA): Addison Wesley

Bandura, A., 1986: Social Foundations of Thought and Action. A Social-cognitive Theory. Englewoods Cliff (NJ): Prentice Hall

Barrow, J.D., 1991: Theories for Everything. The Quest for Ultimate Explanation. Oxford: Oxford University Press

Belew, R.K., McInerney, J., and Schraudolph, N.N., 1992: Evolving networks using the genetic algorithm with connectionist learning. In: Langton, C., Taylor, C., Farmer, J.D., Rasmussen, S. (eds.): Artificial Life II. Redwood City (CA): Addison Wesley

Bell, E.T., 1937: Men of Mathematics. New York (NY): Simon and Schuster

Berger, P. and Luckmann, T., 1967: The Social Construction of Reality. New York (NY): Doubleday

Böhme, D., 1980: Alternativen der Wissenschaft. Frankfurt (M): Suhrkamp

Brisch, K.H., 1980: Arzt-Patient-Gespräche in der Allgemeinpraxis. Theoretische Reflexion, methodische Diskussion und exemplarische Analyse des Arzt-Patient-Gesprächs. University of Ulm: PhD thesis (Doctor – Patient Discourses in a Medical Practice)

Buchanan, B.G., Shortliffe, G.H. (eds.), 1984: Rule-based Expert Systems – The MYCIN Experiment of the Stanford Programming Project. Reading (MA): Addison Wesley

Carnap, A., 1950: Empirism, semantics and ontology. In: Revue Internationale De Philosophie 4, 11

Carroll, S.B., 2006: Endless Forms Most Beautiful. The New Science of Evo Devo and the Making of the Animal Kingdom. London: Weidenfeld & Nicolson

Castellani, B. and Hafferty, F., 2009: Sociology and Complexity. Heidelberg: Springer

Casti, J., 1997: Would-be-Worlds. How Simulation is Changing the Frontiers of Science. New York (NY): Wiley

Chaitin, G.J., 1999: The Unknowable. Singapore: Springer

Chomsky, N., 1959: A review of B. F. Skinner's verbal behavior. In: Language 35(1), 26–58

Churchland, P. and Sejnowski, T., 1992: The Computational Brain. Cambridge (MA): MIT Press

Clifford, J., Marcus, G.E. (eds.), 1986: Writing Culture. The Poetics and Politics of Ethnography. Berkeley-Los Angeles-London: Blackwell

Cube, F.v., 1965: Kybernetische Grundlagen des Lernens und Lehrens. Stuttgart: Klett

Dahrendorf Lord, R., 1958: Homo Sociologicus. Ein Versuch zur Geschichte, Bedeutung und Kritik der Kategorie der sozialen Rolle. Leske + Buderich, Opladen

Dennett, D.C., 1995: Darwin's Dangeorous Idea. New York (NY): Touchstone

Dreyfus, H.L., 1992: What Computers Still Can't Do: A Critique of Artificial Reason. Cambridge (MA): MIT Press

Dreyfus, H.L. and Dreyfus, S.E., 1986: Mind Over Machine: The Power of Human Intuition and Expertise in the Era of the Computer. Oxford: Blackwell

Droysen, J.G., 1960 (first 1858): Historik. Vorlesungen über Enzyklopädie und Methodologie der Geschichte. Frankfurt (M): Fischer

Edelman, G.M., 1992: Bright Air, Brilliant Fire – On the Matter of the Mind. New York (NY): Basic Books

Epstein, J.M., 1997: Nonlinear Dynamics, Mathematical Biology and Social Sciences. Redwood: Addison Wesley

Galland, S., 1993: Neural Network Learning and Expert Systems. Cambridge (MA): MIT Press

Gardner, H., 1985: The Mind's New Science. A History of the Cognitive Revolution. New York (NY): Basic Books

Geertz, C., 1973: The Interpretation of Culture. New York (NY): Basic Books

Gell-Mann, M., 1994: The Quark and the Jaguar. New York (NY): Freeman and Company

Giddens, A., 1984: The Constitution of Society. Outlines of the Theory of Structuration. Cambridge: Polity Press

Greene, B., 2000: The Elegant Universe. Superstrings, Hidden Dimensions, and the Quest for the Ultimate Theory. New York (NY): Norton

Habermas, J., 1968: Wissenschaft und Technik als Ideologie. Frankfurt (M): Suhrkamp

Habermas, J., 1981: Theorie des kommunikativen Handelns. Frankfurt (M): Suhrkamp

Haken, H., 1984: The Science of Structure: Synergetics. New York (NY): Van Nostrand Reinhold Company

Hartley, R.V.L., 1928: Transmission of information. In: The Bell System Technical Journal 7, 535–563

Hebb, D.O., 1949: The Organization of Behavior. New York (NY): Wiley

Hempel, C.G. and Oppenheim, P., 1948: The logic of explanation. In: Philosophy of Science 15, 135–175

Herrmann, M., 2008: Computersimulationen und sozialpädagogische Praxis. Wiesbaden: VS Verlag Für Sozialwissenschaften

Hillermeier, C., Kunstmann, N., Rabus, B., Tavan, P., 1994: Topological feature maps with self-organized lateral connections: a population-coded, one-layer model of associative memory. In: Biological Cybernetics 72, 103–117

Hofstadter, D.R., 1985: Metamagical Themas. Questing for the Essence of Mind and Pattern. Harmondsworth: Penguin

Holland, J.H., 1998: Emergence. from Chaos to Order. Reading (MA): Addison Wesley

Holland, J.H., Holyoak, K.J., Nisbett, R.E., Thagard, P., 1986: Induction. Cambridge (MA): MIT Press

Hörmann, H., 1978: Meinen und Verstehen. Grundzüge einer psychologischen Semantik. Frankfurt (M): Suhrkamp

Huxley, J.S., 1942: Evolution, the Modern Synthesis. London: Allen and Unwin

Ishiguro, H. and Nishio, S., 2007: Building artificial humans to understand humans. In: Journal for Artificial Organs 10, 133–142

Johnson Laird, P.N., 1983: Mental Models: Towards a Cognitive Science of Language, Inference, and Consciousness. Cambridge (MA): Harvard University Press

Jordan, M.I. and Rummelhart, D.E., 2002: Forward models: supervised learning with a distal teacher. In: Polk, T.A., Seifert, C.M. (Hrsg) (eds.): Cognitive Modeling. Cambridge (MA): MIT Press

Kaastra, I. and Boyd, M., 1996: Designing a neural network for forecasting financial and economic time series. In: Neurocomputing 10(3), 215–236

Kamin, L., 1974: The Science and Politics of I.Q. Potomac (MA): Lawrence Erlbaum

Kandel, E., 2006: In Search of Memory. The Emergence of a New Science of Mind. New York (NY): Norton

Kauffman, S., 1993: The Origins of Order. Oxford: Oxford University Press

Kauffman, S.A., 1995: At Home in the Universe. Oxford: Oxford University Press

Kauffman, S.A., 2000: Investigations. Oxford: Oxford University Press

Klafki, W., 1971: Erziehungswissenschaft als kritisch-konstruktive Theorie. Hermeneutik, Empirie, Ideologiekritik. In: Zeitschrift Für Pädagogik 17, 251–385

Klüver, J., 1988: Die Konstruktion der sozialen Realität Wissenschaft: Alltag und System, Braunschweig-Wiesbaden: Vieweg

Klüver, J., 2000: The Dynamics and Evolution of Social Systems. New Foundations of a Mathematical Sociology. Dordrecht (NL): Kluwer Academic Publishers

Klüver, J., 2002: An Essay Concerning Socio-cultural Evolution. Theoretical Principles and Mathematical Models. Dordrecht (NL): Kluwer Academic Publishers

Klüver, J., 2003: The evolution of social geometry. In: Complexity 9(1), 13–22

Klüver, J. and Klüver, C., 2007: On Communication. An Interdisciplinary and Mathematical Approach. Dordrecht (NL): Springer

Klüver, J. and Schmidt, J., 2007: Recent results on ordering parameters in boolean networks. In: Complex Systems 17(1/2), 29–46

Klüver, J. and Stoica, C., 2006: Topology, computational models, and socio-cognitive complexity. In: Complexity 11(4), 43–55

Klüver, J., Stoica, C., and Schmidt, J., 2006: Computersimulationen und soziale Einzelfallstudien. Bochum-Herdecke: w3l Verlag

Kohlberg, L., 1971: From is to ought. In: Mishel, T. (ed.): Cognitive Development and Epistemology. New York (NY): Norton

Krohn, W. and Küppers, G., 1989: Die selbstorganisation der Wissenschaft. Frankfurt (M): Suhrkamp

Kuhn, T.S., 1963: The Structure of Scientific Revolutions. Chicago (IL): University of Chicago Press

Lakoff, G., 1987: Women, Fire and Dangerous Things. What Categories Reveal about the Mind. Chicago und London: The University of Chicago Press

Lakoff, G. and Núñez, R., 2000: Where Mathematics comes from. How the embodied mind brings Mathematics into Being. New York (NY): Basic Books

Latour, B. and Woolgar, S., 1979: Laboratory Life. Beverly Hills-London: Sage

Levy, S., 1993: Artificial Life. The Quest for a New Creation. London: Penguin

Lewin, K., 1969: Grundzüge der tolopogischen Psychologie. Bern: Hans Huber

Lewontin, R., 2000: It Ain't Necessarily So: The Dream of the Human Genome Project and Other Illusions. New York (NY): Review of Books

Libet, B., 2004: Mind Time: The Temporal Factor in Consciousness. Cambridge (MA): Harvard University Press

Maturana, H., 1975: The organisation of the living: A theorie of the living organisation. In: International Journal of Man – Machine Studies 7, 313–332

Mayntz, R., 1990: The Influence of Natural Science Theories on Contemporary Social Science. MPfG Discussion Paper. Köln: Max Planck Institut für Gesellschaftsforschung

McCulloch, W.S. and Pitts, W., 1943: A logical calculus of the ideas immanent in nervous activity. In: Bulletin of Mathematical Biophysic 5, 115–133

McLeod, P., Plunkett, K., and Rolls, E.T., 1998: Introduction to Connectionist Modelling of Cognitive Processes. Oxford: Oxford University Press

Michalewicz, Z., 1994: Genetic Algorithms + Data Structures = Evolution Programs. Berlin: Springer

Minsky, M.L., 1968: Steps Toward Artificial Intelligence. In: Minsky, M.L. (ed.): Semantic Information Processing. Cambridge (MA): MIT Press

Parsons, T., 1977: Social Systems and the Evolution of Action Theory. New York (NY): Norton

Peacock, J.L., 1982: The Third Stream. Weber, Parsons and Geertz. In: Journal of the Anthropological Society of Oxford 12, 122–129

Penrose, R., 1989: The Emperor's New Mind. Concerning Computers, Minds, and the Laws of Physics. Oxford: Oxford University Press

Pinker, S., 1994: The Language Instinct. New York (NY): Morrow

Plunkett, K. and Marchman, V.A., 1996: Learning from a connectionist model of the acquisition of the English past tense. In: Cognition 61(3): 299–308

Poincaré, H., 1902: La science et l'hypothèse. Paris: Flammarion (Science and Hypothesis, 1905)

Polk, T.A. and Seifert, C.M., 2002: Cognitive Modelling. Cambridge (MA): MIT Press

Popper, K.R.,1969: Die Logik der Forschung. Tübingen: Mohr (English translation: The Logic of Scientific Discovery)

Poundstone, W., 1988: Labyrinths of Reason. New York (NY): Anchor Press, Doubleday

Ray, T., 1992: An approach to the synthesis of life. In: Langton, C.G., Taylor, C., Farmer, J.D., Rasmussen, S. (eds.): Artificial Life II. Redwood (CA): Addison Wesley

Read, D. 2004. Mathematical modeling issues in analytical representations of human societies. In: Cybernetics and Systems (Special Issue) 35, 163–172

Ritter, H. and Kohonen, T., 1989: Self-organizing semantic maps. In: Biological Cybernetics 61, 241–254

Rosch, E., 1973: Natural categories. In: Cognitive Psychology 4(3), 328–350

Rosch, E. and Mervis, C.B. 1975: Family resemblances: studies in the internal structure of categories. In: Cognitive Psychology 7(4), 573–605

Russell, S. and Norvig, P., 2003: Artificial Intelligence: A Model Approach. Englewoods Cliff (NJ): Prentice Hall, Pearson Education

Sacks, O., 1985: The Man Who Mistook His Wife for a Hat. New York (NY): Summit Books

Schank, R.C. and Abelson, R.P., 1977: Scripts, Plans, Goals, and Understanding. Potomac (MD): Lawrence Erlbaum

Schank, R. and Riesbeck, C., 1981: Inside Computer Understanding. Hillsdale (NJ): Lawrence Erlbaum

Schütz, A., 1962–66: Collected Papers. Dordrecht (NL): Martinus Nijhoff Publishers

Searle, J.R., 1980: Minds, Brains and Programs. In: The Behavioral and Brain Sciences 3, 417–457

Searle, J.R., 1987: Minds and Brains without Programs. In: Blakemore, C., Greenfield, S. (eds.): Mindwaves. Thoughts on Thoughts on Intelligence, Identity, and Consciousness. Oxford: Basil Blackwell

Sestito, S. and Dillon, T.S., 1994: Automated Knowledge Acquisition. New York-Sydney: Prentice Hall

Shannon, C.E. and Weaver, W., 1949: The Mathematical Theory of Communication. Urbana (IL): The University of Illinois Press

Skinner, B.F., 1953: Science and Human Behavior. London: Macmillan

Snow, C.P., 1963: The Two Cultures, and a Second Look: An Expanded Version of the Two Cultures and the Scientific Revolution. Cambridge: Cambridge University Press

Spencer, H., 1862: First Principles. London: Williams and Norgate

Stanley, K.O. and Miikkulainen, R., 2002: Evolving neural networks through augmenting topologies. In: Evolutionary Computing, 10, 99–127

Stoica, C., 2000: Die Vernetzung sozialer Einheiten. Hybride Interaktive Neuronale Netze in den Kommunikations- und Sozialwissenschaften. Wiesbaden: DUV

Stoica-Klüver, C., Klüver, J., and Schmidt, J., 2007: Besser und erfolgreicher kommunizieren. Herdecke/Witten: w3l Verlag

Stoica-Klüver, C., Klüver, J., and Schmidt, J., 2009: Modellierung Komplexer Prozesse Durch Naturanaloge Verfahren. Wiesbaden: Vieweg-Teubner

Tarski, A., 1956: Logic, Semnatics, Metamathematics: Papers From 1923 to 1938. Oxford (GB): Oxford University Press

Thagard, P., 1996: Mind: Introduction to Cognitive Science. Cambridge (MA): MIT Press

Tipler, F.J., 1994: The Physics of Immortality. New York (NY): Double Day

Turing, A., 1950: Computing machinery and intelligence. Mind, 59, 433–460

Vanberg, V.J., 1994: Rules and Choice in Economics. London: Routledge

Vico, G., 1947 (German – Latin Edition): De nostri temporis studiorum ratione. Godesberg: Verlag Helmut Küpper

Vogt, J., 2005: Tatort – der wahre deutsche Gesellschaftsroman. In: Vogt, J. (ed.): Medienmorde. München: Wilhelm Fink Verlag

Waldrup, M.M., 1992: Complexity: The Emerging Science at the Edge of Cahos and Order. New York (NY): Simon & Schuster

Watzlawick, P., Beavin, J.H., and Jackson, D.D., 1967: Pragmatics of Human Communication. A Study of Interactional Patterns, Pathologies, and Paradoxes. New York (NY): Norton

Weber, M., 1921: Wirtschaft und Gesellschaft. Grundriß Der verstehenden Soziologie. Tübingen: Mohr

Weizenbaum, J., 1966: Eliza – a computer program for the study of natural language communication between man and machine. In: Communications of the ACM 9, 36–45

Weizenbaum, J., 1976: Computer Power and Human Reason. From Judgment to Calculation. New York (NY): Freeman

Widrow, B. and Hoff, M.E., 1960: Adaptive switching circuits. In: WESCON Convention Record. New York (NY): IRE

Wiener, N., 1948: Cybernetics or Control and Communication in the Animal and the Machine. Cambridge (MA): MIT Press

Winograd, T. and Flores, F., 1986: Understanding Computers and Cognition. Norton (NJ): Ablex Publishing Corporation

Wolfram, S., 2001: A New Kind of Science. Champagne (IL): Wolfram Media

Wright, G.H.v., 1974: Erklären und Verstehen. Frankfurt (M): Fischer

Wuensche, A. and Lesser, M., 1992: The Global Dynamics of Cellular Automata: Attraction Fields of One-Dimensional Cellular Automata. Reading (MA): Addison Wesley

Zell, A., 2003: Simulation neuronaler Netze. München: Oldenbourg Verlag

Index